TAKINGS

Land-Development Conditions and Regulatory Takings after *Dolan* and *Lucas*

TAKINGS

Land-Development Conditions and Regulatory Takings after *Dolan* and *Lucas*

David L. Callies, editor

SECTION OF STATE AND LOCAL GOVERNMENT LAW
AMERICAN BAR ASSOCIATION

Cover design by Jim Colao.

The materials contained herein represent the opinions of the authors and editors and should not be construed to be the action of either the American Bar Association or the Section of State and Local Government Law unless adopted pursuant to the bylaws of the Association.

Nothing contained in this book is to be considered as the rendering of legal advice for specific cases, and readers are responsible for obtaining such advice from their own legal counsel. This book and any forms and agreements herein are intended for educational and informational purposes only.

Printed in the United States of America.

Library of Congress Catalog Card Number 95-80054
ISBN 1-57073-233-7

Discounts are available for books ordered in bulk. Special consideration is given to state bars, CLE programs, and other bar-related organizations. Inquire at Publications Planning & Marketing, American Bar Association, 750 North Lake Shore Drive, Chicago, Illinois 60611.

00 99 98 97 96 5 4 3 2 1

SUMMARY OF CONTENTS

Part II

Takings

A. Generally

Part III

Special Issues

Part IV

Comparative Takings Law

CONTENTS

Part III

Special Issues

ABOUT THE AUTHORS

Michael M. Berger is a partner in the Santa Monica law firm of Berger & Norton, where he has specialized in land use, eminent domain, and other varieties of real property litigation since 1969. He represented the property owners in *First English Evangelical Lutheran Church v. County of Los Angeles* and *Preseault v. ICC* and filed amicus curiae briefs in support of property owners in such cases as *Nollan v. California Coastal Commission, Lucas v. South Carolina Coastal Council,* and *Yee v. City of Escondido.* Mr. Berger received his undergraduate degree from Brandeis University, his J.D. from Washington University, and his LL.M. from the University of Southern California. Active as both a lecturer and legal commentator on land use and eminent domain, he devotes most of his time to appellate practice.

Kenneth B. Bley is a partner in Cox, Castle & Nicholson, an eighty-lawyer firm specializing in providing legal services to the real estate community, where he is the head of its land-use department. Mr. Bley is a lecturer at the University of Southern California Law School, has written and lectured extensively on land use, and represents developers in planning and zoning matters before administrative bodies and trial and appellate courts. Mr. Bley graduated magna cum laude from Harvard Law School and holds B.S. and M.S. degrees from the University of California at Berkeley in engineering, as well as a Ph.D. in engineering from UCLA.

Fred Bosselman is a professor of law at Chicago-Kent Law School in Chicago, where he teaches courses on environmental, land-use, and energy law. He received his B.A. from the University of Colorado in 1956 and his J.D. from Harvard Law School in 1959.

David L. Callies is the Benjamin A. Kudo Professor of Law at the William S. Richardson School of Law, University of Hawaii at Manoa, where he teaches land-use, real property, and state and local government law. He received his B.A. from DePauw University, his J.D. from the University of Michigan, and his LL.M. from Nottingham University. Mr. Callies is past chair and present member of Council of the State and Local Government Law Section of the ABA, a member of the American Law Institute and of the American Institute of Certified Planners. He is the coeditor of *Exactions, Impact Fees and Dedications: Shaping Land Use Development and Funding of Infrastructure in the Dolan Era* (American Bar Association, 1995).

Robert G. "Jerry" Converse is a partner in the law firm of Fulbright & Jaworski of Houston, Texas, where his areas of practice include real estate and oil and gas. Mr. Converse received his B.B.A. in 1968 and his LL.B. in 1970 from the University of Texas. He is a member of the American College of Real Estate Lawyers and the Real Estate Advisory Commission to the Texas Board of Legal Specialization. He is also a past chair of the Land-Use Regulation Committee and a current vice-chair of the Public-Private Partnerships and Privatization Committee of the American Bar Association. Mr. Converse is a member of the Travis County Bar Association, Houston Bar Association, and State Bar of Texas.

Daniel J. Curtin, Jr. is a partner in the law firm of McCutchen, Dole, Brown & Enersen of Walnut Creek, California, where he specializes in land-use law, representing both private and public sector clients. Mr. Curtin received his J.D. from the University of San Francisco and is a recipient of the American Planning Association Distinguished Leadership Award (1988) and the National Institute of Municipal Law Officers Charles S. Rhyne Award for Lifetime Achievement in Municipal Law (1992).

Carl-Heinz David is the chair of spatial planning of the Fakultät Raumplanung (Faculty of Spatial Planning) at the Universität Dortmund, where he teaches courses on planning and land-use law with special attention to environmental protection. He is the author of several books on comparative studies of law and the practice of urban renewal, land banking for ecological purposes, and legal and side effects of the European Union in environmental and spatial planning law. Mr. David has studied at the Universities of Bonn, München, and Münster, and he received his J.D. from the University of Muenster. He was made a full member of the (German) Akademie für Raumforschung und Landesplanung. Currently he is the German representative of the Association of European Planning Schools (AESOP).

Christopher Duerksen is the managing director of Clarion Associates of Colorado, LLC, a real estate development consulting firm with offices in Denver and Chicago. He has represented local governments, nonprofits, and the private sector in a variety of land-use and zoning matters and specializes in development code revisions, growth management planning, natural resource and scenic area protection strategies, airport-area development, and market development strategies. A cofounder of the Rocky Mountain Land Use Institute, Mr. Duerksen has written and spoken extensively on land-use issues in Colorado and nationally. He is the author of *Takings Law in Plain English* and *Aesthetics and Land Use Controls.* He also writes a monthly column for *American Angler,* a national fly-fishing magazine. Mr. Duerksen lives in Denver with his wife, Jan, and their two young boys, Benjamin and Matthew.

Robert H. Freilich is a professor of law and partner in the law and planning firms of Freilich, Leitner & Carlisle in Kansas City, Missouri; Freilich, Kaufman, Fox & Sohagi in Los Angeles, California; and Freilich, Morgan, Leitner & Carlisle in Dallas, Texas, specializing in zoning and subdivision law, land-use and takings litigation, and development of comprehensive plans and implementation systems for state, county, and local governments. Professor Freilich received his A.B. degree from the University of Chicago, his J.D. from Yale Law School, and holds M.I.A., LL.M., and J.S.D. degrees from the Columbia University School of Law. He is Editor of THE URBAN LAWYER, a national quarterly journal on urban law published by the Section of State and Local Government Law of the ABA, and sits on a number of planning and land-use committees. His publications include: *Cases and Materials on Land Use* (West Publishing Co., 1994); *Model Subdivision Regulations: Planning* *and Law* (American Planning Association, 1995); *After Lucas: Land Use Regulation and the Taking of Property Without Compensation* (David Callies, ed., American Bar Association, 1993); and *Exactions, Impact Fees and Dedications: Shaping Land Use Development and Funding of Infrastructure in the Dolan Era* (with David Bushek, American Bar Association, 1995).

Elizabeth A. Garvin is an associate in the law and planning firms of Freilich, Leitner & Carlisle in Kansas City, Missouri; Freilich, Leitner Kaufman, Fox & Sohagi in Los Angeles, California; and Freilich, Morgan, Leitner & Carlisle in Dallas, Texas. She specializes in both regulatory litigation and growth management planning and plan implementation. Ms. Garvin received her B.A. in Environmental Studies in 1988, her J.D. in 1991, and a master's in Urban Planning in 1994, all from the University of Kansas. She is a member of the Missouri and Kansas Bars, the ABA, and the American Planning Association. Ms. Garvin's most recent articles include "Economic Development and Public Transit: Making the Most of the Washington Growth Management Act" in the *Puget Sound Law Review* (with Freilich and White, 1994) and "Handling the Inverse Condemnation Case: Challenging Land-Use Regulations" in *Nichols on Eminent Domain* (with Carlisle, 1993).

Kimberly Gough works with Dykema Gossett, PLLC, in Bloomfield Hills, Michigan, with their Litigation Practice Group. Ms. Gough earned her B.B.A. from the University of Michigan with High Distinction in 1991 and her J.D. at Wayne State University, magna cum laude, Order of the Coif, in 1995.

Malcolm Grant is a professor at the University of Cambridge where he heads the Department of Land Economy. He is a fellow of Clare College, Cambridge, and the Deputy Chairman of the Local Government Commission for England. Professor Grant received his LL.B., LL.M., and LL.D. from the University of Otago, New Zealand. He is an honorary member of the Royal Town Planning Institute and an honorary associate of the Royal Institution of Chartered Surveyors.

Otto J. Hetzel, a professor of law at Wayne State University Law School in Detroit, Michigan, has taught Housing and Community Development Law, Land Use, Legislation, and Civil Procedure for more than twenty years. He also practices law in the Washington, D.C., office of Pepper, Hamilton & Scheetz, with its Real Estate Practice Group, specializing in local government matters including housing and community development issues, zoning, regulation of development, and eligibility for federal grant and loan funds. He served as Associate General Counsel of the U.S. Department of Housing and Urban Development and as Deputy Attorney General, State of California. He has a J.D. from Yale and an LL.M. from Harvard.

G. Richard Hill is a partner with Foster, Pepper & Shefelman in Seattle, Washington. A graduate of Yale Law School, he is currently the Chair of the State and Local Government Law Section of the American Bar Association. He is the editor of *Regulatory Taking: The Limits of Land Use Controls* (American Bar Association, 1990).

Gideon Kanner is a professor of law emeritus at the Loyola Law School in Los Angeles, where he has taught courses in property, eminent domain, land-use controls, and appellate advocacy since 1974. Before joining the faculty, Professor Kanner was in private practice in the field of eminent domain and inverse condemnation. He holds a J.D. from the University of Southern California and his B.S. in mechanical engineering from the Cooper Union in New York. He is the editor and publisher of *Just Compensation*, a monthly legal periodical on the law of eminent domain and inverse condemnation, and has served as a consultant on those subjects to the California Law Revision Commission and the Advisory Committee on the Uniform Eminent Domain Code. Professor Kanner is chairman for several programs of the ALI/ABA Committee on Continuing Legal Education and formerly chaired the second annual Southwestern Legal Foundation eminent domain program.

Douglas W. Kmiec is a professor of law at the University of Notre Dame, on leave during 1995–96 as the Dorothy and Leonard Straus Distinguished Professor of Law at Pepperdine University in California. Author of the *Zoning and Planning Deskbook* (Clark Boardman Callaghan), Professor Kmiec is a recognized constitutional and property law scholar and former Assistant Attorney General of the United States (Legal Counsel) to President Ronald Reagan. An honors graduate of Northwestern University, he received his law degree from the University of Southern California, where he served for two years on the *Law Review.* Professor Kmiec is a member of the Bar of the United States Supreme Court and the State Bars of Illinois and California.

Daniel R. Mandelker is the Stamper Professor of Law at Washington University in St. Louis, Missouri, where he has taught land-use law for many years. He has B.A. and LL.B. degrees from the University of Wisconsin and a J.S.D. degree from Yale University. He is the author of *Land Use Law,* coauthor of *Federal Land Use Law,* and coauthor of *Planning and Control of Land Development*, a casebook widely used in law schools.

Duane Martin is a judicial clerk to the Honorable Forest W. Hanna of the Missouri Court of Appeals, Western District, in Kansas City, Missouri. Mr. Martin is a 1995 graduate of the University of Missouri-Kansas City School of Law. While attending UMKC he served as the student editor in chief of *The Urban Lawyer,* the national quarterly on state and local government published by the ABA. His article "The President and the Cities: Clinton's Urban Aid Agenda" appeared in the Winter 1994 issue.

Dwight Merriam is the head of Robinson & Cole's nationally recognized land-use group within the land-use and environmental section. He has published more than fifty professional articles on land-use law and is the senior coeditor of *Inclusionary Zoning Moves Downtown.* Mr. Merriam has served on the faculty of programs of the American Planning Association, ALI/ABA, the Practicing Law Institute, and the National Institute of Municipal Law Officers. He served for two years as a director of APA and President of the American Institute of Certified Planners. Mr. Merriam has taught land-use planning and law at the University of Bridgeport, the University of Connecticut, Western New England College, Memphis State University, and the Vermont Law School. He also has an active and reserve career in the Navy as a Surface Warfare Officer at the rank of Captain, including seven years on active duty, three tours to Vietnam, and twenty years as a drilling reservist. Mr. Merriam received his B.A. in sociology, cum laude, from the University of Massachusetts at Amherst. He received his Master of Regional Planning from the University of North Carolina at Chapel Hill and his J.D. from Yale Law School, where he was awarded the Ivan S. Meitus Prize for his research and writing on land-use law.

Richard A. Paik is a consultant in economic development and real estate market analysis with Coley/Forrest, Inc., in Denver, Colorado. He has provided consulting services regarding economic development strategies, development feasibility, land-use planning and growth management concepts, and land-use law. Mr. Paik received his B.A. from Brown University (1982), a Master of City and Regional Planning from the University of North Carolina at Chapel Hill (1985), and his J.D. from the University of Minnesota (1991).

Thomas E. Roberts is a professor of law at Wake Forest University in Winston-Salem, North Carolina, where he teaches land-use regulation, natural resources, and property courses. Professor Roberts received his B.A. from Hanover College in 1966 and his J.D. from Ohio State University in 1971. He is a coauthor of *Cases and Materials on Land Use,* second edition (with David Callies and Robert Freilich, West Publishing Co., 1994), and he is the Director of Publications of the Section of State and Local Government Law of the American Bar Association.

FOREWORD

This original collection of essays on takings and land-development conditions after the U.S. Supreme Court's landmark decisions in *Lucas v. South Carolina Coastal Commission* and *Dolan v. City of Tigard* grew from a program on takings cosponsored by the Section of State and Local Government Law and the Section of Real Property, Probate and Trust Law at the 1994 Annual Meeting of the American Bar Association. In a sense it replaces the collection of *Urban Lawyer* articles collected and edited by Richard Hill in 1990 (*Regulatory Taking: The Limits of Land Use Controls*) which preceded these decisions. Although not necessarily in perfect balance, the authors by design represent a wide spectrum of views on the appropriate role of government regulation and its effects on the use and value of land. The authors also represent both the academic and the practicing bar. I am indebted to my research assistants Linda Dragas, a practicing attorney in Honolulu to whom goes the credit for what was well done in the editing process; and Lia Reynolds and Julie Tappendorf, who spent part of a summer and fall putting the essays in order and reading proofs for submission to the ABA Department of Publications Planning and Marketing; and to my colleague Professor Thomas E. Roberts of the Wake Forest Law School, whose review of the manuscript and reading proofs in his capacity as Publications Director of the Section of State and Local Government Law vastly improved both the organization of the essays and their internal consistency. Finally, many thanks to the twenty-one authors who drafted and redrafted their essays under tight deadlines to produce truly fine commentary on this most important of land-use issues.

David L. Callies
Honolulu

TAKINGS

Land-Development Conditions and Regulatory Takings after *Dolan* and *Lucas*

PART I

Background

Chapter 1. After *Lucas* and *Dolan:*
An Introductory Essay
David L. Callies

Chapter 2. Land As a Privileged Form of
Property
Fred P. Bosselman

Chapter 3. Ripeness and Forum Selection in
Land-Use Litigation
Thomas E. Roberts

CHAPTER ❖ 1

After *Lucas* and *Dolan:* An Introductory Essay

David L. Callies

I. Introduction

> [W]hile property may be regulated to a certain extent, if regulation goes too far it will be recognized as a taking.[1]

Since 1922 at least, land-use planners and lawyers have had to cope with the notion that land-use controls and the plans upon which they are based can work a taking of property under the Fifth Amendment to the U.S. Constitution. However, after declaring zoning constitutional in principle,[2] but potentially a taking in practice,[3] the U.S. Supreme Court left the work of deciding which regulations were constitutionally protected takings and which were not largely to state courts.[4] By the 1970s, a series of state supreme court cases had pretty much rendered the doctrine of regulatory takings moribund.[5]

Commencing on April Fool's Day in 1974, the U.S. Supreme Court once again dipped its foot, however gingerly, in the land-use regulatory takings quagmire. In *Village of Belle Terre v. Boraas,*[6] the Court struck down a local ordinance prohibiting three or more persons unrelated by blood or marriage from living in the same single-family house. There followed a series of cases in the early 1980s dealing (or failing abysmally to deal) with land-use regulations in which the landowner claimed a taking of property, many of them undecided on grounds of ripeness.[7] However, in a trilogy of cases decided in 1987, the Court signalled an intent to address critical taking issues on the merits. In *Keystone Bituminous Coal Ass'n v. DeBenedictis,*[8] a Court sharply divided along ideological lines set out a series of rules on partial takings, most (if not all) of which are largely overtaken by the holding and notes in the case of *Lucas v. South Carolina Coastal Council,*[9] described below. In *First English Evangelical Lutheran Church of Glendale v. County of Los Angeles,*[10] the Court's conservative majority held that once a regulation is found to be a taking, even if temporary, compensation (as compared with declaratory or injunctive relief) is an available remedy. Lastly, in *Nollan v. California Coastal Commission,*[11] the same conservative majority addressed the issue of conditions on land-development permissions. Holding that a commission's requirement of a lateral beach-access dedication was an unconstitutional condition on the issuance of a building permit to reconstruct a beach house, the Court said:

> It is quite impossible to understand how a requirement that people already on the public beaches be able to walk across the Nollans' property reduces any obstacles to viewing the beach created by the new house. It is also impossible to understand how it lowers any "psychological barrier" to using the public beaches, or how it helps to remedy any additional congestion on them caused by construction of the Nollans' new house. We therefore find that the Commission's imposition of the permit condition cannot be treated as an exercise of its land-use power for any of these purposes.[12]

However, the Court said, it is an altogether different matter if an "essential nexus" exists between the condition and the landowner's proposed use of the property:

> Thus, if the Commission attached to the permit some condition that would have protected the public's ability to see the beach notwithstanding construction of the new house—for example, a height limitation, a width restriction, or a ban on fences—so long as the Commission could have exercised its police power (as we have assumed it could) to forbid construction of the house altogether, imposition of the condition would also be constitutional. Moreover (and here we come closer to the facts of the present case), the condition would be constitutional even if it consisted of the requirement that the Nollans provide a viewing spot on their property for passersby with whose sighting of the ocean their new house would interfere.... The evident constitutional propriety disappears, however, if the condition substituted for the prohibition utterly fails to further the end advanced as the justification for the prohibition.... [T]he lack of nexus between the condition and the original purpose of the building restriction converts that purpose to something other than what it was. The purpose then becomes, quite simply, the obtaining of an easement to serve some

> valid governmental purpose, but without payment of compensation. Whatever may be the outer limits of "legitimate state interests" in the takings and land-use context, this is not one of them.[13]

This brings us to the two blockbuster cases from the 1990s: *Lucas v. South Carolina Coastal Council*[14] and *Dolan v. City of Tigard*.[15] In the former, the Court sets out the rules on total or per se takings and, in footnotes, potential direction on partial takings. In the latter, the Court expands on its essential-nexus requirement from *Nollan*, adding a new "rough-proportionality" requirement. After these cases, the legal landscape is transformed. The essays that follow, particularly those by Mike Berger, Dan Curtin, Chris Duerksen, Robert Freilich, Doug Kmiec, and Dan Mandelker, analyze and review what these cases have to say as well as how they are being interpreted by lower federal and state courts. It is fair to conclude the *Dolan* case is having the greater influence by far, affecting the regulatory permitting process whenever conditions accompany that process. But *Lucas* has some lessons as well, particularly in crafting the basis for exercising those land-use controls that deprive the landowner of most uses, as in conservation areas and the coastal zone.

II. Regulatory Takings after Lucas

A. The Case

1. TOTAL OR PER SE TAKING

In *Lucas v. South Carolina Coastal Council*, the U.S. Supreme Court held that a coastal-protection statute that prevented construction of houses on two beach lots, thus denying the owner all economically beneficial use of the lots, took such lots by regulation (thereby requiring compensation to the owner) unless the regulation fell into one of two exceptions:

1. the regulation prevented nuisances, or
2. the regulation was part of a state's background principles of real property.

The Court suggested that partial regulatory takings may also require compensation if they interfere with the owner's reasonable investment-backed expectations under state law. Moreover, defining which property interests are before the Court may well be crucial in determining whether a regulatory taking has occurred. The Court reaches these issues after redefining the *past* history of regulatory takings.

First, the Court reduced considerably the previously insuperable ripeness barrier to "applied" (as compared with facial) takings cases that it erected in *Williamson County Regional Planning Commission v. Hamilton Bank of Johnson City.*[16] There, the Court required a landowner who challenged a land-use regulation as applied to seek first all available regulatory relief from government (variances, special permits, and so forth) and then use whatever inverse condemnation procedures were available, before the Court would consider the challenge. In many states, this requirement would make regulatory takings challenges difficult. In multipermit jurisdictions like California, Hawaii, and Florida, it makes them nearly impossible. Courts around the country have avoided deciding regulatory takings cases on the merits by concluding they were not ripe under *Hamilton Bank.*

Holding that the "past deprivation" of Lucas's right to develop his beachfront lots was permanent and that Lucas had appropriately alleged an "injury in fact," the Court declined to apply its ripeness rule in this case. As the dissent pointed out,[17] *Hamilton Bank* provides no such exceptions. Therefore, this case could be construed as substantially weakening the ripeness doctrine of *Hamilton Bank,* regardless of the rationale set out by the Court's majority. Professor Tom Roberts addresses this issue at some length in his chapter on ripeness.

Second, the Court rewrote part of the historical background to regulatory takings on the way to crafting some new standards for total takings and suggesting others for partial takings. Beginning with the 1922 case of *Pennsylvania Coal Co. v. Mahon,*[18] the Court correctly observed that there was no such thing as a taking of property by regulation until Justice Holmes said there was: if a regulation went "too far" then it might be a taking. Until then, only physical takings of property (regular or inverse condemnation) needed a public purpose and just compensation required by the Fifth Amendment to the U.S. Constitution. The Court also correctly observed that the 1922 decision failed to describe what "too far" meant. Moreover, for seventy-five years thereafter, the Court eschewed set formulae except to note that physical invasions always required compensation, including such invasions that were the result of a regulation.[19]

But the Court is not on such sound ground in declaring that it had always regarded the taking of all economic use *by regulation* to be a taking requiring compensation. As the dissent points out (and the Court cavalierly dismisses) the history of the takings clause makes clear that it was originally directed at only physical, and not regulatory, takings.[20] Although it is not so clear that the Court made a conscious distinction, the dissent is also accurate in observing that recent "taking all economic use by regulation" cases were for the most part *facial* attacks on land-use regulations, rather than—as here—challenges to regulations *as applied* to a particular interest in land. The Court compounds its skewing of takings clause history by announcing that the "harmful and noxious use" standard (applied, however strangely, by the South Carolina Supreme Court) is really the same as, if not shorthand for, "advancing a legitimate state interest"—which must be news to legions of planners and lawyers who have rightly assumed they are altogether different concepts. While it may be that in difficult cases attempting to distinguish between "preventing public harm" and "conferring a public benefit" the distinction is not analytically useful, in many instances it is obvious and easily made. The dissent is accurate in its conclusion that explaining the "harmful and noxious use" standard away in this case is unnecessary and unprecedented. It is also arguably irrelevant, at least to the ultimate holding in this case.

It is irrelevant because the rule announced by the Court is a fairly narrow one: a regulation that removes all "productive or economically beneficial use" from a discrete, definable interest in property is a taking requiring compensation under the Fifth Amendment—a situation that the Court describes as a "rarity." The Court clearly takes a broad view of instances when a regulation deprives a landowner of "all economic use" of the land. Lucas had purchased two beachfront lots for nearly $1 million to build two houses. Several nearby beachfront lots already had houses on them. The property was zoned for single-family residential use. An amendment to South Carolina's coastal zone protection statute enacted *after* Lucas purchased his lots made developing them illegal. As one dissenting justice pointed out, Lucas could legally put a trailer on each lot, camp out or picnic on the lots, or build some docking and walkways. However, the majority of the Court found none of these uses to be sufficiently "economic" (the current jargon refers to these as "salvage" uses) and so treated the case as one of total economic deprivation by land-use regulation.

The Court requires compensation for such a taking of real property rights by regulation, unless the State of South Carolina can "identify background principles of nuisance and property law that prohibit the uses he [Lucas] now intends in the circumstances in which the property is presently found."[21] The state must show that the prohibited uses "were not part of his [Lucas's] title to begin with."[22] Therefore:

1. If the common law of the state would allow neighbors or the state to prohibit the two houses that Lucas wants to construct because they are either public or private nuisances, then the state can prohibit them under the coastal-zone law without providing compensation. This result occurs because such nuisance

uses are always unlawful and are never part of a landowner's rights, so prohibiting them by statute would not take away any property rights. The Court gives as an example a law that might prohibit a landowner from filling his land to flood his neighbor's land.

2. If the background principles of the state's property law would permit such prohibition of use as the two houses Lucas proposed to construct, then again no compensation is required. However, the Court did not fully describe these principles, nor did it discuss them except in a nuisance context (see number one above).
3. In determining whether the proposed use is a public or private nuisance (and therefore forbidden without payment of compensation) the following three factors are critical, but *only* within the nuisance context:[23]
   — the degree of harm to public lands and resources, or adjacent private property, posed by the claimant's proposed activities
   — the social value of the claimant's activities and their suitability to the locality in question
   — the relative ease with which the alleged harm can be avoided through measures taken by the claimant and the government (or adjacent landowners)

Noting that similarly situated landowners were able to use their property (for houses) in a way that the state coastal-zone statute prohibited for Lucas, the court stopped just short of finding a taking requiring compensation and sent the case back to South Carolina to see if the state could meet the new tests.

The property interest need not be valueless (of the majority, only Justice Kennedy regularly uses the term "value" in analysis) to qualify for compensation. As the dissent points out, the Lucas property still has some value, though probably not nearly as much as it had before the beachfront regulation preventing residential development. The two lots have virtually no economic use, but this would be true regardless of whether the police power were being exercised to prevent a public harm or confer a public benefit, or to prevent a harmful or noxious use. This nearly compels a conclusion that the Court's purpose in rewriting takings history is to lay the groundwork for decisions requiring Fifth Amendment compensation for partial regulatory takings (not before the Court in *Lucas*) as well as for complete ones (the *Lucas* case). In sum, rewriting takings clause history may well serve to justify treating regulatory takings more like physical takings: many more intrusions on real property rights will require compensation.

2. PARTIAL TAKINGS

This conclusion becomes even more inescapable upon examination of that favorite repository (among professors, anyway) of clues to the future: the Court's footnotes. While largely devoted to answering the blistering barrage directed at the Court by the dissent (for example, the dissent's opening salvo is: "Today the Court launches a missile to kill a mouse")[24] the notes evince a clear intention to allow compensation for takings of less than all economic use if and when such a taking is before the Court. At footnote 8, the Court responds to a dissent criticism that compensation for regulatory taking of all economic use is not consistent with lack of compensation for regulatory taking of, say, 95 percent of economic use:

> This analysis errs in its assumption that the landowner whose deprivation is one step short of complete is not entitled to compensation. Such an owner might not be able to claim the benefit of our categorical formulation, but, as we have acknowledged time and again, "[t]he economic impact of the regulation on the claimant and . . . the extent to which the regulation has interfered with distinct investment-backed expectations" are keenly relevant to takings analysis generally.[25]

This "frustration of investment-backed expectations" standard, which the Court chooses not to apply in *Lucas* because it characterized the regulatory taking as total, is clearly not rejected. Indeed, one concurring member of the Court (Justice Kennedy) would have applied it. Moreover, in an earlier footnote, the Court had already alluded to the utility of the "reasonable expectations" standard, though in a slightly different context: that of deciding how thin to slice property interests (or, alternatively, how many sticks in the Holfeldian bundle) for purposes of deciding whether property has been taken:

> Regrettably, the rhetorical force of our "deprivation of all economically feasible use" rule is greater than its precision, since the rule does not make clear the "property interest" against which the loss of value is to be measured. When, for example, a regulation requires a developer to leave 90% of a rural tract in its natural state, it is unclear whether we would analyze the situation as one in which the owner has been deprived of all economically beneficial use of the burdened portion of the tract, or as one in which the owner has suffered a mere diminution in value of the tract as a whole. [The note then criticizes that portion of the New York state court's decision in *Penn Central Transp. Co. v. New York City*,[27]

> which suggested nearby property of the owner could be amalgamated with that portion he claimed was unusable in deciding whether a taking by regulation had occurred.] . . .
>
> The answer to this difficult question may lie in *how the owner's reasonable expectations* have been shaped by the State's law of property—*i.e.,* whether and to what degree the State's law has accorded legal recognition and protection to the particular interest in land with respect to which the takings claimant alleges a diminution in (or elimination of) value.[26]

This language inescapably leads to a second conclusion about the direction the Court may take in future regulatory takings cases: property owners will be increasingly able to "segment" their property interests presented for takings analyses. While approval of cluster developments of the Planned Unit Development (PUD) variety are probably not in much jeopardy, this Court will likely look carefully at claims that land-use regulations prevent the development of large tracts of land, without necessarily considering nearby land that has been successfully developed under the same ownership.

This result will be particularly likely to occur if the rationale for the regulation falls under the welfare clause of the police power and not the health and safety clauses. Already suggested by the Court in *Agins v. Tiburon,*[28] and picked up by a California appellate court on remand from the Supreme Court in *First English,*[29] the *Lucas* Court is obviously leery of

> regulations that leave the owner of land without economically beneficial or productive options for its use—typically, as here, by requiring land to be left substantially in its natural state—carry with them a heightened risk that private property is being pressed into some form of public service under the guise of mitigating serious public harm. . . .
>
> The many statutes on the books, both state and federal, that provide for the use of eminent domain to impose servitudes on private scenic lands preventing developmental uses, or to acquire such lands altogether, suggest the practical equivalence in this setting of negative regulation and appropriation.[30]

The Court concludes:

> We think, in short, that there are good reasons for our frequently-expressed belief that when the owner of real property has been called upon to sacrifice *all* economically beneficial uses in the name

of the common good, that is, to leave his property economically idle, he has suffered a taking.[31]

In sum, any regulation of land that leaves an owner with no economic use will in all likelihood require compensation as a regulatory taking. The inquiry will focus on what amounts to such a total deprivation. Clearly some marginal use of the land is not enough. The land must have some viable economic use. Thus, land-use reclassifications at either the state or local government level which permit only uses that, for policy or practical reasons, have no economic value, are almost certainly takings which require compensation. But those restrictions, however onerous, that leave viable economic use of the land intact, fall outside the takings holding of this case. This would leave intact most local government zoning districts and, depending upon the uses permitted state land use districts. Indeed, the majority appears to have rejected applying a different standard—frustration of legitimate, investment-backed expectations—which would significantly broaden the landowners' rights to compensation. However, the majority's notes read very much as though they would like to apply this test when the occasion arises.

Second, even if the regulation does deprive an owner of all economic use, it requires no compensation if it prevents the equivalent of a public or private nuisance. Preserving historic buildings, coastal views, natural ecosystems, and the like has not been associated with nuisance prevention, so any regulation for these purposes that leaves a landowner without an economic use of the land would almost certainly require compensation. Indeed, the Court took pains to identify natural resource protection ordinances and historic preservation cases as examples of what it regards as police-power overreaching.

In sum, while the Court's majority has probably not "launched a missile to kill a mouse," it has nevertheless substantially altered the rules for regulating land. Virtually nothing but regulations to prevent nuisances will justify leaving a landowner without some economic use of land. Furthermore, in notes and dicta, the Court does tilt toward preserving property rights and not toward governmental regulation of them. Government can still clearly "go on" without violating the Constitution's prohibition against taking property without compensation, but it must do so with greater care and sensitivity to private property rights, a theme addressed with even greater vigor by the *Dolan* majority, as discussed below. Only under the most egregious circumstances can private property be rendered virtually valueless by regulation. The future for land-use regulations may be more ominous still.

B. After *Lucas*

1. THE EXCEPTIONS

There is, of course, no takings at all if a regulation falls within either the nuisance or inherent principles of state property law exceptions. The nuisance exception is potentially difficult to identify, given the explicit language in *Lucas* rejecting "public harm" as an exception to the per se total taking rule, especially if that public harm is of the welfare variety. Taking a somewhat broader view of this exception than specifically warranted by *Lucas,* though probably within the nuisance exception, is *M & J Coal Co. v. United States.*[32] There, the court rejected a takings claim resulting from a cease and desist order entered against a coal company under the Surface Mining Control and Reclamation Act of 1977, preventing the mining of certain coal in West Virginia. Citing language in *Keystone Bituminous Coal Ass'n v. DeBenedictis*[33] suggesting that no one had a right to use property to create a nuisance or otherwise harm others, the court held: "Thus, in accordance with settled precedent, M & J could not have acquired under its deed of title the right to cause damage or a substantial risk of damage to the public health or safety. . . . An 'antecedent' inquiry into the property use interests acquired by M & J thus reveals that M & J never acquired the right to mine in such a way as to endanger the public health and safety. OSM's action to prevent M & J from doing so did not interfere with M & J's property use interests."[34]

Just how state courts might apply the *Lucas* exceptions is illustrated in the recent Colorado Supreme Court decision in *State Dep't of Health v. The Mill.*[35] There, the court found that Colorado and federal law pertaining to the control of uranium mine tailings fell within the "background principles of state law" exception, so that even though the owner of a sixty-one-acre parcel could do virtually nothing with it and might otherwise be able to show a per se taking, the exception made the claim for compensation untenable. There was also some indication that the nuisance exception might apply, given the nature of the previous use and the resulting danger to public health and safety. The dissent, however, observed that the principal statutes making the property unusable were not passed until several years after the property owner had purchased the site, and therefore should not be construed as part of the company's original title.

2. TOTAL TAKINGS

In the context of single-family residences, the U.S. Court of Claims recently held in *Bowles v. United States.*[36] that denial of a Section 404 (Clean Water Act) permit by the Corps of Engineers, for fill to construct a septic system, constituted a per se taking. Deciding that the lot had "no economically beneficial use after the government action . . . pursuant to the 'total takings' rule announced in *Lucas*, the landowner has suffered a taking and must be compensated."[37] Moreover, the court held that these facts would result in a partial taking even if the court had not already decided that a total taking had occurred:

> Even assuming that the alleged taking in this case is less than total, Bowles still has suffered a compensable taking under the pre-*Lucas* regulatory takings doctrine. Under the pre-*Lucas* framework, the relevant inquiry considers the economic impact of the regulation on the lot and whether Bowles' investment-backed expectations were reasonable at the time he acquired Lot 29.
>
> Bowles' investment-backed expectations were to build a permanent retirement residence on Lot 29. . . . In this respect the court concludes that Bowles' expectations were reasonable.[38]

Of course, the per se total taking is the more difficult of the two kinds of takings to prove, as the majority in *Lucas* suggested it might be. Many of the partial takings cases in the following section were also brought by plaintiffs and petitioners as per se takings. However, when the courts found remaining economic uses of any substance, they found that no such per se taking had occurred because the property had some economically beneficial use. An example is *Outdoor Systems, Inc. v. City of Mesa,*[39] in which the plaintiffs attempted to use *Lucas* to strike down a billboard control ordinance as a taking. As the court observed, because a viable land use would remain, the facts dismally failed the test of loss of all economically beneficial use so "[t]his holding has no relevance to these appeals."[40] By and large, many state court cases reach the same conclusion.[41] However, those decisions which carefully examine *Lucas* have concluded that a fundamental attribute of property now includes the right to make some economically viable use of the land.[42]

Also failing a per se test was the landowner in *Redman v. Ohio Department of Industrial Relations.*[43] There, plaintiff claimed a per se taking under *Lucas* because of the disapproval of a permit to drill two oil and gas wells. Noting the *Lucas* test was whether a denial of all economically beneficial use of the affected property has occurred, the court observed that two functioning wells were on the property, and that permits for drilling others were merely delayed. Therefore, plaintiff could not say the permit disapproval resulted in the denial of all economically beneficial use of his leases.

3. PARTIAL TAKINGS

While the *Lucas* case deals primarily with total takings, it also suggests the way in which the U.S. Supreme Court will deal with partial takings. In a footnote response to the dissent's vigorous criticism of the underinclusiveness of the per se takings rule set out for total takings, Justice Scalia for the majority made it abundantly clear that any landowner whose property loss was not total but in the 90 percent range had an excellent case for a partial taking.[44] The rule suggested by the Court was "frustration of legitimate investment-backed expectations." The likely application of this rule is buttressed by the concurring opinion of Justice Kennedy, who would have applied this more lenient standard even to the *Lucas* facts. The rule was prominently discussed by the Court in 1978 in *Penn Central,* in which the Court proclaimed its difficulty in articulating a bright line rule for regulatory takings. Indeed, according to one commentator, the Court has suggested this rule sixteen times in the past fifteen years.[45]

That some variant of the "frustration of investment-backed expectations" rule will be the principal test for deciding partial takings is clear from federal court decisions immediately following the *Lucas* decision. In *Reahard v. Lee County,*[46] the court actually delayed its decision until after *Lucas* was decided, then set out its own multipart criteria based on the investment-backed expectations standard (though it ultimately found that mere plan designation of property in a resource protection zone fell short of such a taking). Similarly, in *Berrios v. Lancaster,*[47] the court cited *Lucas* for the proposition that partial takings should be decided under the rule of "frustration of distinct, investment-backed expectations." In *Golden Gate Hotel Ass'n v. City and County of San Francisco,*[48] the court held that San Francisco's hotel conversion ordinance constituted a taking without compensation. Citing *Lucas,* the court found that while there was too much use left in plaintiff's hotel property to be a total or per se taking, footnote 8 in that case suggested a taking was still possible depending upon the economic impact of the regulation on the claimant and the extent to which the regulation interferes with the claimant's distinct investment-backed expectations. The court found that

> those rights have been deeply trenched-upon. Consequently, the economically viable uses of the hotel owners' land have been significantly diminished. Accordingly, although the plaintiff hotel owners are not denied all economically productive uses of their land, the court finds that the Ordinance so deeply trenches on the hotel owners' investment-backed expectations and their classic

property rights to use, possess, and exclude as to constitute a deprivation of economically productive use, and thus constitute a taking.[49]

Federal cases since *Lucas* do not always find a partial taking has occurred, of course, but when they do not, clear extenuating circumstances exist. Thus, in *Orange Lake Associates, Inc. v. Kirkpatrick,*[50] the court found that reduction in density on plaintiff's land did not constitute a per se taking because there was economic use left in the property, and reduction in density from twelve dwelling units per acre to two per acre did not constitute a partial taking. The court also appeared to be moved by the "unreasonableness" of the investment-backed expectations of the plaintiff, who arguably had notice of the government plans to reduce the density before plaintiff completed the purchase of the property. The court in *Gamble v. Eau Claire County*[51] reached a similar conclusion. Citing *Lucas* for the proposition that a rule or regulation that deprives an owner of economic use can be a taking under the Fifth Amendment, the court nevertheless found no taking here, in part because the court was skeptical that the denial of a permit to construct a gasoline service station could result either in a per se or a partial taking. The court also found that the plaintiff had not adequately availed herself of state inverse condemnation remedies and therefore the claim was not ripe.

Of particular interest in the analysis of partial takings are two decisions by the Federal Circuit, both of which Robert Freilich and Dan Mandelker discuss at some length. *Florida Rock Industries v. United States*[52] and *Loveladies Harbor, Inc. v. United States*[53] both grew from denials of Section 404 (Clean Water Act) dredge and fill permits by the Corps of Engineers. In each case, the court discussed the so-called (after the infamous footnote 7 in *Lucas*) "denominator issue": what is the extent of the landowner's property interest to be considered in deciding whether the interest allegedly damaged is partially taken? Out of 250 acres, the court was willing to consider only the devaluation of 12.5 acres for which the Corps denied a permit in *Loveladies*. With the difference being $2.7 million with the permit and $12,000 without it, the trial court awarded the $2.7 million and the Federal Circuit affirmed.

This denominator theory has come under strong attack by many commentators, including Robert Freilich and Daniel Mandelker in this collection. Of particular interest in this regard is *Concrete Pipe and Products of California, Inc. v. Construction Laborers Pension Trust,*[54] even though so far ignored by the federal court decisions since *Lucas*. The case is not a real property matter at all. Nevertheless, Justice Souter, for a majority that included Justice Scalia, stated that the Court had not and would not permit the segmenting of property interests for the purpose of deciding when a regulation amounted to a partial taking, citing the Court's 1978 *Penn Central* decision that so held in denying the application of New York's landmark preservation law to Grand Central Station amounted to a regulatory taking. This has led Robert Freilich, Elizabeth Garvin, and Dan Mandelker to suggest (1) that only the degree of the economic loss is a proper matter for the courts to consider in the context of partial takings, and (2) that much, if not all, the property held by a landowner (particularly in the vicinity or adjoining the subject parcel) be included in the "denominator." Freilich and Garvin suggest that the entire *Penn Central* test be applied to such partial takings, including the character of the governmental action and the degree of economic loss to the owner (as compared with the importance of the offending regulation to the public), whereas the *Lucas* majority could be construed as using only the legitimate investment-backed expectations portion.

Dan Mandelker makes the same point, based upon pre-*Lucas* decisions such as *Andrus v. Allard*.[55] The argument is that taking of one "strand" is not a taking of property by regulation because the court must consider the aggregate property interests of the owner as the court did in *Andrus*.[56] Of course, the *Concrete Pipe* decision is not a land-use case and one could reasonably argue that the decision therefore does not apply to real property cases. Indeed, one of the recent state court decisions addressing partial takings of land specifically refused to apply *Concrete Pipe* because the "ordinance at issue here is not federal economic legislation [as it is in *Concrete Pipe*] and the *Concrete Pipe* rationale [therefore] does not apply."[57] Mike Berger addresses this interpretation in his chapter.

State court cases decided after *Lucas* are legion in using the "frustration of investment-backed expectation" standard. When the courts fail to find a regulatory taking it is invariably because (when they comprehend the standard) they find the land retains too much development potential despite the regulation. (After all, the federal courts are *not* saying that any diminution in value due to a regulation is a compensable taking). Thus, in *Zerbetz v. Municipality of Anchorage*,[58] the Alaska Supreme Court found no taking of plaintiff's property (located in a bog) when designated conservation wetlands under the state's coastal-zone management plan could still be developed after submission of soil samples, water flow data, and vegetative and habitat information. Indeed, the court observed that the planning and coastal commission charged with enforcing the designation had approved twenty-six of twenty-eight subdivision platting applications for property designated as conservation wetlands in that bog! In *Tim Thompson, Inc. v. Village of Hinsdale,*[59] an Illinois appellate court found that a down-zoning of the plaintiff's property did not amount to a partial taking requiring compensation because of the considerable economic use left in the property. Observing that the *Lucas* case left unresolved the issue of regulatory taking when a regulation deprived a landowner of less than 100 percent of the economically beneficial use, the court held that property owners can make such a claim, but that the owner could not do so here merely because he could not erect the three houses on three individual lots under a new zoning ordinance, as he had previously planned. The court held that the plaintiff showed only that he could not "realize as much profit . . . as originally anticipated" and that he had been denied only "its optimally desired use."[60] In *Dodd v. Hod River County,*[61] the Oregon Supreme Court similarly found no frustration of reasonable investment-backed expectations when the plaintiff's land was placed in a forest zone, because the plaintiff's expectations were not reasonable. Not only did the plaintiff have constructive notice of the zoning as he was purchasing the property, but also the forest zone "does not require that petitioner's land be left substantially in its natural state; numerous forest and agricultural uses are allowed within the [forest] zone."[62] Therefore, the court rejected the plaintiff's claim that the county took a conservation easement by so zoning the subject property.

III. Exactions and Development Conditions after Dolan

A. The Case

In *Dolan v. City of Tigard,* the Supreme Court struck down a municipal building permit condition that the landowner dedicate bike path and greenway/floodplain easements to the city. As the Court pointed out, had Tigard simply required such dedications, it would be required to pay compensation under the Fifth Amendment. Attaching them as building permit conditions required a more sophisticated analysis closely following *Nollan v. California Coastal Commission,* because the police power is implicated rather than the power of eminent domain. In the process, the Court signalled how far local government may go in passing on the cost of public facilities to landowners. The answer: only to the extent that the required dedication is related both in nature and extent to the impact of the proposed development.

The Dolans own and operate a 9,700 square foot plumbing and electrical supply store on Main Street in Tigard's central business district. Seeking to double the size of the store and pave a thirty-nine-space parking lot, the Dolans applied for a building permit from the city's planning commission. Tigard had previously adopted a comprehensive land-use plan required by state comprehensive land-use management statutes, in accordance with statewide goals.[63] Many of the plan's features are codified in Tigard's Community Development Code (CDC). Among the plan's requirements are the following:

1. In accordance with a pedestrian/bicycle pathway plan, new development must dedicate land for pathways where shown on the plan.
2. In accordance with a master drainage plan, to combat the risks of flooding in one hundred-year floodplains, especially as exacerbated by increased impervious surface through development, developers along waterways such as Fanno Creek (which borders the Dolan parcel to the west) must guarantee the floodway and floodplain are free of structures and able to contain floodwaters by preserving the land alongside as greenway.

As a result of the plan and its codification in the CDC, the commission granted the Dolans their building permit upon the condition that they dedicate the portion of their property in the floodplain as a greenway, and that an additional fifteen-foot strip be dedicated adjacent to the greenway as a pedestrian/bicycle path. A series of commission findings form the basis of these requirements.

Regarding the bikeway, the commission found that the pathway system as an alternative means of transportation could offset some of the traffic demand on nearby streets and lessen the increase in traffic congestion. The commission also found it reasonable to assume that some of the Dolans' customers and staff could use the pathway for transportation and recreation.

Regarding the floodplain greenway dedication, the commission found it reasonably related to the Dolans' application because the site would have more impervious surface. This would result in increased stormwater drainage. Therefore, the dedication requirement was related to the applicants' plans for more intensive development of their land.

After appealing to various local and state administrative agencies and to the Oregon courts without success, the Dolans challenged the holding of the Oregon Supreme Court that the City of Tigard could condition the approval of their building permit on the dedication of property for flood control and traffic improvement. The U.S. Supreme Court granted certiorari to set out the "required degree of connection between the exactions imposed by the city and the projected impacts of the proposed development."[64]

The Court essentially adopted a three-part test:

1. Does the permit condition seek to promote a legitimate state interest?
2. Does an essential nexus exist between the legitimate state interest and the permit condition?
3. Does a required degree of connection exist between the exactions and the projected impact of the development?

The Court disposed of the first two parts quickly and affirmatively. Certainly the prevention of flooding along the creek and the reduction of traffic in the business district "qualify as the type of legitimate public purposes [the Court has] upheld."[65] Moreover, the Court held it was "equally obvious" that a nexus exists between preventing flooding and limiting development within the creek's floodplain, and that "the same may be said for the city's attempt to reduce traffic congestion by providing for alternative means of transportation [like a] pedestrian/bicycle pathway."[66] So far, so good: the Court found both a public purpose (which the Court assumed without deciding in *Nollan*) and an essential nexus (which the Court decided was lacking in *Nollan*). Regarding the third part of the test, a question remained about whether "the degree of the exactions demanded by the city's permit conditions bear the required relationship to the projected impact of petitioner's proposed development."[67]

The Court said no: The city's "tentative findings" concerning increased stormwater flow from the more intensively developed property, together with its statement that such development was "anticipated to generate additional vehicular traffic thereby increasing congestion" on nearby streets, were simply not "constitutionally sufficient to justify the conditions imposed by the city on petitioner's building permit."[68]

The Court's test is one of "rough proportionality," described as follows:

> [T]he city must make some sort of individualized determination that the required dedication is related both in nature and extent to the impact of the proposed development.[69]

Applying this test to the Dolan hardware store property, the Court concluded that the City of Tigard demanded too much to pass the third nexus/rough-proportionality test. Simply concluding that a bikeway easement could offset some of the traffic demand that the new hardware store would generate did not constitute sufficiently quantified findings for the taking of an easement. While the Court has "no doubt that the city was correct in finding that the larger retail sales facility proposed by petitioner will increase traffic on the streets . . . the city has not met its burden of demonstrating that the additional number of vehicle and bicycle trips generated by petitioner's development reasonably relate to the city's requirement for a dedication of the pedestrian/ bicycle pathway easement. The city simply found that the creation of the pathway 'could offset some of the traffic demand . . . and lessen the increase in traffic congestion. . . .' The city must make some effort to quantify its findings ... beyond the conclusory statement [quoted above]."[70]

Regarding the greenway easement, while the Court said "[I]t is axiomatic that increasing the amount of impervious surface will increase the quantity and rate of stormwater flow from petitioner's property . . . the city demanded more—it not only wanted petitioner not to build in the floodplain, but it also wanted petitioner's property along Fanno Creek for its Greenway system. The city has never said why a *public* greenway, as opposed to a *private* one, was required in the interests of flood control."[71]

The constitutional problem in both instances is "the loss of [their] ability to exclude," which the Court reminds us is one of the most essential sticks in the bundle of rights that are characterized as property. Indeed, Chief Justice Rehnquist has previously and frequently written about the fundamental nature of property rights: "[We] hold that the 'right to exclude' so universally held to be a fundamental element of the property right, falls within the category of interests that the Government cannot take without compensation."[72] The Court generally has said much the same thing in *Loretto v. TelePrompTer Manhattan CATV Corp.*[73] This is a critical point, to which the Court returns several times. Property rights matter mightily to this Court:

> We see no reason why the Takings Clause of the Fifth Amendment, as much a part of the Bill of Rights as the First Amendment [free speech, press, religion, association, assembly] or the Fourth Amendment [search and seizure] should be relegated to the status of a poor relation in these comparable circumstances.[74]

B. After *Dolan*: The Progeny

Courts since *Dolan*, both state and federal, appear to have adopted completely both the nexus and proportionality tests which mark that decision. An excellent example is the Eighth Circuit decision in *Christopher Lake Development Co. v. St. Louis County*,[75] in which the court applied *Dolan* to strike down a county drainage-system requirement. The county granted the owner of forty-two acres preliminary development approval for two residential communities on the condition that the owner provide a drainage system for an entire watershed. First, the court dealt with the public purpose issue (part one of the *Dolan* test). The court stated that "even assuming the legitimacy of the County's purpose in requiring a drainage system, the application of the Criteria may violate the equal protection clause."[76] Citing *Nollan* for the nexus or second part of the test, the court then opined that although "the County's objective to prevent flooding may be rational, it may not be rational to single out the Partnership to provide the entire drainage system."[77] The court then found such a requirement disproportionate to the drainage problems resulting from the proposed development:

> [F]rom our review of the record, the County has forced the Partnership to bear a burden that should fairly have been allocated throughout the watershed area. "A strong public desire to improve the public condition will not warrant achieving the desire by a shorter cut than the constitutional way of paying for the change."[78]

As for a remedy, the court said as follows:

> We believe that the Partnership is entitled to recoup the portion of its expenditures in excess of its pro rata share and remand to the district court to determine the details and amounts.[79]

An even more egregious case is *Walz v. Town of Smithtown*,[80] from the Second Circuit. There, landowners were denied access to the public water supply when they refused to deed the front fifteen feet of their property to Smithtown for road-widening purposes. Finding a total lack of nexus between water service and road widening, the court found that "[A]s landowners, the Walzes surely had a right not to be compelled to convey some of their land in order to obtain utility service."[81]

Courts are also concretely addressing the level of detail required to meet proportionality and nexus standards. An excellent example of that requirement comes from the New Jersey case of *F & W Associates v. County of Somerset*.[82] Holding that traffic impact fees assessed against a developer met the rational-nexus test, the court held as follows:

> The developer's pro-rata share must be "necessitated or required by the construction or improvements within such subdivision. . . . [citation omitted] The statute is a codification . . . which focused on the "rational nexus" between the needs created by, and the benefits conferred upon, the subdivision and the cost of the off-tract improvements.[83]

Noting that the ordinance assessing the impact fees was adopted "only after a comprehensive study of such factors as existing road facilities, current zoning, projected population growth, and existing commercial uses in the area,"[84] the court dismissed the notion that

> a causal nexus between the necessity for off-tract improvements and the development must be measured with precision. . . . What must be demonstrated is a "rational" nexus, not mathematical certainty. For example, the assessment should not be invalidated simply because there may be residual benefit conferred to the general public in its use of the off-tract road improvement. An assessment is subject to challenge only if the developer is required to pay a "disproportionate share of the cost of improvements that also benefit other persons."[85]

The court set out in detail what the acceptable comprehensive study contained:

> The study devised a volume-capacity ratio, measuring the demand volume and Mountain Boulevard's capacity. Based on projected full development of potential residential, retail and office use, the study adopted vehicle "trip generation" methodology and from this model, predicted incremental traffic impact resulting from future development of the land. The study estimated how much extra traffic would be generated by each development in the target area (Mountain Boulevard and surrounding roadways). The estimates were grounded on industrial standards, observations and empirical data obtained from traffic counts. The study then suggested what roadway improvements would be needed to accommodate the increased demands, and estimated the cost of those improvements.[86]

Noting that the township ordinance adopted the results of this "exacting study," the court observed that the ordinance authorized traffic-impact fees according to the formula for calculating each developer's share of the cost of the needed off-tract improvements. Not only does the ordinance provide for adjustment of the developer's pro rata share if conditions change, but it also exempts a developer from the fee altogether if the development's off-tract impact is negligible, or if the developer does not benefit from the highway improvement.[87]

Even before *Dolan,* the court in *Northern Illinois Home Builders Ass'n, Inc. v. County of DuPage*[88] also set out a procedure for land-development conditions, described by one expert in the field as "overwhelming" and demonstrating "a level of effort that he had never seen before."[89] The county was seeking to meet Illinois's strict "specifically and uniquely attributable" test for road improvement impact-fees provided for by statute. First, the court held that the county met the test of imposing a fee only for road improvements made necessary by the additional traffic generated by the new development:

> The formula used by the county imposes fees only on road improvement costs generated by new development. In order to quantify the amount of travel generated by different types of development, the county used the Chicago Area Transit (CATS) model, which mathematically traces cars as they leave particular developments and enter on the roads. The county also used trip-generation data collected by the Institute for Transportation Engineering.
>
> Furthermore, DuPage County developed its own computer model which gave it the ability to model future travel based on new development. The County did travel surveys which allowed it to determine which road segments were deficient due to existing development. Impact fee funds are not spent on those roads. . . . We hold that the data gathered by DuPage County ensures that it imposes impact fees only for the improvements made necessary by new development.[90]

Then, the court further found that under the county system the new developments receive direct and material benefit from the road improvements financed by their impact fees:

> DuPage County divided itself into 11 districts based on the following criteria: location of existing and proposed municipal boundaries; locations of major developable parcels of land; existing major retail/employment centers; location of potential transportation corridors; CATS one-quarter-section-based zone system; and the existing county highway system. The funds collected from new development in a particular district are used to finance improvements in that same district. Testimony at trial established that fee payers in a district do benefit from the decrease in congestion resulting from the improvements made in that district.[91]

While some have argued that *Dolan* should be applied according to its facts (that is, only to dedication conditions), many courts apply it not only to impact fees but also to other land-development conditions. This latter interpretation is presumably warranted following the Supreme Court's decision to vacate and remand the impact fees case of *Ehrlich v. Culver City*[92] to a court of appeal in California, only days after its decision in *Dolan*. This is an impact fee case, not a dedication case and, as discussed in detail in Dan Curtin's essay, it is now before the California Supreme Court on certiorari from the California Court of Appeal.

Going well beyond impact fees is the application of *Dolan* in *Manocherian v. Lenox Hospital,*[93] in which the New York Court of Appeals struck down a rent-stabilization statute in part because it did not advance "a closely and legitimately connected State interest." Citing both the *Dolan* and *Nollan* cases, the court said that

> the Supreme Court refrained from placing any limitations or distinctions or classifications on the application of the "essential nexus" test. This suggests and supports a uniform, clear and reasonably definitive standard of review in takings cases. . . . Indeed, Justice Brennan, in dissenting in *Nollan,* expressly attributed to the Majority's holding in *Nollan* an impact on *all regulatory takings cases,* stating that the Court's "exactitude, is inconsistent with our standard for reviewing the rationality of a State's exercise of its police power for the welfare of its citizens."[94]

Nor are these post-*Dolan* cases unique. Earlier state court cases have held that at the least, a nexus must exist between the conditions placed on land development permits or zone changes and a legitimate state interest achieved or facility constructed.

In *Sparks v. Douglas County,*[95] the Washington Court of Appeals struck down a road right-of-way dedication on proportionality grounds. The court held that the dedication requirements for sixteen single-family homes or thirty-two duplexes were arbitrary, capricious, and unconstitutional takings because the increase of an estimated twenty-five cars per hour was not a number of sufficient magnitude to support a reasonable inference that the developments would have an adverse impact justifying those dedications. The case is on appeal to the Washington Supreme Court.

Applying a "specifically and uniquely attributable" test (questionable after *Dolan,* however), a Connecticut court in *Timber Trails Corp. v. Planning and Zoning Commission of the Town of Sherman*[96] struck down an off-site road improvement condition on subdivision approval on the ground that problems with existing highways were not so specifically and uniquely attributable to abutting subdivisions. More applicable is the Connecticut Supreme Court case of *Property Group, Inc. v. Planning and Zoning Commission of the Town of Tolland,*[97] striking down a road widening condition on a subdivision approval for only ten lots. The court found that the road problems were preexisting and there was no substantial evidence the widening was necessitated by the proposed development. The Kentucky Court of Appeals also struck down a bridge construction and dedication requirement as a subdivision approval and rezoning requirement in *Lexington-Fayette Urban County Government v. Schneider and Hi Acres Development Co.*,[98] because no reasonable relationship existed between the development and the need for the bridge. Reaching a similar conclusion is *Cobb v. Snohomish County*,[99] in which the court struck down a road-improvement fee because the county could not show the improvements were reasonably necessary for the particular level of service to be provided.[100]

The court in *Lancaster Redevelopment Agency v. Dibley*[101] found housing financed by a traffic-impact fee offset invalid on nexus grounds. The court found no guarantee the program would result in construction of affordable housing for low- or moderate-income persons who would benefit from the overpasses. Somewhat similarly, but raising broader takings issues, is the decision in *Sintra, Inc. v. City of Seattle*.[102]

IV. Conclusion

Clearly there are many principles that can be derived from these landmark cases. Among the most salient:

1. A regulation that leaves a landowner without economically beneficial use (not merely use or value) is a per se taking of property requiring compensation.
2. There are only two exceptions to this rule: nuisance and background principles of state property that inhere in the title. Most of us know what the former is. Few of us know what the latter is.
3. There is no inquiry into how or why the landowner acquired the property. This is irrelevant. That is what a per se rule is all about. "Investment-backed expectations" is a partial taking inquiry, not a total taking inquiry.
4. In all likelihood, partial takings will be measured against the landowner's legitimate, investment-backed expectations, but whether the determination is based on all the owner's land or only that part which is regulated is not yet clear.
5. A land-development condition must advance a legitimate state interest, have a rational or essential nexus to a problem the payor landowner is about to cause by developing land, and be roughly proportional and beneficial to that land development.
6. Local government bean-counting is not required, however.
7. The U.S. Supreme Court does not think much of environmental, coastal, historical, or other welfare-based (as compared with

health and safety) regulations that devalue property without compensation.

Notes

1. Pennsylvania Coal Co. v. Mahon, 260 U.S. 393, 415 (1922).
2. Village of Euclid v. Ambler Realty Co., 272 U.S. 365 (1926).
3. Nectow v. City of Cambridge, 277 U.S. 183 (1928).
4. FRED P. BOSSELMAN, DAVID L. CALLIES, AND JOHN S. BANTA, THE TAKING ISSUE: AN ANALYSIS OF THE CONSTITUTIONAL LIMITS OF LAND-USE CONTROL (1973).
5. *Id.; see also* LAND USE AND THE CONSTITUTION (Brian W. Blaesser and Alan C. Weinstein eds., 1989).
6. 416 U.S. 1 (1974).
7. *E.g.,* Williamson County Regional Planning Comm'n v. Hamilton Bank of Johnson City, 473 U.S. 172 (1985); MacDonald, Sommer & Frates v. Yolo County, 477 U.S. 340 (1986).
8. 480 U.S. 470 (1987).
9. 112 S. Ct. 2886 (1992).
10. 482 U.S. 304 (1987).
11. 483 U.S. 825 (1987).
12. *Nollan,* 483 U.S. at 838-39.
13. *Id.* at 836-37.
14. 112 S. Ct. 2886 (1992).
15. 114 S. Ct. 2309 (1994).
16. 473 U.S. 172 (1985).
17. *Lucas,* 112 S. Ct. at 2906 (Blackmun, J., dissenting).
18. 260 U.S. 393 (1922).
19. *See* Loretto v. Teleprompter Manhattan CATV Corp., 458 U.S. 419 (1982).
20. *Lucas,* 112 S. Ct. at 2914 (Blackmun, J., dissenting) (citing and quoting FRED P. BOSSELMAN, DAVID L. CALLIES, AND JOHN S. BANTA, THE TAKING ISSUE: AN ANALYSIS OF THE CONSTITUTIONAL LIMITS OF LAND-USE CONTROL 80-81 (1973)).
21. *Lucas,* 112 S. Ct. at 2901-02.
22. *Id.* at 2899.
23. *Id.* at 2901.
24. *Id.* at 2904 (Blackmun, J., dissenting).
25. *Id.* at 2895 n. 8 (citing Penn Central Transp. Co. v. New York City, 438 U.S. 104 (1978)).
26. *Id.* at 2894 n. 7 (emphasis added).
27. 42 N.Y.2d 324, 366 N.E.2d 1271, 397 N.Y.S.2d 914 (1977), *aff'd,* 438 U.S. 104 (1978).
28. 447 U.S. 255 (1980).
29. First English Lutheran Evangelical Church of Glendale v. County of Los Angeles, 210 Cal. App. 3d 1353, 258 Cal. Rptr. 893 (Ct. App. 1989), *cert. denied,* 493 U.S. 1056 (1990).
30. *Lucas,* 112 S. Ct. at 2894-95.
31. *Id.* at 2895 (emphasis added).

32. 47 F.3d 1148 (Fed. Cir. 1995).

33. 480 U.S. 470 (1987).

34. *M & J Coal Co.*, 47 F.3d at 1154-55.

35. 887 P.2d 993 (Colo. 1994).

36. 31 Fed. Cl. 37 (1994).

37. *Bowles*, 31 Fed. Cl. at 49.

38. *Id.* at 49-50.

39. 997 F.2d 604 (9th Cir. 1993).

40. *Outdoor Systems*, 997 F.2d at 617.

41. *See e.g.*, Sierra Club v. Dep't of Forestry and Fire Protection, 26 Cal. Rptr. 2d 338 (Ct. App. 1993) (observing that economic uses remain to loggers on land restricted for environmental protection purposes) (case ordered not published on denial of review).

42. *See* Guimont v. Clarke, 854 P.2d 1 (Wash. 1993).

43. Nos. 93APE12-1670, 93APE12-1671, 1994 WL 485750 (Ohio Ct. App. Sept. 6, 1994) (unpublished opinion).

44. *Lucas*, 112 S. Ct. at 2895 n.8.

45. Michael M. Berger, *Property Owners Have Rights; Lower Courts Need to Protect Them, in* AFTER *LUCAS*: LAND-USE REGULATION AND THE TAKING OF PROPERTY WITHOUT COMPENSATION 33 (David L. Callies ed., 1993).

46. 968 F.2d 1131 (11th Cir. 1992). On appeal after remand, the Eleventh Circuit held the claim was not ripe because the landowner failed to bring an inverse condemnation action available under Florida law. 30 F.3d 1412 (11th Cir. 1994).

47. 798 F. Supp. 1153 (E.D. Pa. 1992).

48. 836 F. Supp. 707 (N.D. Cal. 1993), *vacated on other grounds*, 18 F.3d 1482 (1994).

49. *Golden Gate*, 836 F. Supp. at 710-11.

50. 21 F.3d 1214 (2d Cir. 1994).

51. 5 F.3d 285 (2d Cir. 1993), *cert. denied*, 114 S. Ct. 1096 (1994).

52. 18 F.3d 1560 (Fed. Cir. 1994), *cert. denied*, 115 S. Ct. 898 (1995).

53. 28 F.3d 1171 (Fed. Cir. 1994).

54. 113 S. Ct. 2290 (1993).

55. 444 U.S. 51 (1979).

56. Daniel R. Mandelker, *Investment-Backed Expectations in Taking Law*, 27 URB. LAW. 215 (Spring 1995).

57. Guimont v. Seattle, 77 Wash. App. 74, 896 P.2d 70 n.10 (Ct. App. 1995).

58. 856 P.2d 777 (Alaska 1993).

59. 617 N.E.2d 1227 (Ill. App. Ct. 1993).

60. *Tim Thompson*, 617 N.E.2d at 1245.

61. 855 P.2d 608 (Or. 1993).

62. *Dodd*, 855 P.2d at 617.

63. *See* Edward J. Sullivan, *Oregon Blazes a Trail, in* STATE AND REGIONAL COMPREHENSIVE PLANNING: IMPLEMENTING NEW METHODS FOR GROWTH MANAGEMENT (Peter A. Buchsbaum and Larry J. Smith eds., 1993).

64. *Dolan*, 114 S. Ct. at 2312.

65. *Id.* at 2318 (citing Agins v. Tiburon, 447 U.S. 255, 260-62 (1980)).
66. *Dolan,* 114 S. Ct. at 2318.
67. *Id.*
68. *Id.*
69. *Id.* at 2319-20.
70. *Id.* at 2322.
71. *Id.* at 2320 (emphasis added).
72. Kaiser Aetna v. United States, 444 U.S. 164, 179-80 (1979).
73. 458 U.S. 419 (1982).
74. *Dolan,* 114 S. Ct. at 2320.
75. 35 F.3d 1269 (8th Cir. 1994).
76. *Christopher Lake,* 35 F.3d at 1275.
77. *Id.*
78. *Id.* (quoting Dolan v. City of Tigard, 114 S. Ct. 2309 (1994)).
79. *Christopher Lake,* 35 F.3d at 1275.
80. 46 F.3d 162 (2nd Cir. 1995).
81. *Walz,* 46 F.3d at 169 (citing Dolan v. City of Tigard, 114 S. Ct. 2309 (1994)).
82. 648 A.2d 482 (N.J. Super. Ct. App. Div. 1994).
83. *F & W Associates,* 648 A.2d at 486 (citations omitted).
84. *Id.* at 487.
85. *Id.* (citing Holmdel Builders Ass'n v. Township of Holmdel, 121 N.J. 550, 571, 583 A.2d 277, 287 (1990)).
86. *F & W Associates,* 648 A.2d at 487.
87. *Id.* at 488.
88. 621 N.E.2d 1012 (Ill. App. Ct. 1993), *aff'd in part, rev'd in part,* No. 76503, 1995 WL 123705 (Ill. March 23, 1995).
89. *Northern Illinois Home Builders,* 621 N.E.2d at 1020.
90. *Id.*
91. *Id.*
92. 19 Cal. Rptr. 2d 468 (Cal. Ct. App. 1993), *vacated,* 114 S. Ct. 2731 (1994).
93. 643 N.E.2d 479 (1994).
94. *Manocherian,* 643 N.E.2d at 483.
95. 863 P.2d 142 (Wash. Ct. App. 1993).
96. No. 27-21-70, 1992 WL 239100 (Conn. Super. Ct. Sept. 16, 1992).
97. 628 A.2d 1277 (Conn. 1993).
98. 849 S.W.2d 557 (Ky. Ct. App. 1992).
99. 829 P.2d 169 (Wash. Ct. App. 1991).
100. *See also* Dellinger v. City of Charlotte, 441 S.E.2d 626 (N.C. Ct. App. 1994) (striking down a road-dedication requirement because the city planning staff failed to make written findings relating the dedication to traffic from the proposed subdivision).
101. 25 Cal. Rptr. 2d 593 (Cal. Ct. App. 1993).
102. 829 P.2d 765 (Wash. 1992), *cert. denied sub nom.* Robinson v. City of Seattle, 113 S. Ct. 676 (1992).

CHAPTER ❖ 2

Land As a Privileged Form of Property

Fred P. Bosselman

I. Introduction: Differing Treatment of Real and Other Property

The U.S. Supreme Court has taken the position that the Constitution affords greater protection from government regulation to investments in land than to investments in other forms of property. By doing so, the Court has reawakened memories of a division between land property owners and business entrepreneurs that was a volatile issue in the early nineteenth century. The entrepreneurs have long assumed that they won that battle and attained equal status with the landowners, both in legal and economic theory. Now, for reasons left unstated, the Court declares that they remain "second class."

To assign land a privileged status in relation to other categories of investment is particularly ironic at this point in history. In recent years, interests in land have become more like securities and often resemble other forms of investment capital. Mortgage-backed securities and their derivatives have become an important investment vehicle. Real estate managers and developers operate through real estate investment trusts with securities listed on major stock exchanges. And agriculture and forestry are dominated by large corporations that have widely traded securities.

Because the Court has been so cryptic in its decisions, it is not possible to discern why it has chosen to treat land as property with a privileged status. Therefore, after summarizing the Court's recent decisions on the subject, this essay will discuss the issues that were debated when this topic last surfaced in American dialogue over a century ago. Finally, it will conclude by briefly summarizing some of the ways in which modern investment practices have made land and other investments increasingly similar, thus creating a trend that moves in the opposite direction from that of the Court.

II. Recent Cases: Lucas, Concrete Pipe, *and* Dolan

The stage was set for the Court's recent decisions two decades ago, when Congress adopted complex federal legislation governing the operation of pension funds. Pension funds were becoming one of the most important sources of investment capital, and this trend has continued: the median size of retirement accounts doubled between 1983 and 1989.[1] Congress, perceiving the potential for abuse of these funds, adopted the Employee Retirement Income Security Act of 1974 (ERISA),[2] which imposed detailed rules for operating such pension funds.

Since ERISA's enactment, Congress observed in the statute various loopholes that allowed abuses to continue. It kept tightening up the rules in a series of later statutes, particularly the Multiemployer Pension Plan Amendments Act of 1980 (MPPAA).[3] These changes operated to the disadvantage of many pension fund operators, who challenged them in the federal courts under the takings and due process clauses.

Although plaintiffs in these cases were able to show significant losses in reliance on what appeared to be reasonable investment-backed expectations, the Court was wholly unsympathetic to their plight. The Court upheld the revised regulations against claims that they violated substantive due process[4] and the takings clause.[5] "Those who do business in the regulated field," said the Court, cannot object to amendments "to achieve the legislative end."[6]

In *Lucas v. South Carolina Coastal Council,*[7] the Court dealt with a similar claim by the developer of a subdivision of land on the South Carolina coast. Two of his lots adjoined the beach and were undeveloped when the state adopted regulations restricting the construction of buildings in flood-prone areas. He alleged that the new regulations constituted a taking of his property. In deciding for the plaintiff, the Court sought to distinguish its earlier decisions in which it found no taking even though the regulations had a serious impact on the property owner's expectations. It chose the nature of the property as the basis for the distinction:

> It seems to us that the property owner necessarily expects the uses of his property to be restricted, from time to time, by various measures newly enacted by the State in legitimate exercise of its police powers; "[a]s long recognized, some values are enjoyed under an

> implied limitation and must yield to the police power." Pennsylvania Coal Co. v. Mahon, 260 U.S. at 413, 43 S. Ct. at 159. And in the case of personal property, by reason of the State's traditionally high degree of control over commercial dealings, he ought to be aware of the possibility that new regulation might even render his property economically worthless (at least if the property's only economically productive use is sale or manufacture for sale), see Andrus v. Allard, 444 U.S. 51, 66-67, 100 S. Ct. 318, 327, 62 L. Ed. 2d 210 (1979) (prohibition on sale of eagle feathers). In the case of land, however, we think the notion pressed by the Council that title is somehow held subject to the "implied limitation" that the State may subsequently eliminate all economically valuable use is inconsistent with the historical compact recorded in the Takings Clause that has become part of our constitutional culture.[8]

The Court does not further explain the basis for its conclusion that this "historical compact" is applicable to land but not to other property. In a footnote to the above-quoted passage, the Court responds to Justice Blackmun, whose dissent criticizes the Court's historical accuracy, pointing out that the founders had not originally intended the takings clause to apply to any type of regulation. The majority responded by stating that

> Justice Blackmun . . . argu[es] that our description of the "understanding" of land ownership that informs the Takings Clause is not supported by early American experience. That is largely true, but entirely irrelevant. The practices of the States prior to incorporation of the Takings and Just Compensation Clauses, see Chicago, B. & Q.R. Co. v. Chicago, 166 U.S. 226 (1897)—which, as Justice BLACKMUN acknowledges, occasionally included outright physical appropriation of land without compensation—were out of accord with any plausible interpretation of those provisions. Justice BLACKMUN is correct that early constitutional theorists did not believe the Takings Clause embraced regulations of property at all, but even he does not suggest (explicitly, at least) that we renounce the Court's contrary conclusion in Mahon. Since the text of the Clause can be read to encompass regulatory as well as physical deprivations (in contrast to the text originally proposed by Madison, see Speech Proposing Bill of Rights (June 8, 1789), in 12 J. Madison, The Papers of James Madison 201 (C. Hobson, R. Rutland, W. Rachal, & J. Sisson ed. 1979) ("No person shall be . . . obliged to relinquish his property, where it may be necessary for public use, without a just compensation"), we decline to do so as well.[9]

The Court went on to discuss its earlier decisions involving permanent physical occupation of land, apparently suggesting that they provided some support for its position that land is to be treated more favorably than other types of property:

> Where "permanent physical occupation" of land is concerned, we have refused to allow the government to decree it anew (without compensation), no matter how weighty the asserted "public interests" involved, Loretto v. Teleprompter Manhattan CATV Corp., 458 U.S. at 426—though we assuredly would permit the government to assert a permanent easement that was a pre-existing limitation upon the landowner's title. Compare Scranton v. Wheeler, 179 U.S. 141, 163 (1900) (interests of "riparian owner in the submerged lands . . . bordering on a public navigable water" held subject to Government's navigational servitude), with Kaiser Aetna v. United States, 444 U.S. at 178-180 (imposition of navigational servitude on marina created and rendered navigable at private expense held to constitute a taking). We believe similar treatment must be accorded confiscatory regulations, i.e., regulations that prohibit all economically beneficial use of land. . . .[10]

The Court in cases such as *Loretto* and *Kaiser Aetna,* however, did not appear to base its conclusions on any distinction between land and personal property. And the Court has held that the government's permanent physical occupation of personal property violates the takings clause.[11]

Lucas leaves us, therefore, without any rationale for its holding that land is a privileged form of property, other than the unexplained reference to a "historical compact . . . that has become part of our constitutional culture."[12] Such a "naked assertion" of a "free-floating sort of historical fact"[13] is hard to square with Justice Scalia's claim to be a conservative.[14]

The Court had another opportunity to address the issue of land's uniqueness in the following year when it decided another pension fund case, *Concrete Pipe and Products of California, Inc. v. Construction Laborers Pension Trust for Southern California.*[15] In an opinion by Justice Souter, the Court again rejected a pension fund trustee's claim that amendments to ERISA "took" the fund's property. The Court discussed *Lucas* only briefly and without elucidating any rationale for the difference in treatment between land and other assets:

> We reject Concrete Pipe's contention that the appropriate analytical framework is the one employed in our cases dealing with per-

> manent physical occupation or destruction of economically beneficial use of real property. See Lucas v. South Carolina Coastal Council, 112 S. Ct. 2886, 2890-2892 (1992). While Concrete Pipe tries to shoehorn its claim into this analysis by asserting that "[t]he property of [Concrete Pipe] which is taken, is taken in its entirety," Brief for Petitioner 37, we rejected this analysis years ago in Penn Central Transportation Co. v. New York City, 438 U.S. 104, 130-131 (1978), where we held that a claimant's parcel of property could not first be divided into what was taken and what was left for the purpose of demonstrating the taking of the former to be complete and hence compensable. To the extent that any portion of property is taken, that portion is always taken in its entirety; the relevant question, however, is whether the property taken is all, or only a portion of the parcel in question.[16]

In the following year, when the Court took the case of *Dolan v. City of Tigard*,[17] the lawyers for the city hoped that *Lucas* might be distinguished on the ground that because Mr. Lucas had characterized himself as a homeowner, the Court was expressing some higher value for homeownership than for other uses of land. Because *Dolan* involved a plumbing supply store rather than a home, the city's lawyers argued that the land should not be entitled to the special protection given to homeowners.[18] The dissent accepted the validity of the distinction,[19] but the majority, in an opinion by Chief Justice Rehnquist, did not:

> [D]enominating a governmental measure as a 'business regulation' does not immunize it from constitutional challenge on the grounds that it violates a provision of the Bill of Rights.[20]

We are left with an unexplained distinction of great economic significance. Investments in land are given protection from regulations that deprive them of all value while investments in other property are not. Lower courts have cited *Lucas* for this proposition in dismissing claims involving personal property.[21]

Is there any rational argument for such a difference? One of Justice Scalia's former academic colleagues, Judge Frank Easterbrook of the Seventh Circuit Court of Appeals, has offered one possible explanation of the unwritten compact on which Justice Scalia apparently based the distinction. In the case of *River Park, Inc. v. City of Highland Park*,[22] the issue was whether a landowner had a property interest sufficient to bring a constitutional claim when the city changed the zoning of the land. The court, in an opinion by Judge Easterbrook, opined that any landowner seeking to develop land had a property interest under the due process and takings clauses because the right to develop land was "old property" rather than "new property":

> The references to "property" in the Constitution reflect its Lockean heritage. The founding generation viewed "property" in concrete terms—land and chattels acquired by the investment of effort or purchase from another. An owner may build on its land; that is an ordinary element of a property interest. Zoning classifications are not the measure of the property interest but are legal restrictions on the use of property.[23]

The court recognized that it had become "useful to think of some governmental promises as 'property.' "[24] But it said that such promises can only be

> "new property" rather than the "old property." In the main, the Constitution is a charter of negative rather than positive liberties. DeShaney v. Winnebago County Department of Social Services, 489 U.S. 189 (1989). . . . Those things people can hold or do without the government's aid count as property or liberty no matter what criteria the law provides. . . . Otherwise a single local ordinance providing that "we may put your land in any zone we want, for any reason we feel like" would abolish all property rights in land overnight. The due process and takings clauses are made of sterner stuff.[25]

The distinction between new and old property, however, fails to explain why land and personal property should be treated differently, and Judge Easterbrook notes that Locke's concrete conception of property includes both land and chattels.[26]

Perhaps, however, the Judge's preference for old property over new property gives us a clue to the motivation of some modern judges. In these words, one hears echoes of the debate over the special status of land that was an important issue in the political discourse of the early nineteenth century. A review of that debate may shed some light on the current puzzle.

III. Ricardo's Theory of Economic Rent: A Historical Look at Land versus Other Forms of Capital

Shortly after American independence, there arose a group of agrarian pamphleteers who argued that land was the only form of property that should be recognized for voting and other purposes. The most prominent of this group was John Taylor. Taylor argued that land was the only legitimate property—everything else was fictitious property. "Out of paper stock," he proclaimed, "nothing grows."[27]

How could such an idea have attained wide circulation? American attitudes toward land reflected the attitudes of English society. From medieval times, English law had recognized land as the vehicle through which the ruling nobility maintained social control, and English legal institutions sought to inhibit the transfer of landholdings from the upper classes. English emigrants to America saw the new world as an opportunity to obtain control over land—an opportunity that was unavailable at home.[28]

During the time America was being settled, the English nobility maintained tight control over most of English land. Gradually, other individuals who lacked noble birth but possessed substantial amounts of land became identified as a new social class, the "landed gentry." They shared the nobility's desire to maintain the legal uniqueness of land as a key element of the social system.[29] The nobility and the landed gentry together became known as the "landed magnates" and formed the backbone of the Tory party.

The land in England was actually farmed by tenants, who found few opportunities to acquire land. The land remained in the control of the landed magnates through practices like entailment and strict settlement. The tenant farmers could look forward only to generation after generation of labor to pay rent.[30]

Enforcement of the prerogatives of the landowning classes remained a central element of the English legal system. Lawyers were typically drawn from the ranks of the gentry. By the nineteenth century, half the land of England was controlled by two to three thousand individuals, few of whom had the power to sell it.[31] The plight of agricultural workers had been steadily aggravated by the increasing enclosure of common lands and the combination of small holdings into larger units, often held by "doctors, lawyers, clergymen and soldiers all turned farmers."[32]

By the nineteenth century, the Industrial Revolution was making the unique status of land increasingly anachronistic. The landed magnates could maintain the existing social order only by keeping their assets invested in land, which made them dependent on agriculture as an economic base. As a result, most of them were unable to invest in the new manufacturing technologies and transportation improvements that created a new class of business entrepreneurs. These entrepreneurs, resenting the privileges of the nobility and gentry, sought to reform those government policies that favored the old money of the landed magnates over the new money of the manufacturers.[33]

The government policy that provoked the most controversy between landowners and entrepreneurs was the high tariff on foreign agricultural products.[34] Because the primary source of income for the landed classes was rent collected from the tenant farmers, it was in the interest of the landowners to keep the price of farm products high.[35] During the eighteenth century, while tariffs were high, the average value of land in England roughly doubled, and some four million acres of marginal land was brought into cultivation.[36] The new entrepreneurs wanted cheaper imported farm products because they believed the high price of food was forcing them to pay workers higher wages,[37] although they downplayed the potential reduction of wages to avoid antagonizing the workers.[38]

A wealthy retired stockbroker, David Ricardo, led the fight against the high agricultural tariffs. He offered a concise and persuasive argument for reform: each nation should specialize in the thing it does best, and because the British surpassed everyone else in their ability to manufacture products, Britain should import cheap food from abroad and devote the energies of its workers to manufacturing goods.[39]

Ricardo was a cautious reformer. He sought only a gradual reduction of tariffs to reduce potentially drastic impacts on the economy.[40] Nevertheless, when the agricultural economy declined after 1818[41] he argued that landowners had no more right to be protected from changes in market conditions than did the entrepreneurs, who often lost capital to new technology or competition from new geographic areas.[42]

Ricardo's argument was based on his theory of "economic rent," which he first set out in 1815.[43] Rent, he argued, was simply a windfall that was captured by the lucky landowner whose land had been endowed by nature with better productivity or accessibility than a marginal site. When a country is first settled and land is freely available, the produce of land will belong to the owner of such capital invested to produce it without any deduction for rent. But as it becomes necessary to till more distant and less fertile land, the owner of the better land will be able to charge rent; this "rent would rise on the land previously cultivated, and precisely in the same degree profits would fall."[44]

The label "economic rent" was designed to give the landed magnates a less deserving image than that of the entrepreneurs. Ricardo argued that the magnates' fortunes varied with the fortuitous attributes of their land holdings, rather than with the skill of their management. Thus, the high tariffs on farm products were merely adding to the windfall income of the landed magnates at the expense of the other classes:

> If we import [corn,] the portion of the capital last employed on the land, and which yielded no rent, will be withdrawn; rent will fall and profits rise. . . . If corn can be imported cheaper than it can be grown on this rather better land, rent will again fall and profits rise, and another and better description of land will now be cultivated for profits only. In every step of our progress, profits of [capital] stock increase and rents fall, and more land is abandoned. . . .[45]

Other commentators of the day, such as Lord Byron, were even less respectful of the landed class:

> Alas, the country! how shall tongue or pen
> Bewail her now *un*country gentlemen?
> The last to bid the cry of warfare cease,
> The first to make a malady of peace.
> For what were all these country patriots born?
> To hunt, and vote, and raise the price of corn?[46]

In America, an edition of Ricardo's *Principles of Economics* appeared in 1818,[47] and his theories were studied with interest.[48] For many years American writers on political economy used the Ricardian view on any issue as the accepted doctrine to be supported or attacked.[49] Long after most of Ricardo's other theories had become unfashionable, his theory of rent was often cited favorably by American economists.[50]

Some American commentators argued that Ricardo's theory of economic rent was valid for England, but inapplicable to conditions in the United States because the tight restrictions on land ownership in England were nonexistent in the "new world." Others believed that American landowners received no economic rent because they were too distant from markets. Still others accepted the existence of economic rent, arguing that it was economically justified in a country where the government made vast quantities of open land available at low cost, thus preventing existing landlords from raising rents to exorbitant levels.[51]

Meanwhile, the Industrial Revolution in America was rapidly transforming a land-based economy to a paper-based economy.[52] This worried agrarians such as John Taylor, but they were fighting a losing battle: even the Republicans began abandoning the Jeffersonian tradition and diversifying their investments.[53] As a result, power and wealth in the eastern United States began to shift, not to the owners of agricultural land, but to the owners of the capital needed to develop the manufacturing industries required to make the country self-sufficient. By the time of the American publication of Ricardo's *Principles* in 1818, the entrepreneurs were the ones who had the trappings of "aristocracy."[54] Wealthy Americans of that period were beginning to view agriculture as only an intermediate stage of the progression through which societies naturally evolve.[55]

In states such as California, however, land ownership patterns were looking less like Jefferson's vision of a nation of prosperous small farms and more like the concentrated power of large plantations that had characterized Ricardo's England.[56] California was characterized by "a concentrated pattern of ownership of land, a small number of farms in relation to the population, large bonanza farms, and a high proportion of farm laborers and tenants."[57]

A California newspaper editor, Henry George, took Ricardo's characterization of rent as a windfall to the next level. He proposed that the government levy a tax that would eliminate what Ricardo had defined as economic rent because the "monopolistic" nature of landownership in the United States was destroying the Jeffersonian ideal.[58] His proposed tax was to equal 100 percent of the amount by which economic rent from unimproved land exceeded the return that the land would have provided if it had been simply capital. George argued that the growing concentration of land ownership was reversing the trend toward economic equality. By widening the gap between the rulers and the ruled, that concentration of land ownership was following a pattern that had led in the past to the downfall of civilizations.[59] Although George claimed to have arrived at the idea of economic rent independently of Ricardo, he saw himself as a disciple of Ricardian ideas[60] and shared Ricardo's political belief "that workers and investors have a common cause against the landowners, landholders and land speculators."[61]

George's ideas were advocated by a variety of populist and progressive movements that blossomed in the late nineteenth and early twentieth centuries,[62] but most state and local governments regarded his ideas on tax policy as too radical; only a few jurisdictions adopted them, and only in modified form.[63] After Henry George's death, his and Ricardo's writings receded into the background as writers on political economy addressed other issues.[64] After 1870, many economists turned their backs on what they understood to be the Ricardian theory of value and distribution.[65] But the basic tenets of Ricardian economics remained sufficiently dominant in the 1930s that Keynes complained that "Ricardo conquered England as completely as the Holy Inquisition conquered Spain."[66]

In America, however, the social distinction between manufacturing-dependent entrepreneurs and agriculture-dependent gentry, which had dominated British society, quickly became of only minor significance. Consequently, the relevance of maintaining a sharp distinction between land and other capital assets lost its social usefulness.[67] Some American farmers tried to emphasize the distinction between agricultural and mercantile interests through groups like the Grange, but the movement had limited political success.[68] To American economists, Ricardo's tripartite distinction among "land, labor, and capital" became reduced to labor and capital.[69] Economic theory now recognizes no basic distinction between land and other forms of capital.[70]

In summary, the English battle between the Tory landowners and the new middle class never developed into a major conflict in America. Land was too cheap and easily available to provide a defining criterion for the upper classes, and the entrepreneurs rapidly demonstrated that their way of making money was more effective than the farmers' method. Sharp distinctions between land and other forms of capital were not drawn by society, economics, or law.

IV. Wealth in Property Today

As the world economy has developed in practice, the distinction between land and other forms of capital has become even less discernible. As Oxford law professor Bernard Rudden recently noted in his article, *Things as Thing and Things as Wealth,*

> The traditional concepts of the common law of property were created for and by the ruling classes at a time when the bulk of their capital was land. Nowadays the great wealth lies in stocks, shares, bonds and the like, and is not just movable but *mobile,* crossing oceans at the touch of a key-pad in the search for a fiscal utopia. . . . In terms of legal theory and technique, however, there has been a profound if little discussed evolution by which the concepts originally devised for real property have been detached from their original object, only to survive and flourish as a means of handling abstract value. The feudal calculus lives and breeds, but its habitat is wealth not land.[71]

The trend toward turning interests in land into commodities is rapid and undiminishing.

Agricultural land is now heavily concentrated in the hands of large entities. Farms classified as "large commercial" (having annual sales exceeding $100,000) accounted for 76.3 percent of farm sales in 1987, up from 62.9 percent in 1978.[72] Farms having annual sales of over $1 million averaged sales of $3.2 million per year; their sales are expected to approach 40 percent of all farm sales by the year 2000.[73] Thirteen states have imposed restrictions on the extent to which corporations may own land, in a largely futile attempt to protect the family farm.[74] Attempts to prevent business entities from amassing large land holdings have a long history of futility.[75]

The financial interest in most single-family residential property is divided between residents and mortgage holders. The ratio of home mortgages to the total value of owner-occupied real estate has increased virtually every year since 1983, rising from 27.4 percent in that year to 42.4 percent in 1993.[76]

Today, most mortgages have been sold to entities that combine them into mortgage-backed securities. Investment in these securities and their derivatives has been one of the major developments in capital markets in the 1980s. A secondary market for mortgage-backed securities has been created by the Government National Mortgage Association (GNMA), the Federal National Mortgage Association (FNMA), and the Federal Home Loan Mortgage Corporation (FHLMC). First mortgages on one- to four-family residential properties are written to standard specifications; the GNMA, FNMA, and FHLMC purchase them from originating institutions, combine the mortgages into large pools, and then issue debt securities backed by the mortgages.

> Beginning in the late 1980s, more complex structures were developed by pooling larger groups of mortgages and PCs [pass-through certificates] into subordinated tiers, or "tranches," each tranche carrying a different maturity and interest rate. These newer mortgage-backed securities, known as Collateralized Mortgage Obligations (CMOs) and Real Estate Mortgage Investment Conduits (REMICs), created an even wider investor market for mortgage-backed securities.
>
> As a result of this growth, the mortgage-backed securities market has outstripped the corporate bond market. Today, the total amount of outstanding mortgage-backed securities is more than $1 trillion, making residential mortgage loans the most widely securitized financial asset.[77]

Similar efforts to securitize the more complex commercial property market are underway:

> [T]wo recent developments have stimulated significant increases in commercial mortgage securitization. First, the savings and loan crisis of the late 1980s resulted in the transfer to the RTC of the portfolios of hundreds of thrifts; these portfolios often contained significant numbers of commercial mortgages. . . . Borrowing from

> the experience in the residential market, the RTC began combining commercial mortgage loans into large pools and issuing PCs to investors that represent an interest in the cash flow due under the mortgages. To date, the RTC has securitized over $13 billion in commercial mortgages using this technique.
>
> Second, as a result of the savings and loan crisis, regulatory agencies began imposing risk-based capital guidelines on banks and insurance companies . . . [and] assigned commercial mortgage loans to the highest risk-weight categories. . . . At a time when regulators were forcing lenders to increase their overall capital, banks and insurance companies needed a way to dispose quickly of large volumes of commercial mortgages. Securitization offered the answer.[78]

Developers of commercial and multifamily residential buildings are also going to the securities market with real estate investment trusts (REITs) to finance the equity interest in such buildings, and investment bankers are now creating derivatives in those REITs.[79]

On the other hand, real estate's share of direct household investment is falling. The equity interest in one or more homes is the most common form of real estate investment; some 32.2 percent of American families own at least one home.[80] Ironically, the self-interest of these single-family homeowners has usually been blamed for the hardships imposed by regulation on the developers of vacant land.[81]

The number of individual Americans owning real estate for investment purposes is hard to determine; but such investments are clearly a declining share of Americans' overall capital:

> Continuing a trend observed since [1983], an overall rise occurred in the share of financial assets in families' asset portfolios between 1989 and 1992. There were corresponding declines in the shares of primary residences and other non-financial assets.[82]

Although in 1989, 20.4 percent of American families owned real estate other than the family's private home,[83] this figure includes second homes, which are also benefiting from land-use regulations. Consequently, to give land special protection against regulation would be adverse to the interests of the largest category of owners of land—those who own one or more homes.

The changes in the relationship between land and other types of property are part of a worldwide trend toward investment in intangible assets that has been facilitated by technological advances in telecommunications and computing:

> Money is now an image. Simultaneously, it can be displayed on millions of computer screens on millions of desks around the world. But in reality it is located nowhere and needs no vault for safekeeping. Yet, while money has no real location, it has created an environment that is paradoxically everywhere while taking up no physical space. An environment peopled by millions of investors, traders, bankers, money managers, stockbrokers, arbitrageurs, analysts, policymakers, and government officials—all observing and manipulating money from different video terminals around the world. A community where neighbors, colleagues, and competitors are accessible only through electronics.[84]

V. Conclusion

In conclusion, the Supreme Court's decision to reestablish the privileged status of land over other investments is puzzling. The Court cites no precedents or constitutional history for its distinction; it makes only a vague reference to a "historical compact" that it concedes is inconsistent with the original interpretation of the Constitution.

A preferential status for land over other property was, of course, a defining element of the feudal property system of medieval England. But the early years of the nineteenth century saw the decline of this distinction in England, and the explicit rejection of the distinction in the United States. The social distinctions that reinforced land's uniqueness in England two centuries ago seem anachronistic today.

To reinvent the distinction at the dawn of the "age of hyperspace" is peculiarly inappropriate. Today's global economy, with its increasingly free trade and virtually instantaneous international flows of wealth, is an odd environment in which to reinstitute benefits for one form of capital over another. In practice, interests in land are now "commodified" much like other forms of securities.

Whether one believes that the modern regulatory environment is too tight, too loose, or just right, it is difficult to devise logical arguments for applying one standard for land and another for other investments.

Notes

1. Arthur Kennickell & Janice Shack Marquez, *Changes in Family Finances from 1983 to 1989: Evidence from the Survey of Consumer Finances*, 78 FED. RES. BULL. 1 (1992).
2. 29 U.S.C. § 1001 (1985).
3. Pub. L. 96-364, 94 Stat. 1208 (1980).
4. Pension Benefit Guaranty Corp. v. R.A. Gray & Co., 467 U.S. 717 (1984).
5. Connolly v. Pension Benefit Guaranty Corp., 475 U.S. 211 (1986).
6. *Id.* at 227.

7. 112 S. Ct. 2886 (1992).

8. *Lucas,* 112 S. Ct. at 2899-900.

9. *Id.* at 2900 n.15.

10. *Id.* at 2900.

11. Webb's Fabulous Pharmacies, Inc. v. Beckwith, 449 U.S. 155 (1980).

12. *See* William W. Fisher III, *The Trouble With* Lucas, 45 STAN. L. REV. 1393, 1397-1402 (1993); Richard J. Lazarus, *Shifting Paradigms of Tort and Property in the Transformation of Natural Resources Law, in* NATURAL RESOURCES POLICY AND LAW (Lawrence J. MacDonnell & Sarah F. Bates eds., 1993).

13. Frank I. Michelman, *Property, Federalism, and Jurisprudence: A Comment on* Lucas *and Judicial Conservatism,* 35 WM. & MARY L. REV. 301 (1993).

14. *See generally* Fred P. Bosselman, *Scalia on Land, in* AFTER *LUCAS*: LAND-USE REGULATION AND THE TAKING OF PROPERTY WITHOUT COMPENSATION (David L. Callies ed., 1993).

15. 113 S. Ct. 2264 (1993).

16. *Lucas,* 112 S. Ct. at 2290.

17. 114 S. Ct. 2309 (1994).

18. *See Dolan,* 114 S. Ct. at 2321.

19. *Id.* at 2324-25.

20. *Id.* at 2320.

21. *See* Glenn P. Sugamelli, *Taking Issues in Light of* Lucas v. South Carolina Coastal Council, 12 VA. ENVTL. L.J. 439, 461-62 (1993).

22. 23 F.3d 164 (7th Cir. 1994).

23. *River Park,* 23 F.3d at 166.

24. *Id.*

25. *Id.*

26. *See* Kenneth J. Vandevelde, *The New Property of the Nineteenth Century: The Development of the Modern Concept of Property,* 29 BUFF. L. REV. 325, 333-34 (1980). *See also* Michelman, *supra* note 13, at 307 n.25.

27. JOHN TAYLOR, AN INQUIRY INTO THE PRINCIPLES AND POLICY OF THE GOVERNMENT OF THE UNITED STATES 227 (Loren Baritz ed., 1969).

28. *See* JAMES W. ELY, JR., THE GUARDIAN OF EVERY OTHER RIGHT 10-13 (1992).

29. F.M.L. THOMPSON, ENGLISH LANDED SOCIETY IN THE NINETEENTH CENTURY 109 (1963).

30. *See* J.L. HAMMOND & BARBARA HAMMOND, THE VILLAGE LABOURER (1911).

31. HERMANN LEVY, LARGE AND SMALL HOLDINGS: A STUDY OF ENGLISH AGRICULTURAL ECONOMICS 118-19 (1911).

32. *Id.* at 21. *See also* D.W. HASBACH, A HISTORY OF THE ENGLISH AGRICULTURAL LABOURER 57 (1908).

33. *See generally* PAUL JOHNSON, THE BIRTH OF THE MODERN: WORLD SOCIETY 1815-1830, at 370-77 (1991).

34. *See* C.R. FAY, THE CORN LAWS AND SOCIAL ENGLAND (1932).

35. *See* 1 ARTHUR D. GAYER ET AL., THE GROWTH AND FLUCTUATION OF THE BRITISH ECONOMY, 1790-1850, at 792-94, 927-29 (1953).

36. ASA BRIGGS, A SOCIAL HISTORY OF ENGLAND 171 (1983); G.E. MINGAY, A SOCIAL HISTORY OF THE ENGLISH COUNTRYSIDE 6 (1990).

37. MARK BLAUG, RICARDIAN ECONOMICS: A HISTORICAL STUDY 9 (1958).

38. J.D. CHAMBERS & G.E. MINGAY, THE AGRICULTURAL REVOLUTION, 1750-1880, at 152 (1966).

39. See Ricardo's essay, *On Protection of Agriculture, in* 4 THE WORKS AND CORRESPONDENCE OF DAVID RICARDO 2 (Piero Sraffa ed., 1966).

40. *See* Herbert Hovenkamp, *The Political Economy of Due Process,* 40 STAN. L. REV. 379, 407 (1988).

41. *See* 1 GAYER, *supra* note 35, at 929.

42. CHAMBERS & MINGAY, *supra* note 38, at 123.

43. DAVID RICARDO, AN ESSAY ON THE INFLUENCE OF A LOW PRICE OF CORN ON THE PROFITS OF STOCK (1815).

44. *Id.* at 13-14.

45. *Id.* at 38-39.

46. 14 LORD BYRON, THE AGE OF BRONZE 11, 1-6 (1823).

47. 1 JOSEPH DORFMAN, THE ECONOMIC MIND IN AMERICAN CIVILIZATION, 1606-1865, at 369-70 (1946).

48. DOROTHY ROSS, THE ORIGINS OF AMERICAN SOCIAL SCIENCE 44-47 (1991).

49. 2 JOSEPH DORFMAN, THE ECONOMIC MIND IN AMERICAN CIVILIZATION, 1606-1865, at 513, 517-22, 708-10 (1953).

50. *See, e.g.,* GEORGE STIGLER, PRODUCTION AND DISTRIBUTION THEORIES 291-92 (1941).

51. *See* FRANK H. KNIGHT, ON THE HISTORY AND METHOD OF ECONOMICS 24 (1956); 2 DORFMAN, *supra* note 49, at 537-61; Ross, *supra* note 48, at 86-87; Herbert Hovenkamp, *supra* note 40, at 424-31.

52. *See* STEVEN WATTS, THE REPUBLIC REBORN: WAR AND THE MAKING OF LIBERAL AMERICA 220-21 (1987).

53. *See* Fred P. Bosselman, *Four Land Ethics: Order, Reform, Responsibility, Opportunity,* 24 ENVTL. L. 1439, 1470-72 (1994).

54. LOUIS HARTZ, THE LIBERAL TRADITION IN AMERICA: AN INTERPRETATION OF AMERICAN POLITICAL THOUGHT SINCE THE REVOLUTION 99 (1955).

55. FORREST MCDONALD, *NOVUS ORDO SECLORUM:* THE INTELLECTUAL ORIGINS OF THE CONSTITUTION 132-42 (1985).

56. PAUL W. GATES, THE FARMER'S AGE: AGRICULTURE, 1815-1860, at 390 (1960).

57. KEVIN STARR, AMERICANS AND THE CALIFORNIA DREAM, 1850-1915, at 133-41 (1973).

58. *See generally* HENRY GEORGE, PROGRESS AND POVERTY (1879).

59. *See* CHRISTOPHER LASCH, THE TRUE AND ONLY HEAVEN: PROGRESS AND ITS CRITICS 64-67 (1991).

60. CHARLES ALBRO BARKER, HENRY GEORGE 267-77 (1955).

61. EDWARD J. ROSE, HENRY GEORGE 70-71 (1968).

62. *See* STEVEN B. CORD, HENRY GEORGE: DREAMER OR REALIST? 33-37 (1965).

63. *See* Donald Hagman, *Land Value Taxation, in* WINDFALLS FOR WIPEOUTS 399, 411-21 (Donald Hagman & Dean Misczynski eds., 1978); NATIONAL COMMISSION ON URBAN PROBLEMS, BUILDING THE AMERICAN CITY 384-98 (1968).

64. KNIGHT, *supra* note 51, at 150-51.

65. MARK BLAUG, ECONOMIC THEORY IN RETROSPECT 141 (3d. ed. 1978). *See generally* Herbert Hovenkamp, *The First Great Law and Economics Movement,* 42 STAN. L. REV. 993 (1990).

66. JOHN MAYNARD KEYNES, GENERAL THEORY OF EMPLOYMENT, INTEREST AND MONEY 32 (1936). *See* Frank W. Fetter, *The Rise and Decline of Ricardian Economics,* 11 HIST. POL. ECON. 67 (1988).

67. *See, e.g.,* Simon N. Patten, *The Scope of Political Economy,* 2 YALE REV. 264, 286 (1893).

68. *See* WILLIAM CRONON, NATURE'S METROPOLIS: CHICAGO AND THE GREAT WEST 360-65 (1991).

69. Frank H. Knight, *Fallacies in the Interpretation of Social Cost,* 38 Q.J. ECON. 582 (1924).

70. Daniel W. Bromley, *Regulatory Takings: Coherent Concept of Logical Contradiction?,* 17 VT. L. REV. 647, 677-78 (1993).

71. Bernard Rudden, *Things as Thing and Things as Wealth,* 14 OXFORD J. LEGAL STUD. 81, 82 (1994).

72. Kent B. Olson & B.F. Stanton, *Projections of Structural Change and the Future of American Agriculture, in* SIZE, STRUCTURE AND THE CHANGING FACE OF AMERICAN AGRICULTURE 587, 603 (Arne Hallam ed., 1993).

73. *Id.* at 612-13.

74. J. DAVID AIKEN, STATE RESTRICTIONS ON LANDOWNERSHIP BY ALIENS AND BUSINESSES, DECEMBER 31, 1992 (1993).

75. *See generally* CHARLES C. GEISLER & FRANK J. POPPER, LAND REFORM, AMERICAN STYLE (1984).

76. FEDERAL RESERVE BOARD, BALANCE SHEETS FOR THE U.S. ECONOMY, 1945-93, at 24-25 (1994).

77. Peter J. Culver, *The Dawning of Securitization,* PROB. & PROP., March/April 1994, at 34, 36. *See generally* THE HANDBOOK OF MORTGAGE-BACKED SECURITIES 346 (Frank J. Fabozzi ed., rev. ed. 1988).

78. Culver, *supra* note 77, at 37.

79. *See, e.g., Merrill Creates MITTS Issue Tied to Real Estate Index,* 20 CORP. FINANCING WK., August 22, 1994, at 2.

80. Arthur Kennickell & Janice Shack-Marquez, *Changes in Family Finances from 1983 to 1989: Evidence from the Survey of Consumer Finances,* FED. RESERVE BULL., Jan. 1992 (reprint), at 3.

81. *See generally* RICHARD F. BABCOCK, THE ZONING GAME (1966).

82. Arthur B. Kennickell & Martha Starr-McCluer, *Changes in Family Finances from 1989 to 1992: Evidence from the Survey of Consumer Finances,* 80 FED. RESERVE BULL. 861 (1994).

83. Kennickell & Shack-Marquez, *supra* note 80, at 9.

84. JOEL KURTZMAN, THE DEATH OF MONEY 15-16 (1993). The trend toward securitization is worldwide. *See* Rudden, *supra* note 71, at 97:

> [T]he oldest and most stable means of treating a thing as wealth is now the basis for one of the youngest and most mobile, by which first mortgages on English homes are transmuted into floating-rate beaver notes listed on the Luxembourg Stock Exchange: the magic of securitization.

CHAPTER ❖ 3

Ripeness and Forum Selection in Land-Use Litigation*

Thomas E. Roberts

I. A Message Unheard, Misunderstood, or Resisted

The 1985 decision in *Williamson County Regional Planning Commission v. Hamilton Bank of Johnson City*[1] imposed significant ripeness and forum selection requirements on Fifth Amendment takings and Fourteenth Amendment due process and equal protection challenges.[2] While the recent takings decisions in *Lucas v. South Carolina Coastal Council*[3] and *Dolan v. City of Tigard*[4] expand the rights of property owners, they have only a modest effect on the ripeness requirements and on forum selection, which remain formidable hurdles in land-use litigation.

Hamilton Bank sets out two requirements. First, for an "as applied" challenge, a property owner must obtain a final decision from local land-use authorities. Second, if dissatisfied with the development rights denied or limitations imposed in seeking a final decision, or if making a "facial" challenge, the property owner must seek compensation from the state courts. The rationale of prong one, the final-decision requirement, is that a regulation is only a taking if it goes "too far," and a court cannot answer this question without knowing how far the regulation goes.[5] The second prong, the compensation requirement, is based on the nature of the Fifth Amendment claim: the Constitution does not proscribe takings, only takings without compensation. Thus, an inverse condemnation remedy that provides a property owner with an opportunity to obtain compensation must be pursued.

Despite these requirements, case reporters over the past decade are filled with lawsuits that have been filed prematurely in both state and federal courts without a final decision from the local authorities. Likewise, in numerous instances, property owners go directly to federal court seeking compensation. These cases suggest that the requirements of *Hamilton Bank* have either not penetrated the consciousness of property owners and their lawyers, or that their affinity for federal court is so great that they are willing, against great odds, to spend their time and money to try to fall within the narrow exceptions to the rules.

In the 1993 decision of *Celentano v. City of West Haven*,[6] for example, the property owner "insisted emphatically" that he, like other § 1983 civil rights litigants, did not need to seek final action, citing as authority the 1982 decision in *Patsy v. Florida Board of Regents*,[7] in which the Supreme Court held that no exhaustion requirement applies to § 1983 actions. Yet, in the *Hamilton Bank* case, the Court expressly distinguished *Patsy* and held that "as applied" takings claims differ from other constitutional claims. Exhaustion of administrative remedies is not required, but a final decision of the initial decisionmaker is necessary.

Some of these premature litigation efforts are understandable in light of uncertainty regarding when a decision is final for the purposes of prong one and the difficulty in distinguishing finality from exhaustion. It is not obvious how many applications for development must be made, to whom they must be made, or whether applying for development is necessary when doing so seems futile. Clarity is needed in the prong one final-decision rule.

Confusion also exists regarding prong two, the compensation requirement. Despite the fact that a compensation remedy is mandated by the Constitution,[8] some litigants and courts question the availability of such claims in state courts. Matters are made worse by the lack of recognition of the res judicata implications of prong two. In this respect the ripeness label is misleading because it suggests that a matter may be heard in federal court after a state court denies compensation. This suggestion is generally not true. Once the issue is tried in state court, the matter cannot be relitigated in federal court. It is preferable to think of prong two as a forum-restricting rule, rather than a ripeness rule.[9]

II. The Leading Cases

In 1973, the developer in *Hamilton Bank* received from the planning commission preliminary plat approval for a cluster home development. The developer then conveyed open-space easements to the county and began putting in roads and utility lines. Over the next few years, the commission reapproved the preliminary plans on several occasions. In 1977, the county changed the density provisions of its zoning ordinance. In 1978, the commission again approved the plans using the prior ordinance but, in 1979, it reversed itself and advised the developer that the project was subject to the 1977 ordinance. When a revised plat was submitted in 1980, the commission rejected it. The developer then went to a county board of zoning appeals and sought an interpretation of the applicable law. The board determined that the 1973 ordinance should apply. In 1981, the developer resubmitted two plats. The commission, refusing to follow the opinion of the board, rejected the plans for eight reasons, some based on the new law and some based on the old law.[10] The developer then brought suit in federal court.

The Supreme Court found the action was not ripe, noting that a takings claim is premature until the "government entity charged with implementing the regulation has reached a final decision."[11] This had not occurred because the developer had not "sought variances that would have allowed it to develop the property according to its proposed plat. . . ."[12] While the developer contended that it had done " 'everything possible to resolve the conflict with the commission,' "[13] the Court was not convinced that a final decision had been obtained. The Court noted that the board of zoning appeals had the authority to grant variances dealing with five of the eight objections, and that the commission itself had the power to grant variances to solve the other objections. A second problem was that the landowner had not used the inverse condemnation process available in state court. Even assuming the restrictions were so severe that they constituted a taking, the Constitution is not violated unless compensation is not paid. The wrong forum had been chosen.

In 1986, a year after *Hamilton Bank,* the Supreme Court decided *MacDonald, Sommer & Frates v. Yolo County.*[14] In *MacDonald,* the developer submitted a preliminary plan to subdivide its residentially zoned land into 159 lots for multifamily and single-family housing. The planning commission rejected the plan because of inadequate access, police protection, and water and sewer services.[15] The developer then filed suit asserting that its property was being condemned to agricultural, open-space use.

The Supreme Court affirmed the state court's holding that the action was unripe because the developer had not obtained a final decision from the authorities regarding the kind of development that would be allowed. The developer failed to convince the Court that it had, with its one application, done enough. "Unfair procedures"[16] need not be pursued, said the Court, but the "rejection of exceedingly grandiose development plans does not logically imply that less ambitious plans will receive similarly unfavorable reviews."[17] The Court made clear that the effort it was demanding was not "useless"[18] or "futile."[19] Rather, quoting the state intermediate appellate court, the Court observed that the plaintiff " 'applied for approval of a particular and relatively intensive development and the application was denied. The denial of that particular plan cannot be equated with a refusal to permit any development. . . . Land use planning is not an all or nothing proposition.' "[20]

In sum, *Hamilton Bank* and *MacDonald* require a final decision on a meaningful application for development.[21] If a variance procedure exists that might permit the project to proceed, it must be used unless applying would be futile. If development permission is denied, compensation must be sought by way of an inverse condemnation action in state court, to which a property owner's lawyer may respond, "Easier said than done."

III. The Final Decision Requirement

The final-decision requirement raises a number of questions. To what type of takings claims does it apply: only to "as applied" regulatory takings claims, such as those involved in *Hamilton Bank* and *MacDonald,* or to physical and facial regulatory claims as well? Does it apply to exaction cases like *Dolan?* What is the distinction between exhaustion and finality in the context of zoning decisions? When is reapplication required? When is a variance request required? What is needed to show futility?

A. Final Decision Rule Inapplicable to Physical Takings and Facial Regulatory Takings

Hamilton Bank's final-decision rule stems from the nature of an "as applied" regulatory challenge, which involves an ad hoc, fact-based examination of a regulation's economic impact and the regulation's interference with reasonable investment-based expectations. To determine whether economic viability has been taken, a court must know how much development will be permitted. In contrast, a landowner bringing a physical takings claim is not subject to this requirement because the physical invasion itself establishes what has been taken.[22]

Likewise, a property owner making a facial takings claim is not subject to the final-decision rule because, by definition, the mere enactment of the law, and not its application, takes the property. The Supreme Court made this clear in *Yee v. City of Escondido.*[23]

B. Ripeness in Exaction Challenges

Some question has been raised about whether the final-decision rule of *Hamilton Bank* applies to *Nollan*[24]*/Dolan* exaction challenges with the same force as it does to *Lucas* economic-impact cases.[25] The Oregon

Court of Appeals recently debated the issue in *Nelson v. City of Lake Oswego*.[26] There, property owners who sought a permit to construct a house were told by the city manager that they would be required to convey a fifty-five-foot drainage easement to the city as a condition for the permit. The property owners did not appeal the city manager's decision to the city council as was allowed under the code, but conveyed the easement to the city and sued for compensation.

In response to the city's argument that the suit was unripe for failure to obtain a final decision, the court held that the first prong of *Hamilton Bank* did not apply to exaction cases. According to the court, the purpose of the final-decision rule is related solely to the "too far" question of economic-impact takings cases. A court needs to know, it said, "whether the owner has applied for enough uses or decisions so that the scope of what the local regulations permit or prohibit can be known."[27] Here, the court knew the effect of the condition because it had "resulted in the actual acquisition of a private property interest."[28]

A concurring judge in *Nelson* disagreed with the majority, finding no distinction between the two types of regulatory taking cases for the purposes of the final-decision rule. Reading Supreme Court precedent[29] to require that an applicant seek a variance or waiver from the initial decisionmaker (whom the judge regarded as the city council, not the city manager), the concurring judge thought the city council should have had the opportunity to exercise the power it reserved to itself in its ordinances to review and reverse the city manager's decision.

The Supreme Court did not address the issue in *Dolan* because the property owner there complied with the final-decision rule, but the policy considerations that underlie the ripeness rules favor the dissent's approach in *Nelson*. The Supreme Court has insisted on some effort being made to give the local government a chance to finalize the application of its ordinances to specific land-development requests. Pursuit of a final decision gives the government a chance to reevaluate its position. Only in *Lucas*, where state law did not allow the agency to modify the regulation, did the Court treat an "as applied" takings case as ripe without the occurrence of some deliberation between the authorities and the developer.

Because the property owner in *Nelson* first conveyed the easement and then sued the city, there was, in effect, a physical taking and, as noted above, physical takings claims are exempt from the final-decision rule. A difference exists, however, between physical takings that result from unilateral government conduct and those that result from regulations. When the physical takings claim stems from experiencing the flooding of one's land by a dam project or suffering overflights from noisy planes, no advance opportunity exists for the landowner and the government to consult. The invasion occurs, and there is nothing to negotiate. In the exaction case, however, the property owner approaches the city to request development permission, and the parties can then debate the propriety of an exaction. If the purpose of the ripeness rule is, in part, to give the government "an opportunity to change its mind,"[30] as one court put it, then the property owner ought to make some effort to ensure that the government has the chance to do so.

The same rationale ought to apply to monetary exactions or impact fees, whether challenged on Fifth Amendment takings grounds or Fourteenth Amendment due process grounds.[31] The argument that a property owner must seek a final decision is stronger in cases involving the levy of a fee than in those involving a physical exaction, because the resemblance to a physical taking, which was used to support nonapplication of the rule in *Nelson,* is lacking.

Prudence suggests obtaining a final decision and seeking a variance from the condition. The process will likely occupy relatively little time compared with the wasted effort of pursuing a lawsuit that a court might declare unripe.

Putting aside the degree of finality of the exaction condition, a question remains about how a property owner should proceed when confronting a municipal demand for land or money in return for a permit. One can do what the *Nelson* plaintiffs did: convey the land or pay the fee to the government and then sue. While this approach worked in *Nelson,* in some states the property owner who follows it risks a finding of waiver of the right to challenge the exaction.[32] In contrast, one could take the approach used by the property owner in *Dolan:* refuse to convey the land and challenge the city's decision that a permit will be granted only if certain land is dedicated. This avoids the waiver problem but, according to Justice Stevens's dissent in *Dolan,* that approach made the takings claim unripe:

> Dolan has no right to be compensated for a taking unless the city acquires the property interests that she has refused to surrender. Since no taking has yet occurred, there has not been any infringement of her constitutional right to compensation. See Preseault v. ICC, 494 U.S. 1, 11-17, 110 S. Ct. 914, 921-925, 108 L. Ed. 2d 1 (1990) (finding takings claim premature because property owner had not yet sought compensation under Tucker Act); Hodel v. Virginia Surface Mining & Reclamation Ass'n, Inc., 452 U.S. 264, 294-295, 101 S. Ct. 2352, 2370, 69 L. Ed. 2d 1 (1981) (no taking where no one "identified any property . . . that has allegedly been taken").[33]

Acceptance of Justice Stevens's rationale puts a potential inverse condemnation claimant with a *Nollan/Dolan*-type claim in an untenable position. The city may never take the step suggested by Justice Stevens in his opening sentence above; that is, there may be no direct condemnation. Likewise, the city will not grant the permit without the dedication. This leaves the property owner with the following choices:

1. Drop the development proposal. This results in a denial of an otherwise legitimate proposed use.
2. Deliver a deed to the city under protest and obtain the permit. An advantage to this approach is that the developer, by proceeding with the project, mitigates damages. This step is unsatisfactory, however, unless it can be reversed by a legal challenge voiding the condition or ordering the payment of compensation. This would presumably be acceptable to Justice Stevens but, unless state law permits payment under protest,[34] the property owner might waive her claim.[35] Perhaps the Supreme Court would invalidate a state rule that imposed waiver on one who deeded land or paid a fee under duress of an unconstitutional requirement.
3. Without complying with the condition, file suit seeking a declaration that the condition is unrelated to the proposed development and ask the court to void the condition or order the payment of compensation if the city refuses to drop its demand. No risk of waiver exists, but this procedure may delay the project.[36] This is the path followed by the plaintiffs in both *Nollan* and *Dolan*.

Justice Stevens's suggestion, which mandates the second option and risks waiver, should be rejected as unnecessary to meet ripeness concerns and as unfair to the property owner. As long as a final decision is obtained, through pursuit of either the second option (with payment under protest) or the third option (a challenge without compliance), the local governing body is alerted to the risk that it may have to pay compensation and can, if it wishes, decide whether to continue to insist on the condition.

C. Exhaustion, No; Finality, Yes.

Understandably, confusion exists between the finality requirement and the exhaustion requirement.[37] As Justice Blackmun explained in *Hamilton Bank:*

> The question whether administrative remedies must be exhausted is conceptually distinct, however, from the question whether an administrative action must be final before it is judicially reviewable. . . . While the policies underlying the two concepts often overlap, the finality requirement is concerned with whether the initial decision-maker has arrived at a definitive position on the issue that inflicts an actual, concrete injury; the exhaustion requirement generally refers to administrative and judicial procedures by which an injured party may seek review of an adverse decision and obtain a remedy if the decision is found to be unlawful or otherwise inappropriate.[38]

Michael Berger differentiates the two concepts by labeling the exhaustion requirement as "vertical finality" and the finality requirement as "lateral finality."[39] Accordingly, one should not be obligated to climb the administrative ladder to seek review of decisions, but one should seek some confirmation by the initial decisionmaker that the denial is final.

While these characterizations are useful starting points, they must be used cautiously because the course of action one must take is driven by the specific context of local procedure coupled with the purpose of the rule. Resort to a board of adjustment, for example, is not required if the board has the power only to review the application of the regulation (vertical finality), but is required if the board possesses the power to waive or grant a variance from the regulations, and thus participate in the decision (lateral finality). *Hamilton Bank* provides an example. The Court said the developer would not be required to appeal the planning commission's rejection of the plat to the board of adjustment because the board had the power only to review, not participate in, that decision.[40] However, the Court said the property owner had to go to both the board of adjustment and the planning commission to seek variances because those bodies had the power to relieve the property owner of the alleged hardships.[41]

Hedging is necessary, however, because the case law is muddled. For example, a court has held that repeated denials of a building permit by a building inspector do not constitute final action when appeal of the inspector's decisions to a board of adjustment is available.[42] That ruling was based on the court's determination that the board, not the inspector, had the final authority to construe the zoning regulations.[43] What is not required for a final decision, and what will not suffice,[44] is appeal of the action's legality, as a matter of state zoning law, to a state court.[45]

A major difficulty is identifying the initial decisionmaker. The "government entity" or the "initial decisionmaker" may include the local legislative body, the planning commission, the building inspector, and the board of adjustment. As the opinion in *Hamilton Bank* demonstrates,[46] viewing the term "initial decisionmaker" narrowly is a mistake. The plural "decisionmakers," rather than the singular, more accurately expresses the requirement. Depending on local procedure, resort to all four entities (the legislative body, the planning commission, the building inspector, and the board of adjustment) may be required to make a decision final. A rezoning request to the legislative body may be necessary in addition to seeking a variance, especially when the current zoning classification is somewhat dated.[47]

Courts are anxious to give the governing body a "realistic opportunity and reasonable time within which to review its zoning legislation vis-a-vis the particular property"[48] and, with this in mind, tend to broadly construe "local decisionmaker" to carry out that purpose. If one wishes to minimize the chances of a dismissal on ripeness grounds, prudence dictates resort to the various agencies, whether they carry administrative or legislative labels.

D. Application and Reapplication: Meaningful, Grandiose, or Meager?

The *MacDonald* Court's statement that "the rejection of exceedingly grandiose development plans does not logically imply that less ambitious plans will receive similarly unfavorable reviews,"[49] has led to the requirement that a developer submit at least one meaningful proposal. The difficult issue is deciding when, and how often, reapplication is necessary.

In *MacDonald,* the Court said that "a court cannot determine whether a regulation has gone 'too far' unless it knows how far the regulation goes."[50] The phrase has a nice ring to it, but it oversimplifies and confuses the problem, unduly burdening the property owner's quest to ascertain what the city will allow. The land-development permit process typically does not involve the developer merely going to the city and asking, "What will you let me do?" That might occur in a classical, simple, and mythical Euclidean zoning scheme, where the city's response would be, "We allow commercial use on that lot," and that would be the end of the matter. Under most land-use schemes, however, a parcel's current zoning classification is only the beginning. More often, though, some type of flexible zoning tool (such as a conditional-use permit, floating zone, or site review) or subdivision process must be pursued, requiring the developer to submit its proposal to which the city will react by saying yes, no, or maybe. If the answer is yes, there is no problem; the development proceeds.

If the answer is no or maybe, the developer must decide whether its proposal was meaningful or grandiose. If it thinks the proposal might have been grandiose, the developer must reapply. This determination will not be an easy one to make. If the record shows that the city might be receptive to a modified proposal, reapplication is likely necessary. This was the case in both *MacDonald* and *Penn Central Transportation Co. v. City of New York.*[51] More recently, in *Southview Associates, Ltd. v. Bongartz,*[52] the Second Circuit found a claim unripe when a commission denied permission because it determined that the location of the structures on the subject land would interfere with a deer habitat. Critically, the commission indicated that it "would be receptive to a subdivision proposal that placed lots in a different segment"[53] of the parcel, and it also determined that the developer had not "undertaken all feasible and reasonable means of reducing the development's effect on the deeryard."[54] On these facts, the court held that the developer needed to reapply and alter its development request to determine what the commission would allow. Because some development seemed likely to be permitted, the developer had to ask for it.

The Court has given us some examples of grandiose proposals, though they are not especially helpful. The proposal rejected by the county in *MacDonald* was referred to as an "intense type of residential development."[55] The *MacDonald* Court also intimated that the " 'five Victorian mansions' " sought in *Agins v. City of Tiburon*[56] and the nuclear power plant in *San Diego Gas & Electric Co. v. City of San Diego*[57] were of the grandiose variety.[58] The proposed fifty-five–story office tower atop the landmark Grand Central Station in the *Penn Central* case was also likely "grandiose."

Circumstances dictate when and how often reapplication must be made. For example, in *Gil v. Inland Wetlands and Watercourses Agency,*[59] the court found a lack of finality even though four applications had been made:

> Our review of the record, however, convinces us that the plaintiff has not met his burden of demonstrating finality. A number of factors leads us to this conclusion. First, although we agree with the Appellate Court that the plaintiff had a reasonable expectation of developing the property for residential purposes, the wetlands status of a portion of the property should also have warned the plaintiff that development would be difficult and that repeated ap-

> plications might be necessary before the agency would approve an application for a building permit. In this case, although the plaintiff submitted four applications, only three were actually reviewed on their merits.
>
> Additionally, the record discloses that whereas neighboring homes on similarly sized lots varied in footprint size from 800 to 900 square feet, each of the plaintiff's applications proposed single family houses with footprints exceeding 1500 square feet. Furthermore, although the plaintiff's final application reduced the footprint of the proposed house to 1800 square feet from the 2100 square feet of the preceding application, the final application nonetheless represented an increase from an earlier application's 1500 square feet proposed residence. In light of these factors, we cannot say that the agency would have rejected a more modest proposal if one had been offered by the plaintiff.[60]

In addition to the guesswork of whether to reapply, waiver is a concern that must be evaluated. A developer trying to make a case ripe by making meaningful, nongrandiose submissions may ask for less than it wants. If the city says no to one or two "greedy" requests, and says yes to another more moderate request, the developer can proceed to build according to the approved plans. But does the developer have the right to sue for the losses it sustained as a result of the prior denials? Because the city approved the meager request, has the developer waived its right to challenge the prior denials of the "greedy" requests?

If waiver is a realistic risk, the developer should not make the meager request, nor should it be required to do so. Dolan did not do so in her case. She simply sought a variance to proceed with her initial plan, which was denied.[61] Presumably (the issue was not discussed) her request was meaningful, and not grandiose; only when a request is grandiose must the developer accommodate by asking for less.

While the exercise of calculating a meaningful proposal may always be somewhat of a guessing game, the rule ought not force the developer to make repeated, increasingly meager requests to make a claim ripe. Recall that *MacDonald,* the source of the meaningful-application rule, spoke of "relatively intense" and "grandiose" proposals.[62] One need not read the case as requiring repeated submissions. It is one thing to force a developer to submit a request or requests (and thus acknowledge that it is subject to a regulatory authority that clearly can impose some constraints) and make some concessions (surrendering the principle that "it is my land and I will do what I want"); it is quite another to make a local government's decision limiting land use unreviewable in court because the developer is unwilling to concede what it thinks is reasonable under the circumstances.

The "grandiose proposal" concern should be used sparingly to strike claims on the grounds of ripeness. Though *MacDonald* envisions some reapplication process, compelling the developer to repeatedly downsize its project is inconsistent with the variance requirement of *Hamilton Bank,* which used the developer's proposal as the frame of reference. There the Court required the developer only to seek variances that would have "allowed it to develop the property according to its proposed plat."[63]

Even in a case like *Gil,* the wetlands case quoted above,[64] a proposal that requests significantly larger or more intense uses than those existing in the surrounding area may be reasonable. The current zoning may be excessive and the surrounding property may be underused. Under such circumstances, favoring the property owner does not pose unreasonable burdens on government. It simply gives the owner its "day in court." Case law, which makes clear that the property owner who seeks to maximize the development potential of its land runs a very real risk of losing on the merits, ought to deter hasty filings.

E. Prong One Futility

Both *Hamilton Bank* and *MacDonald* state that futile or useless applications are not necessary. But what does it take to convince a court?[65] *Lucas* shows that one need not pursue applications for relief that the authorities lack the power to give. However, likelihood of success is not the test. Relief must be pursued if granting it is theoretically possible.[66]

Suspicions about local hostility or even oral statements by local officials generally cannot be relied upon to release one from the obligation of making formal application. In *Wheeler v. City of Wayzata,*[67] the landowners wished to construct docks on waterfront land as part of a commercial marina but were prevented from doing so because the land was zoned for single-family use. Because the physical characteristics of the land precluded residential structures, the owners were left with no use of their land. Without seeking a variance, special-use permit, or rezoning, the owners brought a takings claim. In response to a challenge that the claim was not ripe under *Hamilton Bank,* the owners said it would have been futile to seek relief from the city because a few years earlier the city manager told the owners that " 'the city does not want any development of that property.' "[68] The court rejected the futility argument, noting that the burden is on the challenger to prove futility. An oral statement made years earlier by one authorized to grant or deny land-use permission does not suffice to reflect the town's current position on development.[69]

While the absence of a variance or other similar procedure may, as to prong one, render the claim ripe on futility grounds,[70] such an absence, standing alone, is not proof of futility. Even when no variance procedure exists, there are instances when a rezoning must be sought. This is particularly true when the currently contested zoning classification is a dated one.[71] In *Celentano v. City of West Haven*,[72] for example, land was zoned for open space in 1967 under the mistaken assumption that it was publicly owned. The property owner's 1990 federal court lawsuit was dismissed on ripeness grounds because the owner failed to formally apply for a rezoning.[73] The court was not going to "permit a disgruntled landowner to bypass or preempt the local agency charged with adjudicating the validity of zoning decisions in favor of a federal district court."[74] The city gets a chance to make a current determination about how the land is to be used before the city is hauled into court.

If the legislation is recent, there may be no reasonable likelihood that the legislative body will change its mind, and a rezoning or variance likely need not be sought. A recent downzoning itself may be evidence of finality. In *Resolution Trust Corp. v. Town of Highland Beach*,[75] for example, the town granted permission in 1980 for a planned-unit development to be constructed by 1990. In 1984, a new town board decided to shorten the completion date to 1985. The developer did not meet the new deadline. In 1987, the town downzoned the land to eight units per acre. The developer sued. In 1990, the town downzoned the land to six units per acre. The town argued that the developer should have appealed the 1984 decision or sought an extension of time, but the court found the later downzonings evidenced a final decision.

Some courts are more stringent. In *Southern Pacific Transportation Co. v. City of Los Angeles*,[76] a strip of railroad land was zoned in varying classifications consistent with the zoning of adjacent land along the railroad route. When the railroad applied to the Interstate Commerce Commission (ICC) for abandonment, the city downzoned the land to a classification allowing only parking lots. The railroad brought a takings claim without first applying for development permission. The court held the claim unripe.

When a moratorium is imposed on development, a claim may be ripe under the futility exception.[77] When a city freezes development pending the resolution of a particular problem (for example, adopting a plan to deal with flooding problems) or to give the city time to study community needs,[78] applying for relief has been held futile.[79] Of course, if the interim ordinance contains a variance procedure or allows some uses, a landowner is obligated to pursue those processes to obtain a final decision.

IV. Seeking Compensation from State Courts

The second prong of *Hamilton Bank* requires takings claimants to seek compensation from the state courts. While *Hamilton Bank,* decided in 1985, made the second step contingent on whether the state provided a procedure for awarding compensation for regulatory takings, that contingency was removed in 1987 when the Court held in *First English Evangelical Lutheran Church v. County of Los Angeles*[80] that the self-executing nature of the Fifth Amendment required a compensation remedy. Under the supremacy clause, state court judges are bound to enforce the Constitution; therefore, after *First English,* no state court may refuse to award compensation when a taking is found.[81]

Before *First English,* some state courts (most notably those in Florida, New York, and California) rejected money damages as possible relief for regulatory takings. They are no longer free to make that choice.[82] No state court can assert that its law does not provide a compensation remedy because federal law, in effect a part of state law, provides that remedy.[83]

A. Prong Two Is Applicable to All Takings Claims

All takings claims, physical and regulatory, are subject to the requirement that the property owner seek compensation from the state. The reason is inherent in the nature of the Fifth Amendment: it does not proscribe all takings, but only those without compensation. The longstanding rule of interpretation is that the mandate of the Fifth Amendment is satisfied by post-taking compensation.[84] Thus, if a property owner thinks that government conduct, by physical invasion or a regulation on use, has taken her property, she must bring an inverse condemnation action.

It should not matter whether the taking occurs by the application of a law or its mere enactment. Only when the state refuses to pay is the Fifth Amendment violated. Thus, prong two applies to facial claims as well as applied claims.[85] Some disputable authority to the contrary exists. In *Adamson Companies v. City of Malibu,*[86] the court found a facial takings claim ripe in federal court without prong two having been met, but did so by mistakenly relying on *Yee v. City of Escondido.*[87] In *Yee,* the Supreme Court heard a facial takings claim and noted that it was not subject to prong one finality. The *Yee* Court, however, had no occasion to address prong two, which in fact had been met. The *Yee* case came to the Court from the state courts.[88]

B. Prong Two in *Nollan/Dolan*-Type Exaction Cases

As discussed above,[89] although some question exists about the application of *Hamilton Bank*'s prong one to exaction cases, apparently no one has specifically questioned the applicability of *Hamilton Bank*'s second prong. This is understandable because there is no good reason to question prong two's applicability, but the issue merits discussion because of the following comment by Justice Stevens in his dissent in *Dolan:*

> If the Court proposes to have the federal judiciary micro-manage state decisions of this kind, it is indeed extending its welcome mat to a significant new class of litigants. Although there is no reason to believe that state courts have failed to rise to the task, property owners have surely found a new friend today.[90]

If Justice Stevens's reference to "micro-management" means the lower federal courts, the apprehension is misplaced. As with economic-impact claimants such as Lucas, *Nollan/Dolan*-type claimants suffering a physical exaction are raising a Fifth Amendment issue. But the Fifth Amendment is not violated by a taking of property, only a taking without compensation. The cause of action is not complete until compensation is sought and denied, and this matter can be litigated in state courts.

With *Lucas*-type economic-impact cases, the property owner asks for compensation and, if a taking is found, the state decides whether to pay temporary or permanent damages. With an exaction case, the property owner can go to state court to ask for invalidation of the exaction or compensation. If the requisite nexus exists, there is no taking. If the nexus is missing, the state can choose to drop the condition or pay for it.[91]

However, some danger of confusion exists, as demonstrated in *Amoco Oil Co. v. Village of Schaumburg*.[92] In *Amoco,* the village conditioned Amoco's request for a special permit on Amoco's dedicating 20 percent of its land for a highway. There appeared to be no nexus, and a federal challenge ensued. While the case was pending, the village revoked the permit. This action left Amoco with no requirement of dedication and no permit. Although the federal district court was convinced that the exaction was invalid under *Nollan,* it nonetheless dismissed the case and directed Amoco to state court. The court was satisfied that the Illinois courts reviewed special permit denials with *Nollan*-like scrutiny[93] and that Amoco was likely to obtain a state court ruling that the reason for the permit denial (the refusal to dedicate land) was arbitrary.

The *Amoco* court opined in dicta that if the state court were to find a nonarbitrary denial, Amoco could return to federal court. Property owners should not count on this. *Hamilton Bank* says that when a city has taken property without paying for it, the owner is to go to the state courts. In an *Amoco*-type case, the owner would go to state court and assert that the denial of the permit was wrong and ask that either a permit be issued without the condition or that the state be ordered to pay compensation for the dedication. If the state court responds to the developer by saying, "I think the condition is validly imposed, so if you want the permit, you dedicate the land," that conclusion is a lower court finding that a nexus exists, which is the equivalent of a determination that no taking has occurred and no compensation is due. That finding renders the case ripe, but it is also appealable directly. It is not subject to collateral attack in federal court.[94]

Nollan and *Dolan* demonstrate the feasibility of trying these issues in state court. Both parties lost at the state level on the issue of legitimacy of the condition. Both appealed directly to the U.S. Supreme Court and prevailed. If the Nollans or Dolan had gone to federal district courts after the state trial or appellate courts had found the conditions valid, the federal courts would have been obliged to give full faith and credit to those findings.

C. The Nature of the Remedy: Federal or State Based

Because the Constitution mandates a compensation remedy, the procedure need not be statutorily authorized.[95] It is sufficient that the courts of the state will hear the claim even if the contours of the action are somewhat uncertain.[96] Some courts have found an available remedy based on independent state constitutional guarantees similar to the Fifth Amendment.[97] This is not only unnecessary, but complicates matters.

There are grounds for confusion. First, *Hamilton Bank* referred to state law as evidence of how to fulfill the requirement. Second, *Hamilton Bank,* preceding *First English* by two years, said that a party had to resort to state remedies when adequate. As proof of adequacy, the Court cited Tennessee statutes that allowed an inverse condemnation action. It happens that these statutes were premised on the Tennessee Constitution's analogue to the Fifth Amendment. But the right to compensation would have existed even if the legislature had not enacted the statute[98] and even if the Tennessee Constitution had lacked a takings clause, because the right to compensation is self-executing.[99]

Although the self-executing nature of the Fifth Amendment's just compensation clause means that state constitutional or statutory authorization is unnecessary,[100] legislatures are free to adopt procedures allowing litigants to pursue this right.[101] A state may establish administrative mechanisms to adjudicate inverse condemnation claims.[102]

When one looks for a state procedure, the search quickly leads to the detailed eminent domain codes that states have enacted.[103] These codes present two difficulties. First, the statutes are developed primarily to address direct condemnations, and typically address inverse condemnation obliquely, if at all. Second, it is not clear whether these statutes are designed solely to administer[104] the state constitution's just compensation requirement or to administer the Fifth Amendment as well.

A look at a few such statutes will show the ill fit with regulatory takings actions. Tennessee's code, § 29-16-123, entitled "Action initiated by owner," provides:

> (a) If, however, such person or company *has actually taken possession* of such land, occupying it for the purposes of internal improvement, the owner of such land may petition for a jury of inquest, in which case the same proceedings may be had, as near as may be, as hereinbefore provided; or he may sue for damages in the ordinary way, in which case the jury shall lay off the land by metes and bounds and assess the damages, as upon the trial of an appeal from the return of a jury of inquest. (emphasis added)[105]

The requirement that the condemnor "has actually taken possession" is easy to apply to some inverse situations such as flood damage or overflights. But what about regulatory limits on use? It happens that the Tennessee courts have interpreted the requirement to apply to zoning restrictions,[106] but that interpretation is hardly a given.

Wyoming's statute, § 1-26-516, entitled "Action for inverse condemnation," provides:

> When a person possessing the power of condemnation takes possession of or damages land in which he has no interest, or substantially diminishes the use or value of land, *due to activities on adjoining land* without the authorization of the owner of the land or before filing an action of condemnation, the owner of the land may file an action in district court seeking damages for the taking or damage and shall be granted litigation expenses if damages are awarded to the owner. (emphasis added)

The statute appears applicable to zoning enactments that destroy use, but only when "due to activities on adjoining land. . . ."[107]

North Carolina's law provides as follows:

> § 40A-51: Remedy where no declaration of taking filed.
>
> (a) If property has been taken by an act or omission of a condemnor listed in G.S. 40A-3(b) or (c) and no complaint containing a declaration of taking has been filed, the owner of the property may initiate an action to seek compensation for the taking. The action may be initiated within 24 months of the date of the taking of the affected property or the completion of the project involving the taking, whichever shall occur later.

Section 40A-3(b) of the North Carolina General Statutes defines local public condemnors as follows:

> For the public use or benefit, the governing body of each municipality or county shall possess the power of eminent domain and may acquire by purchase, gift or condemnation any property, either inside or outside its boundaries, for the following purposes. . . .

The statute then lists as purposes: roads, public enterprises, parks, sewers, hospitals, cemeteries, libraries, drainage, and "acquiring historic properties." On its face, the statute is not designed to deal with excessive exercises of regulatory powers.

Statutes, like the ones above, are not necessarily inappropriate to use when dealing with regulatory takings claims, but they create confusion for litigants trying to identify the proper claim to file. For example, there is a tendency to refer to the fulfillment of prong two as seeking compensation under "state law."[108] Seeking relief under "state law" means that state procedures are used to assert the right, but a Fifth Amendment right is the one being asserted.[109] Yet, because of the unusual nature of the Fifth Amendment (it is not violated by a taking, only by an uncompensated one), some courts have taken the position that the claim presented to the state courts is not a federal claim, because the federal claim, unripe under *Hamilton Bank,* does not yet exist.[110]

Looking at prong two as a matter of "state law" can have unusual and unfortunate results. It led one state court to take the position that it had no jurisdiction over a Fifth Amendment claim until the party sought compensation under the state constitution. In *Drake v. Town of Sanford,*[111] the plaintiff property owners filed an action in state court alleging that the town's shoreland zoning ordinance had taken their property without compensation in violation of the federal and state constitutions. This assertion was in accord with a prior state supreme court opinion,[112] which said that although no Maine statute provided for an inverse condemnation suit, such a right existed at common law based on the federal and state constitution.[113] At trial, the plaintiffs dismissed with prejudice their claim under the state constitution. A jury found a taking based on the Fifth Amendment.

On appeal, the state supreme court overturned the jury's verdict and dismissed the case for lack of jurisdiction. The court said the case was not ripe until the plaintiffs resorted to "the state procedure" for determining compensation, meaning the claim based on the Maine Constitution.[114] The plaintiffs' dismissal of that claim meant they had not completed *Hamilton Bank*'s prong two.[115] This result is unnecessary under *Hamilton Bank* and wasteful.

A state court has an obligation to enforce federal rights, and a property owner has a federal constitutional claim under the Fifth Amendment enforceable in state court independent of the state constitution. Although a state can compel a litigant to follow its procedures, it should not use prong two to force a property owner to rely on the state constitution or some other source of state substantive law. It is true that all states have some counterpart to the Fifth Amendment requiring compensation for takings.[116] It is also true that in some states the protection conferred by the state constitution is greater than that conferred by the federal constitution.[117] Nonetheless, states are not required to have just compensation clauses in their constitutions, nor must they interpret them to provide as much protection as the Fifth Amendment provides.[118]

State statutes, like those discussed above, simply say that when state agents take property the state shall pay. The statutes normally do not identify a source of the right, and state courts may conclude that the source is in the state constitution.[119] But, it may just as well be in the Fifth Amendment.[120] If the state channels such actions through its inverse condemnation procedures, recognizing that the process that exists to implement a state constitutional requirement is also a logical way to litigate a similar federal constitutional requirement, then no harm is done to the federal right. But it does harm the federal right to prevent it from being asserted as was done in *Drake*.

Placing undue emphasis on the label chosen by the property owner pursuing compensation in state court runs a risk of reestablishing the tyranny of the common law forms of action that supposedly were buried years ago. This lack of clarity about whether the state condemnation procedure or a common law action should be used compels property owners' lawyers to study state law in this area carefully.

D. Res Judicata Implications of Pursuing State Court

Once a property owner has completed prong two, the law of res judicata will usually preclude a Fifth Amendment claim from being pursued in federal court.[121] Adjudication of the claim in state court bars a subsequent lawsuit in federal court under 28 U.S.C. § 1738, the full faith and credit statute.[122] Collateral attack of the state court judgment is not available in federal district court.[123] A property owner who is dissatisfied with the results obtained from the state court is limited to appealing directly to the U.S. Supreme Court.

This is true even if a court takes the position discussed above[124] that the state claim must be litigated first because the federal claim is unripe. Once the claim is litigated, the rule of issue preclusion will still likely bar a suit in federal court on the federal claim, as the issues being tried under the state constitution's takings clause would be the same.[125]

The Eleventh Circuit has suggested that a "possible exception"[126] to the res judicata doctrine is a reservation of the right to litigate federal rights in federal courts under the doctrine laid down in *England v. Louisiana State Bd. of Medical Examiners*.[127] There is disagreement, however, about whether a reservation of rights can be made in state-initiated proceedings.[128]

It may seem anomalous that the action necessary to make a claim ripe terminates it. It is certainly surprising to those who are misled by the language of ripeness to think that the state lawsuit is preparatory to a federal suit. The harm of this misleading language is discussed below.[129] First, however, the one narrow instance when the res judicata bar can be avoided should be discussed. That instance is explored in the following section.

E. Prong Two Futility or Inadequacy

The burden on the property owner to establish inadequacy of the state's compensation remedy is difficult to carry.[130] Uncertainty does not equal inadequacy.[131] Also, if the property owner allows the state statute of limitations to run, he or she forfeits any right to seek compensation in federal court.[132] If the property owner's state action is dismissed with leave to amend, and the property owner fails to amend, no federal lawsuit will lie.[133]

In rare instances, prong two futility can be established by proving that the state courts have rejected takings claims that are on all fours with the challenger's case. Because takings claims are usually highly fact-specific affairs, this similarity will not often occur,[134] but it does happen. In *Naegele Outdoor Advertising, Inc. v. City of Durham,*[135] a challenge to a five-and-one-half-year billboard amortization ordinance was deemed ripe in federal court without pursuit of a lawsuit in state court, because the North Carolina state courts had, on several occasions, upheld the same type of amortization ordinance.[136] The federal court concluded that a five-and-one-half-year sign amortization provision would not be viewed as a taking by the North Carolina courts and that asking the state court for relief would be pointless. The Ninth Circuit has made a similar finding regarding certain rent-control statutes as they have been construed in California state courts.[137]

Finally, if the government defendant removes a takings case to federal court, the federal court may appropriately find that prong two cannot be met.

V. Ripeness for Due Process and Equal Protection Claims

In addition to, or instead of, a Fifth Amendment takings claim, property owners often assert Fourteenth Amendment due process and equal protection challenges to land-use restrictions. These include (1) the very suspect "substantive due process" takings claim, (2) a substantive due process arbitrary and capricious claim, (3) a "procedural due process" claim, and (4) an equal protection claim.[138] Property owners are less likely to prevail on the merits of these claims because courts give greater deference to government action under these theories than under the takings clause. The question here is whether the ripeness considerations differ.

Hamilton Bank applied the final-decision rule not only to Fifth Amendment takings claims but also to substantive due process claims that allege, in a manner identical to the Fifth Amendment, that a regulation has gone too far (the so-called due process takings claim).[139]

While the *Hamilton Bank* opinion did not expressly refer to the just compensation prong in its due process discussion, other courts have held that consistency with the rationale of *Hamilton Bank* regarding the Fifth Amendment claim requires that a party asserting a "due process taking" must seek compensation from the state.[140] The point ought not matter because it is unlikely that such a cause of action will continue to be recognized.[141]

Most courts have held that the final-decision requirement applies to "as applied" arbitrary and capricious substantive due process claims.[142] As is the case with the Fifth Amendment, the rule is not applicable to facial claims.[143] The compensation requirement has been held inapplicable to substantive due process arbitrary and capricious claims.[144]

Generally, procedural due process claims have been exempted from the final-decision requirement,[145] but equal protection claims have been held subject to it.[146] Courts have differed about whether the compensation requirement applies to procedural due process[147] and equal protection claims.[148]

VI. Conclusion: Are the Ripeness Rules Undue Burdens? Are They a Hoax?

There is disagreement about whether compliance with the final-decision rule is more analogous to fording a raging river than stepping over a trickle of a stream. One commentator finds that there "is no rationality in the ripeness law" and "anarchy" reigns and suggests that with the absence of sound guidance from the Supreme Court, lower courts' efforts to provide clarity are doomed to futility.[149] For another commentator the courts have developed a "predictable and understandable body of law" and have been "remarkably tolerant of developers' efforts to reach the federal courts."[150]

My own view is that some clarification is needed, and that an accurate reading of *Hamilton Bank* and *MacDonald* would do the job. Much of the stringency of the final-decision rule has come from the lower federal courts' expansion of those cases beyond their bounds. This, I assume, is traceable in large part to the desire of these courts, for good and bad reasons, to keep land-use cases off their dockets.

More troubling from my point of view is prong two and the paradoxical consequences that result from the mixture of ripeness law and the law of full faith and credit. One understandable reaction to the prong two requirement of *Hamilton Bank* is that it perpetrates a fraud or hoax on landowners. The courts say, "Your suit is not ripe until you seek compensation from the state courts," but when the landowner does these things, the court says, "Ha ha, now it is too late." While it is unfortunate that courts continue to use misleading ripeness language, the result is justifiable if one thinks that one lawsuit is enough.

Beyond the misleading ripeness language, no harm befalls the litigant simply because he or she is barred from federal court. If the property owner's lawyer knows the law, a wasted effort in federal court can be avoided or taken with knowledge that the effort is likely to fail if the government defendant or the court raises the jurisdictional defense of ripeness.[151]

Although a denial of a federal forum may occur, our dual system presumes state court competency. No injury to property owners as a class results unless one thinks that state courts are likely to be hostile to property owners' rights. Undoubtedly, state courts vary in the deference they accord local land-use decisions; but, even if some courts display hostility, the same would likely be true in federal courts. Numerous federal judges have often decried being turned into "super" zoning boards of appeal hearing "garden variety zoning dispute[s] dressed up in the trappings of constitutional law."[152] The denigrating tone of these pronouncements suggests that the outcome for property owners in many instances would be no better, and might be worse, in federal court.

If the matter is thought to be in need of change, there are two solutions: rewrite the law of res judicata and full faith and credit, or rewrite the law of the Fifth Amendment.

In rewriting the law of res judicata, the Supreme Court or Congress might address the paradox and conceivably say that the second lawsuit in federal court is not barred by the full faith and credit statute. Such a ruling or statute, however, would require a decision about whether the principles and policies behind full faith and credit and the law of finality of judgments should give way to replication of matters once litigated. Certainly an anomaly exists: an unripe suit is barred at the moment it comes into existence. Like a tomato that suffers vine rot, it goes from being green to mushy red overnight. It can never be eaten. This anomaly, however, is not necessarily bad. The additional lawsuits might not cause the federal judiciary to collapse, but they would use limited resources of courts already busy.

If one insists on opening the lower federal courts to these lawsuits, judicial economy would be better served by having just one lawsuit. This result could be achieved by reexamining the rule that the Fifth Amendment does not require pretaking compensation.[153] This rule lies behind prong two's view of the Fifth Amendment that no cause of action exists until demand is made on the state and the state refuses to pay. The language of the Fifth Amendment does not mandate this rule.

The Fifth Amendment could be read as providing that in the inverse condemnation setting, a taking occurs upon the adoption or application of an excessive or illegal regulation. Regarding "as applied" claims, one would have to obtain a final decision and, once that was done, sue in either state or federal court. Regarding facial claims (prong one not being applicable), the choice of forums would exist upon enactment. With this reinterpretation, at least there would be only one lawsuit. The state (the wrongdoer in the sense that it took property without paying), could hardly complain that it must defend itself in federal court for violating federal rights. The increased workload on the lower federal courts might affect the inclination to overturn this longstanding rule of inverse condemnation. That, in part, may depend on whether those courts are already obligated to hear land-use claims under the due process and equal protection clauses of the Fourteenth Amendment. If so, perhaps the takings claim related to the same facts might be seen as an insignificant addition.

I do not advocate these changes. Federal courts are busy enough. State judges are more familiar with land-use disputes and can do a better job of evaluating local and state interests. The bar is not total. When state courts have definitively ruled out takings claims, a federal action will lie.[154] Finally, I am not convinced that state judges in general harbor hostilities toward property owners that would, if true, support the availability of the more independent federal judiciary.

Notes

*A revised version of this chapter appears as *Ripeness and Forum Selection in Fifth Amendment Takings Litigation,* 11 J. LAND USE & ENVTL. L. (Fall 1995).

1. 473 U.S. 172 (1985).

2. For the rules' application to due process and equal protection claims, see the discussion at text accompanying notes 138-48.

3. 112 S. Ct. 2886 (1992).

4. 114 S. Ct. 2309 (1994).

5. MacDonald, Sommer & Frates v. County of Yolo, 477 U.S. 340, 348 (1986).

6. 815 F. Supp. 561 (D. Conn. 1993). *See also* Provident Mutual Insurance Co. v. City of Atlanta, 864 F. Supp. 1274, 1280 (N.D. Ga. 1994), in which the same argument is made and rejected.

7. 457 U.S. 496 (1982).

8. First English Evangelical Lutheran Church of Glendale v. County of Los Angeles, 482 U.S. 304 (1987). There is confusion about whether the claim pursued in state court is one of state or federal law. *See* discussion *infra* § IV. C. *See also* Dodd v. Hood River County, 59 F.3d 852 (9th Cir. 1995), in which the majority takes the position, contrary to that advocated in this chapter, that the issue is one of state law.

9. The prong two requirement to seek compensation from the state courts is sometimes referred to as an exhaustion of state remedies requirement. *See* Sinaloa Lake Owners Ass'n v. City of Simi Valley, 882 F.2d 1398, 1404 (9th Cir. 1988). This requirement contrasts with exhausting administrative remedies, which is not required to meet the final decision prong of *Hamilton Bank.*

This chapter's focus on choice of forum is limited to *Hamilton Bank*'s prong two. Concerning other issues see Kenneth B. Bley, *Deciding Whether to Sue in Federal Court,* URBAN LAND 39 (Feb. 1995); Thomas E. Roberts, *Forum Selection in Land-Use Cases: Is Federal Court a Viable Option?* 16 URBAN, STATE AND LOCAL LAW NEWSLETTER (Winter 1993).

10. *Hamilton Bank*, 473 U.S. at 178.
11. *Id.* at 186.
12. *Id.* at 188.
13. *Id.*
14. 477 U.S. 340 (1986).
15. *MacDonald*, 477 U.S. at 343.
16. *Id.* at 350 n.7.
17. *Id.* at 353 n.9.
18. *Id.* at 353.
19. *Id.*
20. *Id.* at 347.
21. While *Hamilton Bank* and *MacDonald* are the leading ripeness cases, the Court had, in several prior opinions, expressed concern about the lack of clarity regarding the actual impact of a regulation in finding no taking to have occurred on the merits. In hindsight, these opinions have come to be treated as ripeness cases as well. *See* Penn Central Transportation Co. v. City of New York, 438 U.S. 104 (1978); Agins v. City of Tiburon, 447 U.S. 255 (1980); Hodel v. Virginia Surface Mining & Reclamation Ass'n, Inc., 452 U.S. 264, 294-95 (1981).
22. Sinaloa Lake Owners Ass'n v. City of Simi Valley, 882 F.2d 1398, 1402 (9th Cir. 1989), *cert. denied*, 494 U.S. 1015 (1990). *But see* Harris v. City of Wichita, 862 F. Supp. 287, 291 (D. Kan. 1994) (in dicta, stating that law is unclear).
23. 503 U.S. 519 (1992). *See also* Galbraith v. City of Anderson, 627 N.E.2d 850 (Ind. Ct. App. 1994).
24. Nollan v. California Coastal Comm'n, 483 U.S. 825 (1987).
25. Though some question exists about the final-decision rule of *Hamilton Bank* in exaction cases, it does not appear that anyone has specifically questioned the applicability of *Hamilton Bank*'s second prong, the compensation requirement. Some concern might exist, however, due to a comment by Justice Stevens in dissent in *Dolan*, discussed below at text accompanying notes 89-94.
26. 126 Or. App. 416, 869 P.2d 350 (Ct. App. 1994).
27. *Nelson*, 869 P.2d at 352.
28. *Id.*
29. *Hamilton Bank* and Hodel v. Virginia Surface Mining & Reclamation Ass'n, Inc., 452 U.S. 264, 294-95 (1981).
30. Tinnerman v. Palm Beach County, 641 So. 2d 523 (Fla. Dist. Ct. App. 1994).
31. Conceptually an impact fee fits more appropriately as an "arbitrary and capricious" substantive due process claim than as a Fifth Amendment taking claim.
32. *See* discussion *infra* note 35.
33. 114 S. Ct. at 2328.
34. *See* former CAL. GOV'T CODE § 65913.5 and § 66021 (West 1995). *See also* Balch Enterprises, Inc. v. New Haven Unified School District, 219 Cal. App. 3d 783, 268 Cal. Rptr. 543 (Ct. App. 1990) (suit challenging school fee paid under protest subject to four-year statute of limitations).

35. Trimen Development Co. v. King County, 65 Wash. App. 692, 829 P.2d 226 (Ct. App. 1992), *aff'd on other grounds,* 124 Wash. 2d 261, 877 P.2d 187 (1994) (developer who paid park fee and proceeded with development estopped from challenging legality of ordinance); *but see* Henderson Homes, Inc. v. City of Bothell, 124 Wash. 2d 240 877 P.2d 176 (1994) (in which park impact fee characterized as a tax, suit to recover payment allowed, and use of estoppel by city rejected in light of city's lack of clean hands).

See also Bd. of Supervisors of North Coventry Twp. v. Laurelwood Construction Co. 144 Pa. Commw. 63, 600 A.2d 690 (Commw. Ct. 1991) (state law required developer to appeal condition to zoning board of adjustment or township's legislative body rather than pay fee and seek judicial review); *In re* 1983-84 County Tax Levy v. Box Butte County Bd. of Education, 374 N.W.2d 235 (Neb. 1985); *but see* Nelson v. City of Lake Oswego 126 Or. App. 416, 869 P.2d 350 (Ct. App. 1994) (property owners conveyed easement and then sued; no taking found but court did reach merits).

36. The delay might be compensable under *First English.*

37. Additional confusion exists because of the practice of some courts to refer to *Hamilton Bank*'s prong two requirement to seek compensation from the state courts as an "exhaustion of state judicial remedies" requirement. *See, e.g., Sinaloa Lake Owners Ass'n* 882 F.2d at 1404.

38. *Hamilton Bank,* 473 U.S. at 192. Despite this distinction, Shonkwiler and Morgan observe that many state courts use the phrase "exhaustion of administrative remedies" to include the requirement that government action be final. JOHN W. SHONKWILER & TERRY MORGAN, LAND USE LITIGATION 281 (1986).

39. Michael M. Berger, *The Ripeness Mess in Federal Land Use Cases or How the Supreme Court Converted Federal Judges into Fruit Peddlers,* 1991 INST. ON PLAN. ZONING & EMINENT DOMAIN, ch. 7 at 7-15.

40. *Hamilton Bank,* 473 U.S. at 193.

41. *Id.* at 188.

42. Acierno v. Mitchell, 6 F.3d 970 (3d Cir. 1993).

43. The court noted that the board had plenary review over "any order, requirement, decision, or determination" under the zoning ordinance by any county officer, and authority to hear and decide any "applications for interpretation of any zoning ordinance, code, regulation, or map upon which [it] is empowered to pass." 6 F.3d at 977.

44. Southview Associates, Ltd. v. Bongartz, 980 F.2d 84, 96 (2d Cir. 1992), *cert. denied,* 113 S. Ct. 1586 (1993).

45. *See Hamilton Bank,* 473 U.S. at 193; *Acierno* 6 F.3d at 976 n.17. But distinguish from this the obligation to go to state court for inverse condemnation, where one seeks a declaration that a taking occurred and an award of compensation.

46. Recall that the Court required resort to both the planning commission and the board of adjustment.

47. *See* Hernandez v. City of Lafayette, 643 F.2d 1188 (5th Cir. 1981). In contrast, when an application for development permission was denied and the

land then immediately downzoned, a request for rezoning was not required because the recent nature of the downzoning showed the request would be futile. Hoehne v. County of San Benito, 870 F.2d 529, 535 (9th Cir. 1989). *See also* discussion *infra* notes 71-76 and accompanying text.

48. *Hernandez,* 643 F.2d at 1200.

49. *MacDonald,* 477 U.S. at 353 n.9.

50. *Id.* at 348.

51. 438 U.S. 104 (1978).

52. 980 F.2d 84 (2d Cir. 1992), *cert. denied,* 113 S. Ct. 1586 (1993). Note that reapplication to the initial decisionmakers is required rather than appeal of the initial denial. In *Southview,* a developer filed an application for development permission with a district environmental commission. When the permit was denied, the developer appealed to the state environmental board. After losing that round, the developer appealed to the state supreme court. Again, it lost, as the court affirmed the permit denials. The developer then sued in federal court arguing that it had obtained a final decision rendering the claim ripe. The court held that it was the district commission to which reapplication had to be made.

53. *Southview,* 980 F.2d at 98.

54. *Id.*

55. *MacDonald,* 477 U.S. at 352.

56. 447 U.S. 255 (1980).

57. 450 U.S. 621 (1981).

58. *MacDonald,* 477 U.S. at 353 n.9.

59. 593 A.2d 1368 (Conn. 1991).

60. *Gil,* 593 A.2d at 1374-75.

61. The Court did not discuss ripeness but did note that when Dolan sought a variance after the initial imposition of the exactions, she did not offer to downsize her project to mitigate the harm to the city. She simply argued that her project was consistent with the city's plan. Implicitly, that was enough to meet prong one.

62. *See supra* text accompanying notes 14-20 and 49-58.

63. *Hamilton Bank,* 473 U.S. at 187.

64. *Gil,* 593 A.2d at 1374-75.

65. Futility is a question of law for the court. Kawaoka v. City of Arroyo Grande, 17 F.3d 1227 (9th Cir. 1994).

66. *Hamilton Bank,* 473 U.S. at 188; *Lucas* 112 S. Ct. at 2891.

67. 511 N.W.2d 39 (Minn. Ct. App. 1994). *See also* Sinaloa Lake Owners Ass'n v. City of Simi Valley, 882 F.2d 1398 (9th Cir. 1989), *cert. denied,* 494 U.S. 1015 (1990).

68. *Wheeler,* 511 N.W.2d at 42.

69. Recent rejections of futility claims include a case in which the property owner alleged that city officials were predisposed to voting against any request he might make. Reliance on private or off-the-record comments was found to be insufficient to establish that formal application would be futile. *See* Celentano v. City of West Haven, 815 F. Supp. 561 (D. Conn. 1993).

70. *See Lucas*, 112 S. Ct. 2886; Naegele Outdoor Advertising, Inc. v. City of Durham, 803 F. Supp. 1068 (M.D.N.C. 1992).

71. *See* Hernandez v. City of Lafayette, 643 F.2d 1188 (5th Cir. 1981).

72. 815 F. Supp. 561 (D. Conn. 1993).

73. Celentano acquired the land in 1974. He filed, then voluntarily withdrew, a site development plan in 1986. In 1987 Celentano and the city engaged in informal discussions regarding development of the property.

74. *Celentano*, 815 F. Supp. at 567.

75. 18 F.3d 1536 (11th Cir. 1994).

76. 922 F.2d 498 (9th Cir. 1990).

77. *See* Carpenter v. Tahoe Regional Planning Authority, 804 F. Supp. 1316, 1324 (D. Nev. 1992) (finding prong one met when all permit applications were frozen). One court seems to think that the ripeness rules of *Hamilton Bank* do not apply to temporary takings claims. *See* Alexander v. Town of Jupiter, 640 So. 2d 79 (Fla. Dist. Ct. App. 1994). *Alexander* noted that *First English* did not discuss ripeness and from that concludes that ripeness is not a component of a temporary takings claim, only a permanent claim. There are several problems with this conclusion. First, the *First English* "temporary taking" label is a remedy issue only. It simply describes the option the state has of limiting its damages by lifting the ordinance the court finds to be excessive. Second, *First English* did not need to address the ripeness of the takings claim because it assumed, for the purposes of argument, that a taking had occurred and it dealt solely with the remedy issue. Third, the *First English* Court noted that the church had complied with prong two of *Hamilton Bank*, which it assumed applied. Finally, had the final decision been discussed, the futility doctrine would have applied. The moratorium challenged in *First English* flatly prohibited any use of the property while studies were undertaken to determine what uses eventually should be allowed in light of flooding dangers, and it would have been pointless for the church to seek a development permit.

78. *See* Thomas E. Roberts, *Interim Development Controls*, in 3 ZONING AND LAND-USE CONTROLS ch. 22 (Rohan ed. 1989).

79. *Carpenter*, 804 F. Supp. at 1324. The *Carpenter* court, finding the final decision prong met because a moratorium made it futile to seek development permission, proceeded to the merits of the takings claim without requiring that the plaintiff seek compensation from the state. Whether that decision is correct is unclear. Subsequent to *Carpenter*, the Ninth Circuit held that prong two of *Hamilton Bank* applies to interstate compact commissions as well, which should be sued upon in state court. *See* Brougton Lumber Co. v. Columbia River Gorge Comm'n, 975 F.2d 616, 612 (9th Cir. 1992), *cert. denied*, 114 S. Ct. 60 (1993). A Washington state court, however, has held that the state is not liable for a county's costs in inverse condemnation. *See* Klickitat County v. Washington, 71 Wash. App. 760, 862 P.2d 629 (Ct. App. 1993).

80. 482 U.S. 304 (1987).

81. *See* Carson Harbor Village v. City of Carson, 37 F.3d 468, 474 (9th Cir. 1994) ("The remedy has been available since 1987 when the Supreme Court

ruled in [*First English*] that California's *lack of a damages remedy was unconstitutional*.") (emphasis added). *See also* Tari v. Collier County, 846 F. Supp. 973, 976 (M.D. Fla. 1994).

82. It is thus wrong for the Eleventh Circuit to say that it does not know "whether Florida law now [post-*First English*] recognizes a cause of action wrought by regulatory takings." New Port Largo, Inc. v. Monroe County, 985 F.2d 1488, 1493 n.12 (11th Cir. 1993). *See* New Port Largo, Inc. v. Monroe County, 873 F. Supp. 633 (S.D. Fla. 1994) for the correct analysis. The Eleventh Circuit later found that Florida explicitly recognized a cause of action in inverse condemnation in Reahard v. Lee County, 30 F.3d 1412 (11th Cir. 1994).

83. Howlett v. Rose, 496 U.S. 332 (1990) (state court may not, without a valid excuse, refuse to hear federal claim). The instances when state courts can refuse to hear federal claims are few and far between (*see, e.g.*, Testa v. Katt, 330 U.S. 286 (1947)) and do not include takings claims.

84. *See Hamilton Bank*, 473 U.S. at 194. *See generally* Thomas E. Roberts, *Fifth Amendment Taking Claims in Federal Court: The State Compensation Requirement and Principles of Res Judicata*, 24 URB. LAW. 479, 482 (1992).

85. *See* Southern Pacific Transportation Co. v. City of Los Angeles, 922 F.2d 498, 505 (9th Cir. 1990).

86. 854 F. Supp. 1476 (C.D. Cal. 1994); *see also* Christensen v. Yolo County, 995 F.2d 161 (9th Cir. 1993) (court assumes, without discussion, that facial claim is ripe).

87. 112 S. Ct. 1522 (1992).

88. Other Supreme Court facial takings cases likewise came through the state courts (*Agins* and *Loretto*), were against federal agencies (*Hodel*), or were brought in federal court before *First English* when the state did not provide a compensation remedy (*Keystone*). For a full discussion, see Roberts, *supra* note 84, at 489.

89. *See supra* notes 24-36 and accompanying text.

90. *Dolan*, 114 S. Ct. at 2326.

91. Compensation might be due for the period of the delay under *First English*.

92. (No. 91C4973) 1992 WL 229591 (N.D. Ill. Sept. 11, 1992).

93. The state court would have no choice but to apply *Nollan* and *Dolan* to Fifth Amendment claims.

94. *See* Roberts, *supra* note 84, at 484-88.

95. Southview Associates v. Bongartz, 980 F.2d 84 (2d Cir. 1992); J. B. Ranch, Inc. v. Grand County, 958 F.2d 306, 308-09 (10th Cir. 1992); Lerman v. City of Portland, 675 F. Supp. 11, 16 (D. Me. 1987); Drake v. Town of Sanford, 642 A.2d 367 (Me. 1994).

96. *See Southview Associates*, 980 F.2d at 99, in which the court's research revealed no reported state regulatory takings case. However, the court found a state constitutional provision protecting property from damage and cases providing monetary relief for physical damage. That was enough for the court to conclude that relief would be available. Resort to the Vermont courts was thus required.

97. The Second Circuit, for example, has noted that the Vermont Constitution had been interpreted to require that compensation be paid for property that was physically damaged, and thus found it likely that a remedy for a regulatory taking would likewise be recognized. *Southview Associates*, 980 F.2d at 99-100. The Tenth Circuit has noted that the Utah Constitution provides for compensation and found implicitly that a judicial action was available. *J. B. Ranch*, 958 F.2d at 308; *see also* Anderson v. Alpine City, 804 F. Supp. 269, 273 (D. Utah 1992).

98. Brooksbank v. Roane County, 207 Tenn. 5324, 341 S.W.2d 570, 573 (1960).

99. Alper v. Clark County, 571 P.2d 810, 811 (Nev. 1977).

100. Bacchic v. Board of Control, 23 Cal. 2d 343, 144 P.2d 818 (1943).

101. Horn v. City of Chicago, 403 Ill. 549, 87 N.E.2d 642, 649 (1949) (legislature can require action be pursued within specified period of time).

102. Dep't of Agric. and Consumer Services, 568 So. 2d 24 (Fla. 1990) (no constitutional right to jury trial on inverse condemnation claims when statute provided administrative mechanism for hearing to determine what constituted just or full compensation for destroyed plants). Not just any administrative procedure will suffice. *See* Healing v. California Coastal Comm'n, 22 Cal. App. 4th 1158, 27 Cal. Rptr. 2d 758 (Ct. App. 1994) (petition to review administrative mandate held not to be adequate procedure to determine inverse condemnation issues, in part because administrative agency not vested with adjudicatory powers to decide issues of constitutional magnitude; landowner entitled to present matter to state trial court).

103. Some do not apply to inverse condemnation actions. *See Drake v. Town of Sanborn*, discussed *infra* note 111.

104. I do not say "implement" because the right is self-executing.

105. TENN. CODE ANN. § 29-16-123 (1980). This provision was cited by Justice Blackmun in *Hamilton Bank* to show that an inverse condemnation action was available.

106. Davis v. Metropolitan Gov't of Nashville, 620 S.W.2d 532, 533 (Tenn. Ct. App.) (1981).

107. *See comment*, Rodney Lang, *Wyoming Eminent Domain Act: Comment on the Act and Rule 71.1 of the Wyoming Rules of Civil Procedure*, 18 LAND & WATER L. REV. 739, 761 (1983).

108. *See* Roberts, *supra* note 84 at 492.

109. In Dodd v. Hood River County, 59 F.3d 852 (9th Cir. 1995), the court found that the pursuit of compensation for a taking in state court under the mandate on *Hamilton Bank* was not a Fifth Amendment claim, but mere resort to state substantive law. The court reached this conclusion despite its acknowledgement that *First English* said that claims for compensation are grounded in the Constitution. Still, the limited reading of *Hamilton Bank* was prompted, the majority said, because a contrary ruling would "deny a federal forum to every takings claimant." 1995 WL 383490 at * 6. The *Dodd* court did, however, recognize that pursuit of the state law claim in state court might preclude relitigation in federal court due to claim or issue preclusion rules. The court found that in

the case before it, claim preclusion did not bar the claim because under Oregon law, the state courts had consented to claim splitting. The court remanded the matter for a determination about whether issued preclusion applied.

110. Impinks v. City of Indianapolis, 612 N.E.2d 1125 (Ind. Ct. App. 1993). *See also* Bakken v. City of Council Bluffs, 470 N.W.2d 34 (Iowa 1991), in which a state court dismissed a § 1983 claim due to the property owner's failure to use the state's inverse condemnation procedure.

111. 643 A.2d 367 (Me. 1994). When a party files in state court and the state court adjudicates the claim (as it must) then res judicata normally will prevent relitigation in the federal court. In *Drake* the plaintiffs dismissed their state constitutional claim and proceeded to trial on the Fifth Amendment claim and won. On appeal the court said it had no jurisdiction over the federal claim because it was not ripe. The state court's refusal to hear the Fifth Amendment claim is evidence of an inadequate state procedure entitling the plaintiffs to present a ripe claim in federal court. The dismissal with prejudice of the state takings claim is not relevant to the fact that the Fifth Amendment claim was thrown out of court. In other words, the opinion establishes the plaintiffs' inability to get the state to hear the claim.

In Impinks v. City of Indianapolis, 612 N.E.2d 1125 (Ind. Ct. App. 1993), a claim was dismissed by a state court when the claimant did not use the state inverse condemnation statute for state takings, but apparently directly invoked the general jurisdiction of the court to hear federal claims. Indiana law provides:

> Any person having an interest in any land which has been or may be taken for any public use without having first been appropriated under this or any prior law may proceed to have his damages assessed under this chapter, substantially in the manner herein provided.
>
> IND. CODE § 32-11-1-12 (West 1995).

112. Foss v. Maine Turnpike Authority, 309 A.2d 339 (Me. 1973).

113. *Id.* The *Foss* court said:

> [W]hile it is true that the Legislature may authorize that which otherwise would be a 'nuisance' or 'trespass,' it is equally true that the Fifth Amendment of the United States Constitution [*See also:* Article I, Sec. 21, Constitution of Maine] prohibits the 'taking' of property for public use without 'just compensation.'
>
> 309 A.2d at 343.

114. The *Drake* court's holding that the state's common law remedy was based solely on the state constitution was premised on a federal court decision, Lerman v. City of Portland, 675 F. Supp. 11 (D. Me. 1987), which had said, misreading Maine law, that "Maine law provides relief [in the form of compensation for a taking] under the Maine Constitution. . . ." *Id.* at 15. The federal court's authority for this was *Foss,* but as noted *Foss*'s primary authority for finding that state agencies in Maine would be liable in a common law action for taking property was not the state constitution, as *Lerman* said, but the federal

constitution. Consequently, while the plaintiffs in *Drake* did what prior cases said they could do (that is, sue in state court based on either the federal or state constitution), their claim was dismissed.

115. The court also noted that the dismissal of the state constitutional claim with prejudice might mean the claim could never ripen. *Drake*, 643 A.2d at 369. The claim under the state constitution is independent of the federal claim, and the fact that it was dismissed has no bearing on the plaintiffs' Fifth Amendment right to ask the state (through its state court) to pay them for their loss. The court noted that "the *only* claim requesting damages for the alleged taking *under state law*, was dismissed with prejudice." That is wrong; they also asked for damages *under federal law*.

116. In at least two states, North Carolina and New Hampshire, the right is only implied. *See* JULIUS L. SACKMAN, 1 NICHOLS' THE LAW OF EMINENT DOMAIN § 1.3 (3d. ed. 1995).

117. A number of state constitutions say that property cannot be "taken or damaged" without compensation being paid. JULIUS L. SACKMAN, 2A NICHOLS' THE LAW OF EMINENT DOMAIN §6.02 [2] [c] and [d] (3d. ed. 1995). Whether the word "damage" extends protection beyond a "taking" has been the subject of debate. *Id.* at § 6.20 [2] and [4]. *See* Citizens Utilities Co. of Illinois v. Metro. Sanitary Dist. of Greater Chicago, 25 Ill. App. 3d 252, 322 N.E.2d 857 (App. Ct. 1974) (Illinois constitutional provision regarding "taken or damaged" property broader than Fifth Amendment). *See also* Donaldson v. City of Bismarck, 71 N.D. 592, 3 N.W.2d 808 (1942). Note though, that both of these cases wrongly assume the Fifth Amendment does not apply to the states; it does by incorporation.

118. What they cannot do is refuse to enforce the Fifth Amendment or interpret it in a manner to provide less protection than the Supreme Court requires.

119. Brooksbank v. Roane County, 207 Tenn. 524, 341 S.W.2d 570 (1960).

120. *See* Galt v. Montana, 230 Mont. 327, 749 P.2d 1089 (1988) and Herman v. Southern Pacific Company, 8 Ariz. App. 238, 445 P.2d 186 (Ct. App. 1968), recognizing that the right to just compensation is protected and measured by both the federal and state constitutions.

121. For a complete discussion of this issue, see Thomas E. Roberts, *Fifth Amendment Taking Claims in Federal Court: The State Compensation Requirement and Principles of Res Judicata*, 24 URB. LAW. 479 (1992).

122. *See* Migra v. Warren City School Dist. Bd. of Educ., 465 U.S. 75 (1984); American Nat'l Bank & Trust Co. v. City of Chicago, 826 F.2d 1547 (7th Cir.), *cert. denied*, 484 U.S. 977 (1987).

123. Palomar Mobilehome Park Ass'n v. City of San Marcos, 989 F.2d 362 (9th Cir. 1993); Peduto v. City of North Wildwood, 878 F.2d 725 (3d Cir. 1989).

124. *See infra* notes 110-15 and accompanying text.

125. See the discussion of preclusion in Palomar Mobilehome Park Ass'n v. City of San Marcos, 989 F.2d 362. (9th Cir. 1993).

126. Fields v. Sarasota Manatee Airport Auth., 953 F.2d 1299 (11th Cir. 1992); New Port Largo, Inc. v. Monroe County, 985 F.2d 1488, 1496 (11th Cir. 1993).

127. 375 U.S. 411 (1964).

128. See Roberts, *supra* note 84 at 502, for a discussion of the issue.

129. See the Conclusion, Part VI of this chapter.

130. Belevedere Military Corp. v. County of Palm Beach, 845 F. Supp. 877, 879 (S.D. Fla. 1994) (if state courts have "unequivocally indicated that an individual in Plaintiffs' situation had no cause of action under state law" then they need not bother asking).

131. Aiello v. Browning-Ferris, Inc., No. C-93-0466, 1993 WL 463701 (N.D. Cal. Nov. 2, 1993) (though state law not clear on whether private party acting under color of law was liable in inverse condemnation action, plaintiff is required to resort to state court).

132. Gamble v. Eau Claire County, 5 F.3d 285 (7th Cir. 1993).

133. Belevedere Military Corp. v. County of Palm Beach, 845 F. Supp. 877 (S.D. Fla. 1994).

134. *See, e.g.,* Rockler v. Minneapolis Community Dev. Agency, 866 F. Supp. 415, 417-18 (D. Minn. 1994).

135. 803 F. Supp. (M.D.N.C. 1992).

136. Initially, the state supreme court found such schemes not per se unconstitutional as applied to a three-year provision for the removal of junk yards. State v. Joyner, 211 S.E.2d 320 (N.C. 1975), *appeal dismissed,* 422 U.S. 1002 (1975). Had that been all the law on the subject, a challenge about sign amortization would not have been futile because one premise of the *Joyner* case was that the validity of amortization schemes would be examined on a case-by-case basis. However, two later intermediate court of appeals decisions, had ruled in favor of billboard amortization.

137. *See* Schnuck v. City of Santa Monica, 935 F.2d 171 (9th Cir. 1991); Sierra Lake Reserve v. City of Rocklin, 938 F.2d 951 (9th Cir. 1991).

138. A major impediment to clarity is the confusion that reigns concerning the overlapping nature of these claims. For example, see *Rockler,* 866 F. Supp. at 418, for the enigmatic reference to procedural and substantive due process claims that "fall squarely within the federal takings claim. . . ." Also see the discussion in DAVID L. CALLIES, ROBERT H. FREILICH, AND THOMAS E. ROBERTS, CASES AND MATERIALS ON LAND USE 311-12 (2d ed. 1994).

139. *Hamilton Bank,* 473 U.S. at 197. *See* Eide v. Sarasota, 908 F.2d 716 (11th Cir. 1990) for a discussion of the due process versus the Fifth Amendment takings claim.

140. *See Southview Associates,* 980 F.2d at 98; Rocky Mountain Materials & Asphalt, Inc. v. Bd. of County Comm'rs, 972 F.2d 309 (10th Cir. 1992); Baranowski v. Borough of Palmyra, 868 F. Supp. 86 (M.D. Pa. 1994). *See also Rockler,* 866 F. Supp. at 418 (held procedural and substantive due process claims that "fall squarely within the federal takings claim" to be unripe until compensation sought in state court). *But see Sinaloa Lake Owners Ass'n,* 882 F.2d at 1404.

141. See CALLIES, *supra* note 139, at 311-12, for a discussion about takings and due process claims, and the suggestion that a due process takings claim is subsumed by the explicit guarantees of the Fifth Amendment. *See also* Miller v. Campbell County, 945 F.2d 348 (10th Cir. 1991), *cert. denied,* 112 S. Ct. 1174

(1992); Pearson v. City of Grand Blanc, 756 F. Supp. 314 (E.D. Mich. 1991), *aff'd on other grounds*, 961 F.2d 1211 (6th Cir. 1992).

142. Christopher Lake Dev't Co. v. St. Louis County, 35 F.2d 1269 (8th Cir. 1994); Southview Associates v. Bongartz, 980 F.2d 84 (2d Cir. 1992), *cert. denied*, 113 S. Ct. 1586 (1993); Eide v. Sarasota County, 908 F.2d 716 (11th Cir. 1990), *cert. denied*, 498 U.S. 1120 (1991); Riverdale Realty Co., Inc. v. Town of Orangetown, 816 F. Supp. 937, 942 (S.D.N.Y. 1993). Also see Anderson v. Alpine City, 804 F. Supp. 269 (D. Utah 1992), in which the court explores the Tenth Circuit's view regarding ripeness for due process claims.

143. *Kawaoka*, 17 F.3d at 1231.

144. *Southview Associates*, 980 F.2d at 96; Greenbriar, Ltd. v. City of Alabaster, 881 F.2d, 1570, 1574 n.8 (11th Cir. 1989); *Riverdale Realty Co.*, 816 F. Supp. at 942; Patrick Media Group, Inc. v. City of Clearwater, 836 F. Supp. 833 (M.D. Fla. 1993); Cox v. City of Lynnwood, 863 P.2d 578, 582 (Wash. Ct. App. 1993).

145. Nasierowski Bros. Inv. Co. v. City of Sterling Heights, 949 F.2d 890, 895 (6th Cir. 1991); Landmark Land Co. v. Buchanan, 874 F.2d 717 (10th Cir. 1989); *but see New Port Largo*, 1994 WL 715751 at * 6; Baldini West, Inc. v. New Castle County, 852 F. Supp. 251 (D. Del. 1994).

146. Bannum v. City of Louisville, 958 F.2d 1354, 1362 (6th Cir. 1992); Unity Ventures v. Lake County, 841 F.2d 770, 775 (7th Cir. 1988); Herrington v. County of Sonoma, 834 F.2d 1488, 1494 (9th Cir. 1987); Harris v. City of Wichita, 862 F. Supp. 287, 290 (D. Kan. 1994).

147. *Yes: Riverdale Realty Co.*, 816 F. Supp. at 942; *Rockler*, 866 F. Supp. at 418 (held procedural and substantive due process claims that "fall squarely within the federal takings claim" to be unripe until compensation sought in state court). *No:* Picard v. Bay Area Regional Transit Dist., 823 F. Supp. 1519, 1523 (N.D.Cal. 1993); *New Port Largo*, 1994 WL 715751 at * 6.

148. *Yes: Riverdale Realty Co.*, 816 F. Supp. at 942. *No:* Patrick Media Group, Inc. v. City of Clearwater, 836 F. Supp. 833 (M.D. Fla. 1993).

149. Berger, *supra* note 39, at 37-38.

150. R. Jeffrey Lyman, *Finality Ripeness in Federal Land-Use Cases from* Hamilton Bank *to* Lucas, 9 J. LAND USE & ENVTL. L. 101, 127 (1993).

151. As a matter of subject matter jurisdiction, ripeness can be raised at any time, even on appeal. *See* Unity Ventures v. County of Lake, 841 F.2d 770, 774 (7th Cir. 1988); Thomas E. Roberts, *Ripeness After* Lucas, *in* AFTER LUCAS: LAND-USE REGULATION AND THE TAKING OF PROPERTY WITHOUT COMPENSATION 13-14 (David L. Callies ed. 1993).

152. Coniston v. Village of Hoffman Estates, 844 F.2d 461 (7th Cir. 1988). *See generally* Roberts, *supra* note 9.

153. *Hamilton Bank*, 473 U.S. at 194. *See* Roberts, *supra* note 84 at 481-82.

154. *See supra* notes 134-37 and accompanying text.

PART II

Takings

C. *Dolan* and Progeny

CHAPTER ❖ 4

Takings in the Land-Use Arena after *Lucas* and *Dolan:* How Far Is Too Far in Imposing Exactions?

Daniel J. Curtin, Jr.

I. Takings Law

A. Overview

A land-use regulation or action must not be so unduly restrictive that it causes a "taking" of a landowner's property without just compensation. The Fifth Amendment to the U.S. Constitution states in part, "nor shall private property be taken for public use, without just compensation." Most states have a similar provision (for example, see Article I, Section 19 of the California Constitution). In the land-use context, the argument is that if the ordinance, regulation, or decision is so restrictive that it deprives the owner of economically viable use of the property, then the property, for all practical purposes, has been taken by "inverse condemnation."

The determination of whether a land-use decision amounts to a taking prohibited by the Fifth Amendment has been a difficult task for the courts. The U.S. Supreme Court has candidly admitted that it has never been able to develop a " 'set formula' to determine when 'justice and fairness' require that economic injuries caused by public action be compensated by the government, rather than remain disproportionately concentrated on a few persons."[1] Instead, the high court has observed that "whether a particular restriction will be rendered invalid by the government's failure to pay for any losses proximately caused by it depends largely 'upon the particular circumstances [in that] case.' "[2] The question of whether a regulation has gone too far and a taking has occurred has been an ad hoc, factual inquiry.[3] The highest court reiterated this point in *Lucas v. South Carolina Coastal Council,*[4] and in *Dolan v. City of Tigard.*[5]

B. The U.S. Supreme Court's Taking Test: *Agins*

In *Agins v. City of Tiburon,*[6] the U.S. Supreme Court set forth the basic two-prong legal test for a taking. "A land use regulation does not effect a taking if it 'substantially advances legitimate state interest' and does not 'deny an owner economically viable use of his land.' "[7] This *Agins* test is still used by the Supreme Court. The test sounds simple; however, its application by the courts has been difficult.[8]

In the *Agins* dispute, the city of Tiburon, implementing the open-space policy of its general plan, adopted ordinances modifying existing zoning ordinances, which allowed five units to be built without further land-use approval, and placed the Agins' property in a more restrictive residential planned development and open-space zone. The modified zoning permitted single-family dwellings, accessory buildings, and open-space uses. Density restrictions would have permitted the Agins to build, with city approval, between one and five single-family residences on their five-acre tract. However, the Agins never sought approval for development of their land under the zoning ordinance, deciding instead to file suit in state court and allege a taking of their property. They contended that the city had " 'completely destroyed the value of [appellants'] property for any purpose or use whatsoever. . . .' "[9]

The U.S. Supreme Court, affirming the decision of the California Supreme Court, held that the ordinances did not constitute a taking. The Court stated that the application of a general zoning law to a particular property becomes a taking if the ordinance either (1) "does not substantially advance legitimate state interests" or (2) "denies an owner economically viable use of his land."[10] The *Agins* Court concluded that Tiburon's open-space ordinances substantially advanced a legitimate governmental goal—that of discouraging premature and unnecessary conversion of open-space land to urban uses—and was a proper exercise of the city's police power to protect its residents from the effects of urbanization.[11] Also, the Court held that although the ordinances limited development, "they neither prevent the best use of [the] land . . . nor extinguished a fundamental attribute of ownership."[12]

1. THE REGULATION MUST SUBSTANTIALLY ADVANCE A LEGITIMATE GOVERNMENTAL INTEREST

This first part of the test is labeled the "required nexus" rule. In *Keystone Bituminous Coal Ass'n v. DeBenedictis,*[13] the Court acknowledged that the two *Agins* tests "have become integral parts of our takings analysis."[14] The Court, however, citing numerous precedents and several other factors important to the takings analysis, gave an additional gloss to the first part of the test. It appears that even among those regulations that "substantially advance" a "legitimate state interest," some governmental interests are more "legitimate" than others; that is, the more defensible the state's interest in regulating property, the more likely the regulation will be upheld. The Court cited *Pennsylvania Coal Co. v. Mahon*[15] as recognizing that "the nature of the State's interest in the regulation is a critical factor in determining whether a taking has occurred, and thus whether compensation is required."[16]

> The Court also noted another important factor: [T]he type of taking alleged is also often a critical factor. It is well settled that a "*taking* may more readily be found when the interference with property can be characterized as a physical invasion by the government [citation omitted] than when interference arises from some public program adjusting the benefits and burdens of economic life to promote the common good. *Penn Central Transportation Co. v. New York City*, 438 U.S. 104, 124 (1978).[17]

In *Nollan*, the Supreme Court added still more gloss to the first part of the test. Under consideration was the constitutionality of the California Coastal Commission's development permit condition requiring dedication of a lateral-access easement along the Nollans' private beach. The Court reiterated the two-part test, finding that the lack of nexus between the burdens imposed by the Nollans' development and the permit condition caused the dedication requirement to fail the first part of the test; that is, the dedication did not substantially advance a legitimate state interest. Justice Scalia, who wrote the majority decision, admitted that the Court had not been specific about what was needed to pass the first part of the test, but he noted that a wide variety of land-use tools had passed:

> Our cases have not elaborated on the standards for determining what constitutes a "legitimate state interest" or what type of connection between the regulation and the state interest satisfies the requirement that the former "substantially advance" the latter. They have made clear, however, that a broad range of governmental purposes and regulations satisfies these requirements. See *Agins v. Tiburon, supra*, at 260-262 (scenic zoning); *Penn Central Transportation Co. v. New York City, supra* (landmark preservation); *Euclid v. Ambler Realty Co.*, 272 U.S. 365 (1926) (residential zoning).[18]

The *Nollan* decision did not address the second part of the takings test; it merely embellished the first part of the test focusing on nexus, and struck down the permit condition because there was no nexus. The *Nollan* Court did not discuss the required degree of connection between the exaction imposed and the projected impacts of the proposed development. This was done by the Supreme Court in 1994 in *Dolan,* in which the Court granted certiorari to resolve the question of degree left open by its decision in *Nollan.* After acknowledging the *Agins* rule, the Court in *Dolan* held for the first time that, in making an adjudicative decision, a city must demonstrate a "required reasonable relationship" between the conditions to be imposed on a development permit and the development's impact.

The *Dolan* Court stated that in reviewing a takings claim under the Fifth Amendment, a court must first determine whether an "essential nexus" exists between the "legitimate state interest" and the permit condition exacted by the city. If it finds that a nexus exists, the court must then decide the required degree of connection between the exactions and the projected impact of the proposed development. The Court noted that it was not required to address this question in *Nollan,* because no nexus existed between the condition to dedicate a lateral public easement and a legitimate governmental interest—diminishing the blockage of the ocean view caused by construction of the larger house. The Court stated that the absence of a nexus left the California Coastal Commission in the position of simply trying to obtain an easement "through gimmickry," which converted a valid regulation of land use into an "out-and-out plan of extortion."[19]

In the *Dolan* situation, the Supreme Court stated that no such gimmicks were associated with the permit conditions and the Court found that the nexus did, in fact, exist. However, under the second part of the analysis, the Court had to determine whether the degree of exactions demanded by the city's permit conditions bear the required relationship to the projected impact of the development proposed. The Court then coined the term "rough proportionality" as being one that best summarizes what it holds to be required by the Fifth Amendment. The Court then stated "no precise mathematical calculation is required, but the city must make some sort of individualized determination that the required dedication is related both in nature and extent to the impact of the proposed development."[20]

With that in mind, the Supreme Court reviewed the exactions (the required dedications for a flood plain and a fifteen-foot bicycle pathway) and found that the city did not meet its burden of demonstrating the required relationship. After analyzing the findings upon which the city relied, the Court stated that the city did not show the "required reasonable relationship" between the dedication conditions and the Dolans' proposed new building.

In summary, as long as the required nexus exists that meets the rough-proportionality test, the courts will broadly construe the governmental interests to be advanced.[21]

2. AN OWNER MAY NOT BE DENIED ECONOMICALLY VIABLE USE OF HIS LAND

Government regulations, by their very nature, have an impact on property values. Mere fluctuations in value are "incidents of ownership" and "cannot be considered a 'taking' in a constitutional sense."[22] The Supreme Court has continually "recognized, in a wide variety of contexts, that the government may execute laws or programs that adversely affect recognized economic values."[23]

In *Keystone Coal,* the Court looked to the value that was left in the owner's property, not the value that was taken, to determine whether the owners had been deprived of economically viable use. The plaintiff and appellant in the case was an association of coal mine owners in Pennsylvania who brought suit alleging that the Pennsylvania Bituminous Mine Subsidence and Land Conservation Act (Subsidence Act) constituted a taking of their property.

Although the association alleged that the Subsidence Act required the coal mine owners to forego mining almost 27 million tons of coal in their mines, the Court instead focused on the fact that the total amount of coal in the thirteen mines operated by the companies amounted to over 1.46 billion tons. Noting that the Subsidence Act affected less than 2 percent of the owners' coal, the Court said that the owners "have not shown any deprivation significant enough to satisfy the heavy burden placed upon one alleging a regulatory taking."[24] "[T]here is no showing that petitioners' reasonable 'investment-backed expectations' have been materially affected. . . ."[25]

However, when the owner of real property is called upon to sacrifice all economically beneficial uses in the name of the common good (that is, to leave his or her property economically idle), a taking has occurred. In the 1992 *Lucas* decision, the Supreme Court dealt with a landowner's taking challenge to a South Carolina regulation barring development of two beachfront lots in a developed subdivision. The state regulation findings stated that new construction in the coastal zone threatened a valuable public resource. The Court suggested Lucas was entitled to compensation but sent the case back to the state court for a final determination of the issue. On remand, the state court did find a taking and ordered payment to Lucas.

The *Lucas* decision is a narrow one; it applies only to situations in which owners are deprived of "all economically beneficial use" of their property.[26] The Court itself recognized that such cases are relatively rare.[27] In dissent, Justice Blackmun stated the majority opinion "launches a missile to kill a mouse."[28]

For example, the California courts follow the rule that the court must look at the use of the property that remains to determine whether a landowner has been deprived of economically viable use of the property. In *Terminals Equipment Co. v. City and County of San Francisco,*[29] the court held that plaintiffs were not deprived of all use of their property when they could not demolish an existing building and erect a new multistory office structure, because they were not barred from remodeling the existing building. The court stated:

> In every case in which a landowner seeks compensation for burdensome regulation of his or her property, the standard remains whether the regulations in issue have deprived the landowner of all use of the property. "When, as here, the claim is made that the regulation has significantly diminished the property value, the focus of the inquiry is on the uses of the property which remain. (*Penn Central Transp. Co. v. New York City* (1978) 438 U.S. 104, 131. . . .) Plaintiff cannot contend he was denied all use of his property. He was neither deprived of his right to exclude others from his land nor denied the right to sell the property." (*Guinnane v. City and County of San Francisco* (1987) 197 Cal. App. 3d 862, 868, fn. omitted.)[30]

The Ninth Circuit Court of Appeals' decisions have strictly interpreted the second test. In *Barancik v. County of Marin,*[31] the federal appellate court held that a rezoning that permitted only one residence per sixty acres, with a right to buy development rights, did not violate substantive due process because it did not deny an owner all beneficial use of his land. In upholding the ordinance, the court said it was not irrational or arbitrary. In *Outdoor Systems, Inc. v. City of Mesa*[32] the Ninth Circuit stated that "[a]s for the question whether the sign codes deprive an owner of the economically viable use of the land, we recognize at the outset the term 'economically viable use' has yet to be defined with such precision. We have held, however, that the existence of permissible use [generally] determines whether a development restriction denies a property holder the economically viable use of its property."[33]

In *Moore v. City of Costa Mesa,*[34] the court held that an invalid conditional-use permit (variance) that caused a landowner a three-year delay in developing his property did not amount to a taking under the Fifth Amendment. Gary Moore owned two residential lots in Costa

Mesa. He lived in one of the houses and operated his carpet-cleaning business out of the other. In 1983, he applied to the city for a conditional-use permit and zoning variance, which would have allowed him to develop a large commercial building on the two lots. The city agreed to grant the conditional-use permit if Moore would deed a portion of his land to the city for a proposed street-widening project. The city claimed it needed approximately 10 percent of Moore's land for the project. Moore declined to deed his land and sued the city in state court, claiming the condition was unconstitutional. In a 1985 unpublished state appellate court opinion, the dedication condition was held invalid because of insufficient evidence to support any relationship between the proposed street widening and the expansion of Moore's business.

In 1987, Moore sued the city in federal court, alleging that the delay caused by the illegal conditions was tantamount to a taking under the Fifth Amendment, entitling him to just compensation. Moore argued that the cost of developing the lots had greatly increased during the years he fought the city on the conditional-use permit.

The federal appellate court said there was no taking, holding that temporary regulatory takings that affect only a portion of the property are generally not compensable under the Fifth Amendment. While regulations that hinder use of the entire parcel have been grounds for compensation, a taking that results in merely lowering of property values is not compensable unless it destroys a significant portion of the property's value. Moore's argument (that the delay caused by the illegal condition in the conditional-use permit increased the cost of developing his building) failed to raise the government's interference to the level of a taking worthy of compensation. The conditional-use permit affected only a small portion of Moore's property, and he did not allege that his carpet business was impaired. Moore's allegations failed to establish that the city's actions substantially deprived him of all reasonable use of his property, and therefore the invasion was not a sufficient denial of Moore's property rights. The appellate court specifically stated that the Supreme Court's decisions in *First English Evangelical Lutheran Church v. County of Los Angeles*[35] and *Nollan v. California Coastal Commission*[36] did not support Moore's claim that his inability to develop his property constituted an unconstitutional regulatory taking for which compensation must be paid.

Recently a California appellate court, relying on *Moore,* held that a developer may not recover its lost profits resulting from a growth-control initiative that was void ab initio because it was inconsistent with the city's general plan. In *Del Oro Hills v. City of Oceanside,*[37] the court held that an invalid land-use regulation does not necessarily constitute an unconstitutional taking of private property, even though the regulation may have interfered with the landowner's development plans and caused substantial financial losses. The court stated that to establish that the enactment of a land-use regulation effects an unconstitutional taking of property, one must show that the regulation (1) does not substantially advance legitimate state interests, and (2) denies the owner of all economically viable use of the property. Both elements of this test must be satisfied to establish that the regulation resulted in a taking as a matter of law.

Del Oro Hills was the latest in a series of decisions involving challenges to the City of Oceanside's Proposition A, a zoning-level initiative that placed a numerical cap on the number of dwelling units that could be built each year. In a prior decision, *Building Industry v. City of Oceanside,*[38] (*Building Industry II*), the court invalidated Proposition A because it was inconsistent with the city's general plan, based on the principles of *Lesher Communications, Inc. v. City of Walnut Creek*[39] and the state planning and zoning laws relating to low-income housing.

Before the enactment of Proposition A, Del Oro obtained, for financing and land management purposes, a master tentative subdivision map for a 300-acre property. The project approval recognized that further development plans and/or tentative maps would be required before development. Del Oro subsequently entered into contracts to sell smaller residential neighborhoods or "villages" in the project to other developers who would obtain additional approvals and build out the sites. Proposition A was adopted before the close of escrow on some of the villages. Del Oro was forced to sell four villages at $1.5 million below the price of a tentative agreement reached before the enactment of Proposition A. Del Oro also had to make substantial financial concessions on the sale of other villages to close escrow.

Del Oro sued the city, claiming that Proposition A resulted in an unconstitutional taking of property without just compensation. The appellate court ruled that Del Oro's challenge to this regulation as it applied to the particular property was barred because Del Oro failed to exhaust administrative remedies. The court acknowledged that Del Oro was not the ultimate developer of the property and was not in the usual position of a builder seeking permits or some kind of variance from the regulation. However, the court refused to recognize a new category for developers who serve as wholesalers of land and who would be exempt from the exhaustion requirements.

Del Oro also claimed that Proposition A was facially invalid and constituted a per se taking of private property, because the regulation interfered with the projected timing of the land development deals. In analyzing this claim, the court observed that in *Agins* the Supreme Court developed a two-prong test to evaluate whether a zoning law effects a taking: a taking occurs when (1) the ordinance does not substantially advance a legitimate state interest, *or* (2) the ordinance denies the owner of all economically viable use of the property. However, the court recognized that more recent decisions by the Supreme Court indicate that *both* elements of the *Agins* test must be satisfied to establish a taking.[40]

The *Del Oro* court noted that *Nollan,*[41] relying on the *Agins* test, stated the test in the conjunctive. " 'We have long recognized that land-use regulation does not effect a taking if it "substantially advance[s] legitimate state interests" and does not "den[y] an owner economically viable use of his land," [citing *Agins*].' "[42] Then the court said that in *Dolan,* the Supreme Court reiterated the *Agins* test but stated it in the negative and the conjunctive, "A land use regulation does not effect a taking if it 'substantially advance[s] the legitimate states interests' and does not 'den[y] an owner economically viable use of his land.' "[43] The appellate court then noted that in all of these formulations, both parts of the test focus on whether property has been taken without just compensation, not on whether a regulation is, in the abstract, an invalid one; the inquiry must be about the effect the regulation has on affected property owners.

The court then rejected Del Oro's argument that a taking of property had occurred because the first element of the *Agins* test was satisfied. The court said:

> [W]e cannot accept Del Oro's theory that satisfaction of one element of the *Agins* test (i.e., that there was an invalid regulation) is enough to establish a taking as a matter of law. In *Nollan, Lucas,* and *Dolan,* the United States Supreme Court's analysis of the taking issue inextricably interlinked both the regulation's validity and the question of whether any economically beneficial use of the property remained in light of the regulation. In light of later authority, *Agins* did not establish an "either/or" type of test.[44]

The court then held that because an invalid regulation is not necessarily unconstitutional, the only available remedy for Del Oro was invalidation of the ordinance, as had already been adjudicated in the earlier *Building Industry II* opinion.

Because Del Oro eventually completed the sale of the property and the buyers received all necessary permits under Proposition A, the court concluded that Del Oro failed to show that the regulation deprived it of all economically beneficial use of the property. Thus, Del

Oro could not establish that Proposition A is facially invalid under the taking standard.

Even a substantial diminution in value due to downzoning does not constitute a taking. For example, in *William C. Haas and Co. v. City and County of San Francisco,*[45] the court upheld the validity of a zoning ordinance that reduced the value of Mr. Haas's property by more than 90 percent, from approximately $2,000,000 to $100,000. Even though *Haas* was handed down in 1979, before the Supreme Court decided *First English* and *Nollan* in 1987, it is still cited as authority in California; in *Long Beach Equities v. County of Ventura,*[46] the court stated that the second prong of the *Agins* taking test is whether the regulations deny the property owner substantially all economically valuable use of the land.

II. Nexus Requirement: Exactions

A. In General

In sum, the courts have been stating that to meet the second test of *Agins,* the challenged regulation must deprive the landowner of *all,* or *substantially all,* of the use of the land. The application of the rules from *Nollan* and *Dolan* will be played out mainly in the exactions arena. The major legal issue involving exactions is not whether the dedication or the fee payment as a condition precedent to development can be required, but to what extent and in what amount the dedication or fee can be imposed. Generally, when all the following conditions are met, the courts will uphold the constitutionality of a public agency's ordinance, regulation, or imposition of a dedication or fee as a condition of land-use approval:

1. The public agency is acting within its police power
2. The condition substantially furthers a legitimate governmental interest
3. The condition furthers the same governmental purpose advanced as justification for improving it
4. The owner is not denied economically viable use of its land

The principal area of dispute is the third test—the nexus or connection rule.

B. Supreme Court Nexus Pronouncements: The *Nollan* and *Dolan* Decisions

1. *NOLLAN V. CALIFORNIA COASTAL COMMISSION*

In *Nollan,* the California Coastal Commission approved the construction of a two-story beachfront house, on condition that the owners dedicate a

public-access easement across a portion of their property alor
The easement purportedly would assist the public in viewing the ...
and in overcoming a perceived "psychological barrier" to using the beach. The owners challenged the easement, claiming that the condition violated the Fifth and Fourteenth Amendments' prohibitions against taking private property for public use without just compensation. The Court held that, although protection of the public's ability to see the beach is a legitimate governmental interest, no nexus or connection existed between the identified impact of the project (obstruction of the ocean view) and the easement condition (physical access across the beach). Thus, the exaction constituted a taking of private property without just compensation. The Court did say a condition to dedicate a viewing spot on the Nollan property might be legal, because there would be a nexus.

Thus, the *Nollan* court stressed the importance of a nexus or connection between the dedication condition and the burden imposed by the new development. If no such nexus or connection exists, the decision to impose the condition would not be a proper land-use decision, and therefore could amount to a taking of property for which money must be paid pursuant to the Fifth and Fourteenth Amendments of the Constitution (as affirmed in *First English Evangelical Lutheran Church v. County of Los Angeles*).[47] Apart from holding that the condition did not survive constitutional scrutiny because of its utter lack of the essential nexus, the Court did not decide how close the nexus must be for a regulation to "substantially advance" a "legitimate state interest." This was done by the Court in *Dolan.* The Court did say that its previous cases made clear that a broad range of governmental purposes and regulations satisfies these requirements.[48]

The *Nollan* case does not say that the dedication requirement may be upheld only if the particular subdivision creates the need for the dedication. Instead, the condition will be upheld if it substantially furthers a legitimate governmental purpose, and the condition furthers the same governmental purpose advanced for imposing it. Putting it another way: is the condition likely to alleviate the problem caused by the development? The Court did suggest that the constitutionally required nexus may be even tighter when exactions include the actual conveyance of property; this indicates that mitigation fees might not be subject to as close scrutiny as an actual conveyance of property. In summary, the *Nollan* decision did not, in any fashion, discuss the nature, amount, or size of an excessive dedication, and thus the Court again failed to reach the question, "How far is too far?" In 1994, this was discussed by the Supreme Court in *Dolan.*

2. *DOLAN V. CITY OF TIGARD*

In *Dolan v. City of Tigard,* a sharply divided Supreme Court held that local governments must prove that development conditions placed on a discretionary permit have a "rough proportionality"[49] to the development's impact. If not, a taking could occur. In this five-to-four decision, the Court held for the first time that, in making an adjudicative decision, a city must demonstrate a "required reasonable relationship" between the conditions to be imposed on a development permit and the development's impact. Even though the court coined a new term ("rough proportionality") for such a standard, it is basically the same reasonable relationship test that a majority of states, including California and Wisconsin, have followed for years.

a. Facts and Procedural Background Florence Dolan owned a plumbing and electrical-supply store located in the business district of Tigard, Oregon. Fanno Creek flows through the southwestern corner of the lot and along its western boundary. Dolan applied to the city for a building permit to develop the site. Her proposed plans called for nearly doubling the size of the store and paving a thirty-nine-space parking lot.

The planning commission granted Dolan's permit application subject to conditions imposed by Tigard's Community Development Code (CDC), which contained the city's comprehensive plan. The commission required that Dolan dedicate the portion of her property lying within the 100-year flood plain for improvement of a storm drainage system along Fanno Creek, and that she also dedicate an additional fifteen-foot strip of land adjacent to the flood plain as a pedestrian/bicycle pathway. The commission made a series of findings concerning the relationship between the dedicated conditions and the projected impacts on the Dolan property.

Dolan requested variances and appealed to the Land-Use Board of Appeals (LUBA) on the grounds that the city's dedication requirements were not related to the proposed development and constituted an uncompensated taking under the Constitution's Fifth Amendment. LUBA found a "reasonable relationship" between the proposed development and the requirement to dedicate land along Fanno Creek for a greenway, and also found a reasonable relationship between alleviating the impact of increased traffic from the development and facilitating the pedestrian/bicycle pathway as an alternative means of transportation. The Oregon Court of Appeals affirmed the decision, as did the Oregon Supreme Court.

In her Petition for Writ of Certiorari, Dolan urged, among other things, that the U.S. Supreme Court establish that a precise fit between an exaction and the impacts of proposed development is constitutionally required, instead of the reasonable relationship test used in Oregon and other states, including California. The Supreme Court granted certiorari "to resolve a question left open by our decision in *Nollan v. California Coastal Comm'n* . . . of what is the required degree of connection between the exactions imposed by the city and the projected impacts of the proposed development."[50]

b. Decision The Supreme Court acknowledged the standard rule that a "land use regulation does not effect a taking if it 'substantially advances legitimate state interest' and does not 'deny an owner economically viable use of his land,' " citing *Agins v. Tiburon*.[51] Significantly, the Court noted that in this case, it was not dealing with a legislative determination about land-use regulations but instead with a city having made "an adjudicative decision to condition an application for a building permit on an individual parcel."[52] Also, the Court noted that "the conditions imposed were not simply a limitation on the use that [the] petitioner might make of her own parcel but a requirement that she deed portions of the property to the city."[53]

In evaluating a takings claim under the Fifth Amendment, the Court stated that a court must first decide whether an "essential nexus" exists between the legitimate state interest and the permit condition exacted by the city. If the court finds that a nexus exists, it must then determine the required degree of connection between the exactions and the projected impact of the proposed development. The Court noted that it was not required to address this question in *Nollan,* because no nexus existed between the condition of dedicating a lateral public easement and a legitimate governmental interest (diminishing the blockage of the ocean view caused by construction of the larger house).

In *Dolan,* the Supreme Court stated that no such gimmicks were associated with the permit conditions and it found that the nexus did, in fact, exist. However, under the second part of the analysis, the Court had to determine whether the degree of exactions demanded by the city's permit conditions bear the required relationship to the projected impact of the proposed development. Because state courts have a long history of dealing with this question, the Court then reviewed several of those representative decisions. The Court noted that the decisions fell into three categories: (1) those including a very generalized nexus statement, which the court determined to be too lax (for example, *Billings Properties, Inc. v. Yellowstone County*);[54] (2) those using a very exacting nexus described as the "specific and uniquely attributable test" (the so-called "Pioneer Trust Rule" from an Illinois decision, *Pioneer*

Trust & Savings Bank v. Mount Prospect),[55] which the court rejected; and (3) those taking an intermediate position of a "reasonable relationship" nexus, which was highlighted in *Jordan v. Menominee Falls*[56] and other cases. In *Jordan*, the court upheld a parkland dedication and school impact-fee ordinance. The *Jordan* rule has been the most popular one; for example, the California Supreme Court relied on *Jordan* in *Associated Home Builders v. City of Walnut Creek*,[57] and upheld a "reasonable relationship test" for parkland dedication and in-lieu fees.

The U.S. Supreme Court noted that the "reasonable relationship test" adopted by the majority of states (including California) was closer to the federal constitutional norm than the other two tests. However, the Court stated, "But we do not adopt it as such, partly because the term 'reasonable relationship' seems confusingly similar to the term 'rational basis' which describes the minimal level of scrutiny under the Equal Protection Clause of the Fourteenth Amendment."[58] The Court then coined the term "rough proportionality." As noted earlier, the majority opinion never used this term again in applying the rule to the facts. Instead, it continued to use the words "required reasonable relationship" or "reasonably related." The Court then stated, "No precise mathematical calculation is required, but the city must make some sort of individualized determination that the required dedication is related both in nature and extent to the impact of the proposed development."[59]

With that in mind, the Court reviewed the two exactions (the flood plain and fifteen-foot bicycle path dedications) and found that the city did not meet its burden of demonstrating the required relationship. After analyzing the findings upon which the city relied, the Court stated that the city did not show the "required reasonable relationship" between the flood plain easement and the petitioner's proposed new building.

Noting that Dolan's proposed development would have increased the amount of impervious surface—which in turn would increase the quantity and rate of storm water flowing from the property—the Court determined that the city could have required that Dolan only keep the area open. By requiring a dedication rather than restricting building, the city limited Dolan's ability to exclude other individuals which, the Court stated, is "one of the most essential sticks in the bundle of rights that are commonly characterized as property."[60]

Also, the Court said that "on the record before it, the City had not met its burden of demonstrating that the additional number of vehicle and bicycle trips generated by petitioner's development reasonably related to the city's requirement for dedication of the pedestrian/bicycle pathway easement."[61] The Court noted "the city simply found that the creation of the pathway 'could offset some of the traffic demand . . . and lessen increase in traffic congestion.' "[62] This was a far cry from finding that the system would, or was likely to, offset some of the traffic demand.

"No precise mathematical calculation is required," the Court said, "but the city must make some effort to quantify its findings in support of the dedication for the pedestrian/bicycle pathway beyond the conclusory statement that it could offset some of the traffic demand generated."[63]

The Court concluded,

> "Cities have long engaged in the commendable task of land use planning, made necessary by increasing urbanization particularly in metropolitan areas such as Portland. The city's goals of reducing flooding hazards and traffic congestion, and providing for public greenways, are laudable, but there are outer limits to how this may be done. 'A strong public desire to improve the public condition [will not] warrant achieving the desire by a shorter cut than the constitutional way of paying for the change.' "[64]

The dissenting Justices stated that the Court made a serious error by abandoning the traditional presumption of constitutionality and imposing a novel burden of proof on a city implementing an admittedly valid comprehensive land-use plan. In his dissent, Justice Souter stated that "having assigned the burden, the court concludes that the city loses based on one word ('could' instead of 'would') and despite the fact that this record shows the connection the court looks for."[65]

III. Duty of the Public Agency to Demonstrate Relationship

Clearly, the Supreme Court in *Dolan* has put some limitations on a public agency's exercise of its police power to require dedication of land as a condition for issuing a development permit. This decision requires that documenting the connection between the dedication and the projected impact of the proposed development now must be made on an individualized basis. Not only must the required nexus exist, but findings must justify the required reasonable relationship between the dedication and the impact. In many states, as the Court indicated in *Dolan,* the courts have always required a nexus based on a reasonable relationship.[66] In 1971, the California Supreme Court in *Associated Home Builders, Inc. v. City of Walnut Creek* abandoned whatever *direct* nexus theory might have existed for dedications in land-use permit approval in California. The court rejected Associated Home Builders, Inc.'s argument based on the *Pioneer Trust* rule from Illinois that a dedication requirement may be upheld only if the particular subdivision creates the need for dedication. The court stated that in the absence of a more restrictive statute, dedication can be required based on a general and broad "public welfare measure" standard—however, there still must be a nexus. *Dolan* reiterates that point, but emphasizes that there must be something more than generalized or conclusive findings to support that relationship or connection.

As a result of *Dolan*, if a public agency requires a dedication of land as a condition of a land-use adjudicatory approval (for example, building permits, map approvals, and so on) rather than a legislative enactment (for example, a general plan amendment, or impact-fee ordinance), these rules should be followed:

1. The public agency must adopt findings demonstrating that each dedication condition with which the permit applicant must comply is reasonably related to the impact of the proposed development.
2. The agency can meet its burden by quantifying its findings in support of the particular dedication, but it must not rely on a conclusory statement that the dedication "could" offset the burden. In *Dolan*, the Court criticized the finding that the creation of a pathway "could offset some of the traffic demand . . . and lessen the increase in traffic congestion."[67]
3. Although no precise mathematical calculation is required to show the required reasonable relationship, the public agency must make some sort of individualized determination that the required dedication is related both in nature and extent to the impact of the proposed development. The agency cannot rely only on the fact that the statute or local ordinance requires dedication. In *Dolan*, the city argued unsuccessfully that its comprehensive plan codified in a community development code required a dedication to be imposed. The condition must also be factually justified.
4. The public agency has the burden of showing why a dedication is necessary and why a land-use regulation restricting the use of the property cannot achieve the same purpose. For example, did the agency in *Dolan* actually need to own a floodplain? Could the same result be achieved by zoning the affected property and limiting development on the property?
5. The conditions must be tailored to address only the types of impacts expected from the development.
6. If an impact is part of a community-wide problem, other contributors who add to the problem should be identified, along with the relative contributions of the applicant.

IV. Application of Dolan *to Development Fees and Legislative Acts*

A. Impact Fees (Nonpossessory "Takings"): *Ehrlich* on Remand and *Trimen Development*

A reading of *Dolan* indicates that the Court is ruling only on possessory takings—that is, dedications of land. For example, in California, most courts have stated that *Nollan*'s higher scrutiny is not applicable to impact fees.[68]

However, on June 27, 1994, the Supreme Court granted a writ of certiorari in *Ehrlich v. Culver City*,[69] vacated the judgment, and remanded the case to the California appellate court. On December 23, 1994, the appellate court held in an unpublished opinion that *Dolan* was applicable to impact fees (nonpossessory "takings").[70] In March 1995, the California Supreme Court granted review. Even though this case is pending before the California Supreme Court, its background is of interest to those who practice in the land-use field.

In *Ehrlich*, the developer challenged the city's requirement that he pay a $280,000 mitigation fee for the city's loss of private recreational facilities occasioned by his request for land-use changes to build townhouses (General Plan, Rezoning, Specific Plan, Tentative Map, and Development Plan), and a $33,220 in-lieu art fee. The $280,000 mitigation fee was made a condition of the rezoning ordinance. In the 1993 decision, the appellate court upheld the mitigation fee as complying with *Nollan* and the state statutes. Ehrlich then filed a writ of certiorari to the U.S. Supreme Court.

After remand the appellate court said the "constitutionality of the mitigation fee must be determined under the two-prong test set forth in *Nollan v. California Coastal Comm'n* . . . as expanded by *Dolan v. City of Tigard* . . . (1) the governmental entity could have denied the request without the denial constituting a taking; and (2) the condition imposed substantially furthers the governmental goal furthered by a denial and is roughly proportional to the impact of the proposed development."[71]

Ehrlich contended that the land-use regulations requiring that his property be used as community recreational facilities deprived him of all economically beneficial use of his property. The court said that this argument was seriously flawed. Ehrlich, as trustee for certain family trusts, purchased a 2.4-acre parcel of vacant land in Culver City. The property was zoned commercial and was restricted to the construction of recreational facilities when he purchased it. Ehrlich initially operated the property as a private tennis club but later closed the club because it was not a financial success. Ehrlich applied to the city to change the property's land-use designation, including a request for general plan and zoning amendments to allow construction of thirty townhomes with a value of $10 million. The city denied the application on the ground that the land-use restrictions provided needed recreational facilities for the city. On reconsideration, the city decided to approve the development project if Ehrlich paid a $280,000 mitigation fee and a $33,220 in-lieu art fee. Ehrlich then challenged those fees.

The court said the first prong of the *Nollan* test had been met. The city was not required to approve the development project and denial of the request would not have effected a compensable taking. The court noted that Ehrlich had purchased the property with knowledge of the restrictions and with the intent to develop the property as a private tennis club, in compliance with the restrictions. The court stated that under these facts, the land-use regulations could not constitute a taking even if the property could not be operated profitably.

The court then held the city met the second prong of the *Nollan* test. Upon finding that the essential nexus exists between the legitimate governmental interest and the permit conditions, the court must determine whether the proper degree of connection exists; that required degree is a "rough proportionality" or essentially a "reasonable relationship" test. That test requires a city to make some sort of individualized determination that the conditions are related both in nature and extent to the impact of the proposed development. In *Ehrlich,* the city made that determination.

The court said it was beyond dispute that the city had a legitimate governmental interest in making available community recreational facilities, and the city made the nexus finding. The court did "note that the mitigation fee was not imposed as a condition relating to the development project's burden on the community for increased community services, such as community recreational facilities. . . . The mitigation fee was imposed to compensate the City for the burden on the community resulting from the loss of recreational facilities. The proper inquiry is whether the mitigation fee bears a reasonable relationship to the projected impact of rezoning, i.e., loss of recreational facilities, rather than to the projected impact of the proposed development on the need for recreational facilities."[72]

After its *Dolan* analysis, the court also upheld its earlier decision that the fee was not a special tax and that it complied with a statute (Government Code section 66000–07) relating to a reasonable relationship test set forth by the legislature.

The court then stated that the city's art program was essentially based on a legislative determination applicable to all large development projects. In light of that, the in-lieu art fee was not an adjudicative decision conditioning a developer's permit on an individual parcel; therefore, the court held that *Dolan* had no applicability. The court then reaffirmed its earlier decision that this fee was a valid exercise of the city's police power. This position was also taken by another appellate court in *San Mateo County Coastal Landowners Assn. v. County of San Mateo,* 95 DAILY JOURNAL D.A.R. 12558 (Sept. 20, 1995), where the court said the *Dolan* test was not applicable to agricultural and open-space easement development requirements which were imposed as part of a legislatively adopted land-use and zoning scheme.

Also, in *Trimen Development Co. v. King Co.,*[73] the Washington Supreme Court, in an action brought by a subdivider who challenged an in-lieu fee, held that a county's ordinance requiring reservation or dedication of land for parks, or payment of a fee in lieu of dedication of land, was valid under *Dolan*'s rough-proportionality test. The court noted that the county had conducted a comprehensive assessment of park needs. The court concluded that the fees imposed in lieu of dedication were reasonably necessary because of Trimen's development.

B. Legislative Acts: *Ehrlich* and *Home Builders Ass'n of Central Arizona* on Remand

A reading of the *Dolan* decision clearly implies that it does not apply to legislative acts.[74] This was also the conclusion in *Ehrlich* (after remand, regarding in-lieu art fees) and in *Home Builders Ass'n of Central Arizona v. City of Scottsdale.*[75] In *Home Builders,* the Arizona Court of Appeals concluded that because the Scottsdale development-fee ordinance under attack was a legislative determination affecting the entire city, the ruling in *Dolan* did not affect a prior opinion in this matter upholding the fee.

In *Home Builders,* the payment of the fee was a condition to the city's issuance of the building permit. The fee charged by the city was for the express purpose of providing future water to the subject property. In an earlier opinion, the court had concluded that the development fee was a regulatory fee rather than a tax, on the grounds that (1) the fee was to be used to benefit the property on which the fee was imposed rather than for general revenue, and (2) the property's need for future water was directly related to the development.

The court stated that the *Dolan* decision had no bearing upon the Scottsdale development-fee ordinance because the special circumstances of *Dolan* were not present. First of all, the *Dolan* Court recognized the distinction between a legislative decision affecting entire areas of a city and an adjudicative decision affecting only an individual parcel. Here, the Scottsdale ordinance was a legislative act. Second, the court said that the *Dolan* Court distinguished between a dedication of land and a mere limitation on the use of property.[76] The court concluded that the Scottsdale development fees were more akin to a limitation. Similarly, in *Parking Association of Georgia, Inc. v. Atlanta*,[77] the Georgia Supreme Court upheld Atlanta's zoning ordinance requiring landscaping and trees in surface parking lots against a takings challenge. In that case, the court said *Dolan* was not applicable because unlike the circumstances in *Dolan*, Atlanta made a legislative decision affecting many property owners.

V. Dolan *Principle Upholds Open-Space, Scenic-View, Flood-Plain, and Low-Density Legislative Land-Use Regulations*

The *Dolan* court said that the right to exclude is "one of the most essential sticks in the bundle of rights that are commonly characterized as property." Thus, the types of legislative land-use designations/regulations for open space, scenic views, flood plains—made through adoption of a general plan amendment or rezoning—now seem to be legally justified by *Dolan* as alternative methods to mitigate a burden (even though building on the property would thus be severely restricted) because a city enacting this method would not be interfering with an owner's ability to exclude others and would not be a taking of all of the property. The city would not be requiring a public easement for flood plain, for example, but instead would be zoning property for flood plain use leaving the property in private ownership with some compatible uses.

These principles were enunciated in two earlier California cases: *Barancik v. County of Marin*,[78] in which zoning that permitted one dwelling unit per sixty acres was upheld; and *Guinnane v. City and County of San Francisco*,[79] in which the court said that despite severe land-use restriction, the right to sell or exclude prevents a taking claim based on denial of all use of the property. In *Barancik*, the federal appellate court responded to petitioner Barancik's argument that zoning allowing only one residence per sixty acres violated his substantive due process rights:

> The district court found that the County had a reasonable purpose in zoning as it did and applying the zoning as it did to Loma Alta Ranch. We agree. To prove his case Barancik had to show that the County's zoning was arbitrary and irrational. *Usery v. Turner*

Elkhorn Mining Co., 428 U.S. 1, 15, 96 S. Ct. 2882, 2892, 49 L.Ed.2d 752 (1975). He attempted to do so by concentrating on the zoning in relation to his own property and arguing that just as many cows would graze there if there were 28 residences as would if there were nine. The argument, of course, is myopic. Zoning is of an area. The planner wants to preserve an area for a given use. Yielding to Barancik's arguments would set a precedent which, followed, would lead to the emulative destruction of agriculture in Nicasio Valley. The cowboy and the farmer may be friends as the song has it, but not the rancher and the urban commuter, at least not if commuters, with the roads they need and the cars they drive and the tastes they have, begin to predominate in the countryside. Marin's zoning no doubt preserves a bucolic atmosphere for the benefit of a portion of the population at the expense of those who would flow into the county if there was no zoning. The Constitution lets that decision be made by the legislature. The Countywide Plan is a legislative declaration that there will be a corridor in Marin agricultural in its use. The choice was not irrational, the application to Barancik not arbitrary.[80]

VI. Conclusion

A public agency can achieve most of the goals of its comprehensive general plan by doing its homework and crossing all "t"s and dotting all "i"s, but it cannot go beyond outer limits. If the agency has not done its homework in justifying its fees, it might want to enter into a development agreement; thus, no legal question would arise about the validity of conditions if a developer accepts them.[81]

As a result of *Dolan,* if a public agency is going to require a dedication of land or payment of impact fees (exaction) as a condition of a land-use adjudicatory approval (for example, building permits, map approvals), instead of making a "legislative determination applicable to all large development projects," then the agency has the burden of showing, on an individual basis, the required reasonable relationship ("rough proportionality") between the exaction required and the impact of the proposed development. Moreover, it must adopt findings that demonstrate that each of the conditions with which the permit applicant must comply is reasonably related to the impact of the proposed development.

The *Dolan* decision will no doubt cause public agencies to require more thorough applications for all types of development and to require that applicants address the impact of development. This is now being done by the city of Tigard, Oregon.[82]

Notes

1. Penn Central Transp. Co. v. New York City, 438 U.S. 104, 124 (1978).
2. *Id.*
3. *Id.*
4. 112 S. Ct. 2886 (1992).
5. 114 S. Ct. 2309 (1994).
6. 447 U.S. 255 (1980).
7. *Agins,* 447 U.S. at 260.
8. *See* Keystone Bituminous Coal Ass'n v. DeBenedictis, 480 U.S. 470 (1987); Nollan v. California Coastal Comm'n, 483 U.S. 825 (1987); *Lucas,* 112 S. Ct. 2886 (1992); *Dolan,* 114 S. Ct. 2309 (1994).
9. *Agins,* 447 U.S. at 258.
10. *Id.* at 260.
11. *Id.* at 261-62.
12. *Id.* at 262.
13. *Keystone,* 480 U.S. 470 (1987).
14. *Id.* at 485.
15. 260 U.S. 393 (1922).
16. *Keystone,* 480 U.S. at 488.
17. *Id.* at 488-89 n.18.
18. *Nollan,* 483 U.S. at 834-35.
19. *Dolan,* 114 S. Ct. at 2317.
20. *Id.* at 2319.
21. See Part II of this chapter for a detailed discussion of the nexus issue in *Nollan* and *Dolan*.
22. Danforth v. United States, 308 U.S. 271, 285 (1939).
23. *Penn Central,* 438 U.S. at 124.
24. *Keystone,* 480 U.S. at 493.
25. *Id.* at 499.
26. *Lucas,* 112 S. Ct. at 2899.
27. *Id.* at 2894.
28. *Id.* at 2904.
29. 221 Cal. App. 3d 234, 270 Cal. Rptr. 329 (Ct. App. 1990).
30. *Terminals Equipment,* 270 Cal. Rptr. 329. *See also* City and County of San Francisco v. Golden Gate Heights Investments, 14 Cal. App. 4th 1203, 18 Cal. Rptr. 2d 467 (Ct. App. 1993) (court found *Lucas* principles not applicable because not all property taken).
31. 872 F.2d 834 (9th Cir. 1988).
32. 997 F.2d 604 (9th Cir. 1993).
33. *Outdoor Systems,* 997 F.2d at 616.
34. 886 F.2d 260 (9th Cir. 1989).
35. 482 U.S. 304 (1987).
36. 483 U.S. 825 (1987).
37. 31 Cal. App. 4th 1060, 37 Cal. Rptr. 2d 677 (Ct. App. 1995).

38. 27 Cal. App. 4th 744 , 33 Cal. Rptr. 2d 137 (Ct. App. 1994).

39. 52 Cal. 3d 531, 802 P.2d 317 (1990).

40. *Del Oro Hills,* 37 Cal. Rptr. 2d at 686.

41. 483 U.S. 825 (1987).

42. *Nollan,* 483 U.S. at 834.

43. *Del Oro Hills,* 37 Cal. Rptr. 2d at 686.

44. *Id.* at 689.

45. 605 F. 2d 117 (9th Cir. 1979).

46. 231 Cal. App. 3d 1016, 1036-38, 282 Cal. Rptr. 877 (Ct. App. 1991).

47. 482 U.S. 304 (1987).

48. *See Agins,* 477 U.S. at 260-62 (scenic zoning); *Penn Central, supra* note 1 (landmark preservation); Euclid v. Ambler Realty Co., 272 U.S. 365 (1926) (residential zoning); *Nollan,* 483 U.S. at 834-35.

49. After coining the term "rough proportionality," the Court, in its majority opinion, never used that term again when it applied its decision to the facts; instead it continued to use the words "required reasonable relationship" or "reasonably related."

50. *Dolan,* 114 S. Ct. at 2312.

51. *Id.* at 2316.

52. *Id.* at 2316.

53. *Id.*

54. 144 Mont. 25, 394 P.2d 182 (1964).

55. 22 Ill. 2d 375, 380, 176 N.E.2d 799, 802 (1961).

56. 28 Wis. 2d 608, 137 N.W.2d 442 (1965).

57. 4 Cal. 3d 633, 484 P.2d 606 (1971).

58. *Dolan,* 114 S. Ct. at 2318.

59. *Id.* at 2318-19.

60. *Id.* at 2319.

61. *Id.* at 2321.

62. *Id.*

63. *Id.* at 2322.

64. *Id.*

65. *Id.* at 2331.

66. *See* Ayres v. City Council, 34 Cal. 2d 31, 207 P.2d 1 (1949).

67. *Id.* at 2321-22.

68. *See* Blue Jeans Equities West v. City and County of San Francisco, 3 Cal. App. 4th 164, 168-71, 4 Cal. Rptr. 2d 114 (Ct. App. 1992).

69. 15 Cal. App. 4th 1737, 19 Cal. Rptr. 2d 468 (Ct. App. 1993).

70. Ehrlich v. Culver City, 15 Cal. App. 4th 1737, 19 Cal. Rptr. 2d 468 (Ct. App. 1993). Petition for review granted by Cal. Supreme Court on June 27, 1994.

71. *Id.*

72. *Id.*

73. 124 Wash. 2d 261, 877 P.2d 187 (1994).

74. *Dolan,* 114 S. Ct. at 2316.

75. (No. 1 CA-CV 92-0210) 1995 W.L. 61490 (Ariz. Ct. App. Feb. 16, 1995).
76. *See Dolan,* 114 S. Ct. at 2316.
77. 450 S.E.2d 200 (1994), *cert. denied,* 63 U.S.L.W. 3703 (1995).
78. 872 F.2d 834 (9th Cir. 1988).
79. 197 Cal. App. 3d 862, 241 Cal. Rptr. 787 (Ct. App. 1987).
80. *Barancik,* 872 F.2d at 836.
81. County of Imperial v. McDirigal, 19 Cal. 3d 505, 564 P.2d 14 (Ct. App. 1977).
82. *See* John Tibbetts, *Everybody's Taking the Fifth,* PLANNING, Jan. 1995, at 4.

CHAPTER ❖ 5

At Last, the Supreme Court Solves the Takings Puzzle

Douglas W. Kmiec

I. Introduction: A Move toward Responsible Judicial Review

The purpose of the takings clause is "to bar government from forcing some people alone to bear public burdens which, in all fairness and justice, should be borne by the public as a whole."[1] The takings clause thus serves as a fulcrum upon which private property interests are balanced against the police power. The balance is a difficult one because both property and the police power are indeterminate concepts that change over time and from place to place. Two other structural complexities come into play: federalism, which traditionally has left the definition of property largely to state common law; and separation of powers, which is a check against the federal judiciary usurping functions that are better left to majority legislative determination.

Many commentators and practitioners, ranging from property advocates to police-power hawks, have viewed the Supreme Court's takings cases as incoherent, piecemeal, or categorical. Some of the criticism is deserved, some not. Indeed, I will argue that with its decision in *Dolan v. City of Tigard*,[2] the Court has largely solved the takings puzzle. It has calibrated the property/police power balance in a way that has yet to be achieved, or even acknowledged, in other areas of economic regulation. Since *Lochner*[3] and the decline of substantive economic due process, the Court has been reluctant to review economic regulations in a meaningful way. If there is any conceivable rational basis for the regulation, the Court has been silent, even when that basis appears to be neither conceivable nor rational.

Thus, in economic matters, the Court has refrained from substituting its will for that of the legislative majority, even if specific textual provisions of the Constitution—such as the privileges and immunities[4] or contract[5] clauses—seemingly invite, or even obligate, the Court to do just that. This lack of judicial review is partially responsible for the dominating federal presence in much of daily life, from the workplace to schools. And the perception of that federal presence as bloated or unwarranted or worse has now triggered a seismic political change, the likes of which have not been seen in over four decades.

With *Nollan v. California Coastal Commission,*[6] *Lucas v. South Carolina Coastal Council,*[7] and now *Dolan,* the Court has awakened to its responsibility under the takings clause to actively maintain the property/police power balance. What explains this conquering of judicial timidity? I submit it is the Court's growing recognition that an objective standard exists by which it can responsibly respect and check the legislative process. This standard is not a problematic judicial creation, as is so much of the Court's most controverted caselaw,[8] but the product of hundreds of years of refinement, ongoing reevaluation, and modification. Most importantly, the standard originates primarily at the state level, and thus is highly responsive to the federalist structure of the republic. What is this standard? None other than the common law.

In particular, the common law of nuisance simultaneously negatively defines property and positively outlines the general scope of the police power, at least in the Constitution's original understanding,[9] which is premised more upon stability and order than social engineering. This was as implicit in *Mugler*'s[10] denial of the noxious use without compensation as it was in *Euclid*'s[11] express linkage of the police power to the *sic utere* maxim. For the better part of this century, however, this understanding was lost. Wholesale schemes of wealth redistribution took hold unfettered by a judiciary that had been overcowed into submission by a misstated notion of judicial restraint. In the property field, the Court mustered only the weak admonition that such schemes better not go "too far."[12] As recently as the late 1970s, the Court could do no more than speculate about a set of ad hoc factors that might limit the police power.[13]

The Court's lame response to the excess of police power was analytically cut adrift from the common law of nuisance which, however imprecisely, gives meaning to both property and police power. The Court's focus on diminution in value has proven to be unworkable and unprincipled because the concept of property is not fully definable. More importantly, to gauge the constitutionality of a taking by asking how much a person has lost is an analytical non sequitur, even though such an inquiry is helpful in assessing damages or speculating about the judiciary's willingness to rectify particular takings claims.

II. Recent Cases

A. *Loretto:* The Right to Exclude

Loretto[14] was one of the first modern takings cases to reattach the takings analysis to the common law of property. Here, the categorical protection of the right to exclude emerged from the ancient protection against trespass. At first, *Loretto* seemed both jolting and puny. The constitutional need to provide compensation for a four-inch-square box and accompanying cable wire seemed downright silly in the face of the million dollar diminutions that had not merited compensation. Yet, *Loretto*'s significance was great because it served to remind the Court that no matter how high-minded the justifications for a public regulatory scheme might be, in our democratic republic, those schemes are limited by the objective reality of privately held property resources.

As important as *Loretto*'s reminder was, its practical significance was less: not much land-use regulation directly depends upon physical occupation. Thus, neither the Court nor land-use players realized how directly the analytical line based upon the common law of property connected *Loretto* with *Nollan.*[15] Indeed, the Supreme Court term that produced *Nollan* coughed up *Keystone,*[16] a precedential hiccup of Holmes's "too far" limitation repackaged in the ad hoc balancing factors of *Penn Central.*

B. *Nollan:* Substantially Advancing Legitimate State Interests

With *Nollan,* the Court returned to a sounder course, defining property and police power in relation to a state's common law. The Court's emphasis on the formulation of "substantially advancing a legitimate governmental interest," as distinct from the reasonableness or mere rational basis standards applied in other economic contexts, was the legal equivalent of a surveyor restaking parcel corners that had become imperceptible by overgrowth. And of course, like neighbors who had grown accustomed to encroachment of an indeterminate lot line, police-power hawks groused about *Nollan*'s seeming break with precedent.[17] But it was the intervening "diminution in value" cases that were the aberration from the common law plat dividing private and public interests.

Yet, *Nollan*'s primary requirement that there be a nexus between regulatory means and ends failed to convey its important reassertion of the common law definition of property and police power. Both the opinion and the opinion's author were denigrated.[18] Some argued the opinion should be confined to cases in which a property concession occurred.[19] Land-use regulators concluded that all that was required was a facile matching of regulatory means and ends. Thus, if the public end was a bikepath on a permit applicant's property, it should be a simple matter to require the conveyance of an easement or fee interest underlying the path.

C. *Lucas:* Returning to Common Law Roots and State Courts

Or so it was mistakenly thought. But I am getting ahead of the story, and a critical part needs telling. *Lucas*[20] is that part. In argument, *Lucas* was portrayed as the ultimate "diminution in value" case. In fact, Lucas's argument uncomfortably—and wrongly—conceded a virtually limitless police power. Lucas just wanted to be paid, when regulation effectively took his property rights from him. Ironically, the state resurrected the analytical connection to the common law to justify this total deprivation of value. Calling upon the harm/benefit distinction, South Carolina declared Lucas's homebuilding plans on a barrier island to be a harm. The Court partially agreed with South Carolina (see below), in 1,575,000[21] ways that the state now regrets.

Yes, said the Court in *Lucas,* the harm/benefit distinction does matter. But Justice Brennan taught us in *Penn Central* that one person's harm is another's benefit.[22] Thus, the distinction must be connected not to landowner or regulator assertion, but to the objective reality of the state's common law. To justify its regulation, South Carolina must show by antecedent inquiry that what Mr. Lucas planned to do was never part of his common law property bundle in the first place.

With this one bold stroke, the Court solved the takings puzzle. It had seemingly returned the land-use power to its roots, as a reasonable codification of the *sic utere* principle, the law of nuisance. This principle was indeed the "helpful clue" that Justice Sutherland said in *Euclid* it always would be for determining the acceptable scope of the police power in relation to private property. With the distracting and unhelpful "diminution in value" factor functionally eliminated from the case, the Court could see clearly that judicial intervention as a constraint against the exercise of police power was not unwarranted judicial activism, but a duty borne of the takings clause itself. This was not judicial predilection displacing majority will, but a judicial reminder within a federalist structure (drawing directly upon a federalist source—state common law) that ours is not a democracy simpliciter, but a democracy bounded by human and, necessarily, property right.[23]

It is possible to argue that *Lucas* is an incomplete acknowledgment of federalism, because it accepts the property definition implicit in state common law, while rejecting (or at least limiting) its redefinition by state or local legislatures.[24] But this is nothing more than the constitutional recognition that the state police power is always bounded by private right. As a *Harvard Law Review* appraisal of *Lucas* put it, "The majority [in *Lucas*] allocated this authority to the state judiciary rather than the state legislature or the federal courts. Considerations of institutional competence, predictability, and federalism support the Court's decision."[25]

The *competence* of state courts to strike a proper balance between individual right and majoritarian desire is manifest in traditional nuisance analysis,[26] which gradually develops within a precedential system of law that invites reliance, investment, and initiative. In contrast, state legislative bodies, or their local delegates, are not limited by prior decision or enactment and are highly responsive to the shifting interests of their political constituencies. This is too much of a conflict of interest to overlook. "To allow the state legislature that enacts a regulation . . . also to determine when the federal constitution will require compensation unduly concentrates power in the hands of the legislature."[27] No state or local legislative body can fairly appraise and neutrally balance public desire and private right. "Without the protection that the Court provides in *Lucas* [premised upon the independent handiwork of the state judiciary], a state legislature could too easily use sleight-of-hand to convert benefit-conferring regulations into harm-preventing regulations and thus avoid the requirement of compensation for what would otherwise be a compensable regulatory taking."[28]

Importantly, nuisance determinations are both local and dynamic. If the aphorism "all politics are local" is correct, it surely applies to political efforts to re-allocate property, which is necessarily local. A house on a barrier island susceptible to erosion and hurricane gales may not be the equivalent of a house on the prairie in Indiana. So too, as the subtleties of local ecology are better understood by modern science and incorporated into local conceptions of harm, the house built yesterday may not be the equivalent of the house built today.

Some landowners may think this concession to the dynamic understanding of reality advantages the state too greatly. Yet, even with this dynamism, the fairness of looking to the state judiciary to sort out competing private and public claims is evident. The *Lucas* opinion enhances that fairness in two ways. First, *Lucas* places the burden of establishing that a landowner's use is nuisancelike on the state, which has the best appraisal of its regulatory interests and the greatest incentive to demonstrate any private incompatibility with them. Second, *Lucas* properly reserves some federal supervision of state nuisance determinations. Ripeness and abstention doctrines will hold these occasions to a minimum, but the fact that the takings clause is a *federal* assurance of property rights means it cannot be nonexistent. Such federal review logically follows as well from the implicit distinction between the independent reality of a state's common law of property and the rare possibility that any court, even a state court, may misapply it.[29]

Nuisance law is imprecise.[30] Yet, the common law of nuisance cannot be meaningfully asserted as too imprecise to govern the constitutional acceptability of land-use regulation. The imprecision cannot be denied, because it is at the heart of the concepts of property and the police power. Neither property nor police power is an absolute right; each evolves in context and over time. The state courts are in the best position to monitor this evolution, and the federal courts—by recognizing property as largely defined in this "independent source of state law"[31]—are in the best position to assay any takings claim that results from this evolution. This is true whether the dispute arises from state or federal regulation.

D. *Dolan:* No Affirmative Obligations without Cause

Lucas should have decided *Dolan.*[32] It did, but not as explicitly or definitively as it might have. On the surface, *Dolan* appears to extend the nexus analysis begun in *Nollan*. As the Court noted in a footnote in *Nollan,*[33] the nexus required must connect not only regulatory means and ends, but also the need for this particular regulatory imposition on this particular landowner. One hears complaints about the imprecision of the Court's "rough proportionality" language, but it is precise enough to convey two unmistakable points: the government has the burden of justifying the regulation and the justification must be reconciled with the common law of property. The greenway dedication failed for the same reason the *Loretto* cable box failed—the right to exclude holds an important place in the common law definition of property. The bikepath dedication failed because there was no relationship between the landowner's activity and the public purpose sought to be furthered. The common law does not impose an affirmative obligation without cause.

Lucas and *Dolan* are siblings. When the takings analysis in *Dolan* is linked to the search for causation, it is also linked to the takings analysis in *Lucas* premised upon property's common law definition. A landowner is not the proportionate cause of a public land-use problem, and by parity of reasoning no public harm is created, by undertaking a common law use. We may want our neighbors to furnish bikepaths, beautiful buildings, recreational amenities, artwork, or open space for an aesthetic view, and the charitable impulse may prompt individual landowners to make these welcome contributions to their community. The rule of law, however, secures such goods from public confiscation.

Although *Dolan* and *Nollan* are rooted in the common law analysis begun in *Loretto* and made explicit in *Lucas*, these cases do appear to continue an unfortunate contextual limitation: namely, that by happenstance of the facts presented in *Nollan, Dolan* and *Lucas*, the Court's resolution of the takings puzzle is nominally confined to either property concession or total diminution in value cases. Both factors are remnants of the lame "too far" or ad hoc approach, and both now deserve outright repudiation by the Court.

There is no constitutional basis to confine the *Lucas* analysis or the derivative *Dolan* and *Nollan* nexus analysis to cases of complete value deprivation or property concession. The Court implicitly recognized this concept in declining to review and remanding a case involving fee exaction.[34] The common law of property recognizes property in many forms, physical and monetary; specious arguments should not obscure that point. For this reason, the Court was arguably mistaken to include dicta in *Dolan* suggesting that the "rough proportionality" standard might not be applicable to general land-use limitations.[35] It is error to conclude that concessions/exactions and total deprivations differ in kind from the garden variety of land-use restriction; they differ in degree only. They involve matters of diminution in value, which, unlike the common law of property, are not the explanatory heart of the purpose of the takings clause.

E. *Penn Central:* Investment-Backed Expectations in Discrete Parcels

The "diminution in value" formulation may temporarily forestall the Court's recognition that *Loretto, Nollan, Lucas,* and *Dolan* are all of a piece; the odd man out is *Penn Central* and its distant ancestor, *Pennsylvania Coal*. Diminution in value is a side issue, an early surrogate for the more searching inquiry into whether the police power has been asserted in league with, or in opposition to, the common law. Even *Penn Central* recognized this concept with its reference to "reasonable investment-backed expectations." These expectations are common law ones. If the Court is to find the proper denominator for the loss calculation fraction, the answer is to be found in them.

The *Penn Central* position that landowners cannot conceptually sever their property for purposes of demonstrating regulatory loss will not hold. It should not hold because it is fundamentally at odds with the common law nature of property where expectations are often (but not always) formed with respect to discrete aspects or segments of property. Property investment, development, sale, and descent rely on the flexibility and utility of such property segmentation; therefore it is artificial for the Court to maintain an antiseverance conceptual posture. This feature of *Lucas*, along with the parallel dictum in *Dolan* that general-use limitations are not subject to heightened scrutiny, should gradually recede now that the takings puzzle has been solved.

III. Conclusion

There is no constitutional limitation preventing the Court from removing the antiseverance concept or general-use regulation exceptions from the Court's successful balancing of the property and police power. But there is a pragmatic one: the limits of judicial resources. It will take time, but several ways to meet this concern are open to the Court. First, a high ripeness hurdle is already in place.[36] Second, state common law is already developing in ways that give greater identification and precision to the property segments that, in proper cases, should form the denominator against which to measure loss.[37] Once this happens, it is a minor step to the recognition that general-use limitations can result in compensable losses every bit as much as property invasions, concessions/exactions, or total deprivations.

Yes, the takings puzzle has been solved. Of course, its specific applications will always remain contentious. Like other features of our constitutional system, a "machine that would go by itself," there is constant push and counterpush; the same is true with the destiny of the countervailing property and police power forces. What is a modern work of genius, however, is the clever way in which the Supreme Court worked its way out of a judicially complacent posture that was as untenable as it was dangerous to one of the cornerstones on which the republic was first built—the preservation of property.[38] Perhaps, however, the genius lies less with the individual men and women who write in our present day, than with they who "built better than they knew," the framers of our Constitution.

Notes

1. Armstrong v. United States, 364 U.S. 40, 49 (1960).
2. 114 S. Ct. 2309 (1994).

3. Lochner v. New York, 198 U.S. 45 (1905) (the much-criticized high point of substantive economic due process).

4. U.S. CONST. art. IV, § 2; U.S. CONST. amend, XIV, § 1.

5. U.S. CONST. art. I, § 10; *see* Douglas W. Kmiec and John O. McGinnis, *The Contract Clause: A Return to the Original Understanding,* 14 HASTINGS CONST. L. Q. 525 (1987).

6. 483 U.S. 825 (1987).

7. 112 S. Ct. 2886 (1992).

8. *See* Roe v. Wade, 410 U.S. 113 (1973); Planned Parenthood v. Casey, 112 S. Ct. 2791 (1992).

9. *See* Douglas W. Kmiec, *The Original Understanding of the Taking Clause is Neither Weak nor Obtuse,* 88 COLUM. L. REV. 1630 (1988).

10. Mugler v. Kansas, 123 U.S. 623 (1887).

11. Village of Euclid v. Ambler Realty Co., 272 U.S. 365 (1926).

12. Pennsylvania Coal Co. v. Mahon, 260 U.S. 393 (1922).

13. Penn Central Transp. Co. v. City of New York, 438 U.S. 104 (1978).

14. Loretto v. Teleprompter Manhattan CATV Corp., 458 U.S. 419 (1982).

15. Nollan v. California Coastal Comm'n, 107 S. Ct. 3141 (1987).

16. Keystone Bituminous Coal Ass'n v. DeBenedictus, 107 S. Ct. 1232 (1987).

17. Norman Williams, *A Narrow Escape?,* 16 ZONING & PLAN. L. rep. nos. 4-5 (1993).

18. Jerold Kayden characterizes Justice Scalia's analysis for the Court in *Nollan* as based upon "shoddy scholarship and misguided analysis." Jerold S. Kayden, *Judges as Planners: Limited or General Partners? in* ZONING AND THE AMERICAN DREAM 223, 233 (Charles M. Harr and Jerold S. Kayden eds. 1989).

19. Frank Michelman, *Takings, 1987,* 88 COLUM. L. REV. 1600, 1608 (1988).

20. 112 S. Ct. 2886 (1992).

21. The Court agreed with South Carolina only to the extent that it could prove that Mr. Lucas's homebuilding plans were a nuisancelike activity not part of his antecedent title. South Carolina did not make this proof on remand, but rather entered into a negotiated settlement whereby Mr. Lucas received $425,000 for each of his two lots and $725,000 in interest, attorneys' fees and costs. South Carolina later resold Mr. Lucas's property to another developer for $785,000.

22. *Penn Central,* 438 U.S. at 133 n.30.

23. In *Lynch v. Household Finance Corp.,* 405 U.S. 538, 552 (1972), the Court stated:

> Property does not have rights. People have rights. The right to enjoy property without lawful deprivation . . . is in truth a 'personal' right. . . . In fact, a fundamental interdependence exists between the personal right to liberty and the personal right in property. Neither could have meaning without the other. That rights in property are basic civil rights has long been recognized.

24. In order to prevail in *Lucas,* South Carolina was instructed by the Court to "identify background principles of nuisance *and property law* that pro-

hibit" Mr. Lucas's homebuilding. 112 S. Ct. at 2901-02 (emphasis supplied). Does the reference to "property law" apart from nuisance include state legislative limitations on use? Perhaps. Clearly, it would be circular to include the very legislative limitation under challenge. On the other hand, well-established legislative limitations in place at the time of acquisition have a better claim for being included (and thus qualifying a landowner's common law property bundle), especially if they reinforce or reasonably extend a common law nuisance limitation.

25. Survey, *The Supreme Court, 1991 Term: Leading Cases,* 106 HARV. L. REV. 163, 274 (1992).

26. Joseph W. Singer, *The Reliance Interest in Property,* 40 STAN. L. REV. 614, 747 (1988) (courts "develop moral principles to govern the proper exercise of power in the marketplace" and are "experts in such principles").

27. Survey, HARV. L. REV., *supra* note 25, at 275.

28. *Id.*

29. *See, e.g.,* Jeremy Paul, *The Hidden Structure of Takings Law,* 64 CAL. L. REV. 1393, 1412-13 (1991) (federal review implies a federal component to a state definition of property); Henry P. Monaghan, *Of 'Liberty' and 'Property',* 62 CORNELL L. REV. 405, 435-38 (1977) (recognizing the distinction between state property law and its interpretation); Barton H. Thompson, Jr., *Judicial Takings,* 76 VA. L. REV. 1449, 1450-51 (1990) (suggesting federal review for takings that result from radical reversals of precedent by a state court).

30. W. Page Keeton, Dan B. Dobbs, Robert E. Keeton, and David G. Owen, PROSSER AND KEETON ON THE LAW OF TORTS, § 86 at 616 (5th ed. 1984).

31. Board of Regents v. Roth, 408 U.S. 564, 577 (1972).

32. For a suggested alternative opinion written and published *before* the case was decided, see Douglas W. Kmiec, *Clarifying the Supreme Court's Taking Cases—An Irreverent but Otherwise Unassailable Draft Opinion in* Dolan v. City of Tigard, 71 DENV. U. L. REV. 325 (1994).

33. *Nollan,* 107 S. Ct. at 3147 n.4. Justice Scalia, foreshadowing the Court's opinion in *Dolan,* wrote, "[i]f the Nollans were being singled out to bear the burden of California's attempt to remedy [the various regulatory] problems, although they had not contributed to [them] more than other coastal landowners, the State's action, even if otherwise valid, might violate either the incorporated Takings Clause or the Equal Protection Clause."

34. Ehrlich v. Culver City, 15 Cal. App. 4th 1737, 19 Cal. Rptr. 2d 468 (Ct. App. 1993), *rev. denied,* No. 5033642, 1993 Cal. LEXIS 4467 (Cal. August 1993), *cert. denied,* 114 S. Ct. 2731 (1994) (remanding in light of *Dolan* a $280,000 "mitigation" fee when a landowner desired to convert his unprofitable private tennis club to townhomes—an act the city asserted would "harm" its recreational interests. An "in lieu" art fee of $30,000 was also imposed. One would expect that the notion that private owners must maintain private recreational uses or supply "art" on their private property for public enjoyment would be a novel one even under the common law of California, but perhaps not. On remand, the California Court of Appeal sustained the exactions, notwithstanding *Dolan,* in

an opinion that it (wisely) directed to remain unpublished. Ehrlich v. Culver City, B055523 (Cal. Ct. App. 2d Dist., Div. 5 Dec. 23, 1994).

To reach its result, which is quite jarring to those of us residing in less exotic environments, the California appellate court asserted that "it is beyond dispute that the City has a legitimate governmental interest in making available [*private*] community recreational facilities." (unpublished opinion at 19, emphasis and adjective supplied for clarity of context). Reading this, one is tempted to say, sure, that's right, cities do have unquestioned authority to buy parkland and put up public tennis courts and tax all its residents for these amenities. But on second reading, in context, it is apparent that this well-established common law authority is not what the city is asserting, but instead the extraordinary notion that once a private landowner has undertaken a permitted common law use, like a private swimming pool or tennis court, it must either continue that use or pay to stop, or, as the appellate court notes blithely several times, go out of business or sell the property.

The appellate court's analysis well illustrates the danger—warned against in the text—of not seeing *Lucas*'s reliance upon the common law of nuisance as the premise to *Dolan*'s inquiry of whether a landowner can in any credible way be said to be the "cause" of harm that can then legitimately be addressed by the police power.

In theory, of course, a given community might refine its common law, over an extended period of litigation, to include affirmative recreational and artistic exhibition duties within the common law conception of private property ownership. Theoretically, as I say, this can be imagined, though given the loss of personal freedom entailed by such coerced duties, this would not be a community in which I would care to live. As best as I can discern, however, this is not the present state of the common law of ownership in California, even as the appellate court disingenuously asserted that requiring recreational mitigation and art fees is no different from routine subdivision requirements for storm drains, curbs, and gutters.

35. In discussing Mrs. Dolan's situation, the Court observes that it differs from a case involving "essentially legislative determinations classifying entire areas of the city. . . ." *Dolan*, 114 S. Ct. at 2316. The Court also notes that the *Dolan* case involved a property concession. As argued here, these distinctions are partially beside the point if they are used to distract the Court from the most fundamental taking inquiry—whether there has been a disproportionate imposition of public burdens in light of common law property. A property concession may be an example of a disproportionate burden, but it is not the only example. A general law, in application, can disproportionately burden as well, regardless of whether it involves a property concession. The Court seems to grasp this point by characterizing Mrs. Dolan's circumstance as involving an "adjudicative decision." *Id.* Later, the Court uses this "adjudicative" label again to explain why the burden of proof is on the city. *Id.* at 2320 n.8. This "adjudicative" label and burden shift should apply to a circumstance in which a general-use restriction is used to justify a permit denial, provided the plaintiff has made

a prima facie showing that the restriction and denial are inconsistent with the common law property interest involved.

36. Williamson County v. Hamilton Bank, 473 U.S. 172 (1985).

37. *See* DOUGLAS W. KMIEC, ZONING AND PLANNING DESKBOOK § 7.02 [5] [b] (1995) and cases cited therein. The Federal Circuit has also begun to outline factual circumstances in which a discrete segment may be the relevant focus of analysis. *Id.* at § 7.02 [5] [a]; Loveladies Harbor, Inc. v. United States, 28 F.3d 1171 (Fed. Cir. 1994).

38. James Madison wrote, "Government is instituted to protect property of every sort. . . . This being the end of government, that alone is a *just* government, which *impartially* secures to every man, whatever is his *own*." JAMES MADISON, PROPERTY (1792), *reprinted in* 14 PAPERS OF JAMES MADISON 266-68 (Robert A. Rutland et al., eds., 1983) (emphasis in the original). *See also,* Douglas W. Kmiec, *The Coherence of the Natural Law of Property,* 26 VAL. U. L. REV. 367 (1991); JAMES W. ELY, JR., THE GUARDIAN OF EVERY OTHER RIGHT, (Oxford 1991).

CHAPTER ❖ 6

Investment-Backed Expectations in Takings Law

Daniel R. Mandelker

In *Penn Central Transportation Co. v. New York City,*[1] the Supreme Court added "investment-backed expectations" as a factor a court should consider in land-use cases involving takings. Unfortunately, the Court is confused about the meaning of this term, federal and state courts divide on how to apply it, and its role in takings law remains a puzzle.[2] This article reviews judicial treatment of investment-backed expectations in takings law. It proposes a regulatory risk theory courts can use to decide cases when landowners claim investment-backed expectations in takings controversies.[3]

Part I reviews the investment-backed expectations factor as it developed in Supreme Court cases before 1987. Part II reviews the Court's 1987 takings trilogy and later Supreme Court cases that elaborated on the meaning of this takings factor. Part III critiques the use of investment-backed expectations in takings cases and proposes the regulatory risk theory to evaluate expectations claims in takings controversies. Part IV reviews lower federal and state court decisions that applied the investment-backed expectations factor after the trilogy. The article concludes that the decisions provide substantial support for the regulatory risk theory as the basis for considering landowner expectations in takings cases.

I. Investment-Backed Expectations in the Supreme Court before the Trilogy

A. *Penn Central:* Introducing Investment-Backed Expectations

In *Penn Central Transportation Co. v. City of New York,*[4] the Supreme Court upheld the designation of Grand Central Terminal as a historic landmark. It also upheld the city's rejection of a proposal to build a high-rise office building using air rights over the terminal. Writing for the majority, Justice Brennan introduced a new multifactor balancing test in takings law. He noted that the Court had not adopted a "set formula" for takings cases and stated:

> In engaging in these essentially ad hoc, factual inquiries, the Court's decisions have identified several factors that have particular significance. The economic impact of the regulation on the claimant and, particularly, the extent to which the regulation has interfered with distinct, investment-backed expectations are, of course, relevant considerations. So, too, is the character of the governmental action.[5]

Justice Brennan's explanation of investment-backed expectations in *Penn Central* did not fully clarify the Court's role in takings law.[6] Brennan illustrated the term's meaning by discussing *Pennsylvania Coal Co. v. Mahon*,[7] in which Justice Holmes held that a statute prohibiting coal mining that caused subsidence was a taking. The coal company had reserved subsurface mining rights to property it sold on which defendant constructed a residential dwelling. Justice Brennan interpreted *Pennsylvania Coal* to mean a taking occurred because the statute made it commercially impracticable to mine coal and therefore "had nearly the same effect as the complete destruction of the property rights" reserved by the coal company.[8] This holding suggests that property owners have investment-backed expectations only when they possess formally reserved rights in property.

Most of Justice Brennan's discussion of investment-backed expectations in *Penn Central* considered exceptions to this takings factor. Unfortunately, these exceptions overlap and add more, rather than creating less, confusion to the role of investment-backed expectations in takings law.

Brennan did not extend the expectations factor to divisible property interests that are unprotected, as in *Pennsylvania Coal*, by formal reservation. In a significant holding, he said that " 'taking' jurisprudence does not divide a single parcel into discrete segments and attempt to determine whether rights in a particular segment have been entirely abrogated."[9] In *Penn Central*, this holding countered a claim by the terminal owners that the city's refusal to allow an office building in the airspace over the terminal took their property rights. This holding, known as the "whole property" rule, means that courts need not give takings clause protection to every strand a property owner has in the bundle of property rights.

Justice Brennan further narrowed the scope of investment-backed expectations by holding that "the submission that [the terminal owners] may establish a 'taking' simply by showing that they have been denied the ability to exploit a property interest they heretofore had believed was available for development is quite simply untenable."[10] This holding also countered the argument by the terminal owners that they should be allowed to build in the airspace. The "exploitation" holding limits landowner reliance on investment-backed expectations because it appears to mean that a subjective intention concerning the use of property is not enough to support a taking claim.

Justice Brennan also rejected the taking claim because the landmark law did not interfere with the "primary expectation concerning the use of the parcel" as a railroad terminal.[11] This holding implies a landowner can claim his investment-backed expectations are frustrated if a land-use regulation does interfere with his primary expectations concerning his property. If so, the holding modifies the rejection of subjective expectations by the exploitation exception, if the holding means a landowner's subjective intentions concerning his property decide whether they are primary.[12]

B. The "Bundle of Property Rights" Cases

Other Supreme Court cases before the trilogy elaborated on the meaning of investment-backed expectations, but only confused their role in takings cases.[13] One group of cases considered the "bundle of property rights" problem raised in *Penn Central. Andrus v. Allard*[14] upheld a federal statute prohibiting the sale of Indian artifacts. The Court applied *Penn Central* to hold the destruction of one strand in the bundle of property rights is not a taking, because courts must consider the aggregate property interests of property owners when they make takings claims. Owners of the artifacts could still possess, transport, donate, or devise them. In another holding that limits investment-backed expectations, the Court said that loss of profits without physical restriction of property is not a taking because "prediction of profitability is a matter of reasoned expectation that courts are not especially competent to perform."[15]

The Court qualified *Andrus* in *Kaiser Aetna v. United States.*[16] After a private developer improved a coastal pond and dredged a channel to provide private access to the ocean, the U.S. Army Corps of Engineers sued to prevent denial of public access to the channel. The Court held the government's attempt to create public access was a taking of the property owner's "right to exclude." This holding means the takings clause protects this right in the bundle of property rights.[17] The Court also based its decision on the Corps' failure to require permits for the developer's improvements to the pond and channel. Although this failure did not estop the government, it created expectancies entitled to protection under the takings clause. This holding suggests that reliance on tacit or explicit government approval is a factor courts should consider when deciding whether investment-backed expectations are frustrated.

C. *Monsanto:* The Notice Rule

Ruckelshaus v. Monsanto Co.[18] added a new element not considered in *Penn Central* by adopting a notice rule to decide when courts should recognize investment-backed expectations. A federal environmental statute authorized a federal agency to disclose data submitted by applicants seeking registration of a pesticide. Monsanto claimed the statute was a taking of property because it required the disclosure of trade secrets.

The Court held that the "force" of the investment-backed expectations factor partly defeated the taking claim, even though the takings clause protects trade secrets as property. Monsanto did not have reasonable investment-backed expectations in trade secrets disclosed after the adoption of the statute, because the statute put Monsanto on notice that it required disclosure of trade secrets. Furthermore, the disclosure requirement did not impose an unconstitutional condition on a valuable government benefit. The Court found Monsanto was aware of the conditions, which related rationally to a legitimate governmental interest, and voluntarily submitted data in return for an economic advantage.

Monsanto adds an important qualification to investment-backed expectations, even though it is not a land-use case, because it held that notice of a government regulation can limit landowner investment-backed expectations in takings cases. *Monsanto* suggests that actual notice is not necessary, by holding that the statute put the company on notice it might have to disclose trade secrets. This is constructive notice. Land-use cases before the trilogy relied on the *Monsanto* constructive notice rule to dismiss takings claims based on investment-backed expectations.[19] The Court later rejected the *Monsanto* constructive notice rule in a land-use trilogy case.

II. The Supreme Court's 1987 Trilogy and Beyond

The Supreme Court's *Penn Central* decision held that the "investment-backed expectations" concept is one of the three factors courts must consider when they apply a multifactor balancing test to land-use takings cases. The Court's 1987 trilogy of land-use cases took a different approach to takings law. The Court introduced[20] a two-part test for takings cases, without suggesting how courts should correlate the two-part test with the three-factor balancing test the Court adopted in *Penn Central*.

A. *Keystone:* The Unit of Property Considered

Keystone Bituminous Coal Ass'n v. DeBenedictus[21] introduced the two-part taking test. It held that courts should find a land-use regulation is a taking if it " 'does not substantially advance legitimate state interests . . . or denies an owner economically viable use of his land.' "[22] The requirement that a regulation "substantially advance legitimate state interests" is an elaboration of the holding in *Penn Central* that a court should take the character of the land-use regulation into account. A 1987 trilogy case, *Nollan v. California Coastal Commission*,[23] made it clear that most interests advanced by land-use regulation are legitimate. It noted the Court had approved a "broad range" of governmental purposes, such as scenic zoning, landmark preservation, and residential zoning.[24] *Keystone* also stated, as an alternate test, that a taking occurs if a regulation denies a landowner all "economically viable use" of the land.[25] The Court held in a later case that a per se taking occurs in this situation.

Keystone's treatment of investment-backed expectations is confusing. The Court had before it a statute that prohibited coal mining if it would cause dwellings and other structures to subside. The Court had held a similar statute was a taking almost seventy years earlier in *Pennsylvania Coal*,[26] partly because the statute made the mining of coal commercially impracticable. The Court reached the opposite result in *Keystone* because there the statute affected only 2 percent of the coal left in place for mining. The Court applied the *Penn Central* "whole property" rule in holding it would not treat this percentage of coal as a separate segment of property for taking purposes. The plaintiffs' duty to retain this "small percentage" of coal, when considered with any "reasonable unit" of the plaintiffs' statewide coal-mining operations, did not deny all economically viable use or frustrate plaintiffs' reasonable investment-backed expectations. The Court concluded there had been "no showing that petitioners' reasonable 'investment-backed expectations' have been materially affected by the additional duty to retain the small percentage that must be used to support the structures protected by [the statute]."[27]

This holding on investment-backed expectations is confusing. Perhaps the Court meant the "whole parcel" rule defines the unit of property that determines whether a landowner has investment-backed expectations. Because the appropriate unit of property in *Keystone* was statewide coal mining, the limited restriction on coal removal throughout the state was insignificant and did not affect plaintiffs' investment-backed expectations. This problem usually is important only in wetlands takings cases. A court may have to decide whether to evaluate the effect of a development prohibition on the "whole property" and not just that part that is wetlands and subject to wetlands restrictions.[28]

B. *Nollan:* The Death of the Notice Rule?

Nollan v. California Coastal Commission,[29] a 1987 trilogy case, adopted an important revision of the constructive notice rule as applied to investment-backed expectations. The California Coastal Commission granted a permit under the California Coastal Act to build a beachfront home, but required as a condition an easement that allowed the public to cross the beach. The commission imposed the condition to provide opportunities for public views of the beach, but the Court held there was no nexus and that a taking occurred because the access condition did not advance this purpose. Justice Brennan's dissent states that he would have applied *Monsanto*'s constructive notice rule to hold plaintiffs did not have investment-backed expectations entitled to protection under the takings clause. He applied *Monsanto* to argue that plaintiffs were aware that "stringent regulation of development along the coast" had been in place for many years, and that a condition requiring access had been placed on all other development projects in their tract. Plaintiffs thus were on notice the commission would approve development only if they made provision for lateral beach access. They could have no "reasonable expectation" of, or "entitlement" to, approval without the access condition.[30]

Justice Scalia, writing for the majority, disagreed. He dealt with the notice problem in a footnote,[31] in which he noted Justice Brennan's application of the notice rule but distinguished *Monsanto.* There, he explained, a taking did not occur because the government announced that an application for a "valuable Government benefit" would confer on the government a "license" to use and disclose trade secrets the application contained:

> But the right to build on one's own property—even though its exercise can be subjected to legitimate permitting requirements—

> cannot remotely be described as a "government benefit." And thus the announcement the application for (or granting of) the permit will entail the yielding of a property interest cannot be regarded as establishing the voluntary "exchange" that we found to have occurred in *Monsanto*.[32]

Scalia added that the Nollans' property rights were not "altered because they acquired the land well after the Commission had begun to carry out its policy."[33]

This footnote makes clear that the right to build on land is not a government benefit, and that requiring a property owner to give up a property interest in return for the right to build is not a voluntary exchange that escapes the takings clause. Scalia did not mention the investment-backed expectations of property owners in his footnote; but he implies a government limitation on property rights in return for the approval of a "right" to develop does not extinguish these expectations.

Scalia's footnote also suggests a court can find a taking even though a landowner has purchased land subject to a restrictive regulatory program. It is not clear whether Scalia would take a different view if a landowner, at the time of purchase, had actual notice of a land-use regulation, and the government later applied this regulation to frustrate the landowner's expectations. It is also unclear whether Scalia's footnote prohibits courts from considering constructive notice of a land-use regulation in takings cases. Justice Scalia may have meant only that constructive notice of a restrictive regulation is not an absolute bar to a taking claim.

Although *Nollan*'s footnote may limit the effect of notice on investment-backed expectations, it is at odds with the Court's treatment of ownership expectations in a different constitutional setting. In *Nordlinger v. Hahn*,[34] a property tax limitations case, the Court rejected an equal protection challenge to California's Proposition 13, an amendment to the state constitution that placed limits on general real property taxes. The Court upheld a provision that applies the amendment's tax limitation only to persons owning property at the time the amendment was adopted, and not to persons who buy property later.

The Court upheld this distinction partly because it concluded a new owner who acquires property "does not have the same reliance interest warranting protection against higher taxes as does an existing owner."[35] It added that "an existing owner rationally may be thought to have vested expectations in his property or home that are more deserving of protection than the anticipatory expectations of a new owner at the point of purchase."[36] The Court then noted it had "not hesitated to recognize the legitimacy of protecting reliance and expectational interests" outside the context of the Equal Protection Clause. As an example it cited the *Penn Central* holding that investment-backed expectations are considered in determining whether a taking has occurred. *Nordlinger* is a property tax rather than a takings case, and this difference may have affected the Court's decision.[37] The case illustrates, nonetheless, that the Court is not consistent in the constitutional protection it gives to reliance and expectation interests in property.[38]

C. *Lucas:* More Confusion about Expectations

Five years after the 1987 trilogy, in *Lucas v. South Carolina Coastal Commission,*[39] the Court decided another land-use case that affects the role of investment-backed expectations in takings law. In *Lucas,* the plaintiff bought two lots on a barrier island on which he intended to build homes similar to those on immediately adjacent parcels. At the time of purchase the lots were not subject to the state's coastal building permit requirement, but the Beachfront Management Act, adopted later, prohibited permanent structures on the property.[40]

Justice Scalia held that a taking occurred. After reviewing the Supreme Court's takings law, he concluded there are "at least two discrete categories" of regulation that are compensable "without case-specific inquiry into the public interest advanced in support of the restraint."[41] One is a physical occupation of property,[42] and the other is a regulation that denies "all economically beneficial or productive use of land."[43] This holding clearly means courts are not to apply the *Penn Central* balancing test if a land-use regulation is a taking per se.[44] When a per se taking does not occur, the *Penn Central* balancing test applies.

Justice Scalia reinforced his *Nollan* footnote stating that the constructive notice rule does not apply to real property by making an exception for personal property. In *Lucas,* he held an owner of personal property should be aware, "because of the traditionally high degree of control over commercial dealings," that a new regulation might render his or her property economically worthless. This is an application of the rule that constructive notice of a regulation will defeat a takings claim, and implies that real property is not so heavily regulated that the constructive notice rule should apply.[45]

Another part of the *Lucas* decision contradicts these holdings. It suggests a failure of investment-backed expectations can prevent a taking, even though a regulation is totally restrictive and a per se taking should have occurred. Justice Scalia held a per se taking does not occur if the "logically antecedent inquiry into the nature of the owner's estate shows" the uses prohibited by the regulation were not part of the owner's "title."[46] Restrictions imposed under the common law of nuisance are one example.

Scalia added that this limitation on the per se taking rule is consistent with takings jurisprudence, "which has traditionally been guided by the understandings of our citizens" concerning the state's power over the "bundle of rights" landowners acquire when they obtain title to property.[47] He then said a property owner necessarily expects that measures "newly enacted" by the state in exercising its police power will restrict the use of the property from time to time, and he quoted *Pennsylvania Coal* for the proposition that "some values" are under an "implied limitation and must yield to the police power."[48]

This recognition of an "implied" police power limitation is surprising in an opinion that held a per se taking occurs when all economically viable use is denied. What is more surprising is Justice Scalia's admission that a landowner should expect newly-enacted regulations to restrict the use of the property. This admission could mean a newly-enacted land-use regulation "inheres" in the title and is not a per se taking if it was in effect when the landowner purchased the land, even if the regulation denies all economically viable use.[49] The Court did not decide this question in *Lucas,* because no restriction on development applied to the land when Lucas purchased it.

III. A Critique of Investment-Backed Expectations as a Taking Factor

A. The Role of Expectations in Takings Law

Supreme Court decisions have not been coherent in their treatment of investment-backed expectations in takings cases. The Court has concentrated almost entirely on deciding when investment-backed expectations do not exist rather than when they can provide a basis for a takings claim.

A major problem in the decisions may be the choice of terms to describe this takings element. Justice Brennan introduced investment-backed expectations as one of three factors in his balancing test, but the word "expectations" has a wider meaning in our understanding of the rights that make up property. Justice Scalia's *Lucas* decision provides an example. Scalia noted that he had not clearly defined the property interest to which courts should apply the "denial of all economically viable use" rule. He then added:

> [T]he answer to this difficult question may lie in how the owner's reasonable expectations have been shaped by the State's law of property—i.e., whether and to what degree the State's law has accorded legal recognition and protection to the particular interest in land with respect to which the takings claimant alleges a diminution in (or elimination of) value.[50]

If state law shapes the expectations that determine property interests protected by takings law, courts should not have to reconsider expectations in property as a discrete factor in "as applied" takings cases. The requirement that "expectations" be "investment-backed" does not eliminate this redundancy. All expectations in privately held property are investment-backed by purchase or acquisition.[51]

Despite, or perhaps because of, this redundancy, an understanding of how history shapes expectations in property will help explain the role of investment-backed expectations in takings cases. As Professor Tarlock has noted,[52] two competing traditions in American history take different views of expectations in property. The federalist natural law tradition holds that property rights generate firm expectations entitled to judicial protection from excessive government regulation. The republican positivist tradition stresses the relationship between the individual and the civil community and holds that all claims to property are subject to an implied public interest limitation.

These competing historic traditions express different views of how the takings clause protects expectations in property. Professor Tarlock adds that common law expectations in property have never been absolute and have eroded over time. The state's decision about when it will prohibit the unrestricted use of property to avoid harm diminishes compensation expectations. Landowners, for example, have historically held title to property subject to government control of common resources, such as navigable waterways. A government action that prevents property owners from impeding or restricting the flow of navigable waters, such as a decision to impair or destroy a riparian owner's access, does not require compensation.[53] Property owners are on notice of government ownership in common property resources. This notice defeats a takings claim when government asserts its interest in common property to restrict private use.

A major question is whether courts should extend to new categories the constructive notice rule they have applied to protect common property resources from takings claims.[54] The objection to such an extension is that a refusal to recognize investment-backed expectations in these market environments again raises an unresolved normative problem.[55] Markets become risky only because government regulation makes them so, and government can increase market uncertainties such that opinions about land-development opportunities diverge widely and risk increases.[56] Risk increases and investment-backed expectations diminish as government regulation becomes increasingly restrictive, because uncertainty about expectations is highest when government approval of development is doubtful.[57]

An answer to this objection should begin with the implied limitations on property entitlements that historically have put landowners on notice they do not have takings claims. These implied limitations are normative. An example is the public's interest in navigable waters. Landowners are on notice they do not have takings claims when government protects navigable waters by limiting private use. A strong normative case exists for extending these historic, implied limitations to deny protection of investment-backed expectations when landowners assume regulatory risk.

Investment-backed expectations held by property owners arise at the time of purchase, and the information the owners have then about their property gives them meaning. For example, if a landowner knows at the time she enters a land market that she is, or might be, covered by a regulatory program in which government can deny permission to develop her land, it is only fair that she assume the regulatory risk this program creates. She also should be charged with constructive notice of regulatory barriers when the market sends a signal that regulatory risk is high. The market sends such a signal when a wide divergence in opinion exists about whether the landowner will realize her expectations for development.

Regulatory uncertainty shapes the validity of landowner expectations, and judicial protection of expectations should diminish as regulatory uncertainty increases. To recognize the reasonableness of investment-backed expectations in this situation by allowing a landowner to succeed in a takings claim improperly allows her to "gamble" against the market. Speculators do not have reasonable investment-backed expectations entitled to protection under the takings clause.

B. Landowner Reliance as a Factor in Recognizing Investment-Backed Expectations

The discussion so far has emphasized how courts should decide when government rejects landowners' expectations in the development of their land. The notice rule also should apply when government intervenes to raise, rather than lower, landowners' expectations. This situation occurs when, following an initial purchase, government intervenes to allow, rather than deny, development. A government decision to allow development changes a landowner's information because it creates an expectation that the landowner can put the land to a more intensive use. A landowner's expectations should include reliance on government approvals that allow development to go on. There is no uncertainty about expectations in this type of situation: the property owner has an expectation that she or he can go on with the project.

Problems arise with protecting landowner expectations in this situation only when the government changes its mind and either rescinds the previous approval or adopts a regulation that nullifies what the previous approval allowed. Change of this kind is another form of the transition problem, and the question is whether courts should protect a landowner's expectations from a governmental change of mind. The takings law question is whether and when a landowner's expectations become investment-backed and reasonable once government has approved the development.

The answer to this question is not difficult. Zoning law protects an owner's reliance when courts find the owner has obtained a vested right in property. State courts recognize vested rights under the majority rule when a zoning agency has given a landowner a building permit, and the landowner relied on the permit by making substantial expenditures on the development the permit allows.[58] A later change in zoning does not prevent a landowner from proceeding to completion. A similar reliance rule is appropriate in deciding when investment-backed expectations are reasonable and entitled to protection under the takings clause.

IV. Investment-Backed Expectations in the Post-Trilogy Era in the Lower Federal and State Courts

A. Some Introductory Comments

Post-trilogy lower federal and state court cases reflect the confusions evident in Supreme Court decisions that apply investment-backed expectations as a factor in takings law. These cases, like the pre-trilogy decisions, avoid the ambiguities inherent in investment-backed expectations by adopting specific decision rules to decide takings cases when landowner expectations are an issue.

The post-trilogy cases also illustrate the circularity commentators have found in the use of investment-backed expectations as a takings factor. Some cases are concerned solely with a landowner's expectations at the time of purchase. They hold a taking occurs if landowner expectations at this time are frustrated. Other cases protect landowner expectations when the court finds a vested right created by landowner reliance on a land-use approval. These cases do not consider regulatory risk as a factor in deciding whether landowner expectations are reasonable. Another significant group of cases rejects investment-backed expectations, by holding that landowners must assume regulatory risk. These cases hold investment-backed expectations did not exist, because landowners had or should have had notice of the regulatory program under which approval of their development was denied.

B. Vested Rights and the "Economically Viable Use" Rule

A landowner's expectations are investment-backed and reasonable when he or she proceeds substantially in good faith after government approval of the development.[59] Government action creates a vested right in property in this situation and, like a property right privately reserved,[60] courts should protect it as a landowner's investment-backed expectation. Several decisions either recognized[61] or held that vested rights can create investment-backed expectations protected by the takings clause.[62] A few cases merged investment-backed expectations with the vested rights doctrine. They held courts should find protected investment-backed expectations only when landowners have vested rights.[63]

These decisions are consistent with the view that regulatory risk determines whether courts should protect expectations under the takings clause. Landowners have every right to expect protection when government action takes away reserved property rights or interferes with government-created vested rights.[64] The vested rights decisions also are consistent with the protection of landowner expectations when a landowner responds properly to government action that changes the information on which he or she relies. In the vested rights cases, a landowner's expectations are reasonably based on a government decision approving a development for which the landowner applied.

An influential, pre-trilogy, Third Circuit decision, *Pace Resources v. Shrewsbury Township*,[65] applied the constructive notice rule to decide whether the court should protect vested rights as part of a landowner's investment-backed expectations. After the plaintiff began development of an industrial park, the township blocked its completion (in part by downzoning) when residents became concerned about industrial development in the community. The plaintiff appealed to a state court, which invalidated the downzoning. The plaintiff then sued in federal court claiming a taking had occurred because the town denied it the economically viable use of its land until the state court reached a decision.

The court of appeals held the downzoning was not a taking. It applied *Penn Central*'s multifactor balancing test, holding that the purpose of the rezoning was legitimate and that the downzoning did not deny plaintiff the economically viable use of its land. On the investment-backed expectations issue, the court applied the holding in *Penn Central* that a statute can "frustrate distinct investment-backed expectations" when it has "nearly the same effect as the complete destruction of rights [a party] had reserved from the owners of the surface land."[66] The reference is to *Pennsylvania Coal,* in which the Supreme Court found a taking because a statute that prohibited subsidence totally destroyed the right to mine coal the plaintiff had reserved as a property right.

Pace also claimed it had investment-backed expectations because of expenditures it made in reliance on the preliminary approval of its development. This assertion was essentially a vested rights claim. The court recognized that "distinct expenditures" of this kind could provide the basis for a takings claim. It then applied the constructive notice rule to hold investment-backed expectations "are reasonable only if they take into account the power of the state to regulate in the public interest."[67] A state statute defined the plaintiff's expectations by limiting the time during which a developer has vested rights in preliminary development approval. The plaintiff could not claim investment-backed expectations because the statutory period had expired.

Pace is correct because it recognizes courts should protect vested rights at the time they arise. In *Pace,* a state statute limited vested rights to three years. It gave plaintiff constructive notice of a restriction that limited the plaintiff's vested rights expectations when they were created. An expectation that a vested right would continue after the statutory period expired was a regulatory risk that did not require protection under the takings clause.

Later cases in the Third Circuit and elsewhere give *Pace* a different interpretation. They quote its holding that investment-backed expectations are frustrated only if a regulation has nearly the same effect as the destruction of a property right. They interpret this holding to mean a landowner's investment-backed expectations are not frustrated unless he or she is denied all economically viable use of the land.[68] Other courts have taken the same position, but do not rely on *Pace.*[69]

These cases may reflect Justice Brennan's decision in *Penn Central,* in which destruction of a reserved property right was the only example he gave of a case in which investment-backed expectations can be frustrated. Later courts may believe the only cases raising investment-backed expectations claims comparable to the destruction of a reserved property right are cases in which a regulation has denied all economically viable use.

C. Protecting Landowner Expectations at the Time of Purchase

Another group of cases solves the circularity inherent in investment-backed expectations by recognizing landowner expectations at the time of purchase as the basis for a takings claim. Government intervention in these cases later denied the landowner a more intensive use than he or she contemplated. Courts did not consider the regulatory program, or any notice it might have given, when deciding whether a refusal to approve a development frustrated a landowner's expectations. These cases find support in Justice Brennan's *Penn Central* holding that a taking did not occur in that case because the historic landmark designation did not interfere with the "primary expectation concerning the use of the parcel" as a railroad terminal.[70] The implication is that courts should protect expectations if they are primary.

These decisions do not always protect a landowner's subjective expectations at the time of purchase. They reject an investment-backed expectations claim if the expectations were not primary, or if the refusal to allow development interfered only with the right to "exploit."[71]

Gil v. Inland Wetlands and Watercourses Agency,[72] a Connecticut case, illustrates the type of cases that protect landowner expectations at the time of purchase.[73] Plaintiff owned a 3.36-acre lot that was almost entirely a wetland in an area zoned for residential use. The trial court held a taking occurred when, after four applications, the town wetland agency denied a permit to build a single-family home. On appeal, the supreme court upheld the trial court's "factbound determination" that the plaintiff had reasonable investment-backed expectations he could build upon the lot. The supreme court also held the plaintiff's purchase was not speculative, even though the lot would be worth 60 percent more than the purchase price if buildable. The court held the discount from market value was a "prudent evaluation" of how to resolve tension between the residential designation and the restriction on wetland development. This holding disregards the regulatory risk imposed by the wetland designation to favor the landowner's expectations based on the residential designation of the property.

The court downplayed the environmental qualities of the wetlands property the plaintiff wanted to develop. It held the landowner's investment-backed expectations were not limited to the natural wetlands status of the land at the time of purchase. After discussing earlier Connecticut cases, the court concluded, "It is evident from these cases that a landowner, who purchased property with a reasonable expectation of residential or commercial development, has suffered a taking if regulatory constraints allow him to use his land only in its natural state without any economically viable alternative use thereof."[74]

The court then held the case was not ripe for decision. It noted other homes in the area were smaller than the home the plaintiff proposed, that he should have applied for a more modest proposal, and that the wetlands status of the property was a warning development would be difficult and repeated applications would be necessary before the agency would give its approval.

Gil is an important case because the property was in a wetlands and subject to wetland permit approval on which opinion would diverge widely at the time of plaintiff's purchase. A court could have held the plaintiff did not have reasonable investment-backed expectations in the development of his land under the regulatory risk theory. The court's willingness to recognize the landowner's expectations despite this risk solves the circularity problem inherent in investment-backed expectations. It favors the landowner's argument that ownership in property is an entitlement that protects against regulatory change.

The presence of other single-family homes in the area may have influenced the *Gil* court's willingness to recognize the landowner's investment-backed expectations. These homes showed that plaintiff's expectation of building a single-family home was reasonable. By holding the case not ripe because plaintiff's home was larger, the court could send the case back with a clear signal that approval of a more modest dwelling would eliminate the takings claim. This holding gave some weight to the warning notice the wetland regulatory program gave the plaintiff.

Other cases applied the "time of purchase" rule to hold a property owner's investment-backed expectations were not frustrated if they arose after the owner purchased the property.[75] In these cases the purchaser could continue uses that existed on the property at the time of purchase, and the courts sometimes noted they were economically viable.[76] In one case,[77] for example, a landowner acquired its property for mining purposes and decided to develop the property as a waste-disposal site much later. The court held a zoning ordinance that prohibited use of the site for waste disposal did not frustrate the owner's investment-backed expectations.

These cases apply the regulatory risk theory to investment-backed expectations by holding a landowner's expectations arise at the time of purchase, when the risk factor affects the purchase decision. Courts do not protect expectations if landowners acquire them later. These cases also are consistent with Supreme Court holdings that only primary expectations are protected, and that investment-backed expectations do not include development that simply makes land more profitable.[78]

D. Actual Notice Cases

Although Justice Scalia rejected the notice rule in *Nollan*,[79] cases since then held that actual notice of a regulatory program defeated an investment-backed expectations claim arising from a denial of development in that program.[80] Landowners may not admit to having actual notice of a regulatory program in these cases, but courts inferred notice from their behavior.[81] For example, a landowner who owns land that includes wetlands may begin development on land outside the wetland area and propose development of the wetlands later.[82] This behavior suggests the landowner knew a law regulating the use of wetlands could prevent him from developing his wetland property.

Plaintiff's prior development experience can also provide a basis for implying actual knowledge. For example, a developer might have prior experience with the dredge-and-fill permit program for wetlands authorized by the Clean Water Act.[83] A court can infer from this experience that the developer knew the land was subject to this program and would not recognize investment-backed expectations if a development he or she proposed in a wetland did not obtain approval.[84]

Injection of an ad hominem disqualifier into a takings law intended to protect property interests may at first appear incorrect; but precedent exists for considering personal behavior as a factor in land-use law. Self-inflicted hardship cannot be the basis for a hardship zoning variance.[85] Nor is a landowner who relies in bad faith on a building permit entitled to a vested right based on substantial construction authorized by that permit.[86]

Denial of investment-backed expectations when an owner has actual notice of a land-use regulation also is consistent with the regulatory risk theory of investment-backed expectations. As noted earlier, investment-backed expectations presumably are part of takings law because landowners require some protection from risk when they enter property markets; but a landowner should assume the risk if he or she knows about it and courts should not afford protection. The reasonableness of investment-backed expectations should depend on the information the landowner has at the time of acquisition. If this information contains knowledge of a regulatory program that may frustrate the landowner's expectations, courts should not protect him or her. Justice Scalia's *Nollan* footnote does not foreclose this interpretation. Scalia held merely that purchase of property alone is not sufficient to foreclose a claim under the takings clause. He did not address the actual notice problem.

E. Constructive Notice Cases

The vast majority of cases reject investment-backed expectations claims when a property owner has constructive notice of a regulatory program.[87] These decisions disregard and undercut Justice Scalia's *Nollan* footnote. They come full circle from cases in which courts recognize landowner expectations at the time of purchase.[88]

A bit of backtracking is helpful here. Scalia's footnote rejected the constructive notice rule adopted in *Ruckelshaus v. Monsanto Co.*[89] The Court did not find a taking in *Monsanto* when a federal law required the disclosure of trade secrets because the company had constructive notice of the law's disclosure requirements. Scalia held that purchase, alone, is not enough to foreclose a claim that a land-use regulation is a taking. Cases after *Monsanto* but before *Nollan* applied the *Monsanto* constructive notice rule to deny recognition of investment-backed expectations in land-use takings cases.[90] Scalia did not cite these cases when he held the *Monsanto* rule did not apply to land-use takings. His clear rejection of the dissent's argument, that the coastal regulatory program gave constructive notice that limited plaintiffs' investment-backed expectations, suggests he does not agree with them.

Since the *Nollan* footnote, the Supreme Court and many lower federal and state courts applied *Monsanto*'s constructive notice rule to reject takings claims in cases when land use was not an issue.[91] Some, but not all, of these cases resembled *Monsanto* because the courts found the plaintiff had constructive notice of conditions attached to a government benefit. In other cases, the courts found a plaintiff had constructive notice of a regulation carrying out safety or similar concerns in which the public interest was especially critical. Because the takings claim in these cases challenged a regulatory program, the courts could not base constructive notice on a waiver inherent in an application for government benefits. These cases weaken Justice Scalia's rejection of the constructive notice rule in *Nollan* as applied to land-use regulation, unless land-use regulation somehow is different from other regulatory programs.

A few land-use takings decisions did not apply the constructive notice rule to defeat investment-backed expectations. The courts did not provide a detailed explanation of their holdings and did not mention the

Scalia footnote.[92] Most land-use cases applied the constructive notice rule to defeat a takings claim based on a landowner's investment-backed expectations.[93] These cases cover a wide range of land-use regulations, including zoning, sign, subdivision, and wetlands regulations. Again, none of these cases mentions the Scalia footnote in *Nollan,* and most do not provide detailed explanations for their holdings.

The cases sometimes isolate factors, such as the character of an area, that put a landowner on constructive notice that a regulatory program applied to the land or that government might adopt such a program. In one case, for example, the land was located in a vast area where population was increasing. The court held the plaintiff should have been on notice that government might adopt regulations to manage growth in this area.[94] Other cases that found constructive notice emphasized the plaintiff paid a discounted price for land because it was subject to regulatory controls.[95] In many of these cases the regulation served important environmental values, such as the protection of wetlands.

A case upholding an ordinance that restricted development in a coastal dune area, *McNulty v. Town of Indialantic,*[96] provides a good explanation of the constructive notice rule. The court held a beach-setback ordinance that prohibited plaintiff from constructing a single-family home was not a taking. At the time plaintiff purchased his lot the town had not adopted the beach-setback ordinance, but the town's zoning ordinance required the town's permission to develop land in the beach area. Holding that the plaintiff had constructive notice of the beach-setback ordinance even though the town adopted it after the plaintiff's purchase, the court stated, "The reasonableness of . . . [plaintiff's] expectation is undermined by the fact that the land has been subject to land-use regulation since its purchase, and those regulations are subject to change from time to time as circumstances change."[97]

The court noted that the town could not know the "effect storms, construction and erosion would have on the beach, the value of the dune system, and how it would be undermined."[98] The state had adopted strong regulations to protect the dune system and "Indialantic properly may change its land-use regulations to address these concerns."[99] The price plaintiff paid for the lot was another factor in the court's decision. Plaintiff purchased his lot for 95 percent less than the prices paid for similar residential lots in the neighborhood. This difference, the court said, should have alerted him that he could not use his lot for all the uses allowed on complying lots.

McNulty is consistent with the regulatory risk theory. Although the town had not adopted the prohibition on development in the setback area when plaintiff purchased his property, it was possible that the town later would adopt such a prohibition. Opinion at the time of purchase would have diverged widely on whether the town would adopt a prohibition. In these circumstances, McNulty took the risk the town would later adopt a development prohibition in the setback ordinance. The court was correct in refusing to recognize his expectations.

Many cases in which courts applied the constructive notice rule to reject a landowner's investment-backed expectations claim were cases, like *McNulty,* in which government applied environmental regulations to reject development. It is in just these cases that opinions about regulatory risk are likely to diverge widely. Many will believe government will apply its regulations to prohibit development. Others will believe government will eventually change its mind and allow development. To put it another way, there is an implied public interest limitation that government may regulate sensitive environmental resources in the public interest without facing takings claims.

Other cases applied the constructive notice rule when landowners made takings claims against subdivision control, sign, and zoning regulations. Although these were not cases in which the location of land in environmental resource areas made development approval uncertain, comparable risks were present. Subdivision control ordinances require agency approval of a subdivision application. A court could conclude that uncertainties concerning approval create a regulatory risk that should give landowners constructive notice and defeat investment-backed expectations.

In sign control and zoning cases, the ordinance often prohibited the use the landowner contemplated. A change in the regulations or favorable action on a development proposal was necessary before development could proceed. Uncertainties concerning these changes again created regulatory risk that put landowners on notice and defeated investment-backed expectations.

V. Conclusion

No problem is more intractable in land-use law than defining the boundaries of regulation protected from attack under the takings clause. Investment-backed expectations play an important role in applying the takings clause to land-use regulations; courts must decide whether a landowner's investment-backed expectations were frustrated when the courts apply *Penn Central*'s balancing test to takings claims.

Despite the importance of investment-backed expectations in takings law, the Supreme Court has not clarified the meaning of this term, and lower federal and state courts divide on how it should apply. Some courts have given up. They effectively eliminate investment-backed expectations from takings law by holding expectations are frustrated only when a land-use regulation denies all economically viable use of the land.

If investment-backed expectations are to play a role in takings cases, courts must resolve the inherent ambiguities and develop a clear idea of the meaning of the term. The regulatory risk theory proposed in this article makes investment-backed expectations depend on the risks landowners take when they enter property markets. Divergence in opinion about regulatory uncertainty determines the degree of risk that is present. Courts should recognize landowner expectations when risks are minimal. They should refuse to recognize landowner expectations when risks are high.

No monolithic unitary theory supports this view of the role of investment-backed expectations in takings law. It reflects a pragmatic judgment about the property interests that courts decide are worth protecting under the takings clause. Nothing else is possible.

Notes

I would like to thank Jennifer Cook, Frances Foster, Jeffrey Frieden, Richard Lazarus, Peggy McDermott, and C. Ford Runge for their assistance with this article. This article is reprinted with permission from *The Urban Lawyer,* 27 URB. LAW. 215 (1995).

1. 438 U.S. 104 (1978).

2. For discussion of investment-backed expectations as a factor in takings law, see the following sources in addition to articles cited later in this article: Jack M. Beermann, *Government Official Torts and the Takings Clause: Federalism and State Sovereign Immunity,* 68 B.U. L. REV. 277 (1988); William A. Fischel & Perry Shapiro, *Takings, Insurance and Michelman: Comments on Economic Interpretations of "Just Compensation" Law,* 17 J. LEGAL STUD. 269 (1988); Ruddick C. Lawrence, *Bright Lines in the Big City: Seawall, Tenant Succession Right, and the Jurisprudence of Takings,* 91 COLUM. L. REV. 609 (1991); Andrea L. Peterson, *The Takings Clause: In Search of Underlying Principles Part I—A Critique of Current Takings Clause Doctrine,* 77 CAL. L. REV. 1301 (1989); Craig A. Peterson, *Land Use Regulatory "Takings" Revisited: The New Supreme Court Approaches,* 39 HASTINGS L.J. 335 (1988); Joseph L. Sax, *Property Rights and the Economy of Nature: Understanding* Lucas v. South Carolina Coastal Council, 45 STAN. L. REV. 1433 (1993).

3. This article updates an earlier one on investment-backed expectations published just before the Supreme Court decided, in 1987, three major takings cases known as the takings trilogy. Daniel R. Mandelker, *Investment-Backed Expectations: Is There a Taking?,* 31 J. URB. & CONTEMP. L. 3 (1987) [hereinafter *Expectations*].

4. 438 U.S. 104 (1978).

5. *Penn Central*, 438 U.S. at 124.

6. Courts need to consider investment-backed expectations only in "as applied" takings cases in which factual analysis is necessary. *See* Seawall Assocs. v. City of New York, 542 N.E.2d 1059, 1066 n.6 (N.Y.) *cert. denied*, 493 U.S. 976 (1989).

7. 260 U.S. 393 (1922). Justice Brennan also relied on an article by Professor Frank Michelman. *See* Frank Michelman, *Property, Utility and Fairness: Comments on the Ethical Foundations of "Just Compensation" Law*, 80 HARV. L. REV. 1165 (1967), discussed in *Expectations, supra* note 3, at 10-13.

8. *Penn Central*, 438 U.S. at 127.

9. *Id.* at 130.

10. *Id.*

11. *Id.* at 136.

12. Justice Brennan did not state whether a landowner's primary expectations are determined at the time he or she purchases the land or at some later date. In *Penn Central*, the reliance on the use of the property as a terminal to defeat the taking claim suggests Brennan may have meant the primary expectation at the date of purchase is decisive.

13. *See also* Kirby Forest Indus. v. United States, 467 U.S. 1 (1987) (eminent domain case holding expectations frustrated when regulatory burdens "substantial and unforeseeable"). *Kirby* indicates that one of the reasons for introducing investment-backed expectations as a factor in takings cases is to protect against arbitrary change in regulations.

14. 444 U.S. 51 (1979). *But see infra* text accompanying note 45.

15. *Andrus*, 444 U.S. at 66.

16. 444 U.S. 164 (1979).

17. *But see* PruneYard Shopping Center v. Robins, 447 U.S. 54 (1980) (right to exclude students distributing political literature from shopping center not protected under takings clause).

18. 467 U.S. 986 (1984).

19. *See, e.g.*, Furey v. City of Sacramento, 592 F. Supp. 463 (E.D. Cal. 1984), *aff'd on other grounds*, 780 F.2d 1448 (9th Cir. 1986); Sucesion Suarez v. Gelabert, 541 F. Supp. 1243 (D.P.R. 1982), *aff'd*, 701 F.2d 231 (1st Cir. 1993).

20. The Court first adopted this rule in Agins v. City of Tiburon, 447 U.S. 255 (1980), a land-use takings case, but the rule did not receive much judicial attention until the Court restated it in the trilogy cases.

21. 480 U.S. 470 (1987).

22. *Keystone*, 480 U.S. at 484 (quoting Agins v. City of Tiburon, 447 U.S. 255, 260 (1980)).

23. 483 U.S. 825 (1987).

24. *Nollan*, 483 U.S. at 834. The Court presumably meant these interests are facially legitimate. A land-use regulation also must "substantially advance" a legitimate interest as applied to a particular property.

25. This holding reaffirms the clear implication in *Penn Central* that a mere diminution in value is not enough, standing alone, to serve as the basis for a taking.

26. 260 U.S. 393 (1922).

27. *Pennsylvania Coal*, 260 U.S. at 499.

28. *See, e.g.*, Loveladies Harbor, Inc. v. United States, 28 F.3d 1171 (Fed. Cir. 1994).

29. 483 U.S. 825 (1987).

30. *Nollan*, 483 U.S. at 860.

31. *Id.* at 833 n.2.

32. *Id.*

33. *Id.* The Court added that "[s]o long as the Commission could not have deprived the prior owners of the easement without compensating them, the prior owners must be understood to have transferred their full property rights to conveying the lot."

34. 112 S. Ct. 2326 (1992).

35. *Nordlinger*, 112 S. Ct. at 2333.

36. *Id.* The Court stated, "A new owner has full information about the scope of future tax liability before acquiring the property, and if he thinks the future tax burden is too demanding, he can decide not to complete the purchase at all." The same observation applies to a landowner who purchases land with notice that a land-use regulation that might frustrate his development expectations covers the property.

37. The majority rule is that an increase in a general ad valorem real estate tax is not a taking of property. *See, e.g.*, Superior Oil Co. v. City of Port Arthur, 628 S.W.2d 94 (Tex. Ct. App. 1981), *appeal dismissed*, 459 U.S. 802 (1982).

38. *See also* Concrete Pipe & Prods. v. Constr. Laborers Pension Trust, 113 S. Ct. 2264 (1993). The Court held the company's collective bargaining agreement did not protect it from an amendment to a federal statute requiring an increase in pension liabilities. Applying earlier decisions (*see* Connolly v. Pension Benefit Guar. Corp., 475 U.S. 211 (1986)), the Court noted that pensions had been regulated for a long time, and held that anyone who does business in a regulated field cannot object to statutory change.

Concrete Pipe is consistent with the holding in *Nollan* that the notice rule still applies in cases that do not raise land-use takings issues. However, it is difficult to reconcile *Concrete Pipe* with the *Nollan* dictum that the notice rule applies only when an applicant requests a governmental benefit. The statute in *Concrete Pipe* did not confer a benefit unless the "benefit" of regulation qualifies.

39. 112 S. Ct. 2886 (1992).

40. After briefing and oral argument in the state court, but before that court's decision, the legislature authorized the council to grant special permits for dwellings subject to the act's restrictions.

41. *Lucas*, 112 S. Ct. at 2893.

42. Loretto v. Teleprompter Manhattan CATV Corp., 458 U.S. 419 (1982) (permanent physical occupation by private entity held per se taking when authorized by statute).

43. *Lucas*, 112 S. Ct. at 2893.

44. *See* Loretto v. Teleprompter Manhattan CATV Corp., 458 U.S. 419 (1982) (investment-backed expectations do not apply to taking per se by physi-

cal occupation when statute authorized cable television company to install cable lines and box on roof of apartment building without compensation); Bowles v. United States, 31 Fed. Cl. 37 (1994) (same holding, when there is a taking per se under *Lucas*).

45. *Lucas,* 112 S. Ct. at 2899-900.

46. *Id.* at 2899.

47. *Id.*

48. *Id.* (quoting *Pennsylvania Coal,* 260 U.S. at 413).

49. *See* Hunziker v. State, 519 N.W.2d 367 (Iowa 1994) (statutory restrictions on development in Indian burial-mound area inhere in title as required by *Lucas* and defeat taking claim). *See also* Bernardsville Quarry, Inc. v. Borough of Bernardsville, 608 A.2d 1377 (N.J. 1992) (no taking because landowner had notice of land-use regulation; quoted *Lucas* language that landowners should expect regulation of their property).

50. *Lucas,* 112 S. Ct. at 2894 n.7.

51. This statement applies to land that is inherited or acquired through gift as well as purchased. Even if no consideration is paid, the land become part of an owner's asset base and regulations controlling its use affect the owner's economic status.

52. A. Dan Tarlock, *Local Government Protection of Biodiversity: What Is its Niche?* 60 U. CHI. L. REV. 555, 588 (1993).

53. United States v. Rands, 389 U.S. 121 (1967). *See also* United States v. Willow River Power Co., 324 U.S. 499 (1945).

54. Tarlock, *supra* note 52, at 519. *See also* Carol M. Rose, *Mahon Reconstructed: Why the Takings Issue Is Still a Muddle,* 57 S. CAL. L. REV. 561 (1984).

55. *See, e.g.,* Richard A. Epstein, Lucas v. South Carolina Coastal Council: *A Tangled Web of Expectations,* 45 STAN. L. REV. 1369 (1993).

56. *See, e.g.,* Michael D. Dorum, *Takings Claims Involving Pre-Condemnation Land-Use Planning: A Proposal for Means-Ends Analysis,* 43 RUTGERS L. REV. 457, 489 (1991); Richard G. Wilkins, *The Takings Clause: A Modern Plot for an Old Constitutional Tale,* 64 NOTRE DAME L. REV. 1, 39 (1989).

57. Constitutional discipline to remedy this problem also exists outside the takings clause. Excessively stringent regulation may be arbitrary and subject to attack as a substantive due process violation. The presence of regulatory risk does not prevent a similar claim under the takings clause that a land-use regulation does not substantially advance a legitimate governmental interest.

58. *See* Minch v. City of Fargo (I), 297 N.W.2d 785 (N.D. 1980), *cert. denied,* 464 U.S. 829 (1983).

59. *See infra* text accompanying note 86.

60. Courts may also find investment-backed expectations when there is an interference with the right to exclude. Golden Gate Hotel Ass'n v. City & County of San Francisco, 836 F. Supp. 707 (N.D. Cal. 1993) (ordinance limiting conversion of hotels denied investment-backed expectations because it interfered with right to "to use, possess, and exclude"). *See supra* text accompanying note 16 (discussing Supreme Court's *Kaiser Aetna* decision).

61. Pace Resources v. Shrewsbury Twp., 808 F.2d 1023, 1033 (3d Cir. 1987); Finch v. City of Durham, 384 S.E.2d 8 (N.C. 1989) (vested right not found); Presbytery of Seattle v. King County, 787 P.2d 907, 915 n.29 (Wash.), *cert. denied*, 498 U.S. 911 (1990); Tekoa Construction, Inc. v. City of Seattle, 781 P.2d 1324 (Wash. Ct. App. 1989), *review denied*, 788 P.2d 1079 (Wash. 1990) (vested right not found). *But see* Midnight Sessions, Ltd. v. City of Philadelphia, 945 F.2d 667 (3d Cir. 1991) (downplaying importance of investment).

62. Resolution Trust Corp. v. Town of Highland Beach, 18 F.3d 536 (11th Cir. 1994); County of Kauai v. Pacific Standard Life Ins. Co., 653 P.2d 766 (Haw. 1982). *See also* Hoffman v. City of Town and Country, 831 S.W.2d 223 (Mo. Ct. App. 1992) (recognizing investment-backed expectations, city official indicated support of landowner proposal).

63. *See, e.g.*, Seattle v. King County, 787 P.2d 907, 915 n.29 (Wash.), *cert. denied*, 498 U.S. 911 (1990).

64. *See* Florida Rock Indus. v. United States (IV), 18 F.3d 1560 (Fed. Cir. 1994) (arbitrary action by government interferes with investment-backed expectations).

65. 808 F.2d 1023 (3d Cir. 1987).

66. *Penn Central*, 438 U.S. at 127, *quoted in* Pace, 808 F.2d at 1033.

67. *Pace*, 808 F.2d at 1033.

68. *See* Midnight Sessions, Ltd. v. City of Philadelphia, 945 F.2d 667 (3d Cir. 1991); Elsmere Park Club L.P. v. Town of Elsmere, 771 F. Supp. 646 (D. Del. 1991); Offen v. County Council for Prince George's County, 625 A.2d 424 (Md. Ct. Spec. App. 1993) (extensively reviewing and approving *Pace*), *rev'd and remanded on other grounds*, 639 A.2d 1070 (Md. 1994).

69. *See* Martin v. United States, 30 Fed. Cl. 542 (1994); O'Connor v. Corps of Engineers, 801 F. Supp. 185 (N.D. Ind. 1992); Fitzgarrald v. Iowa City, 492 N.W.2d 659 (Iowa 1992), *cert. denied*, 113 S. Ct. 2343 (1993); Moroney v. Mayor & Council of Borough of Old Tappan, 633 A.2d 1045 (N.J. Super. Ct. App. Div. 1993), *cert. denied*, 640 A.2d 851, 642 A.2d 1004 (N.J. 1994). *See also* Formanek v. United States, 26 Cl. Ct. 332 (1992) (dramatic reduction in value along with interference with investment-backed expectations held a taking).

70. *Penn Central*, 438 U.S. at 136.

71. Long Beach Equities, Inc. v. Superior Court of Ventura County, 282 Cal. Rptr. 877 (Cal. Ct. App. 1991) (orderly development guidelines delayed development of land). *Accord* MacLeod v. County of Santa Clara, 749 F.2d 541 (9th Cir. 1984) (denial of right to harvest timber), *cert. denied*, 472 U.S. 1009 (1985); Flynn v. City of Cambridge, 418 N.E.2d 335 (Mass. 1981) (ordinance prohibiting condominium owner from evicting tenants so owner could take possession). *See also* B.W. Parkway Assocs. L.P. v. United States, 29 Fed. Cl. 669 (1993) (no showing that developer could have completed development or found tenants); Mock v. Dep't of Envtl. Resources, 623 A.2d 940 (Pa. Commw. Ct. 1993) (could put property to alternative use).

72. 593 A.2d 1368 (Conn. 1991).

73. *See also* 1902 Atlantic, Ltd. v. United States, 26 Cl. Ct. 575 (1992) (denial

of wetlands permit frustrated landowner's expectations because it purchased property for development, but delay until permit denial reversed not a taking).

74. *Gil*, 593 A.2d at 1373-74.

75. Indiana Dep't of Natural Resources v. Indiana Coal Council, Inc., 542 N.E.2d 1000 (Ind. 1989), *cert. denied*, 493 U.S. 1078 (1990); Iowa Coal Mining Co., Inc. v. Monroe County, 494 N.W.2d 664 (Iowa), *cert. denied*, 113 S. Ct. 2415 (1993); Bernardsville Quarry, Inc., v. Borough of Bernardsville, 608 A.2d 1377 (1992).

76. *See also* Vatalaro v. Dep't of Envtl. Regulation, 601 So. 2d 1223 (Fla. Dist. Ct. App.), *review denied*, 613 So. 2d 3 (Fla. 1992). In holding a denial of a wetlands permit was a taking, the court distinguished permit denials from cases in which a landowner is denied a change in zoning. It indicated a landowner has protected investment-backed expectations in the permit denial but not in the zoning denial case. In the zoning denial case, the court held, property is not taken because the landowner still has whatever land use the zoning ordinance allowed before the denial.

77. Iowa Coal Mining Co., Inc. v. Monroe County, 494 N.W.2d 664 (Iowa), *cert. denied*, 113 S. Ct. 2415 (1993).

78. *See supra* text accompanying notes 14-15.

79. *See supra* text accompanying notes 29-33.

80. Nello L. Teer Co. v. Orange County, 810 F. Supp. 679 (M.D.N.C. 1992) (moratorium), *aff'd & rev'd in part without opinion*, 993 F.2d 1538 (4th Cir. 1993), reported in full, No. 92-2270, 1993 U.S. App. LEXIS 12525 (4th Cir. May 26, 1993); Naegele Outdoor Advertising, Inc. v. City of Durham, 803 F. Supp. 1068 (M.D.N.C. 1992) (billboard controls), *aff'd without opinion*, 19 F.3d 11 (4th Cir. N.C. 1994), reported in full, No. 92-2321, 1994 U.S. App. LEXIS 3531 (4th Cir. March 1, 1994); Mid-Gulf, Inc. v. Bishop, 792 F. Supp. 1205 (D. Kan. 1992) (oil drilling regulations); Ciampitti v. United States, 22 Cl. Ct. 310 (1991) (wetlands); National Advertising Co. v. Village of Downers Grove, 561 N.E.2d 1300 (Ill. App. Ct. 1990) (sign regulations), *appeal denied*, 567 N.E.2d 333 (Ill.), and *cert. denied*, 501 U.S. 1261 (1991); Parranto Bros., Inc. v. City of New Brighton, 425 N.W.2d 585 (Minn. Ct. App. 1988) (downzoning); Kelly v. Tahoe Regional Planning Agency, 855 P.2d 1027 (Nev. 1993) (denial of development plans); Finch v. City of Durham, 384 S.E.2d 8 (N.C. 1989) (downzoning). *See also* Loveladies Harbor, Inc. v. United States, 28 F.3d 1171 (Fed. Cir. 1994) (owner who bought with knowledge of restraint has no reliance interest and assumed risk of any economic loss).

81. The line between actual and constructive knowledge often is difficult to draw. A landowner seldom will admit he or she knew a regulatory program existed under which government might deny permission for development. A court will then have to infer actual notice from circumstances. It could find, for example, that a landowner had actual knowledge of a wetlands program because he or she knew the land was located in a wetlands. These facts also could support a finding of constructive notice.

If a wide divergence of opinion about development opportunities exists in a land market because of regulatory uncertainty, a landowner who enters that market will likely know this uncertainty is created by an existing regulatory program or one that might be adopted later. If a court is unwilling to find actual notice on these facts, it can hold the landowner has constructive notice.

82. Ciampitti v. United States, 22 Cl. Ct. 310 (1991).

83. *Id.*

84. Other regulatory programs may require landowners who sell property to give notice to buyers of land that the regulatory requirements of the program apply. *See, e.g.,* FLA. STAT. ANN. § 161.57(2) (West 1990) (state coastal management law).

85. DANIEL R. MANDELKER, LAND USE LAW, § 6.18.

86. *Id.* at § 6.18.

Denying investment-backed expectations because of personal notice also is consistent with Professor Michelman's speculator exception to the investment-backed expectations takings factor. Michelman, *supra* note 7, at 1238. Professor Michelman based this exception on what appear to be fairness concerns. A buyer will discount the price he or she pays for land to take into account the possibility that government will disapprove development. If government rejects the development later, the buyer got only what he or she meant to buy, society has not imposed a redistribution, and a taking has not occurred. See *Expectations, supra* note 3, at 12.

87. The constructive notice rule does not require government rejection of a landowner's development proposal. All that is required is a regulatory program under which rejection can occur.

88. The Iowa Supreme Court took a similar position in applying the *Lucas* holding that property rights limitations inherent in title to land determine property rights. In Hunziker v. State, 519 N.W.2d 367 (Iowa 1994), a state statute prohibited plaintiffs from developing their land as a subdivision because an Indian burial mound was on the site. The statute prohibited disinterment of the mound and required a buffer zone around it to insure its protection. Because the law was in effect ten to twelve years before the purchase of the land, the court held plaintiffs took title to the land subject to the statutory prohibition.

This holding is problematic, although it is based on language in the *Lucas* decision. *See supra* text accompanying notes 46-49. It is not clear that *Lucas* meant a regulation under attack as a taking could define land rights in a way that limits a landowner's takings claim.

89. 467 U.S. 986 (1984), discussed in *supra* text accompanying notes 18-19.

90. *See, e.g.,* Furey v. City of Sacramento, 592 F. Supp. 463 (E.D. Cal. 1984), *aff'd on other grounds,* 780 F. 2d 1448 (9th Cir. 1986); Graham v. Estuary Props., Inc., 399 So. 2d 1374 (Fla.), *cert. denied,* 454 U.S. 1083 (1981); Claridge v. New Hampshire Wetlands Bd., 485 A.2d 287 (N.H. 1984). *See also Expectations, supra* note 3, at 29 nn. 110, 111.

91. *See, e.g.,* Concrete Pipe & Prods. v. Construction Laborers Pension Trust, 113 S. Ct. 2264 (1993) (pensions); Golden Pacific Bancorp v. United States, 15 F.3d 1066 (Fed. Cir. 1994) (no reasonable expectation that federal agency would not take over insolvent bank); Atlas Corp. v. United States, 895 F.2d 745 (Fed. Cir. 1990) (statute required uranium producers to take costly action to decontaminate production sites and stabilize residue from uranium production

that was potentially hazardous to public health); Barrick Gold Exploration, Inc. v. Hudson, 823 F. Supp. 1395 (S.D. Ohio 1993) (retiree health benefits); B & F Trawlers, Inc. v. United States, 27 Cl. Ct. 299 (1992) (danger to navigation); State of Alaska Dep't of Natural Resources v. Arctic Slope Regional Corp., 834 P.2d 134 (Alaska 1991) (requirement that oil driller submit well data).

92. Carpenter v. Tahoe Regional Planning Agency, 804 F. Supp. 1316 (D. Nev. 1992) ("the court does not accept the analogy to regulated markets"); Bowles v. United States (II), 31 Fed. Cl. 37 (1994) (plaintiff did not have notice of regulation and reasonable investor would not have had notice); Lopes v. City of Peabody, 629 N.E.2d 1312 (Mass. 1994) (wetlands case; notes purchase does not defeat takings claim but does not mention investment-backed expectations as takings factor). *See also* Vatalaro v. Dep't of Envtl. Regulation, 601 So. 2d 1223 (Fla. Dist. Ct. App.) (constructive notice rule does not apply to wetlands permit denial though may apply to zoning), *review denied*, 613 So. 2d 3 (Fla. 1992).

93. Midnight Sessions, Ltd. v. City of Philadelphia, 945 F.2d 667 (3d Cir. 1991) (dance hall license; investment-backed expectations reasonable only if consider power of state to regulate in public interest); *Nello L. Teer Co.*, 810 F. Supp. at 688 ("sophisticated" construction company must be deemed to have knowledge "that local governments may adopt or amend zoning regulations at any time"); Naegele Outdoor Advertising, Inc. v. City of Durham, 803 F. Supp. 1068 (M.D.N.C. 1992) (sign regulation; reasonable property owner must expect use of property may be restricted from time to time by state in legitimate exercise of police power), *aff'd without opinion*, 19 F.3d 11 (4th Cir. 1994), reported in full, No. 92-2321, 1994 U.S. App. LEXIS 3531 (4th Cir. March 1, 1994); Elias v. Town of Brookhaven, 783 F. Supp. 758 (E.D.N.Y. 1992) (downzoning); McNulty v. Town of Indialantic, 727 F. Supp. 604 (M.D. Fla. 1989) (coastal setback); Parranto Brothers, Inc., v. City of New Brighton, 425 N.W.2d 585 (Minn. Ct. App. 1988) (downzoning); White v. City of Brentwood, 799 S.W.2d 890 (Mo. Ct. App. 1990) (zoning); Elam v. City of St. Ann, 784 S.W.2d 330 (Mo. Ct. App. 1990) (same); Gazza v. New York State Dep't of Envtl. Protection, 605 N.Y.S.2d 642 (Sup. Ct. 1993) (wetlands; landowner "factored" regulatory limitations into purchase of property by paying reduced price); Weichert AD&P Inc. v. Dep't of Transp., 631 A.2d 1106 (Pa. Commw. Ct. 1993) (state Outdoor Advertising Control Act); Mock v. Department of Envtl. Resources, 623 A.2d 940 (Pa. Commw. Ct. 1993) (wetland held to be riparian land subject to regulation for centuries); Orion Corp. v. State of Washington, 747 P.2d 1062 (Wash. 1987) (dredge-and-fill project subject to public trust), *cert. denied,* 486 U.S. 1022 (1988). *See also* Southview Assocs. Ltd., v. Bongartz, 980 F.2d 84, 107 (2d Cir. 1992) (dictum, landowner "could not have reasonably expected" to proceed with development without review under state environmental act), *cert. denied,* 113 S. Ct. 1586 (1993); Dodd v. Hood River County, 855 P.2d 608 (Ore. 1993) (forest zone; notes court has never recognized investment-backed expectations under state constitution's taking clause).

94. Elias v. Town of Brookhaven, 783 F. Supp. 758 (E.D.N.Y. 1992).

95. Gazza v. New York State Dep't of Envtl. Protection, 605 N.Y.S.2d 652 (Sup. Ct. 1993). Relying on a discounted price paid for land as an indicator of

constructive notice may not be reliable. Landowners may overpay for land knowing they have a chance at compensation if their expectations for development of the land are not realized. *See supra* text accompanying note 65.

96. 727 F. Supp. 604 (M.D. Fla. 1989).

97. *Id.* at 612. Plaintiff also had relied on a change in the zoning that placed his land in a tourist zone four years after he purchased it, but the court held plaintiff could not have it both ways: "By relying on the Tourist designation, therefore, McNulty relies on subsequent change in zoning and is heard to complain of later changes." *Id.*

98. *Id.*

99. *Id.* The court also relied on an extended application of the "reciprocity of advantage" principle, holding "the burdens imposed on an individual in a regulated environment are often simply the cost of 'living and doing business in a civilized community.' " *Id.* (quoting Andrus v. Allard 444 U.S. 51, 67 (1979)).

CHAPTER ❖ 7

Lucas v. South Carolina Coastal Council: Yes, Virginia, There Can Be Partial Takings

Michael M. Berger

One of the most tantalizing things about the Supreme Court's decision in *Lucas* three years ago was the suggestion that the Court was prepared to consider a regulatory taking of substantially less than all of the subject property.[1]

In footnote 7,[2] the Court not only apologized for the lack of "precision" in its "economically viable use" formulation, but also took on the "unit of property" or "parcel as a whole" analysis which had been spawned a decade and a half earlier in *Penn Central Transportation Co. v. City of New York.*[3] In *Penn Central,* the owner of Grand Central Terminal conceded that the use of the property as a railroad station was yielding a reasonable return on investment and the city's landmarks law had not interfered with that. Thus, in upholding denial of plans to cantilever a large office building over the terminal, the Court rejected the notion of considering the development rights in the airspace separate from those lower down. The unit of property to be evaluated was the entire ownership.

Evidently concerned about some practices which had taken place since the 1978 decision in *Penn Central,* the Court took the opportunity in footnote 7 of *Lucas* to try to clamp some limits on how to determine what constitutes the unit of property being examined. Purporting to do no more than sketch the boundaries of the idea, the opinion notes one example that it says is beyond the pale: the decision of the New York Court of Appeals in *Penn Central.* There, rather than merely uniting the terminal and its superadjacent air rights, as the Supreme Court did, to determine the unit of property being regulated, New York's court examined *all* of the property owner's real estate holdings in the vicinity.

Then, by analyzing the impact on that substantial collection of property, the New York court concluded that no taking had occurred. That sort of assemblage, says *Lucas*, is "extreme—and we think unsupportable."[4]

Adverting to a more ordinary situation, the Court posed the question of how to analyze a case in which a developer was required to leave 90 percent of a rural tract in its natural state. Would that be analyzed as depriving the owner of 90 percent of the total, or of 100 percent of the burdened portion? The question is hardly an idle one. As the Court was undoubtedly aware, it is a rare regulation that operates to stultify completely 100 percent of the ability to use land.[5] If regulatory takings are now examined by looking at the property restricted, without adding to the formula the portion of the property still available for use, then regulatory takings cases will change dramatically.

Before *Lucas,* for example, we would tend to analyze a property owner's plight by asking what the regulation had left him with. That was in line with the typical formulation that there was no taking unless the regulation denied the property owner economically viable use. Thus, regardless of the magnitude of the impact of, for example, a severe downzoning, if what remained was still economically viable, no taking would be found. However, if the focus of the inquiry shifts to the owner's expectations for use when the property was acquired and the extent of the regulation's impact on those expectations, then the stage has been set for a dramatic shift in results.

The question addressed here is whether anything has changed in the last two years.

I. Prescience on the Pacific Coast

But first, some note ought to be made of the fact that the Washington Supreme Court arrived at the *Lucas* footnote 7 position four years ahead of schedule in *Allingham v. Seattle.*[6] *Allingham* dealt with Seattle's greenbelt zoning ordinance. In an oversimplified nutshell, that ordinance required developers of residential lots greater than 5,000 square feet to leave 50 percent of the area of each lot in natural vegetation and to replant an additional 20 percent.

The *Allingham* opinion makes short, clear shrift of the case, easily concluding that the ordinance effected a taking and declaring the ordinance invalid:

> We find . . . that the ordinance deprives certain landowners of all profitable use of a substantial portion of their land. Under the ordinance, 50 to 70 percent of certain lots must be preserved in or re-

> turned to a natural state. The owner of a lot located within a greenbelt zone cannot make any profitable use of that portion of his land required to be reserved under the ordinance. . . . Although he still holds title to the property reserved as greenbelt land, he is denied the control over his property typically accorded landowners. We deem this to be a taking.[7]

The court wasted little time on the city's argument that the ordinance restricted "only" 70 percent of the lot, leaving the owner with the unfettered use of the remaining 30 percent:

> We find this argument unpersuasive. If the City were to take a portion of certain properties for the purpose of building a road, clearly we would hold that the City must pay for the land so taken. Likewise where, as here, the City takes a portion of certain properties for the purpose of preserving greenbelts, the City must pay for the land taken. To permit the City to accomplish the same purpose under the guise of a zoning regulation would be inequitable and would constitute an unconstitutional taking of private property without just compensation.[8]

Allingham thus thrust Washington into a leadership role by arriving at the *Lucas* Court's analysis of partial takings (that is the taking of all use of part of the property) before anyone else. Unfortunately, the Washington Supreme Court apparently did not feel comfortable in that role and overruled *Allingham* a scant two years after its birth.[9] Pity. If the Washington Supreme Court could have waited another two years, it would have seen its *Allingham* analysis vindicated in *Lucas*.

II. The Federal Circuit Heats Things Up

A. *Florida Rock*—One More Time

Sometimes good litigation, like fine wine, needs to be aged. This is not a concept to take to extremes, however, lest someone like Charles Dickens write a bleak, turgid tome about it. The Court of Appeals for the Federal Circuit has been nurturing two cases for quite a number of years. Each began before the decision in *Lucas,* and each involved facts which could invoke the footnote 7 idea of a partial regulatory taking. Each opinion reanalyzed the trial court's conclusions in light of the intervening *Lucas* decision.

Thus far, there have been four published opinions in the *Florida Rock* saga.[10] The question in the case is whether a Fifth Amendment taking occurred of 98 acres of a 1,560-acre tract of land because the 98 acres diminished in value after the U.S. Army Corps of Engineers denied the property owners a permit to mine limestone.

Astute followers of takings law will have noted several issues in that statement of the question: first, whether there can be a regulatory taking of less than an entire parcel of land; second, whether there can be a regulatory taking of less than all the value of the property; and third, whether a case is ripe for litigation after only a single permit denial.

This is not a mystery novel, so I will cut to the chase and spare you the suspense. In light of each of those factors, the decade-long litigational epic of *Florida Rock* has reached the point of holding that a partial regulatory taking of the 98 acres may have occurred even though the property may be worth $4,000 per acre after denial of the permit. The case has been remanded once again so the trial court can redetermine the remaining value and decide whether reducing the value that far is a taking. The case is being highlighted here because of the importance of the Federal Circuit's recent analysis. We will get to that after a brief review of the factual and procedural setting.

Florida Rock Industries bought its 1,560 acres of wetlands in a rural part of Dade County, Florida (west of Miami), in 1972. Its purpose was to mine the limestone deposits on the property. After purchase, Congress passed the Clean Water Act. Still later, the Corps of Engineers adopted regulations to effectuate that act. The Corps required a permit from anyone seeking to dredge or fill wetlands. The property owner's effort to apply for a permit for the entire property was thwarted by the Corps, which would not accept a permit application for more than three years' worth of mining activity—thus, the application for only a 98-acre parcel. In 1980, to guard against loss of valuable wetlands and the danger of creating turbidity in the water the application was denied.

Remember one of your old professors describing how medieval writmongers would "waive the tort and sue in assumpsit" (whatever that meant)? Well, something similar occurred here. The property owner declined the opportunity to sue in U.S. district court to challenge the validity of the Corps's permit denial. Instead, suit was filed in the U.S. Claims Court, accepting the validity of the governmental action, but charging that the consequence was a taking which required compensation. (Prescient choice.) The Supreme Court recently held that a district court suit challenging the permit denial would have barred a suit for compensation.[11]

In "*Rocky I*," the claims court held that the Corps had taken the 98 acres. The court found that the only economically viable use of the property was for limestone mining. The court further found that, to the extent there was a "market" for properties of this type that could not be put to productive use, that market was fueled by speculators. Because the definition of market value (in federal, as well as state, court) contemplates willing, informed buyers and sellers acting thoughtfully and without pressure, the court concluded that prices of properties inflated by speculative pressure were not indicative of market value. Further proceedings were scheduled to determine the cost of this government acquisition.

The government appealed. In "*Rocky II*," the Federal Circuit Court of Appeals partially affirmed and then remanded for further proceedings. The court held that restricting analysis to the 98-acre parcel was appropriate. After all, it was the Corps that refused to accept a permit application for more than 98 acres. Moreover, the court likened the Corps's argument that use of the remainder of the tract might eventually be permitted to "the possibility one might put a pot of water on a hot stove and have it freeze."[12] At the same time, because the property owner had no immediate use for the remainder of the property, the court would not hold that it had all been taken immediately.

The court of appeals also derided a valuation argument made by the government, a type of argument that property owners see all too often. The government argued that sales of comparable property were only truly comparable if subjected to the same severe regulations that the property owners claimed reduced the value of their land to nothing. Thus, said the court, "if the regulation constituting the taking reduced the value of land subject to it to zero, the very severity of the economic injury would relieve the taker of all but nominal fifth amendment liability. We suppose appellant added this contention to provide a little humor. . . ."[13]

The court of appeals ordered the trial court to reconsider its valuation approach. The trial court had focused only on the use value of the property (essentially nil) and disregarded the market created by speculators. On retrial, the claims court again found a taking. The government's appraisers testified that, based on sales of similar land in the area, the property—even after the Corps's permit denial—was worth more than $4,000 per acre. The president of Florida Rock testified that he believed it was still worth $10,000 per acre.

The claims court discounted all of these sales. Based on survey data presented by the property owner, the court concluded that the purchasers in these transactions were not suitably informed. Thus, they could not be used as the basis for the legal standard of fair market value. Assigning only nominal value to the land, the court awarded more than a million dollars for the taking of the 98 acres, plus attorneys' fees, plus interest.

The Federal Circuit was not yet satisfied. It remanded for further evidence, findings, and consideration. The fundamental disagreement was about valuation methodology. The appellate court refused to accept the notion that a substantial number of speculators cannot make a market. In the court's words, "dollars are fungible." Money coming from the wallet of a speculator spends just the same as money from a prudent investor. Thus, the case called for reconsideration.

The importance of "*Rocky IV*" lies in the substantive legal analysis in the opinion. First, in describing a regulatory taking, the court focused on the economic impact of the regulation on the property owner's ability to make productive use of the land. The U.S. Supreme Court has periodically emphasized the relationship between a property owner's right to economic productivity and the protections afforded by the Bill of Rights.[14] However, *Florida Rock* makes the rule come to life in ways that the more oracular Supreme Court opinions generally do not.

Second, the court built on the economic impact base by holding that a property owner's constitutional rights can be violated by a taking of substantially *less* than all the value of the land. As the court appropriately put it, the Fifth Amendment prohibits the uncompensated taking of private property without reference to the owner's remaining property interests. This is a critically important holding. Many judges (and all government lawyers) believe that a taking cannot occur if the government takes only a pound of flesh while leaving the property owner with a pound or two of his or her own. Their focus is on what the government has *not* interfered with. Here, in contrast, the court places the focus squarely on what the government *has* done, as the Fifth Amendment contemplates. Thus, of central importance is the court's conclusion that a regulatory taking could have occurred even though the evidence appeared to show a value of more than $4,000 per acre remained after application of the regulation. Notwithstanding the significant residual value, a taking occurred if the regulation went too far and took too much away—regardless of how much value was left.

Analytically, *Florida Rock* treats all takings alike, refusing to differentiate because of the tool selected by the government. Thus, if the government openly set out to acquire a portion of a large parcel of land, it would plainly have to pay for it. The Federal Circuit's holding is that the same rule applies whether the taking is through a direct condemnation action or through regulatory means. As the Fifth Amendment does not distinguish among causative agents, neither should the courts. The purpose of the Fifth Amendment is to protect property owners from governmental overreaching.

Third, *"Rocky IV"* likewise refuses to follow different rules for regulatory takings than for takings accomplished by physical occupation. The courts have always had an easier time finding a taking when there is a permanent physical occupation (for example, if you fence something off, physically plant yourself on it, or destroy it, the taking is obvious; if you enact a regulation that prevents productive use, the picture seems a bit fuzzier). But there is no reason in law or logic to provide protection from takings caused only in one of the myriad possible ways. The Constitution makes no such distinction.

Years ago, Justice Brennan saw through the fallacy of distinguishing among takings because of their method of accomplishment. His focus was on the protection afforded to the property owner by the Fifth Amendment, "From the property owner's point of view, it may matter little whether his land is condemned or flooded, or whether it is restricted by regulation to use in its natural state, if the effect in both cases is to deprive him of all beneficial use of it."[15]

Thus, in its overall evaluation, the Federal Circuit concluded that—regardless of the means used by the government—a taking occurs when the government deprives the owner of a substantial part, but not essentially all, of the economic use or value of the property. Moreover, when determining the compensation due the owner, the award "should be proportional to the value of the interest taken as compared to the total value of the property, up to and including total deprivation, whether the taking is by physical occupation for the public to use as a park, or by regulatory imposition to preserve the property as a wetland so that it may be used by the public for ground water recharge and other ecological purposes."[16]

The opinion is an appropriate follow-up to the Supreme Court's decision in *Lucas*. There the Court dealt with another environmental protection regulation, one that accomplished its goal of shoreline preservation by preventing a property owner from making productive use of his land. Environmental protection is a hot topic these days. In many ways, that is justifiable. The message of *Lucas* and *Florida Rock,* however, is that this country still distinguishes between ends and means. Regardless of the importance of environmental protection, it must be accomplished in ways that spread the cost among all those who benefit, which is to say, all of us. Too many regulators believe that it is okay to follow the path of lesser resistance and foist the cost onto the backs of a few—especially if the few do not have voting clout. It is not okay. It never has been.

The issue in cases like this was aptly put by the Federal Circuit toward the end of its opinion, "It should be clear that the question in cases such as this is not whether the government has power to regulate the development of wetlands. . . . The only question here is, when the Government chooses to act in the manner it did, must it pay the just compensation mandated by the Fifth Amendment."[17]

Stay tuned. We shall revisit this issue after "*Rocky V*" and the inevitable appeal in "*Rocky VI*."

B. *Loveladies Harbor*—One More Bite

The decision in *Loveladies Harbor, Inc. v. United States*,[18] picked up where *Florida Rock* left off. (That result becomes less surprising when one realizes that they were authored by the same judge.) The case involves the last 12.5 acres of a 250-acre tract the owner had acquired in 1958. Before 1972, 199 acres had been developed. Resolving a dispute with the state, the owner agreed to limit its development to 12.5 acres of those remaining. After settling with the state, the owner sought a federal permit from the Corps. The first strange twist came when the Corps asked the state its opinion of the application. In the teeth of its settlement agreement, the state denied that the project complied with state law and urged that denial of a federal permit would be appropriate. The obvious question of the extent of the relevant parcel also occupied much time and wrangling.

When the Corps denied the permit, Loveladies sued under the Administrative Procedure Act to overturn the denial and obtain its permit. Then Loveladies filed suit in the U.S. Claims Court, seeking compensation for a taking of its property. After a number of years, Loveladies obtained a judgment in its favor.[19] Meanwhile, the U.S. Supreme Court decided *Keene Corp.*, noted earlier, which called into question the jurisdiction of the U.S. Claims Court (now the U.S. Court of Federal Claims) to entertain the suit at all because of the previous suit to overturn the permit denial. (The perversity that says a property owner must choose between (1) seeking review of a permit denial on its merits, or (2) accepting the denial and suing for compensation, can be found in 28 U.S.C. § 1500.)

Thus, by the time *Loveladies* reached the appellate level, the first question to address was whether the federal courts had jurisdiction to hear a compensation suit. That part was handled en banc. By a vote of 8-3, the court (through an opinion by Judge Plager) held that the litigation could proceed. The case was then returned to the three-judge panel where Judge Plager, for a unanimous panel, affirmed the compensatory award. Among the noteworthy matters in the opinion are the following.

First, the court reiterated very plainly (from the end of *Florida Rock*) what the question in regulatory taking cases is and is not:

> What is not at issue is whether the Government can lawfully prevent a property owner from filling or otherwise injuring or destroying vital wetlands. . . .
>
> The question at issue here is, when the Government fulfills its obligation to preserve and protect the public interest, may the cost of obtaining that public benefit fall solely upon the affected property owner, or is it to be shared by the community at large.[20]

Second, the court explained that the Supreme Court's decision in *Lucas,* also decided after *Loveladies* was on appeal, had altered the required analysis. In this court's view, the law before *Lucas* required a balancing test to determine whether the public's rights outweighed those of the property owner. After *Lucas,* the court found the balancing test to have been replaced by a more simple determination of whether state property law vested the owner with an interest that the state could not eliminate under nuisance law.

Third, the court treated the case as though all that was involved was the 12.5-acre remnant, rather than the 250-acre parcel with which the owners started out. Here, because 199 acres had been developed before the state began to regulate development in the wetlands, the court held that 199 acres could not be considered part of the relevant parcel. Of the remaining 51 acres, the state was to receive 38.5 acres as a dedication in exchange for a permit to develop the other 12.5 acres. As the court put it:

> This is only logical since whatever substantial value that land had now belongs to the state and not to Loveladies. It would seem ungrateful in the extreme to require Loveladies to convey to the public the rights in the 38.5 acres in exchange for the right to develop 12.5 acres, and then to include the value of the grant as a charge against the givers.[21]

Thus the court held that this was not a partial regulatory taking case, but a case in which all economically feasible use of the relevant parcel had been taken. However, the court's analysis of the facts shows how the last remnant of a larger parcel can be treated as a separate entity for takings purposes. As the courts have repeatedly told us, the facts in these cases are nearly always unique and must be individually analyzed.

C. Other Federal Cases of Note

Two other federal cases bear mention.

Reahard v. Lee County[22] was a case the Court of Appeals for the Eleventh Circuit waited to decide while *Lucas* was pending. It involved a 40-acre parcel of land that was once part of a 540-acre parcel. The Reahard family had developed the other 500 acres, leaving this 40-acre remnant the subject of litigation about prevention of its use. The court was plainly disappointed that the Supreme Court had left *Lucas*'s footnote 7 unresolved,[23] and it remanded the matter to the trial court to determine whether a taking had occurred. The court posed eight matters it thought should be addressed in resolving that issue:

1. The history of the property (time of purchase, purchase price, location, nature of title, use, and so on)
2. The history of development (what, when, how, by whom, and so on)
3. The history of zoning and regulation
4. Any change in development when title passed
5. The present nature and extent of the property
6. The reasonable expectations of the owner under state law
7. The reasonable expectations of the neighbors under state law
8. The diminution in the owner's investment-backed expectations after the regulatory action

Thus, one might have expected pertinent guidance from the continuation of *Reahard*. And many people in this field did just that. Alas, the court of appeals flinched even before the ink was dry on its remand order. Less than four months later, the court supplemented its opinion by telling the trial judge to consider the issue of ripeness before going further, even though the ripeness issue had not been raised or considered on appeal.[24]

On remand, the trial court refused to take the hint, reexamined the issues, and reinstated the original liability determination in favor of the property owners. On appeal, the Eleventh Circuit concluded the case was not ripe and therefore declined to delve into the substantive issues.[25]

Ripeness issues are convoluted enough in general, with their bewildering and continually expanding hoops for property owners to jump through before being able to obtain the substantive attention of a court.[26] One thing we thought was clear was that federal courts preferred plaintiffs start out in the state court systems. The twist here is that the plaintiff did just that, then the government removed the case to federal court. When things started going sideways in federal court, however, it appears that the government had no objection to returning to state court—resulting in a curious judicial endorsement of forum-shopping and a grotesque unfairness to the property owner who must now start over again.

Another recent federal case worth reading is *Bowles v. United States*,[27] a decision by Chief Judge Smith of the Court of Federal Claims finding a regulatory taking and awarding compensation. It is a useful analysis of post-*Lucas* law in general. The case involves the effects of the Corps of Engineers' denial of Section 404 permit concerning a wetland lot in a coastal subdivision. The tangential relevance of the case to this partial-taking discussion is that the property owner held title to nine other contiguous lots. The opinion notes that the government did not seek to evaluate the effect of permit denial on the value of all ten lots, and goes on to say that such analysis would seem improper under *Lucas*.

III. Some Interesting State Cases

The state courts have generally lagged behind the federal courts in responding to recent Supreme Court holdings. Here are several state court decisions worth noting. Some find partial takings, and some reject the idea.

In *Ramona Convent of the Holy Name v. City of Alhambra*,[28] an order of nuns sued when a city refused to remove 1.97 acres of the order's 19.17-acre property from open-space zoning so it could be sold. The property was used for a school, with the open-space parcel used for outdoor sports. The nuns decided they needed to sell the empty 1.97 acres to raise funds to remain solvent. When the city refused, suit was filed.

The nuns argued that forcing the property to remain open space was the same as conscripting the property for park purposes. They relied on *Lucas* for the proposition that all use cannot be drained from property without compensation. The court rejected the argument, and concluded that the open-space parcel was zoned for use as an educational institution and had viable uses as part of the larger educational parcel.

In *Dodd v. Hood River County*,[29] the county denied a permit to build a single house on 40 acres of land in a forestry zone. The property owners urged that the property was worth next to nothing if they could not build. The county urged that it was worth $10,000 for forestry (even though the purchase price had been $33,000). The property owners argued that the analytical factors in *Lucas* gave them a right to compensation even if the property was worth $10,000. The Oregon Supreme Court's response was that "[t]he dictum in *Lucas* went far beyond what the majority opinion in that case needed to say to decide the issue presented."[30]

Sometimes it is easier to deal with constitutional concepts when land is not involved. *U.S. West Communications, Inc. v. Public Utilities Commission,*[31] involved telephone switching facilities. The state Public Utilities Commission (PUC) had granted a South Dakota network (a competitor of U.S. West) a monopoly over switching. The new arrangement meant not only that U.S. West had to use its rival's facilities, but also that many of U.S. West's existing facilities were rendered worthless. Relying on *Lucas,* the South Dakota Supreme Court had no trouble in finding a total taking of part of U.S. West's property. Compensation was ordered.

BSW Development Group v. Dayton Board of Zoning Appeals[32] involved the constitutionality of a local historical-designation ordinance. After the city designated its building a historical landmark, BSW sought permission to demolish it because the cost to bring the building up to code in its historic configuration would exceed the market value of the building. The trial court agreed with the property owner and declared the ordinance unconstitutional as applied to this property.

On appeal, the government urged that the appropriate unit of property was the historic building *and* an adjacent parcel owned by these same people. Viewed that way, argued the regulators, the property owners were left with sufficient value to avoid a taking. The court of appeals affirmed. Finding that the only connection between the two parcels was that they were accidentally located next to each other and owned by the same parties, the court held that relationship insufficient to link the properties together for takings analysis.

In something of a middle ground, an Illinois appellate court indicated its openness to the partial-taking theory of *Lucas,* but found it inapplicable to the facts before it.[33]

IV. A Parenthetical Discussion of Concrete Pipe

Some mention probably ought to be made of *Concrete Pipe & Products of California, Inc. v. Construction Laborers Pension Trust,*[34] if only because some people have suggested it has some bearing on regulatory takings of land. This discussion is labelled "parenthetical" because that is all I think the case is worth in this context. It is not a land case and should not control land cases.

Why do I say that? Let us start with the *Concrete Pipe* decision itself. It is (as you can see from its title) one of those pension fund cases. Congress amended the Employee Retirement Income Security Act of 1974 (ERISA) to require that employers withdrawing from the plan pay to the plan a fixed sum representing the employer's share of vested, but unfunded, benefits. Concrete Products challenged the validity of the act and included a claim that the act was a taking of its property. (I wish there was a way to stop everyone from thinking that a Fifth Amendment claim is the ideal "catch-all" to throw in amongst the welter, but that is a different parenthetical discussion for a different day.)

In any event, among the things that happened in *Concrete Pipe* was that the company tried to convince the Court to analyze the case as though it were a land case. In refusing, here is what the High Court said:

> We reject Concrete Pipe's contention that the appropriate analytical framework is the one employed in our cases dealing with permanent physical occupation or destruction of economically beneficial use of real property. [Citing *Lucas*.][35]

A good reason for rejecting the analytical framework used in land cases is demonstrated in the next portion of the *Concrete Pipe* opinion, in which the Court reiterates its *Penn Central* idea that property cannot be divided into segments for Fifth Amendment purposes. Aside from the fact that property is divided for Fifth Amendment purposes all the time (anybody know the owner of any discrete property interest—a landlord, tenant, or lender, for example—who does not insist on his or her portion when the property is condemned?), the concept of partial takings makes little analytical sense when you are talking about money. Yet that is what happened here.[36]

More importantly, the Court used the case to expand on the "expectations" concept it had brought to the fore in *Lucas*. The Court noted that the basic regulatory scheme was in place when Concrete Products acquired the company, that this was merely business regulation anyway, and that Congress had a relatively less fettered hand in regulating the economics of business.[37] Thus, on its face, *Concrete Pipe* is just another reasonable expectations case, one in which the regulatory matrix was in place when the property was acquired, and thus the purchase price presumably reflected potential regulatory impacts.

And that business (the *Penn Central* factor) about not dividing property into slices? It did not survive the next occasion for Supreme Court review. That part of *Concrete Pipe* made a cameo appearance in *Dolan v. City of Tigard*,[38] but only in Justice Stevens's dissent. There, complaining bitterly that the Court had apparently abandoned its old test, Justice Stevens noted that it had been reiterated as recently as *Concrete Pipe*.[39] Obviously, a majority of the Court believed it appropriate to analyze the taking of small slices of Mrs. Dolan's property, even though she was plainly left with economically productive use of the rest.

And do not forget *Florida Rock.* That series of opinions is discussed earlier in this chapter. Suffice it to note for now that the most recent decision of the Federal Circuit Court of Appeals found there could be liability for interference with less than all the value of less than all the property owner's holdings. *Concrete Pipe* makes an appearance—again in a dissent. In contrast to the majority opinion discussed earlier, the dissenting judge thought that *Concrete Pipe* showed the need to examine the impact "on the totality of an owner's rights in the property."[40] But that theory did not prevail.[41] The Washington Court of Appeals probably came closest to the mark when it refused to apply *Concrete Pipe* in a land regulation context because "[t]he ordinance at issue here is not federal economic legislation."[42] In short, *Concrete Pipe* may be useful in pension fund analyses. It may even be useful as an "expectations" case or a "business regulation" case. But it is not much help as a regular takings case.

V. Conclusion

This analysis has focused on those cases in which partial takings have been recognized. That is not to say there are not others that go the other way. For example, in the *Tabb Lakes* litigation, the court refused to examine whether wetlands regulations had rendered individual lots, or even the entire wetland portion of the tract, unsalable because the "parcel as a whole" retained substantial value.[43] To do otherwise, said the court, would render any wetland permit denial a per se taking of that portion of the property, something the court was not yet ready to do.[44] Curiously, although citing *Lucas* in other places, the court failed to analyze the impact of the *Lucas* footnotes on the partial taking issue where there is a 100 percent loss of use of a part of the property.

The most recent of the North Carolina billboard decisions is in the same vein.[45] There, the court may have been spared the necessity of close analysis of *Lucas* due to the way in which the billboard company did business. Although insisting that each billboard must be evaluated separately, the company leased its billboards in packages related not to particular signs, but to the percentage of the local driving public that would view the signs each day. Thus, if a customer bought what was called a "fifty showing," he or she would receive coverage on sufficient billboards to expose the advertising to 50 percent of the driving public. Still, one was left with a feeling of being cheated of the proper analysis due to the last footnote in the opinion, which read:

> The court is not unmindful of the significance of its determination that each individual sign does not constitute a separate unit of

property. If it did, the *Lucas* inquiry into the nature of Naegele's title could be determinative.[46]

For that reason, cases like *Tabb Lakes* and *Naegele* are of little interest. They are of the dog-bites-man variety. They have happened for years. It is the other cases—the ones that pick up the challenge expressed by the Supreme Court in *Lucas*—that seek to find an answer.

The development of the common law has never been accomplished in a smooth fashion. The nature of the beast is that courts use different analyses to reach different conclusions until at some point either a concensus is reached or a resolution is imposed by the Supreme Court. The interesting cases to watch are those seeking to break free of old patterns suspected of having lost their vitality. When the Supreme Court consciously placed footnote 7 into its *Lucas* opinion, it was no accident. It was an invitation to the lower courts to try a different approach. Although moving with fits and starts, that new approach has substantial justice behind it. Time will tell whether it has the intellectual staying power to provide relief to property owners who have heretofore been ordered to suffer in silence while large chunks of their land has been rendered useless and valueless.

Notes

1. Lucas v. South Carolina Coastal Council, 112 S. Ct. 2886 (1992). The author's discussion of this issue immediately after *Lucas* was decided appears in Michael M. Berger, *Property Owners Have Rights; Lower Courts Need to Protect Them, in* AFTER LUCAS: LAND USE REGULATION AND THE TAKING OF PROPERTY WITHOUT COMPENSATION, ch. 2 at 41-45 (David Callies ed., 1993).

2. *Lucas,* 112 S. Ct. at 2894, n.7.

3. 438 U.S. 104 (1978).

4. *Lucas,* 112 S. Ct. at 2894, n.7.

5. That is why Justice Blackmun (one can only presume with a straight face) was able to find less than complete prohibition even in *Lucas* because "Petitioner can picnic, swim, camp in a tent, or live on the property in a movable trailer." (*Id.* at 2908, Blackmun, J., dissenting.) One can only wonder how the owners of the million dollar homes next door would have reacted had Mr. Lucas attempted to place trailers on his lots.

6. 749 P.2d 160 (1988).

7. *Id.* at 163.

8. *Id.* at 163-64.

9. Presbytery of Seattle v. King County, 787 P. 2d 907 (1990).

10. The most recent is reported in Florida Rock Indus., Inc. v. United States, 18 F.3d 1560 (Fed. Cir. 1994). Alternating between the U.S. Claims Court and the

U.S. Court of Appeals for the Federal Circuit, the first three installments may be found at 8 Cl. Ct. 160 (1985), 791 F.2d 893 (1986), and 21 Cl. Ct. 161 (1990).

11. Keene Corp. v. United States, 113 S. Ct. 2035 (1993).

12. *Florida Rock,* 791 F.2d at 904.

13. *Id.* at 905.

14. United States v. James Daniel Good Real Property, 114 S. Ct. 492 (1993); Lucas v. South Carolina Coastal Council, 112 S. Ct. 2886 (1992).

15. San Diego Gas & Elec. Co. v. San Diego, 450 U.S. 621, 652 (1981) (Brennan, J., dissenting).

16. Florida Rock Indus., Inc. v. U.S., 18 F.3d 1560, 1569 (Fed. Cir. 1994).

17. *Id.* at 1568, n.18.

18. 27 F.3d 1545 (Fed Cir. 1994) (procedural decision, in banc) and 28 F.3d 1171 (Fed. Cir. 1994) (merits).

19. 21 Cl. Ct. 153 (1990).

20. *Loveladies,* 28 F.3d at 1175.

21. *Id.* at 1181.

22. 968 F.2d 1131 (11th Cir. 1992).

23. *See Reahard,* 968 F.2d at 1134, n.5.

24. 978 F.2d 1212 (11th Cir. 1992).

25. 30 F.3d 1412 (11th Cir. 1994).

26. *See, e.g.,* Michael M. Berger, *The "Ripeness" Mess in Federal Land Use Cases or How the Supreme Court Converted Federal Judges into Fruit Peddlers,* 1991 INST. ON PLAN. ZONING & EMINENT DOMAIN ch. 7.

27. 31 Fed. Cl. 37 (1994).

28. 26 Cal. Rptr. 140 (Ct. App. 1993).

29. 855 P.2d 608 (Or. 1993).

30. It is not nice to get snippy with the Supreme Court. Although *Dodd* was not reviewed by the High Court, all three decisions of the Oregon Supreme Court reviewed during the Term resulted in reversal. The Ninth Circuit Court of Appeals recently held a parallel federal suit ripe after these state proceedings ended. Dodd. v. Hood River County, 59 F.3d 852 (9th Cir. 1995).

31. 505 N.W.2d 115 (S.D. 1993).

32. No. 13218, 1993 Ohio App. LEXIS 2544 (Ohio Ct. App., May 7, 1993).

33. Tim Thompson, Inc. v. Village of Hinsdale, 617 N.E.2d 1227 (App. Ct. 1993).

34. 113 S. Ct. 2264.

35. *Concrete Products, Id.* at 2290.

36. *Id.*

37. *Id.* at 2291-92.

38. 114 S. Ct. 2309.

39. *Dolan, Id.* at 2324.

40. Florida Rock Indus., Inc. v. U.S., 18 F.3d 1560, 1573 (Fed. Cir. 1994) (Nies, C.J., dissenting).

41. Two other recent Federal Circuit decisions cite *Concrete Pipe* for the proposition that it is an "expectations" case. *See* Creppel v. U.S., 41 F.3d 627, 632 (Fed. Cir. 1994); Loveladies Harbor, Inc. v. U.S., 28 F.3d 1171, 1177 (Fed. Cir. 1994).

42. Guimont v. City of Seattle, 896 P.2d 70, 79, n. 10 (Wash. App., 1995).

43. Tabb Lakes, Ltd. v. U.S., 10 F.3d 796 (Fed. Cir. 1993).

44. *Id.* at 802.

45. Naegele Outdoor Advertising v. City of Durham, 803 F. Supp. 1068 (M.D.N.C. 1992).

46. *Id.* at 1080 n.7.

CHAPTER ❖ 8

Regulatory Takings: Factoring Partial Deprivations into the Taking Equation

Robert H. Freilich, Elizabeth A. Garvin, and Duane A. Martin

I. Introduction

For years, the U.S. Supreme Court has promulgated land-use opinions that commentators have attempted to fashion into a set of rules defining a "taking equation" applicable to all forms of land-use regulation resulting in "regulatory takings."[1] A key component of the taking equation that has generated considerable commentary is the question of whether a taking has occurred when a regulation deprives a property owner of less than all of the use or value of that owner's relevant property. While that question has been answered by the courts, the *Lucas v. South Carolina Coastal Council*[2] decision appears to have sparked renewed confusion in this area. In particular, it has created the misconception that a "partial regulatory taking" is now a category of regulatory takings analysis.[3] This article will explore the impact of the *Lucas* decision on economic regulatory takings involving less than total deprivation of use and value. It will show that there is no valid reason to use the term "partial regulatory takings" for economic (as opposed to title or possessory) cases, and that the U.S. Supreme Court in *Concrete Pipe*[4] has definitively settled this issue.

II. The Taking Equation and the Classifications of Regulatory Takings

A. The Taking Equation

Traditional takings analysis focuses on the character of the government action and on what the government has acquired or taken.[5] The earliest attempt to formulate a regulatory taking equation was made by Justice Holmes in the Supreme Court's decision of *Pennsylvania Coal Co. v. Mahon*.[6] In an oft-quoted opinion, Justice Holmes posited that "while property may be regulated to a certain extent, if regulation goes too far it will be recognized as a taking."[7] Although the Supreme Court determined that a regulation that goes "too far" would result in a taking, it was not until the mid-1970s that the factors of the modern taking equation began to emerge.[8]

Because the Court will not use a set formula, it engages in essentially a two-tier inquiry. The first tier explores the legitimacy of the governmental action, asking (1) whether the purpose of the regulatory action is a "legitimate state interest"; and (2) whether the means used to achieve the objective "substantially advances" the intended purpose.[9] Legitimacy review is particularly important when the government acquires incidents of ownership or title ("title" takings). The analysis for title takings is expanded to determine the remoteness and proportionality of the government's actions.[10]

If the regulatory action passes muster under legitimacy review, only then must the court undertake the second inquiry into the impact of the regulation on the property owner. This is essentially a two-part test. First, the court will inquire whether a per se taking has occurred, either through permanent physical (possessory) occupation of the property[11] or through the deprivation of *all* economic use or value.[12] In a third category of cases, diminution of title (as in mandatory dedication accompanying development approval), the Court has developed a "higher scrutiny" test but not an outright per se test.[13] If either of these per se situations has occurred, the court will decree a taking and the inquiry will cease. If the government action does not fit into either of these two discrete categories (that is, it is an *economic* regulatory deprivation), then the court must make a *Penn Central* taking determination based upon an ad hoc, factual inquiry. This inquiry involves a balancing of three basic factors: the character of the governmental action, the economic impact on the property owner resulting from a loss of all reasonable use or value in the entirety of the property, and the regulation's interference with the property owner's investment-backed expectations.[14]

It is significant that in title or physical occupation ca impact on the property owner is not a factor. In those cat tial" taking will clearly exist, the same as in a direct cond compensation is paid for the portion of property taken, damages for the remainder, if any. In an economic regulatory taking, when economic impact (loss of all reasonable use or value) is an essential element in determining whether there is a taking in the first place, we must look to the entirety of the property and not to a part being regulated.

B. Classifications of Regulatory Takings

Because major differences in analysis exist regarding regulatory takings, we must first analyze the classifications before looking at the rule. Three types of regulatory takings are recognized: physical, title, and economic.[15] In two of three, the U.S. Supreme Court has recognized a distinction between a per se taking and a de facto taking;[16] if there is no per se taking, the case shifts to de facto takings analysis that will be governed by case-by-case, ad hoc, factual inquiries.[17] This is somewhat analogous to the distinction in nuisance law between a nuisance per se and a nuisance per accidens.[18]

The key to understanding partial regulatory takings lies in how they are classified. A partial deprivation may equate to a physical, title, or (in rare cases) an economic regulatory taking, but the analysis for each class varies significantly.

1. PHYSICAL TAKINGS

A regulatory activity producing a physical invasion sufficient to support an action for inverse condemnation is the oldest and most easily recognized category of regulatory takings. If the government, through a regulation, physically invades land,[19] the regulation will be held a taking unless the possessory intrusion secured a private benefit to the landowner, abated private development burdens imposed on the public, or was a "temporary deprivation," to which a balancing test is applied.[20] The partial taking theory is easiest to conceptualize in the context of physical takings. Essentially, the physical invasion the government has authorized may amount to the taking of a portion of the property, thereby effectuating a partial physical taking.

An example of a partial physical invasion occurred in *Kaiser Aetna v. United States*,[21] in which a privately owned pond was made accessible to navigable waters. The government claimed the pond was thus made available for public use. The Court responded that under the commerce clause, the public could assert a navigable servitude to use the pond; however, the action was a taking which required compensation to the landowner. According to the Court, an infringement on the owner's right to exclude others from the property constituted a taking, "[W]e hold that the 'right to exclude,' so universally held to be a fundamental element of the property right, falls within this category of interests that the Government cannot take without compensation."[22]

The physical invasion involved in the *Kaiser Aetna* case intruded upon only one of the sticks in the bundle of the owner's property rights. Nevertheless, the Court found that a taking had occurred. Although the easement of passage, not being a permanent occupation of land, was not a per se taking, *Kaiser Aetna* demonstrates that a partial physical deprivation can amount to a taking.

After *Kaiser Aetna* came *Loretto v. TelePrompTer Manhattan CATV Corp.,*[23] in which the Court provided a per se rule requiring that an enactment authorizing a "permanent physical occupation" of a landowner's property constitutes a taking regardless of the economic impact or the nature of the governmental interest involved.[24] In *Loretto,* an apartment owner claimed a taking had occurred because a New York statute authorized a cable television company to install cable lines and boxes with roof cables on the roof of the owner's apartment building. The Supreme Court held that a *permanent* physical occupation authorized by the government was a per se taking, even though the physical and economic interference with the landowner's property was minimal, and that no balancing test was required. The Court found that the taking in *Loretto* destroyed the apartment owner's right to exclude.

Note, however, that the Court held the per se taking rule does not apply to temporary physical invasions or cases when a regulation merely restricts the use of property. The Supreme Court reaffirmed in *Loretto* that when a permanent physical invasion has not taken place, the Court will engage in an ad hoc, multifactor inquiry into the "economic impact of the regulation, the extent to which it interferes with investment-backed expectations and the character of the government action."[25]

The *Loretto* decision highlights the importance of the various ways to view, and subsequently segment, property. When property is viewed from a spatial perspective, the regulation may impact a minimal portion of the property yet fall within the category of the *Loretto* per se rule. But if property is viewed from a temporal perspective, the regulation must impact the entire property interest (that is, the deprivation must be permanent) for the per se rule to apply.

2. TITLE TAKINGS

Title taking differs from physical taking in that the regulating body does not physically invade the land but still restricts property use, resulting in the government acquiring incidents of ownership or title to the property.[26] The Court addressed title taking in one of the "trilogy" cases of 1987, *Nollan v. California Coastal Commission*.[27] It held that drafting and implementing regulatory conditions in the development approval process that lead to title acquisition or interference with possession may result in a finding that private property has been taken for public use, requiring the payment of just compensation.

Following *Nollan*, the Court decided *Dolan v. City of Tigard*,[28] the latest addition to the taking equation. The Dolans sought a building permit to demolish a 9,700-square-foot building and construct a replacement 17,600-square-foot building for an electric and plumbing supply business on 1.67 acres in Tigard's downtown central business district. The property lies within an "action area" overlay zone, which allowed the city to attach conditions to the Dolans' development at the building permit stage to accommodate projected transportation and public facility needs.

To comply with Oregon's comprehensive land-use management program, the City of Tigard codified its comprehensive plan in a Community Development Code (CDC). The CDC required the Dolans and all others located within the central business district to comply with a 15 percent open-space requirement. Tigard granted the Dolans' application, but required them to dedicate a fifteen-foot easement that was within the 100-year flood plain to install a storm drainage system. The city also required, as a condition of the permit, an eight-foot easement to construct a pedestrian and bicycle pathway. The exactions amounted to approximately 10 percent of the Dolans' total property.

The Tigard Planning Commission based the two conditions for easement dedication on the Comprehensive Master Drainage Plan and the Pedestrian/Bicycle Pathway Plan, each of which created a "reasonable relationship" between the Dolans' developmental impacts and the need for increased drainage and alternative means of transportation, respectively.[29] The commission specifically found that "[i]t is reasonable to assume that customers and employees of the future uses of this site *could* utilize a pedestrian/bicycle pathway adjacent to this development for their transportation and recreational needs."[30] Concerning the anticipated increase in storm-water runoff, the commission concluded that "the requirement of dedication of the floodplain area on the site is related to the applicant's plan to intensify development of the site."[31]

The Oregon Supreme Court upheld the district court's finding that Tigard's exaction did not create a taking of the Dolans' property.[32] The Oregon court accepted the planning commission's conclusions that the bicycle path requirement was reasonably related to the Dolans' business expansion and the anticipated increase in traffic, and that the drainage system reasonably related to the increased impervious surface of a larger parking lot. The Oregon court rejected the Dolans' argument that *Nollan*[33] abandoned the "reasonably related" test (substituting an "essential nexus" requirement) for the connection between the city's condition for permit approval and the needs created by the new development. Despite accepting *Nollan* as representing only the "essential nexus" requirement, the Oregon court concluded that there was an essential nexus between the Dolans' developmental needs and the bikepath and drainage system dedications.[34]

Dolan reached the U.S. Supreme Court on a question about the type of connection required between the impact caused by land-use development and the exactions demanded by a city as a condition of approving the landowner's building permit.[35] The Supreme Court held that to avoid a taking, a "reasonable relationship" (denominated as "rough proportionality") must exist between a city's conditions and a new development's impacts.[36] This reasonable relationship nexus test, Justice Rehnquist opined, is an adoption of the "intermediate position" developed by state courts that have considered the same question.[37]

Nollan and *Dolan* stopped short of creating a per se rule for title taking. The two cases have, however, established a two-step nexus test to be applied during legitimacy review. First, the *Nollan* "essential nexus" must exist between the asserted "legitimate state interest and the permit condition exaction imposed by the government."[38] Second, if the required nexus exists, the court must analyze the "degree of connection" between the exaction and the "projected impact" of the proposed development[39] to ensure a "rough proportionality" exists between the two.[40] There is, therefore, no per se rule, but instead a heightened scrutiny within the ad hoc, factual inquiry balancing test of *Penn Central*.[41] A partial title taking may occur when government acquires incidents of ownership or title to only a portion of the property owned. Most government regulations that may rise to the level of a title taking generally involve a transfer of title to merely a portion of the property owned.

Dolan exemplifies a partial title taking. As discussed, in *Dolan,* the City of Tigard conditioned its approval of a building permit on the dedication of two easement strips: one for a storm drainage ditch, the other for a pedestrian and bicycle pathway. The exactions amounted to approximately 10 percent of the Dolans' property. However, the Court found that a taking had occurred.

3. ECONOMIC TAKINGS

Although the issue of partial regulatory takings may be applicable to physical and title takings,[42] it is most often raised and rejected in the context of an economic taking. Economic takings constitute the vast majority of regulatory takings cases. An economic taking occurs when a regulation deprives a property owner of the reasonable or beneficial economic value or use of property. Under "economic impact" review, the court determines whether a permanent, reasonable beneficial value remains for the property, *when viewed as a whole.*

Economic impact analysis was greatly affected by *Lucas v. South Carolina Coastal Council.*[43] *Lucas* changed the economic inquiry, fractionally, into a two-part test based on the amount of value left to the landowner. If the regulation has taken *all* permanent value of the property, *Lucas* holds that the landowner must be compensated, unless the regulation is based on antecedent common law nuisance principles or is in accordance with the state's background principles of property law. If, however, the landowner is left with some property value, the inquiry returns to the balancing of interests.[44] Landowner proponents see this double test as a major victory. In fact, it is only a pyrrhic victory.[45] The decision in *First English Evangelical Lutheran Church v. County of Los Angeles,*[46] in which the Court granted the remedy of compensation, was based on the finding that permanent deprivation of *all* use had occurred.[47] In subsequent opinions, both federal and state courts have held that when it is shown that less than a permanent deprivation of *all* use has occurred, *no* taking has occurred.[48] *Lucas*'s categorical per se test may now accelerate that trend.

There are three key points to understand about applying the *Lucas* per se rule. First is the limited role of the *Lucas* categorical formulation. For it to apply, a landowner must be deprived of *all* economically beneficial use of the property. Second, if the *Lucas* per se rule does not apply, the court must revert to a balancing of the *Penn Central* factors. Finally, applying this rule requires determining the unit of property to be evaluated. We will examine the final point first. The problem is whether to segment the property in some way and view only a discrete segment, or to compare that segment to the property as a whole, sometimes referred to as the "denominator problem."

a. The Denominator Problem To carry out economic impact analysis, a court must first determine the unit of property to be evaluated. In other words, the court must first define the deprivation denominator. As stated by Chief Justice Rehnquist, "The need to consider the effect of regulation on some identifiable segment of property makes all important the admittedly difficult task of defining the relevant parcel."[49]

Defining the relevant property is critical in determining whether a taking is found. A broad definition of the relevant mass of property allows the economic impact of a regulation to be diluted and thus less likely to be a taking. Conversely, a narrow definition allows the economic impact of the regulation to be concentrated, thus making a taking more likely.

Traditionally, to determine economic impact, the property interest is viewed in its totality.[50] If only a portion of the total property has been taken, then the court's balancing inquiry must center on the totality of the property using the *Penn Central* factors. In *Penn Central,* the Court made the totality rule clear by stating that:

> '[t]aking' jurisprudence does not divide a single parcel into discrete segments and attempt to determine whether rights in a particular segment have been entirely abrogated. In deciding whether a particular governmental action has effected a taking, this Court focuses rather both on the character of the action and on the nature and extent of the interference with rights in *the parcel as a whole*—here, the city tax block designated as the 'landmark site.'[51]

After *Penn Central,* the Court repeatedly acknowledged the totality rule as the general rule for defining the relevant property.[52] Justice Scalia, however, called this traditional view into question in *Lucas*.[53] He pointed out (in a footnote) that when a regulation requires a developer to leave 90 percent of a rural tract in its natural state, it is unclear whether a court should analyze the situation as one in which the owner has been deprived of all economically beneficial use of *the burdened portion of the tract,* or as one in which the owner has suffered a mere diminution in value of the tract as a whole.[54] Although Justice Scalia expressly refrained from announcing a new definition of the deprivation denominator, he questioned the utility of the totality rule. This view is troublesome for several reasons.

First, state law has always determined the nature of the property interest that has been taken.[55] When property is subdivided into lots before the regulation is passed, state law may treat the single lot as the entire property to be examined under the law.[56] Except in this unusual circumstance and in deliberate intents to evade,[57] a reviewing court should view the property as a whole under state law, just as it has always done.[58]

Second, defining the relevant property as less than the whole has dramatic implications. Adopting such a suggestion would significantly expand the number of land-use regulations vulnerable to a takings challenge. Narrowly defining the deprivation denominator would cause many minor regulations to completely destroy the economic value of discrete property interests, and thus require compensation. Justice Holmes recognized this problem in *Pennsylvania Coal,* when he wrote that "[g]overnment could hardly go on if it had to compensate property owners every time a regulation negatively affected property values."[59]

Moreover, a narrow definition of the deprivation denominator would allow property owners to strategically parcel their property to ensure the finding of a taking. As Justice Stevens pointed out in his *Lucas* dissent,

> [t]he smaller the estate, the more likely that a regulatory change will effect a total taking. Thus, an investor may, for example, purchase the right to build a multi-family home on a specific lot, with the result that a zoning regulation that allows only single-family homes would render the investor's property interest "valueless."[60]

A more narrow definition of the relevant parcel would allow owners to take advantage of the rule and structure specialized property interests so that compensation could rarely be avoided. This elaborate and socially useless structuring of property interests would eventually force courts to redefine the deprivation denominator to view the property as a whole.[61]

Unfortunately, Justice Scalia's questioning of the totality rule in *Lucas* has led to considerable confusion about the proper definition of the deprivation denominator. This is true despite the Supreme Court's return to the issue in its 1993 decision in *Concrete Pipe*.[62] In that case, the Court reaffirmed the totality rule and the essence of its holdings in both *Penn Central*[63] and *Keystone*[64] that loss of value in a regulatory economic takings case is to be measured against the value of the entire property.

Concrete Pipe, a wholly owned subsidiary of Concrete Pipe and Products Company, purchased the assets of a company named Cen-Vi-Ro in 1976. At the time of the purchase, Concrete Pipe was aware Cen-Vi-Ro had entered into a trust agreement creating a multiemployer retirement plan[65] in 1962 and that it continued to make contributions to the plan after the purchase.

Due to abuses of the Multiemployer Pension Plan Amendments Act[66] (MPPAA), Congress enacted provisions requiring penalties for early withdrawal from the program.[67] As a result, "'any employer withdrawing from a multiemployer plan was subject to a contingent liability that was dependent upon the plan's termination in the next five years and the PBGC's [Pension Benefit Guarantee Corporation] decision to exercise its discretion and pay guaranteed benefits.'"[68] It soon became evident, however, that these provisions had not solved the problem of early withdrawal. Therefore, Congress enacted a new rule requiring a withdrawing employer to pay the share of the plan's unfunded liabilities attributable to that employer's participation.[69] Under the amendments, an employer's withdrawal liability could be calculated in fixed and certain terms.[70]

In 1981, Concrete Pipe ceased operations and payments to the plan. As a result, the plan notified Concrete Pipe in January 1982 of a $268,168.81 withdrawal liability. Concrete Pipe objected to this amount, claiming that it "completely withdrew" from the plan. After an unsuccessful attempt at arbitration, Concrete Pipe filed a complaint alleging, among other claims, that the MPPAA provisions violated its Fifth Amendment rights regarding withdrawal liability. The essence of Concrete Pipe's takings challenge was that it had entered into a contractual agreement that legislative regulations could not later alter. Furthermore, to allow such regulation to retroactively affect the company's contract rights, resulting in increased liability, would amount to a taking of property.[71]

The Court rejected Concrete Pipe's *Lucas* per se claim[72] and instead reviewed the challenge under the *Penn Central* factors. In evaluating the economic impact, the majority makes clear that the relevant property is the property as a whole. The Court specifically rejected Concrete Pipe's attempt to segment its property for takings purposes, stating:

> [W]e rejected this analysis years ago in *Penn Central Transportation Co. v. New York City,* where we held that a claimant's parcel of property could not first be divided into what was taken and what was left for the purpose of demonstrating the taking of the former to be complete and hence compensable. To the extent that any portion of property is taken, that portion is always taken in its entirety; the relevant question, however, is whether the property taken is all, or only a portion of the parcel in question.[73]

As Justice Souter's opinion makes clear, the "parcel as whole," or "totality" rule, is the proper denominator for the deprivation fraction. Notably, the Court was unanimous in rejecting the concept of splitting property interests for the purposes of the takings clause.

Although the Supreme Court clarified its definition of the deprivation denominator in *Concrete Pipe,* the lower courts continue to puzzle over Justice Scalia's views of the relevant property interest, even though he concurred in *Concrete Pipe,* in which the decision on the totality rule portion was unanimous. A prime example of this obfuscation is found in *Florida Rock Industries, Inc. v. United States.*[74] In its latest consideration of *Florida Rock,* the Court of Appeals for the Federal Circuit remanded the "partial" regulatory takings case for the second time, compounding the confusion. The court posed the question of whether a "partial deprivation" resulting from a regulatory imposition that deprives the owner of a substantial part, but not necessarily all, of the economic use or value of the property constitutes a compensable "partial taking."[75]

The case arose in 1980 when Florida Rock Industries, pursuant to section 404 of the Clean Water Act (Section 404), applied to the Army Corps of Engineers for a permit to mine limestone located underneath a tract of wetlands.[76] Initially, Florida Rock sought a permit for its entire tract of 1,560 acres. The Corps refused, because permits were limited to parcels with a maximum three-year potential for mining. Florida Rock acquiesced and applied for a permit for a 98-acre parcel, the size required to serve its anticipated needs for three years.

The permit was denied on the basis that the mining would destroy the surface wetlands and create undesirable water turbidity.[77] In *Florida Rock I,* the U.S. Court of Federal Claims[78] found a regulatory taking, assessed the value of the property "taken" at $10,500 per acre, and concluded that the property was valueless because mining was the only viable economic use of the property.[79] It ruled that the landowner was entitled to just compensation of $1,029,000, plus attorneys' fees and simple interest.[80] On appeal, the Court of Appeals for the Federal Circuit vacated the finding that a taking had occurred and remanded for further consideration (*Florida Rock II*).[81] On remand, the Court of Federal Claims found that the permit denial deprived Florida Rock of all value of its land, and again found a taking (*Florida Rock III*).[82] The government appealed and again the Federal Circuit vacated the judgment but, in doing so, promulgated a partial takings theory contrary to the totality rule.

Florida Rock requested a permit for only 98 acres of the 1,560 acres it owned. Nevertheless, Judge Plager opined that a partial taking of a percentage of property may equal a taking if the regulation prohibits all economically beneficial use of the partial portion of the land taken.[83] The court, apparently refusing to consider the remaining 1,462 acres Florida Rock owned, disregarded the totality rule. In his dissent, Chief Judge Nies took the majority to task for promulgating a partial takings theory that is contrary to Supreme Court precedent, particularly *Concrete Pipe.*[84]

Judge Plager continued his assault on the totality rule in *Loveladies Harbor, Inc. v. United States.*[85] After noting that *Lucas* has effected a "sea change" in regulatory takings analysis, Judge Plager framed the issue as whether there has been a partial or total loss of economic use. *Loveladies* involved a dispute about 250 acres that were part of a wetland. The development of 199 of those acres occurred before the enactment of Section 404 in 1972. Loveladies Harbor, Inc. owned a 51-acre parcel that was part of the original 250-acre tract of land acquired in 1958. Litigation began when Loveladies was denied a permit under Section 404 to finish the real estate development project by filling the remaining 51 acres.

After years of negotiations with the New Jersey Department of Environmental Protection (NJDEP) and the Army Corps of Engineers, NJDEP granted Loveladies a permit to develop only 12.5 acres and to fill and construct thirty-five residential homes. However, the Army Corps of Engineers denied the Section 404 permit, notwithstanding the fact that the State of New Jersey granted a permit under its Coastal Act.

The Court of Federal Claims awarded Loveladies $2,658,000, plus interest, based on a finding of a $2,658,000 fair market value of the land before denial of the permit and a $12,500 fair market value after denial of the permit. The government appealed this decision to the U.S. Federal Court of Appeals, arguing that the Supreme Court's decisions in *Lucas* and *UNR Industries, Inc. v. United States*[86] directly applied to the case.

The federal appeals court agreed to examine the issue of whether the government may impose the cost of preserving and protecting the public's interest in wetland preservation solely on the affected property owner, or whether such costs should be imposed on the community.[87] In its analysis, the court acknowledged the denominator problem and expressly sought to resolve the question.

Loveladies urged the court to adopt a bright-line rule that the denominator of the takings fraction is that parcel for which the owner seeks a permit.[88] Conversely, the government argued that the proper denominator was the original 250-acre parcel, or at least the 51 acres remaining unsold in 1982 when the permit was denied.[89] Instead of turning to Supreme Court precedent,[90] the court relied on its own precedent to adopt "a flexible approach, designed to account for factual nuances."[91] Under this approach, the court ruled that the relevant property applicable to the takings analysis was the 12.5 acres. The regulation had deprived the owner of all economically feasible use of that acreage and thus constituted a total taking of that parcel.[92] The court reached this conclusion despite the fact that the Supreme Court had reaffirmed the totality rule the year before in *Concrete Pipe.*

In short, *Loveladies* and *Florida Rock* are incorrectly decided. The analysis by the Federal Court of Appeals is based on an inaccurate definition of the deprivation denominator. The court based its decisions on the notion that Justice Scalia's questioning of the totality rule in a footnote of the *Lucas* opinion was tantamount to overruling the Court's traditional regulatory takings jurisprudence, which has consistently focused on the property as a whole. Moreover, the Federal Court of Appeals shows a total disregard for the Supreme Court's post-*Lucas* affirmation of the totality rule in *Concrete Pipe.*

b. Deprivation of All Use Required When a court appropriately applies the totality rule, it becomes immediately clear that the *Lucas* per se rule is applicable to only a minimal number of cases. In *Lucas,* the Court emphasized at least eighteen times that no categorical taking occurs unless the owner is permanently deprived of *all* value and use. This means all use and value when viewed in light of the entire property.

Despite the *Lucas* Court's emphasis on the limited applicability of the categorical rule, litigants still attempt to present their claim to fall within the per se rule when they have been deprived of less than *all* use. A prime example is found in *Concrete Pipe,* in which the company tried to fashion its claim into a *Lucas* per se challenge.[93] The Court flatly rejected the claim as an attempt to "shoehorn" the challenge into the *Lucas* analysis.[94]

It is also important to remember the conceptual parameters of the phrase "all value." This phrase means all value, both physical and temporal. A case illustrating the limited scope of the *Lucas* rule is *Woodbury Place Partners v. City of Woodbury.*[95] The *Woodbury* case involved a city ordinance that placed a moratorium on all planning permits from March 23, 1988, to March 23, 1990. The plaintiff developer contended that the moratorium deprived him of all the economically viable use of his property during the two-year period.

The *Woodbury* court's determination of whether the moratorium was a deprivation of *all* use centered on evaluating the depth, width, and length of the governmental action. The court held that a taking for two years did not deprive the developer of all economically viable use of his land. Following the two-year period, the developer would be free to use his land in any manner he sought. Thus, a two-year period of deprivation was insufficient to maintain a takings claim based on the *Lucas* per se rule. As a result, the court reversed the lower court's determination that a categorical taking had occurred and remanded for a balancing under the *Penn Central* factors.[96]

c. Application of the Penn Central *Multifactor Test* If the *Lucas* per se rule does not apply, then the court must revert to the ad hoc, factual inquiry delineated by *Penn Central* and consider the following: the character of governmental action, the economic impact on the property owner, and the regulation's interference with the property owner's investment-backed expectations. Because the *Lucas* per se rule applies only when a total taking occurs, all partial economic takings must be analyzed under this *Penn Central* test.

Some courts, however, are unclear about this reversion to the *Penn Central* balancing test. This confusion seems to arise when courts fail to recognize that if the *Lucas* per se rule does not apply, the court must analyze the economic impact of the regulation by balancing it against the other *Penn Central* factors.

Again, *Florida Rock* is instructive. The court there failed to use the analysis required for economic takings. Instead, it asserted that if no categorical taking under *Lucas* is found, the claimant may recover proportional compensation if the impairment of economic use passes a threshold beyond "diminution in value." The court supports this view with citations to *Loretto*[97] and *Hendler*,[98] both involving physical takings where the size of the property interest taken was irrelevant to the courts' analyses. In effect, the *Florida Rock* court adopts an analysis that says that if the *Lucas* categorical rule does not apply, the analysis for physical takings does.

Consequently, the court ruled that a partial taking of a percentage of property may equal a taking if the regulation prohibits all economically beneficial use of the partial portion of the land taken.[99] According to the court,

> Nothing in the language of the Fifth Amendment compels a court to find a taking *only* when the Government divests the total ownership of the property; the Fifth Amendment prohibits the uncompensated taking of private property without reference to the owner's remaining property interests.[100]

The analysis is problematic for several reasons. First, this formulation departs significantly from traditional economic regulatory takings jurisprudence, which has always focused on what the property owner has left after the regulatory action, rather than what has been taken away. The court, in remanding to the Court of Federal Claims, states that the amount of just compensation should be "proportional to the value of the interest taken as compared to the total value of the property" whether the taking results from physical occupation or from regulation.[101] This characterization of the issue leads to the conclusion that a mere diminution of economic value caused by government regulation requires compensation.[102] The Supreme Court, however, has long rejected this position.[103] It has stated that the regulatory takings equation "is resolved by focusing on the uses the regulations permit," rather than the uses restricted.[104]

A second problem with this formulation is that it does not acknowledge that *Concrete Pipe* has prescribed the analysis required when a takings challenge does not fit into one of the discrete categories described in *Lucas*. If neither of the categorical rules applies, the court should revert to the *Penn Central* factors, just as the Supreme Court did in *Concrete Pipe*.

Most importantly, the *Florida Rock* court fails to recognize how the Court distinguished various types of takings. Its analysis varies significantly for each type of taking, particularly when partial deprivations are involved. One reason why economic takings analysis differs from physical and title takings analysis is because the latter two have an identifiable property interest that can be transferred to the government.

If the court recognizes a mere diminution in value as a taking, there is no specific property interest to be transferred. The right taken must also be identified because compensation is fixed at the fair market value of the transferred property right.[105] This fundamental requirement forecloses the likelihood of successive claims to the taking of a single property interest. As Chief Judge Nies noted in dissent,

> [A] lost value damage claim would impose not even an easement on the land. Successive claims are not only possible but likely. If loss of value alone created a claim, Florida Rock not only would receive the damage award, but also would keep the land. In effect, takings jurisprudence would become a novel type of Fifth Amendment tort claim for regulatory injury to the landowner under which the United States must pay damages while receiving no quid pro quo. *This is not the law.*[106]

The majority's response to this point seems to call for property lawyers to create their own property interests. According to the court, "Identification of a specific property interest to be transferred to the Government should pose no problem for property lawyers. Property interests are about as diverse as the human mind can conceive."[107]

III. Conclusion

The Supreme Court appears to be moving toward a clearer definition of property for the purposes of regulatory economic takings analysis. In so doing, it is removing the obfuscatory partial takings issues. Although some would interpret Justice Scalia's action in *Lucas* to have opened the partial takings question, it would be landmark legal practice for footnote dicta to overturn existing precedent and also negate a later decision by the Court. Following *Concrete Pipe*, therefore, land-use practitioners should interpret the partial takings denominator to include the property as a whole, both physically and temporally. When, and whether, some of the lower courts will clearly interpret this message remains to be seen. The best result would be for the Supreme Court to clarify this issue itself, once and for all.

Notes

1. *See* Robert H. Freilich, *Solving the "Taking" Equation: Making the Whole Equal the Sum of Its Parts*, 15 URB. LAW. 447 (1983); *see also* Robert H. Freilich and Stephen P. Chinn, *Finetuning the Taking Equation: Applying it to Development Exactions*, 40 LAND USE L. & ZONING DIG., pt. I, Feb. 1988, at 3, pt. II, Mar. 1988, at 3; Robert H. Freilich & David W. Bushek, *Thou Shalt Not Take Title Without Adequate Planning: The Takings Equation after* Dolan v. City of Tigard, 27 URB. LAW. 187 (1995).

2. Lucas v. South Carolina Coastal Council, 112 S. Ct. 2886 (1992); Robert H. Freilich & Elizabeth A. Garvin, *Takings After Lucas: Growth Management Planning and Regulatory Implementation Will Work Better Than Before*, 22 STETSON L. REV. 410 (1993).

3. Note that the term "partial regulatory taking" is an oxymoron. Justice Scalia in *Lucas* refers to the "total takings" inquiry, but care should be exercised in using this term. Because a total restriction is a taking, it is apparently acceptable to call it a taking. But if the phrase leads to calling *all* partial deprivations "partial takings," the phrase assumes the conclusion that a taking has occurred. Yet, a partial deprivation, as this article will demonstrate, in most instances does not constitute a taking—partial or total. Woodbury Partners v. Town of Woodbury, 492 N.W.2d 25 (Minn. Ct. App. 1993). Nevertheless, the term "partial regulatory taking" has been improperly used by the lower courts. *See* Florida Rock Indus., Inc., v. United States, 18 F.3d 1560, 1568 (Fed. Cir. 1994).

4. Concrete Pipe & Prod. of Calif., Inc. v. Constr. Laborers Pension Trust, 113 S. Ct. 2264, 2290 (1993).

5. *See* Kaiser Aetna v. United States, 444 U.S. 164 (1979) (holding owners of private lagoon subject to a taking when United States makes lagoon accessible to navigable water and public use).

6. 260 U.S. 393 (1922).

7. *Pennsylvania Coal*, 260 U.S. at 415.

8. The landmark case of Penn Central Transp. Co. v. City of New York, 438 U.S. 104 (1978), established the criteria to be used in assessing when a regulation goes "too far." The Court acknowledged that it had been unable to develop any set formula and that the cases necessarily involved "essential ad hoc, factual inquiries." *Id.* at 124.

9. For an extensive discussion of the legitimacy analysis in light of the Supreme Court's recent takings decision of Dolan v. City of Tigard, 114 S. Ct. 2309 (1994), see Freilich and Bushek, *supra* note 1.

10. *See* Nollan v. California Coastal Comm'n, 483 U.S. 825 (1987); Dolan v. City of Tigard, 114 S. Ct. 2309 (1994). *See also* Robert H. Freilich and Terry D. Morgan, *Municipal Strategies for Imposing Valid Development Exactions: Responding to* Nollan, 10 ZONING AND PLAN. L. REP., Dec. 1987, at 169.

11. Loretto v. TelePrompTer Manhattan CATV Corp., 458 U.S. 419 (1982). *Loretto* established a categorical rule for permanent physical occupations. Under the *Loretto* rule, any permanent physical invasion by, or authorized by, the government equates to a taking.

12. *See* Lucas v. South Carolina Coastal Council, 112 S. Ct. 2886 (1992), in which the Court promulgated a categorical rule for permanent deprivations of all economic use of the relevant property.

13. Nollan v. California Coastal Comm'n, 483 U.S. 825 (1987).

14. *Penn Central,* 438 U.S. at 124; *see also* Agins v. City of Tiburon, 447 U.S. 255, 261 (1980) (adopting and reiterating the *Penn Central* balancing test); Concrete Pipe & Prod. of Calif., Inc. v. Construction Laborers Pension Trust, 113 S. Ct. 2264 (1993) (reaffirming the use of the *Penn Central* balancing test in the wake of the Court's *Lucas* decision).

15. *See* Freilich & Garvin, *supra* note 2, at 411; *id. in* AFTER LUCAS: LAND USE REGULATION AND THE TAKING OF PROPERTY WITHOUT COMPENSATION 53-81 (David L. Callies ed., 1993).

16. In the third category, although there is no categorical per se taking, the court may require a higher scrutiny of the governmental action.

17. In physical taking and economic taking, the Court has put a definitive per se rule into place (Loretto v. TelePrompTer Manhattan CATV Corp., 458 U.S. 419 (1982) (physical taking); Lucas v. South Carolina Coastal Council, 112 S. Ct. 2886 (1992) (economic taking). In the third category of title taking there is no per se takings category, only ad hoc factual inquiry. But when the facts reveal that a title impairment (or exaction in lieu of a title impairment—that is, dedication) has occurred, the court will require higher scrutiny and will ease the balancing test's heavy presumption of validity toward the character of the governmental action. *See* Nollan v. California Coastal Comm'n, 483 U.S. 825 (1987); Freilich & Morgan, *supra* note 10, at 169.

18. *See generally* Bove v. Donner-Hanna Coke Corp., 258 N.Y.S.2d 299 (App. Div. 1932) (discussing the type of action that constitutes a nuisance per se); J.H. Beuscher & Jeffrey W. Morrison, *Judicial Zoning Through Recent Nuisance Cases,* WIS. L. REV. 440 (1955); A. Mitchell Polinsky, *Resolving Nuisance Disputes: The Simple Economics of Injunctive and Damage Remedies,* 32 STAN. L. REV. 1075 (1980).

19. The line between physical invasions and economic taking is not always clear, but has consistently been interpreted, except under extreme cases, to fall into the latter category. In Seawall Associates v. City of New York, 542 N.E.2d 1059 (N.Y.), *cert. denied,* 493 U.S. 976 (1989), a New York City ordinance established a five-year moratorium on conversion or demolition of single-

resident occupancy multidwelling units, and compelled rehabilitation and rental of all units at controlled rates. The court found this to be a surrender of the right to exclusive possession and therefore a per se or facial compensable physical taking, citing *Nollan*. The finding in *Seawall* has not been followed in other states or in subsequent cases in New York. *See* Yee v. City of Escondido, 503 U.S. 519 (1992).

20. *See* Hodel v. Irving, 481 U.S. 704 (1987); Griggs v. Allegheny County, 369 U.S. 84 (1962); United States v. Causby, 328 U.S. 25 (1946).

21. 444 U.S. 164 (1979).

22. *Kaiser Aetna*, 444 U.S. at 179-80 (citations omitted).

23. 458 U.S. 419 (1982).

24. *Loretto*, 458 U.S. at 426.

25. *Id.* at 432.

26. The Supreme Court's recent decision in Dolan v. City of Tigard, 114 S. Ct. 2309 (1994), reaffirms the existence of a category of takings referred to here as "title" takings. In *Dolan*, the Supreme Court emphasized that the case was distinguishable from other types of takings cases because the property owner was required to deed portions of the property to the city to receive a building permit. *Id.* at 2316. Additional support for this classification is found in the lower court cases following *Dolan*. For instance, Harris v. City of Wichita, 862 F. Supp. 287 (D.Kan. 1994), reviewed upon an Order On Reconsideration due to the release of the *Dolan* opinion, reinforces the concept of a title takings category. The *Harris* Court emphasized that *Dolan* was different from earlier land-use regulation cases, because the City of Tigard required that the Dolans deed property to the city upon an adjudicative decision. *Id.* at 294-95.

27. 483 U.S. 825 (1987).

28. 114 S. Ct. 2309 (1994).

29. Dolan v. City of Tigard, 854 P.2d 437, 539-40 (Or. 1993).

30. *Dolan*, 114 S. Ct. at 2314 (emphasis added).

31. *Id.*

32. *Dolan*, 854 P.2d at 444.

33. 483 U.S. 825 (1987). *See also* Freilich & Morgan, *supra* note 10, at 169.

34. *Dolan*, 845 P.2d at 443-44.

35. *Dolan*, 114 S. Ct. at 2313.

36. *Id.* at 2321.

37. *Id.* at 2319. The Court divided the nexus tests into three categories. The easiest test requires "very generalized statements about the necessary connection between the required dedication and the proposed development. . . ." *Id.* At the other extreme, "[o]ther state courts require a very exacting correspondence, described as the 'specific and uniquely attributable'" test. *Id.* Despite some confusion in the literature about the various labels that apply to each test, the "reasonable relationship" test was the intermediate position for the Court. The Court erred in this regard, because "reasonable relationship" has always been the most liberal or expansive test. *See* Wald Corp. v. Metro. Dade County, 338 So. 2d 863 (Fla. Dist. Ct. App. 1976).

38. *Dolan*, 114 S. Ct. at 2317.

39. *Id.* at 2317.
40. *Id.* at 2311.
41. *See* Freilich & Morgan, *supra* note 10, at 169.
42. A court's analysis differs for each takings classification. Its analysis for physical takings begins with the *Loretto* per se rule that a permanent physical occupation of property results in a taking. Under this rule, a partial regulatory taking can occur if the segment of property taken is less than total in the spatial sense, but cannot occur if the segment of property is less than total in the temporal sense. In *Loretto,* the Supreme Court held that a permanent physical occupation authorized by government is a per se taking even though the physical interference is minimal. In other words, if the partial deprivation is spatial, a court may find a taking. Nevertheless, if the partial deprivation is temporary, the *Loretto* per se rule does not apply and the inquiry will return to the balancing of interests.

The Court's analysis for title takings centers around the legitimacy of the government action rather than the impact of the action on the relevant property. Nevertheless, a partial regulatory taking may be found when the government acquires title to only a part of the relevant property.

43. 112 S. Ct. 2886 (1992).
44. The majority contemplates giving landowners two bites at the takings apple. First the landowner can seek to establish entitlement to a liability determination under the new categorical rule in which the character of the governmental action is disregarded and, if unsuccessful, may still present a takings claim under the traditional multifactor test of *Penn Central:*

> This analysis [Justice Stevens's criticism of the categorical rule as establishing an all-or-nothing approach to regulatory takings] errs in its assumption that the landowner whose deprivation is one step short of complete is not entitled to compensation. Such an owner might not be able to claim the benefit of our categorical formulation, but, as we have acknowledged time and again, "the economic impact of the regulation on the claimant and . . . the extent to which the regulation has interfered with distinct investment-backed expectations" are keenly relevant to takings analysis generally.

Lucas, 112 S. Ct. at 2895 n.8 (quoting *Penn Central,* 438 U.S. at 124).

45. Freilich & Garvin, *supra* note 2, at 420.
46. 482 U.S. 304 (1987).
47. "We merely hold that where the government's activities have already worked *a taking of all use* of property, no subsequent action by the government can relieve it of the duty to provide compensation for the period during which the taking was effective." *First English,* 482 U.S. at 321 (1987) (emphasis added).
48. *See* Faux-Burhans v. County Comm'rs, 674 F. Supp. 1172 (D. Md. 1987), *aff'd,* 859 F.2d 149 (4th Cir. 1988), *cert. denied,* 488 U.S. 1042 (1989); Terminal Equip. Co. v. City of San Francisco, 270 Cal. Rptr. 329 (Ct. App. 1990) (restating California rule that "all" reasonable use must be denied); De Bottom v. Marble Township, 689 F. Supp. 477 (E.D. Pa. 1988) (finding no taking because plaintiff

not deprived of "all" use(s) of property); City of Virginia Beach v. Virginia Beach Land Inv. Ass'n No. 1, 389 S.E.2d 312 (Va. 1990) (downzoning of 403-acre parcel from planned-unit development to agriculture not a taking—no deprivation of "all" economically viable use). *See also* Herrington v. County of Sonoma, 834 F.2d 1488 (9th Cir. 1987), *modified,* 857 F.2d 567 (9th Cir. 1988) (*First English* interpreted to require property owners to "demonstrate that all or substantially all economically viable use of the property ha[d] been denied"), *cert. denied,* 489 U.S. 1090 (1989); Citizen's Ass'n v. Int'l Raceways, Inc., 833 F.2d 760 (9th Cir. 1987) (*First English* interpreted as consistent with view that a taking does not occur unless owner is deprived of "economically viable use of the property," and that mere reduction in property's value not enough to constitute a taking). These factors have also been expressed in dollar or percentage value, since Village of Euclid v. Ambler Realty Co., 272 U.S. 365 (1926), in which the court found no taking despite 78 percent reduction in land value. *See also* Haas & Co. v. City of San Francisco, 605 F.2d 117 (9th Cir. 1979) (finding 95 percent reduction in value is not a taking), *cert. denied,* 445 U.S. 928, *reh'g denied,* 446 U.S. 929 (1980); Pace Resources, Inc. v. Shrewsbury Township, 808 F.2d 1023 (3d Cir.) (stating a 90 percent reduction—$495,000 to $52,000—not a taking), *cert. denied,* 482 U.S. 906, *reh'g denied,* 483 U.S. 1040 (1987); Hadacheck v. Sebastian, 239 U.S. 394 (1915) (an 85 percent reduction—$800,000 to $60,000—not a taking).

49. Keystone Bituminous Coal Ass'n v. DeBenedictis, 480 U.S. 470, 514 (1987) (Rehnquist, C.J., dissenting).

50. Pennsylvania Coal v. Mahon, 260 U.S. 393 (1922); Keystone Bituminous Coal Ass'n v. DeBenedictis, 480 U.S. 470 (1987); Hodel v. Irving, 481 U.S. 704 (1987); Andrus v. Allard, 444 U.S. 51 (1979); Penn Central Transp. Co. v. City of New York, 438 U.S. 104 (1978); Pennell v. City of San Jose, 485 U.S. 1 (1988); McNulty v. Town of Indialantic, 727 F. Supp. 604 (M.D. Fla. 1989); Presbytery of Seattle v. King County, 787 P.2d 907 (Wash. 1990) (expressly overruling *Allingham v. Seattle,* which had allowed a partial taking challenge to rear-yard setback; after uproar within entire state, Supreme Court overruled *Allingham,* holding that takings must be determined by viewing statute's effect on entire physical parcel); Deltona Corp. v. United States, 228 Cl. Ct. 476, 657 F.2d 1184 (1982), *cert. denied,* 455 U.S. 1017 (1982) (total prohibition of development on three wetland neck areas not a taking when total property of five neck areas allowed for development on two neck areas).

51. *Penn Central,* 438 U.S. at 130-31 (emphasis added).

52. *Keystone,* 480 U.S. at 497. The Court acknowledged that when the takings inquiry compares the value taken from the property with the value that remains, "one of the critical questions is determining how to define the unit of property 'whose value is to furnish the denominator of the fraction.'" *Keystone* acknowledges the general rule in *Penn Central* and the holding in *Andrus,* 444 U.S. at 65-66 (destruction of one strand in bundle of rights is not a taking "because the aggregate must be viewed in its entirety"); however, the *Keystone* decision goes on to state: "[T]hese verbal formulations do not solve all of the definitional issues that may arise in defining the relevant mass of property." *Keystone,* 480 U.S. at 497.

53. 112 S. Ct. 2886 (1992) (recognizing that "deprivation of all economically feasible use" is an imprecise test for takings because it "does not make clear the 'property interest' against which the loss of value is to be measured").

54. *Id.* at 2894 n.7 (emphasis supplied).

55. *Lucas,* 112 S. Ct. at 2901 (citing Board of Regents v. Roth, 408 U.S. 564, 577 (1972)) (Justice Scalia's reliance on the Supreme Court's "traditional resort to 'existing rules or understandings that stem from an independent source such as state law' to define the range of interests that qualify for protection as 'property' under the Fifth (and Fourteenth) Amendments would suggest that the answer to the question be resolved under state eminent domain or inverse condemnation law.").

56. *See generally,* Fulling v. Palumbo, 233 N.E.2d 272, 21 N.Y.2d 30 (1967) (court found a taking when development on subdivided one-half-acre lot prevented because minimum lot size changed to one acre after subdivision, even though property owner had contiguous half-acre lot that was already developed).

57. In his dissent in *Lucas,* Justice Stevens suggested that the majority's footnote 7 formulation could lead to considerable mischief:

> On the other hand, developers and investors may market specialized estates to take advantage of the Court's new rule. The smaller the estate, the more likely that a regulatory change will effect a total taking. Thus, an investor may, for example, purchase the right to build a multi-family home on a specific lot, with the result that a zoning regulation that allows only single-family homes would render the investor's property interest "valueless." In short, the categorical rule will likely have one of two effects: Either courts will alter the definition of the "denominator" in the takings "fraction," rendering the Court's categorical rule meaningless, or investors will manipulate the relevant property interests, giving the Court's rule sweeping effect. To my mind, neither of these results is desirable or appropriate, and both are distortions of our takings jurisprudence.

112 S. Ct. at 2919-20 (Stevens, J. dissenting). In *Keystone,* the Supreme Court specifically held that the subsurface estate in land to be mined for coal should not be considered a separate segment of property for takings law purposes, because it constitutes just one part of the mine operator's bundle of property rights, notwithstanding that Pennsylvania law recognizes the support estate as a separate property interest. Given the potential problems posed by Justice Stevens, and in light of the fact that *Keystone* was not reversed, this aspect of the majority opinion (which was, after all, dicta and relegated to a footnote) should not be given great weight. Nevertheless, the footnote has resulted in considerable confusion about this issue.

58. In fact, since *Lucas* was decided, several significant decisions have reached that conclusion, rejecting the segmenting of the property interest. *See, e.g.,* Bernardsville Quarry, Inc. v. Borough of Bernardsville, 608 A.2d 1377 (N.J. 1992) (restriction of subsurface quarrying operation not a separate taking of subsurface property when surface and subsurface taken as a whole); McAn-

drews v. New Bank of New England, 796 F. Supp. 613, 619 (D. Mass. 1992) (restriction on termination of separate leasehold not a taking "because the aggregate must be viewed in its entirety" (citing *Keystone,* 480 U.S. at 497, and *Andrus,* 444 U.S. at 65-66)). Earlier, the Washington Supreme Court reversed a decision that found a taking in a rear-yard restriction of 68 percent of the property, holding that the property must be viewed in its entirety. Presbytery of Seattle v. King County, 787 P.2d 907 (Wash. 1990). *Presbytery* expressly overruled Allingham v. City of Seattle, 749 P.2d 160 (Wash. 1988), which had allowed "partial" taking challenges. Thus, state law in Washington will not allow the property owner to claim that he or she has been deprived of 100 percent of a partial interest.

59. *Pennsylvania Coal,* 260 U.S. at 413.

60. *Lucas,* 112 S. Ct. at 2919-20 (Stevens, J., dissenting).

61. *Id.* at 2920.

62. 113 S. Ct. 2264 (1993) (rejecting attempt to simply divide property into what was taken and what was left; relevant issue is whether property taken is all, or only a portion of, the parcel in question; critical inquiry is how to define the unit of property).

63. *Penn Central,* 438 U.S. at 130-31.

64. *Keystone,* 480 U.S. at 497, (holding "that a claimant's parcel of property could not first be divided into what was taken and what was left for the purpose of demonstrating the former to be complete and hence compensable.").

65. Such a plan, generally established as part of a collective bargaining contract, is created through the combination of employers who hire a pool of employees. All contributions to the plan are placed in a fund for the benefit of all these employees. An employee who has not worked for any one of the group's employers for ten years, but who has worked for the group for ten years, has attained vested benefit status under the Employee Retirement Income Security Act, 29 U.S.C. § 1001—§ 1461 (1988).

66. Pub. L. No. 96-364, 94 Stat. 1208 (1980).

67. 29 U.S.C. §§ 1362(b), 1364 (1988).

68. *Concrete Pipe,* 113 S. Ct. at 2272 (citing Pension Benefit Guar. Corp. v. R.A. Gray & Co., 467 U.S. 717 (1984)).

69. *Id.*

70. *Id.* The equation for determining liability was as follows:

> [The employer's] "proportionate share of the plan's 'unfunded vested benefits,'" that is, "the difference between the present value of vested benefits" (benefits that are currently being paid to retirees and that will be paid in the future to covered employees who have already completed some specified period of service, 29 U.S.C. § 1503) "and the current value of the plan's assets. 29 U.S.C. §§ 1381, 1391." *Id.*

71. The Court distinguished Concrete Pipe's challenge from the challenge in Connelly v. Pension Benefit Guar. Corp., 475 U.S. 211 (1988), as an "as applied" challenge rather than a facial challenge. Due to the similarities between

the contract provisions of *Connelly* and *Concrete Pipe,* the Court begins its evaluation of the takings challenge with a review of some of the *Connelly* principles, giving it the opportunity to reaffirm that the power of Congress to regulate cannot be undone by private contractual agreements.

72. Concrete Pipe attempted to shoehorn its claim into a *Lucas* challenge, which the Court flatly rejected. In doing so, the Court confirmed the limited application of the *Lucas* per se rule.

73. *Concrete Pipe,* 113 S. Ct. at 2291 (citing *Keystone,* 480 U.S. at 497) ("Our test for regulatory taking requires us to compare the value that has been taken from the property with the value that remains in the property, and one of the critical questions is determining how to define the unit of property 'whose value is to furnish the denominator of the fraction'") (citation omitted).

74. 18 F.3d 1560 (Fed. Cir. 1994).

75. *Florida Rock,* 18 F.3d at 1568.

76. *Id.* at 1562.

77. *Id.* at 1563.

78. The Federal Courts Administration Act of 1992, Pub. L. No. 102-572, §902, 106 Stat. 4506 (1992), changed the name of the U.S. Claims Court to the U.S. Court of Federal Claims.

79. *Florida Rock,* 18 F.3d at 1563.

80. *Id.* at 1562.

81. *Id.*

82. *Id.*

83. *Id.* at 1564-65.

84. *Id.* at 1573.

85. 28 F.3d 1171 (Fed. Cir. 1994).

86. VNR Industries, Inc. v. United States, 962 F.2d 1013 (Fed. Cir.), aff'd sub nom., Keene Corp. v. United States, 113 S. Ct. 373 (1992).

87. 28 F.3d 1171 (Fed. Cir. 1994).

88. *Loveladies,* 28 F.3d at 1181.

89. *Id.* at 1180.

90. Ironically, Judge Plager cites to *Concrete Pipe* to support the proposition that use of the investment-backed expectations factor is a way of limiting takings recoveries to owners who can demonstrate that they bought their property in reliance on a state of affairs that did not include the challenged regulatory regime. But he fails to acknowledge *Concrete Pipe*'s instructive discussion of the totality rule.

91. *Loveladies,* 28 F.3d 5th Cir. at 1181. The court cites to Deltona Corp. v. United States, 657 F.2d 1184 (Ct. Cl. 1981), and Whitney Benefits, Inc. v. United States, 926 F.2d 1169 (Ct. Cl. 1981), in support of this flexible approach. Notably, the court ignored one of its own precedents that may have been instructive. In Tabb Lakes Ltd. v. United States, 10 F.3d 796 (Fed. Cir. 1993), the Federal Circuit refused to allow a takings claimant to subdivide his property into five distinct units so he could assert that all economic value of three parcels had been taken by the denial of a wetlands permit. The court explained, "Clearly, the quantum

of land to be considered is not each individual lot containing wetlands or even the combined area of wetlands. If that were true, the Corps's protection of wetlands via a permit system would, *ipso facto*, constitute a taking in every case where it exercises its statutory authority." *Id.* at 802.

92. *Loveladies*, 28 F.3d at 1181.

93. The petitioner's brief states in pertinent part:

> *Lucas* is instructive. In fact, CP&P finds itself in a worse position than Mr. Lucas vis-a-vis the impact on property. Lucas complained that the land-use regulation deprived him of all reasonable uses thereby stripping all economic value from the property. Here CP&P is to be deprived of approximately 46% of its book net value permanently and without any compensation. Had the statute in *Lucas* been upheld, the landowner could still have built a patio and walkway, and enjoyed the view from his beach. Here, if the statute is upheld, CLPT seizes the assets and CP&P retains no property interest in the seized assets.

Brief for Petitioner, at 39.

94. *Concrete Pipe*, 113 S. Ct. at 2290.

95. 492 N.W.2d 258 (Minn. Ct. App. 1993) (*review denied*).

96. In its decision, the court distinguishes *First English Evangelical Lutheran Church v. County of Los Angeles*, 482 U.S. 304 (1987), on the basis that the case held "where the government's activities have already worked a taking of all use of property, no subsequent action by the government can relieve it of the duty to provide compensation for the period during which the taking was effective." According to the *Woodbury* court, the Supreme Court's decision did not specify that every regulation constituted a temporary taking. Therefore, although temporary deprivations *may* form the basis of a takings claim, not every temporary deprivation meets the requirements. Thus, based on the facts, the court was justified in finding no taking.

97. Loretto v. TelePrompTer Manhattan CATV Corp., 458 U.S. 419 (1982).

98. Hendler v. United States, 952 F.2d 1364 (Fed. Cir. 1991).

99. *Florida Rock*, 18 F.3d at 1564-65.

100. *Id.* (Emphasis added).

101. *Id.* at 1569.

102. *Id.* at 1576 (Nies, C.J., dissenting).

103. *Penn Central*, 438 U.S. at 131; Welch v. Swasey, 214 U.S. 91 (1909).

104. *Penn Central*, 438 U.S. at 131.

105. Yuba Natural Resources, Inc. v. United States, 904 F.2d 1577, 1580 (Fed. Cir. 1990).

106. *Florida Rock*, 18 F.3d at 1576 (Nies, C.J., dissenting).

107. *Id.* at 1572 n.32.

CHAPTER ❖ 9

Partial Takings after *Dolan*

G. Richard Hill

I. Introduction

Regulatory takings are like car accidents. They fascinate us. We cannot help slowing down to look. What a disaster, we say to ourselves. We are so glad it did not happen to us. But we wonder if we could be next. We think about who is at fault, who should pay for the damages, and how it all could have been avoided in the first place. And we question how the rules of the road could be improved so that such collisions in the future could be averted.

In fact, it is quite simple for the government to steer clear of takings problems. By following a few clear rules, governmental entities will almost always be successful at insulating themselves from liability: in land-use decisions, the government should act in a fair manner, both substantively and procedurally; the government should base its decisions on adequate study and evaluation; and the government should make an easily reviewable record of its fairness and its study.

Although it is quite simple for the government to avoid liability, in practice governments find it difficult to assure fairness, clarity, studiousness, and thorough administrative records. As a result, it has become necessary for the government and for private property owners to confront the issue of regulatory taking, and the question of when regulations go "too far," entitling property owners to an award of damages equal to the value of the property taken.

The U.S. Supreme Court has defined two bright-line tests. First, if a regulation requires a conveyance of a real property interest to the government, independent of any permit application, it will be deemed a per se taking for which compensation will be due.[1] Second, even in connection with a permit application, if the regulation causes a permanent loss of all economic value of a relevant parcel of real property (assuming the proposed use is not enjoinable as a nuisance under the background principles of the state's law of property), the regulation will be deemed a per se taking for which compensation will be due.[2]

The currently vigorous "property rights movement" proposes yet another bright-line test. For example, Initiative 164, presented to the Washington state legislature in January 1995, provides that most governmental land-use regulations that decrease property values must, to be valid, compensate property owners for that loss of value. If adopted, Initiative 164, and others like it currently being proposed around the country, could drastically change land-use law.

Under the two Supreme Court tests, most land-use regulations fall shy of either of the bright lines. If these regulations are to be challenged successfully under the takings clause, the challenge must be based on a "partial takings" theory.

For the purposes of this chapter, "partial takings" refers to governmental regulations that take less than all economic use of an entire parcel of real property but, under one of several theories, may be deemed to constitute takings nonetheless. This chapter explores "partial takings" involving regulatory conditions that (1) impose dedication requirements, payment of fees, and on-site or off-site improvements; (2) take less than all economic value of a parcel; and (3) take all use of a parcel for a defined period of time.

The Supreme Court Quintet

Five recent U.S. Supreme Court cases set the stage for the jurisprudence of partial takings.

A. *Keystone* and the Problem of the Relevant Parcel

Keystone Bituminous Coal Ass'n v. DeBenedictis[3] addressed a challenge to Pennsylvania's Bituminous Mine Subsidence and Land Conservation Act, which prohibited coal mining that caused subsidence damage to preexisting public buildings, dwellings, and cemeteries. The complaint alleged that Pennsylvania recognizes three separate estates in land: the mineral estate, the surface estate, and the "support estate." The plaintiffs claimed the act "took" all of their support estate in certain discrete parcels of land. The act prevented the mining of 27 million tons of coal owned by the plaintiffs.

The 5-to-4 majority upheld the validity of the act. As part of its analysis, the majority concluded that not "all" value was taken, because the act affected only 2 percent of the plaintiffs' coal and because it was overly formalistic to separate the support estate from the bundle of property rights owned by the plaintiffs.

The four members in the minority, however, would have found that the act deprived the plaintiffs of "all" use of a discrete property interest—the support estate. That deprivation resulted in a taking of 27 million tons of coal for which compensation would have been due, according to their analysis.

Thus, *Keystone* epitomizes the difficulty of defining the relevant parcel. The definition of the parcel can lead to placement of a particular factual situation on one side or the other of the court's "bright-line" test. Even if no per se taking is found, however, and even if "all use" is not taken, the definition of the relevant parcel will be pertinent to a court's ad hoc, factual analysis of whether a taking has occurred.

B. *First English Evangelical Lutheran Church* and the Issue of Delay

In *First English Evangelical Lutheran Church v. County of Los Angeles,*[4] the Supreme Court held that a property owner who claims that his or her property has been taken by a land-use regulation may recover damages for the period of time before a final determination is made that the regulation constitutes a taking of the property.

The appellant owned a 21-acre parcel of land in Los Angeles County that was subjected to flood regulations that allegedly denied "all use" of the property. After reviewing cases involving the appropriation of private property by the United States during World War II, Chief Justice Rehnquist noted "the fact that 'temporary' takings which, as here, deny a landowner all use of his property, are not different in kind from permanent takings, for which the Constitution clearly requires compensation."[5] Chief Justice Rehnquist emphasized that the majority holding was limited to a case in which the appellant was denied "all use" of its property, "We limit our holding to the facts presented, and of course do not deal with the quite different questions that would arise in the case of normal delays in obtaining building permits, changes in zoning ordinances, variances, and the like which are not before us."[6]

This limitation in the opinion raised the question of whether "abnormal delays" in obtaining building permits, changes in zoning ordinances, variances, and the like may be deemed to constitute "regulatory takings." The opinion also raises, but does not answer, the question of whether moratoria on land-use approvals, interim zoning, and phased growth controls, which temporarily take all use of property, could be deemed regulatory takings for which temporary damage compensation is due.

C. *Nollan* and Regulatory Conditions

In *Nollan v. California Coastal Commission,*[7] the Supreme Court confronted the validity of permit conditions on development projects. The Nollans owned a beachfront lot in Ventura County, California. The building on the lot was a small bungalow that fell into disrepair. The Nollans applied for a permit to replace the bungalow with a three-bedroom house. The California Coastal Commission conditioned its grant of permission to rebuild the house on the Nollans' transfer of a public easement across their property. The Nollans claimed imposition of that condition violated the takings clause of the Fifth Amendment.

Writing for the majority, Justice Scalia noted that had there been no permit application, the State of California would have had to pay compensation to the Nollans for the easement. Thus, the issue at hand was whether conditioning the issuance of a permit on the grant of an easement changed the character of the governmental action in such a way that no compensation was required.

While Justice Scalia noted that the condition in this case could be classified as a "physical" taking, the rest of the decision does not focus on that characterization. Rather, the standards set forth in the opinion appear to apply to all governmental permit conditions, not merely to those involving property transfer or physical appropriation.

According to the Court's analysis in *Nollan,* three separate factors must be evaluated to determine the validity of governmental permit conditions:

1. The "legitimate state interest" allegedly furthered by the condition at issue
2. The governmental condition
3. The adverse impacts of the proposed project

First, to justify a proposed condition, the government must establish a "legitimate state interest."[8] While "a broad range of governmental purposes and regulations satisfies the requirement" for a legitimate state interest, the court will nevertheless scrutinize the interest to assure that it is "legitimate."[9]

Second, the condition imposed on the project must "substantially advance" the legitimate state interest cited as the justification for the condition. If it does not do so, the condition is invalid.[10]

Third, the project must itself cause impacts which "substantially impede" the legitimate state interests offered by the state as justification for the condition.[11]

In *Nollan,* the commission argued that it was entitled to protect the public's ability to see the beach, help the public overcome the "psychological barrier" to using the beach created by a developed shorefront, and prevent congestion on public beaches.[12] The condition imposed by the commission failed because Justice Scalia concluded that it did not substantially further these permissible purposes and that the proposed project did not substantially impede the purposes, assuming without deciding that those purposes were "legitimate."[13]

Nollan imposed tough standards on governmental agencies to justify conditions imposed on projects. They must be able to articulate the "legitimate state interest" that the condition is intended to further and also show a nexus between the condition imposed and the adverse impacts of the project. It was left to future cases, however, to determine the actual scope of the *Nollan* decision, how far it would apply beyond regulations that result in a physical taking, how legitimate the state purpose must be, and how substantial the nexus must be between the condition and the project impacts.

D. *Lucas* and the Denominator Uncertainty Principle

Five years after the decisions in *Keystone, First English,* and *Nollan,* the Supreme Court issued its opinion in another landmark case, *Lucas v. South Carolina Coastal Council.*[14]

In 1986, David Lucas paid $975,000 for two residential lots on the Isle of Palms in Charleston County, South Carolina. He planned to build a single-family house on each lot. Two years later, however, the South Carolina legislature enacted the Beachfront Management Act, which prohibited Lucas from building any houses on the two lots.

Writing for the Court, Justice Scalia observed that in the seventy-odd years of regulatory taking jurisprudence, the Court has generally eschewed any set formula for determining how far is too far, preferring to engage in essentially ad hoc, factual inquiries. However, he concluded that the Court has identified at least two discrete categories of regulatory action as compensable without case-specific inquiry into the public interest advanced in support of the restraint. The first category involves those cases in which governmental regulation requires the property owner to suffer a physical "invasion" of his or her property. In such cases, no matter how minute the invasion or how weighty the public purpose behind it, the Court has required compensation. The second category concerns cases in which a regulation denies an owner all economically beneficial or productive use of land.

The Court found that Lucas's claim fell into the second category and held that because the South Carolina regulation denied him all economically beneficial use of his land, the regulation constituted a per se taking of his property regardless of the governmental interest supporting the regulation. The government could avoid paying compensation only if it could show that Lucas's proposed use is prohibited under the state common law of nuisance and property.

Although the case focuses on the rare factual situation of a complete taking of all economically beneficial use, the Court does discuss how the takings inquiry should proceed when less than all use is taken. In footnote 7, the Court observes:

> Regrettably, the rhetorical force of our "deprivation of all economically feasible use" rule is greater than its precision, since the rule does not make clear the "property interest" against which the loss of value is to be measured. When, for example, a regulation requires a developer to leave 90% of a rural tract in its natural state, it is unclear whether we would analyze the situation as one in which the owner has been deprived of all economically beneficial use of the burdened portion of the tract, or as one in which the owner has suffered a mere diminution in value of the tract as a whole. . . . Unsurprisingly, this uncertainty regarding the composition of the denominator in our "deprivation" fraction has produced inconsistent pronouncements by the Court.[15]

The Court suggested that the answer to this question lies in "how the owner's reasonable expectations have been shaped by the State's law of property—i.e. whether and to what degree the State's law has afforded legal recognition and protection to the particular interest in land with respect to which the takings claimant alleges a diminution in (or elimination of) value."[16]

The Court also emphasized, in footnote 8, that even if a property owner is not able to convince a court that the value of his or her property interest has been completely eliminated, that simply means that the *Lucas* categorical rule is inapplicable. The property owner is still entitled to an ad hoc, factual inquiry that would explore the economic impact of the regulation on the claimant and the extent to which the regulation has interfered with distinct investment-backed expectations. Thus, a property owner whose property value has been reduced 95 percent, although unable to avail himself or herself of the categorical rule, still might be entitled to compensation after an ad hoc, factual inquiry.

E. *Dolan* and Rough Proportionality

In *Dolan v. City of Tigard,*[17] the Supreme Court resolved a q
open by its decision in *Nollan:* What is the required degree
tion between the exactions imposed by the governmental agency and the projected impacts of the proposed development?

Dolan had applied to the city to expand her plumbing supply store and to pave her parking lot. The City Planning Commission conditioned its approval on her compliance with dedication of land (1) for a public greenway along the creek to minimize flooding that would be exacerbated by the proposed increase in impervious surfaces and (2) for a pedestrian/bicycle pathway intended to relieve traffic congestion.

Applying *Nollan,* the Court first evaluated whether the "essential nexus" existed between the legitimate state interest asserted by the government and the permit condition exacted by the city. In *Dolan* the nexus existed. There was a legitimate state interest in minimizing flooding. There was a nexus between that interest and the condition requiring a greenway. There was also a legitimate state interest in relieving traffic congestion and a nexus between that interest and the condition requiring a pedestrian/bicycle pathway.

Because the nexus existed, the Court was then obliged to determine the degree of connection required between the exactions and the project impacts. After reviewing state court standards, the Court concluded:

> We think a term such as "rough proportionality" best encapsulates what we hold to be the requirement of the Fifth Amendment. No precise mathematical calculation is required, but the City must make some sort of individualized determination that the required dedication is related both in nature and extent to the impact of the proposed development.[18]

The burden falls on the governmental agency to justify the condition.

In *Dolan,* the city failed to show any impacts of Dolan's project that required granting of a public easement; therefore, that condition constituted an uncompensated taking. The requirement for a pedestrian/bicycle pathway failed because the city failed to meet its burden of showing actual traffic impacts from the project that would be quantifiably mitigated by the pathway.

Dolan's "rough proportionality" test is far from specific. It will be left to future, mainly state court, cases to provide more meaningful content to the test. And *Dolan* still does not answer the question of whether the *Nollan* nexus is applicable only to physical takings or also to development fees and mitigation conditions placed on projects.

II. Partial Takings Today

Partial regulatory takings today arise primarily in three contexts: when governmental agencies condition project approvals, when regulations deprive property owners of all use of less than all their parcels, and when regulations deprive property owners of all use of all their parcels for a temporary period of time. This section will discuss several key cases regarding partial takings.

A. Regulatory Conditions

Regulatory conditions on project approval can involve requirements for land dedication, payment of development fees, and construction of physical improvements on-site or off-site. Recent cases show that actual land-dedication requirements are uniformly suspect, that successful challenges to payment of development fees vary from jurisdiction to jurisdiction, and that challenges to conditions requiring physical improvements only rarely succeed.

Three recent cases from the Northwest challenge land-dedication requirements. In *Sparks v. Douglas County,*[19] a short subdivision application approval was conditioned on dedicating strips of land abutting existing roads for a future right-of-way. Relying on Washington state constitutional law as well as *Nollan,* the court of appeals stated the applicable rule, "[P]ermission to develop land may be conditioned on the owner's agreement to dedicate a portion of his property to public use if the regulatory exaction reasonably prevents or compensates for, in a specific and proportional fashion, . . . adverse public impacts *of the proposed development.*"[20] Because the record did not show any specific or direct impact of the proposed development that would require widening of the road, the court invalidated the condition and held that it constituted a taking.

In *Luxembourg v. Snohomish County,*[21] the county conditioned a subdivision application on the plaintiff's dedicating a right-of-way to neighboring property. Citing *Nollan,* the Washington Court of Appeals held that the exaction of property must address some problem arising from the development under consideration. Because the subdivision did not create the neighboring property's access problem, the county was prohibited from conditioning subdivision approval on dedicating right-of-way for access.

Similarly, an Oregon case decided since *Dolan* invalidated a subdivision condition that required dedication of a ten-foot right-of-way to the county.[22] The Oregon Court of Appeals held that under *Dolan,* no presumption of validity applied to the condition and that the record showed no connection between the proposed subdivision and the necessity for road widening; therefore, the city failed to meet *Dolan*'s "rough proportionality" test. It now appears clear that unless a jurisdiction can show a meaningful connection between the impacts of a project and a dedication requirement, the requirement will not be upheld.

Development fees, however, are another story. Neither *Nollan* nor *Dolan* made clear whether the heightened scrutiny required for dedication conditions is also necessary when courts review challenges to development fees. California courts and the Ninth Circuit have gone in one direction and ruled the *Nollan* heightened scrutiny approach inapplicable to development fees. Other state courts have assumed *Nollan* is applicable.

In *Commercial Builders v. Sacramento,*[23] the Ninth Circuit upheld the validity of fees on nonresidential developments to pay for low-income housing. In its analysis, the Ninth Circuit observed that no court to date had interpreted *Nollan* to change the level of scrutiny to be applied to regulations that do not constitute a physical encroachment on land.[24] According to the Ninth Circuit, only if there is "no evidence of a nexus between the development and the problem to be addressed" will the regulation be invalidated.[25] Because the Ninth Circuit found there was a sufficient nexus in *Commercial Builders,* the fees at issue were upheld.

The California state courts have taken a similar approach. In *Blue Jeans Equities West v. City & County of San Francisco,*[26] the California Court of Appeal reviewed the validity of a traffic impact fee ordinance. It held that the heightened scrutiny test of *Nollan* is limited to possessory, rather than regulatory, takings cases.[27] Under the more lenient standard, the fee ordinance was easily upheld.[28]

Immediately after deciding *Dolan,* however, the Supreme Court granted certiorari in *Ehrlich,* vacated the judgment, and remanded the case to the California Court of Appeal for further consideration in light of *Dolan.* It appears likely this action by the Court shows that the *Nollan* heightened scrutiny test is also applicable to development fees.

If that was the intent of the Supreme Court in remanding *Ehrlich,* the California Court of Appeal failed to discern it. On remand, both a recreational mitigation fee and an in-lieu art fee were upheld. The recreational fee was upheld as satisfying both the *Nollan* and *Dolan* tests—there was no recognition of heightened scrutiny and the court applied a very loose nexus and proportionality standard. The in-lieu art fee was deemed an essentially legislative determination and therefore *Dolan* was held inapplicable.[29] If the Supreme Court agrees to accept review of this decision again, it is unlikely the appellate court's decision will be affirmed—the fees at issue appear preposterous.

New York and Washington have both found the *Nollan/Dolan* tests applicable to development fees. In *Weingarten v. Town of Lewisboro,*[30] property owners filed a challenge to the town's requirement that payment in lieu of reservation of parkland be provided as a condition of development. The court reviewed the *Nollan* test, did not question its applicability to the fees at issue, and found that the necessary nexus was present. Similarly, in *Trimen Development Co. v. King County,*[31] the Washington Supreme Court reviewed a similar subdivision requirement, found that the *Dolan* "rough proportionality" requirement was applicable, and concluded that the county had met its burden of showing that the fees in lieu of dedication were reasonably necessary as a direct result of Trimen's proposed development.

Even less clear than development fees is whether the *Nollan/Dolan* heightened scrutiny tests apply to general project conditioning and on-site and off-site mitigation requirements. Three recent cases discuss this question. In *Harris v. City of Wichita,*[32] a federal district court affirmed the validity of an airport-overlay zoning district against a takings challenge. In its analysis, the court distinguished *Dolan* on two grounds. First, *Dolan* dealt with adjudicative rather than legislative action. The zoning district at issue, however, was clearly a legislative determination. Second, *Dolan* dealt with a dedication requirement. No such dedication requirement was present in *Harris.* Because most project conditions do not involve dedications, if *Dolan* is limited to dedications, as the *Harris* court suggests, its significance will be considerably reduced.

In a recent decision, the Ninth Circuit also emphasizes the dedication component of *Dolan.* In *Carson Harbor Village, Ltd. v. City of Carson,*[33] the court dismissed a challenge to the constitutionality of ordinances that imposed rent control and restrictions on conversion of property to other uses. In ruling that the plaintiff did not have standing to pursue a facial challenge to the ordinances because the law does not substantially advance any legitimate government interest, the court, citing *Dolan* and *Nollan,* summarized the law as follows, "Under this theory of takings, the law is invalid if the required dedication of property is unrelated in nature, or disproportionate in extent, to the problem that the government seeks to mitigate or control."[34]

The Eighth Circuit takes a more expansive view of *Nollan* and *Dolan.* It sustained an equal protection challenge to a county development condition that required the applicant to construct and pay for a drainage system to serve the entire watershed area in which it was located.[35] The court cited *Nollan* for the proposition that singling out this developer to bear the burden of the government's attempt to remedy a broad public problem could constitute an equal protection violation. It also cited *Dolan* for the proposition that a strong public d prove the public condition will not warrant achieving the shorter cut than the constitutional way of paying for the cha

As of today, then, dedication requirements must cert heightened scrutiny and will be upheld only if the government shows that a sufficient nexus exists and that there is a rough proportionality between the exaction and the project's impacts. It is unclear whether development fees will face similar scrutiny, although the Court's vacating and remanding of *Ehrlich* suggest that they will. General project conditioning, on the other hand, will most likely receive more generous review by the courts, unless conditions appear to be wholly unrelated to project impacts.

B. All Use of Less Than All the Parcel

The courts have had several opportunities to address regulatory takings claims when a regulation takes all use of less than all of the parcel.

The most prominent, and thoughtful, of the recent cases is *Florida Rock Industries, Inc. v. United States*.[36] Florida Rock sought, and was denied, a permit under section 404 of the Clean Water Act (Section 404) to mine the limestone that lay beneath a tract of wetlands. While the court concluded the permit denial caused a substantial reduction in value, it was not so great a reduction that the *Lucas* categorical takings rule could be invoked. Thus, on remand, the trial court will be left with "the difficult task of resolving when a partial loss of economic use of the property has crossed the line from a noncompensable 'mere diminution' to a compensable 'partial taking.' "[37] The question, according to the court, will depend on the particular facts and will require a "classic exercise of judicial balancing of competing values."[38]

The court sets forth the following questions that, on remand, the trial court should answer to balance appropriately the pertinent competing values:

> In addition, then, to a demonstration of loss of economic use to the property owner as a result of the regulatory imposition . . . the trial court must consider: are there direct compensating benefits accruing to the property, and others similarly situated, flowing from the regulatory environment? Or are benefits, if any, general and widely shared through the community and the society, while the costs are focused on a few? Are alternative permitted activities economically realistic in light of the setting and circumstances, and are they realistically available? In short, has the Government acted in a responsible way, limiting the constraints on property ownership to

> those necessary to achieve the public purpose, and not allocating to some number of individuals, less than all, a burden that should not be borne by all?[39]

Thus, the key issues, according to the *Florida Rock* court, are the extent of loss of economic use, the presence or absence of reciprocity of advantage, and the availability of alternative, realistically available, economic activities.

In *Bowles v. United States*,[40] the U.S. Claims Court found that the Corps of Engineers' refusal to issue a Section 404 permit to fill a single-family lot to install a septic system was a taking, as no economic use remained. The court analyzed the case as a total taking under *Lucas*, but also addressed the facts in the context of a partial taking.

Under the government's analysis, there was residual value to the lot even after the Corps's permit denial. There was only a 91.8 percent reduction in property value, according to the government. That was enough for the court to find a sufficiently severe economic impact to warrant compensation. The court also found that Bowles had reasonable investment-backed expectations, because all other lots in the subdivision had been filled without any regulatory involvement by the Corps. The court awarded just compensation damages amounting to the value of the lot just before the permit denial, plus interest compounded annually from the date of the taking.

In *Miller Bros. v. Department of Natural Resources*,[41] the director of the Michigan Department of Natural Resources prohibited oil and gas development in a dunes area. Owners of such rights claimed a regulatory taking. The Michigan Court of Appeals held that all the claimants' oil and gas rights were taken, that these were a separate, valid property interest, and that therefore a taking had occurred. The court refused to consider the fact that the claimants owned many other oil and gas rights that were not subject to this regulation; it focused instead on the fact that these particular rights, covering thousands of acres, were taken. The case included a thoughtful discussion of just compensation. Because the director might lift the regulation at any time, the court concluded that the state should be obligated to pay "rent," the fair market rental value of the property, until such time as the regulation is lifted.

The Oregon Supreme Court refused to acknowledge as a taking a city ordinance that removed one strand of property rights from the total bundle.[42] The ordinance prohibited transient rentals (including existing ones) of fewer than fourteen days. The plaintiffs argued that because the right to continue an existing legal use is a property right, removal of that existing use is a taking without regard to other economically viable uses. The court rejected that claim, relying on *Keystone* for the proposition that removal of only one strand in the bundle will not be viewed as a taking.

The final key case in this area is *Reahard v. Lee County.*[43] A property owner challenged the county's designation of his property as a resource protection area, claiming the designation constituted an uncompensated taking. The U.S. Magistrate Judge agreed and ruled the property owner was entitled to compensation. The Eleventh Circuit reversed and remanded, stating the proper test that the lower court should employ on remand to determine whether a partial taking occurred:

> [A] proper takings analysis would address a number of questions. . . . [T]hose questions are: (1) the history of the property—when was it purchased? How much land was purchased? Where was the land located? What was the nature of title? What was the composition of the land and how was it initially used?; (2) the history of development—what was built on the property and by whom? How was it subdivided and to whom was it sold? What plats were filed? What roads were dedicated?; (3) the history of zoning and regulation—how and when was the land classified? How was use proscribed? What changes in classifications occurred?; (4) how did development change when title passed?; (5) what is the present nature and extent of the property?; (6) what were the reasonable expectations of the landowner under state common law?; (7) what were the reasonable expectations of the neighboring landowners under state common law?; and (8) perhaps most importantly, what was the diminution in the investment-backed expectations of the landowner, if any, after passage of the regulation?[44]

While these questions are obviously not pertinent to every fact situation, they show the type of detail that must be explored in an ad hoc factual inquiry in a partial taking context.

C. All Use of the Parcel for a Temporary Period of Time

First English left open the question of whether damages for an interim taking could be assessed for more than normal delays in the regulatory process. Based on that question, doubts have been raised about the validity of zoning moratoria, phased growth controls, and the like. To date, the courts have been unsympathetic to challenges based on temporary taking arguments. Unless the regulatory restriction is permanent or the regulatory delay is so great that it shocks the conscience, the courts are unlikely to find a taking.

Palm Beach County v. Wright[45] dealt with the constitutionality of a county thoroughfare map that designated potential locations of future roadways and forbade land-use activity that would impede future roadway construction. The map was adopted incident to a comprehensive plan.

The Florida Supreme Court ruled the map was not unconstitutional on its face. The court analogized the roadway-corridor construction prohibition to building-setback requirements, which have traditionally been upheld. It emphasized the importance of the map for the county's planning purposes, and it acknowledged the county's willingness to ameliorate concerns by permitting flexibility that would ease the hardships imposed by the map's restrictions. The court also acknowledged that, as applied, the map might constitute a taking. Any "as applied" challenge would arise from a specific development application and would require consideration under the Supreme Court's ad hoc takings formulations.

In *Tabb Lakes, Ltd. v. United States,*[46] the property owner sought temporary taking damages for the three-year period between a Corps of Engineers' denial of a permit application and the district court's reversal of that denial. The Federal Circuit answered the question by finding that the Corps's denial did not effect a taking. Although the refusal to issue a permit prevented the property owner from developing the property, the Corps specifically had invited the property owner to submit a revised application. In addition, the court found that a three-year period of governmental decisionmaking is not such an extraordinary delay that finding a taking would be justified—rather, it is merely an "incident of ownership" in a regulated society.

The Federal Court of Claims reached a similar result in *1902 Atlantic, Ltd. v. United States.*[47] A federal district court ordered that a permit application be issued in 1986, after the Corps of Engineers denied the issuance in 1981. The property owner sought temporary taking damages. The court found no taking, because the property owner never had a property right in the permit until it was actually issued. The court stated, "The temporary harms suffered by Atlantic during the period its permit was denied were certainly significant, but the Government cannot be charged with the delay necessary to complete the review process."[48]

The Minnesota Court of Appeals denied a temporary takings claim in the context of a two-year zoning moratorium in *Woodbury Place Partners v. Woodbury.*[49] The property owners claimed that the moratorium took all use of their property during the two-year period and that therefore, under *Lucas* and *First English,* they were entitled to temporary takings damages. The Minnesota Court of Appeals focused on the "parcel as a whole" within the two-year period and concluded that the time restriction was too modest to merit compensation:

> We acknowledge that no case has specifically addressed the dimension of length of time as it applies to the totality of a taking. Nonetheless the Supreme Court's inclination to measure the economic burden against the value of the property as a whole, rather than against discrete segments, compels us to reject the partnership's argument. . . . When measured against the value of the property as a whole, rather than against only a two-year time frame, the moratorium did not deny the partnership "all economically viable use" of its property. Delaying the sale or development of property during the governmental decision-making process may cause fluctuations in value that, absent extraordinary delay, are incidents of ownership rather than compensable takings.[50]

Thus, absent truly extraordinary delay, courts are reluctant to assess damages against the government for the time it takes to plan for future development or to review projects. The delay is deemed an incident of property ownership. Although property owners are entitled to develop their property, that right is limited by the dimension of time.

III. The Emergence of Predictability

From this review of recent partial takings cases, it is surprising to see the emergence of a modest amount of predictability.

Regulatory conditions that require the dedication of property to the government will receive searching review for nexus and rough proportionality. Development impact fees will likely be approved if they are based on proper study and evaluation and are reasonably related to the actual, direct project impacts; if they are not, they are likely to be invalidated. On-site and off-site project conditions are likely to be approved under a minimal scrutiny standard; they will be invalidated only if they are clearly designed to offset existing infrastructure deficiencies or to serve the public as a whole rather than to address the impacts of the particular project.

Regulatory takings claims asserting that governmental regulations have taken less than all the use of property will be recognized when the facts justify them. A searching factual inquiry that explores (1) the economic impact on the property owner, (2) the significance of the governmental interest, and (3) whether a reciprocity of advantage exists to benefit the property owner, will be necessary. The rule of reason, based on the common law of the state, is likely to be applied to determine the relevant parcel of property for the takings analysis.

The delay associated with governmental planning and review of projects is most unlikely to result in a damages award. Only when such delay is truly extraordinary and unconscionable is it likely that courts will lend a sympathetic ear to property owner complaints.

Despite the predictions of many, the Supreme Court regulatory takings quintet has been neither a disaster for government nor a particular boon to property owners. What these decisions have accomplished, however, is a necessary rebalancing, providing property owners with claims in appropriate equitable situations when government has gone too far in its regulatory zeal.

Notes

1. Loretto v. TelePrompTer Manhattan CATV Corp., 458 U.S. 419 (1982).
2. Lucas v. South Carolina Coastal Council, 112 S. Ct. 2886 (1992).
3. 480 U.S. 470 (1987).
4. 482 U.S. 304 (1987).
5. *First English*, 482 U.S. at 318.
6. *Id.* at 321.
7. 483 U.S. 825 (1987).
8. *Id.* at 834.
9. *Id.* at 834-35.
10. *Id.* at 834.
11. *Id.* at 835.
12. *Id.*
13. *Id.* at 835-839.
14. 112 S. Ct. 2886 (1992).
15. *Lucas*, 112 S. Ct. at 2894 n.7.
16. *Id.*
17. 114 S. Ct. 2309 (1994).
18. *Dolan*, 114 S. Ct. at 2318-19.
19. 863 P.2d 142 (Wash. Ct. App. 1993), *review granted*, 881 P.2d 254 (Wash. 1994).
20. *Sparks*, 863 P.2d at 144 (emphasis added).
21. 76 Wash. App. 502, 887 P.2d 446 (Ct. App. 1995).
22. Schultz v. City of Grants Pass, 884 P.2d 569 (Or. Ct. App. 1994).
23. 941 F.2d 872 (9th Cir. 1991); *cert. denied*, 112 S. Ct. 1997 (1992).
24. *Commercial Builders*, 941 F.2d at 874.
25. *Id.* at 875.
26. 4 Cal. Rptr. 2d 114 (Ct. App.), *review denied*, No. 50 25468, 1992 Cal. LEXIS 2234 (Cal. Apr. 29, 1992), *cert. denied*, 113 S. Ct. 191 (1992).
27. *Blue Jeans*, 4 Cal. Rptr. 2d at 118.

28. *Accord* Ehrlich v. Culver City, 19 Cal. Rptr. 2d 468 (Ct. App.) (mitigation fee and in-lieu art fee upheld based on minimal scrutiny for nonpossessory governmental conditioning), *review denied*, No. 5033642, 1993 Cal. LEXIS 4467 (Cal. Aug. 25, 1993), *motion granted, vacated, remanded*, 114 S. Ct. 2731 (1994), *aff'd in part, rev'd in part, remanded*, No. B055523 (Ct. App. 2d Dist., Div. 5 Dec. 23, 1994), *review granted*, No. 5033642, 1995 Cal. LEXIS 1959 (Cal. Mar. 16, 1995); Tahoe Keys Property Owners Ass'n v. State Water Resources Control Bd., 28 Cal. Rptr. 2d 734 (Ct. App.) (lake pollution mitigation fees upheld because not entitled to "heightened scrutiny that a physical taking would entail"), *review denied*, No. 5039720, 1994 Cal. LEXIS 3274 (Cal. Sup. Ct. June 16, 1994), *cert. denied*, 115 S. Ct. 485 (1994).

29. Ehrlich v. Culver City, No. B055523 (Ct. App. 2d Dist., Div. 5 Dec. 23, 1994).

30. 542 N.Y.S.2d 1012 (Sup. Ct. 1989), *aff'd without opinion*, 559 N.Y.S.2d 807 (1990).

31. 877 P.2d 187 (Wash. 1994).

32. 862 F. Supp. 287 (D. Kan. 1994).

33. 37 F.3d 468 (9th Cir. 1994).

34. *Carson Harbor*, 37 F.3d at 476.

35. Christopher Lake Dev. Co. v. St. Louis County, 35 F.3d 1269 (8th Cir. 1994).

36. 18 F.3d 1560 (Fed. Cir. 1994), *cert. denied*, 115 S. Ct. 898 (1995).

37. *Florida Rock*, 18 F.3d at 1570.

38. *Id.*

39. *Id.* at 1571.

40. 31 Cl. Ct. 37 (1994).

41. 513 N.W.2d 217 (Mich. Ct. App. 1994).

42. Cope v. City of Cannon Beach, 855 P.2d 1083 (Or. 993).

43. 968 F.2d 1131 (11th Cir. 1992).

44. *Reahard*, 968 F.2d at 1136.

45. 641 So. 2d 50 (Fla. 1994).

46. 10 F.3d 796 (Fed. Cir. 1993).

47. 26 Cl. Ct. 575 (1992).

48. *1902 Atlantic*, 26 Cl. Ct. at 581.

49. 492 N.W.2d 258 (Minn. Ct. App. 1992), *review denied*, No. C2-92-670, 1993 Minn. LEXIS 20 (Minn. Jan. 15, 1993), *cert. denied*, 113 S. Ct. 2929 (1993).

50. *Woodbury*, 292 N.W.2d at 262.

CHAPTER ❖ 10

A Planner's View of *Dolan*

Dwight H. Merriam, AICP

The *Dolan v. City of Tigard*[1] decision reminds me of the New Englanders' comment about the weather—if you do not like it, wait a bit, because it will change soon. For planners, a retrospective suggests that the impact of the *Dolan* decision will quickly fade into the rapidly changing landscape of land-use law.

In the fall of 1966 when I was first introduced to planning law as a junior in undergraduate school, the subject was much simpler. A major court decision of that era was *Udell v. Hass*,[2] which established the "cutting edge" theory that local zoning boards must give more than "mock obeisance" to the comprehensive plan. A quick check on our computers recently revealed that case has been cited 111 times so far.

There were no planning computer programs, such as GPS, GIS, ARCINFO, or CAD. I had a great set of Prismacolor pencils in all kinds of numbered colors that I used to prepare existing land-use, future land-use, and zoning maps. Cutting edge (literally and figuratively) technology was the Zipatone plastic, which we would stick onto our tracing paper base maps. There were no electronic calculators. The next summer, when I was fortunate enough to get a job as a planner, we did our cohort survival method population forecasts on enormous "coffee grinder" mechanical calculators that had the miserable habit of jamming right in the middle of running a calculation, after we had spent an hour or two punching in data.

Think about it. Point systems and performance zoning were not in use and growth management had yet to be fully conceptualized. Frankly, we knew we were progressives, and thought we might even be radicals, for pushing the concept of clustering in the urbanizing rural communities of the Pioneer Valley of western Massachusetts. (We are still pushing those concepts in the same area today.)

After being impressed into the navy for Vietnam duty, I returned to study planning, getting my master's degree in 1974. That is just two decades ago, but the leading case then, *Golden v. Ramapo*,[3] dealt with growth management. It was highly touted, seldom followed, and eventually abandoned. But much has happened in growth management and development regulation in the twenty years since *Ramapo*. Numerous West Coast communities adopted adequate public facilities ordinances, which have, probably through the effects of some yet unknown, non-ionizing radiation, mutated into such creatures as the payment-in-lieu-of-art fee imposed on the developer in the case of *Ehrlich v. Culver City*,[4] remanded by the U.S. Supreme Court in light of its *Dolan* decision, and upheld again, of course, by the California courts.[5]

The technology for doing good and evil has so shaped our lives in these past two decades that we would do well to reflect on those changes and consider their impact. Personal computers did not exist. The University of North Carolina had a "statistics lab" with a bank of tube light calculators that students reserved for their use days in advance. I bought my first Texas Instruments five-function calculator (the kind they give you with an oil change today) for about seventy dollars, which was real money in 1973. There was no Federal Express, no voice mail, no fax service, no Lexis, no Nexis, no Westlaw, no CD ROM, no Internet. The "throughput" of change was much slower than today.

The fact that the U.S. Supreme Court did not decide a major land-use case for fifty years, between *Nectow v. City of Cambridge*[6] in 1928 and *Penn Central Transportation Company v. City of New York*[7] in 1978, actually helped the development of land-planning theory and innovative regulation because fifty states, some more active than others, all developed independent bodies of land-use law. Professor Norman Williams, Jr., sees the reentry of the U.S. Supreme Court into land-use law as ending this long and great period of state-by-state experimentation. The reentry has not necessarily been good or helpful, and has come at a time of truly "Tofleresque" future shock, with instant analysis and application of U.S. Supreme Court decisions, even though their interpretation and use is problematic given their evolutionary and often ambiguous nature. In short, we have been forced to adjust to one bed after another, without knowing the dimensions of any one of them as we lay down upon it. The courts are becoming our Procrustes.

Supreme Court decisions have whipsawed planners all along. Fortunately for planners, the Court's tentative tomfoolery with the likes of *Agins v. City of Tiburon*,[8] *San Diego Gas and Electric v. City of San Diego*,[9] *Williamson County Regional Planning Commission v. Hamilton Bank of Johnson City*,[10] *McDonald, Sommers & Frates v. Yolo County*,[11] and the like were not forced upon the regulators. This is probably due to the media's lack of interest and the decisions' failure to advance the law much. Another reason may be that there were fewer land-use lawyers and commentators writing and speaking about the issues. Regardless of the reasons, the early U.S. Supreme Court decisions, at least through the 1978 case of *Penn Central*, had little effect on the way planners conducted their business.

Perhaps the real watershed era was 1978 through the early 1980s, with the *Monell v. Department of Social Services*[12] and *Owen v. City of Independence*[13] decisions infecting municipal law, including land-use regulation, with the remedy of 42 U.S.C. § 1983, the Civil Rights Act of 1871 (Section 1983). By the early 1980s, I noticed a dramatic shift away from volunteerism by members of local councils, boards, and commissions, who became increasingly fearful that their land-use decisions would result in liability under Section 1983, which provides for money damages and attorneys' fees for prevailing plaintiffs.

The flood of such cases in the mid-1980s abated only when some of the leading U.S. courts of appeals (principally the First, Second, and Ninth Circuits) erected judicial detention basins to hold back these actions. Eventually the landowner/developer community realized that it was much better to make money doing developments than it was to sue over developments that were denied, because property owners won so few of the Section 1983 cases.

As Section 1983 actions slowed in the late 1980s, the property rights movement emerged and spurred a not-so-silent majority (or is it a minority?) to champion the owners and developers of property upset by the loss of value caused by public regulation. The movement came of age with President Reagan's Executive Order 12630 of 1988, which I have never heard addressed at the several dozen U.S. Army Corps of Engineers proceedings I have been involved with since that date. A source within the Corps of Engineers for the New England division told me that the takings review under the Executive Order is routinely done whenever a permit application may be denied. The Corps of Engineers reportedly considers the takings analysis done by its Office of Counsel to fall within the attorney-client privilege; thus, the analysis is not available to the public. Interesting.

I. Planners Are Smart and Have Already Learned to Run the Maze Very Well

The point of my little retrospective report on the big changes in planning practice over the past three decades probably has only one good lesson—planning continues, pretty much as before, but with some improvements.

Planning law, on the other hand, has changed so fast that it is difficult to tell if planners have actually been able to keep up with the changes. It does appear from my work with planners around the country, however, that they have learned to run each of the new mazes with great alacrity.

The expansion of liability under Section 1983 during the 1980s taught planners to think a little more like trial lawyers, to keep good records, and to document what they were doing. Practices before then had been sloppy, but planners quickly learned how to create the necessary paper trails to prove their cases.

For example, planners have learned to go head-to-head with landowners/developers in "papering" the file. With the advent of word processing, we see very few instances of files that contain unrebutted letters. Planners now routinely shoot back rebuttals to applicants who make unsubstantiated claims, and occasionally outright lies, in correspondence to the planning office. Fifteen years ago, things were different. When asked to defend municipalities, we would often come upon files that, when considered in total, represented rather one-sided views of the world.

About keeping files, planners have become downright cagey compared with what they used to do. As an example of how bad it used to be, in one case we were defending some years ago we had to produce files going back two decades, and in those files were internal staff memos that referred to a certain prominent business person as being like Mu'ammar Gadhafi, and another memo that speculated, believe it or not, on the sexual preferences of the Lone Ranger and Tonto. Shocking and stupid? Sure, but such banter was typical of the free-wheeling office chatter that was prominent in the 1960s and 1970s. All of that is gone today, in most instances, because planners know how to keep records that solidify defensive positions.

The same holds true for sign regulation, following the many First Amendment cases of the past two decades, which have clarified old law and created new law. Few planners are getting in trouble these days for regulating temporary signs; most planners have mastered practices that respect the difference between content-based regulation and regulation of the time, place, and manner of speech.

But the sharply upward learning curve has not carried all planners and public officials with it. The inertia of local custom and past practices is often great. Just this year, I observed—to my amazement—the chairperson of a local land-use commission asking for a show of hands from the audience to indicate those who supported, and those who objected to, a project. I also still see too many instances in which a local commission will have a discussion about a pending matter outside a hearing room during a break. So, there is still work to be done.

II. Planners Have Become Less Quick to React and More Willing to Take a "Wait-and-See" Attitude Regarding Dramatic New Cases, Such as Dolan

Initially, the decision in *First English Evangelical Lutheran Church v. County of Los Angeles*[14] did create some unwarranted consternation in the planning community; but, for the most part, planners have discovered that *First English* really has had little or no practical effect on their day-to-day work. Similarly, they have found that *Nollan v. California Coastal Commission*[15] has had no measurable effect. Now they see the *Lucas v. South Carolina Coastal Council*[16] decision for what it is—a case of unusual facts that the government should have avoided litigating.

First English, Nollan, and *Lucas* all deserve a retrospective view of their own before putting *Dolan* in context. Perhaps what is most remarkable about these cases is not the decisions themselves (important as they have been), but how the cases were reported in the press and handled by landowners and regulators, and how most of us failed to follow up to see how the cases really turned out.

For example, the *First English* case was a straightforward one, even though the facts and the legal situation were a little complicated. There had been a drought of many years in southern California. The drought resulted in a massive forest fire in the Angeles Forest and the government (remember the government—"we are here to help you") came in with a cloud-seeding operation to bring an end to the drought. In the face of forecasts of pending rain, the government kept seeding and an enormous rainstorm occurred. Because there was little vegetation left, the ground was hard with charred remains and the soot caused a bulking factor (the interesting science-of-run-off stuff is reported only in the intermediate California court decision following the remand from the U.S. Supreme Court), the flood damage was extraordinary.

This flood wiped out a small church camp for handicapped children. Fortunately, the camp had not opened on time that year, so no one was there. A fact not reported in the Supreme Court's decision, however, was that several people were killed as a result of the flood. Consequently, the county adopted a moratorium until it could figure out where the base flood elevation was located and set new regulations for places where habitable buildings could be safely developed. To allow the church camp and others to rebuild immediately would have exposed those groups to almost certain danger and therefore would have been unconscionable.

But the church camp sued almost immediately and the case made its way to the U.S. Supreme Court. What nearly everybody did not realize, however, is that the case was never tried before it went to the Supreme Court. Instead, it went to the Court on a motion to strike a portion of the complaint that made a claim for money damages. California had never paid money damages for a taking, and the issue before the U.S. Supreme Court was only whether the property owner could recover money damages if the property had been taken by the moratorium. Sure, said the Supreme Court. This brought California, always at the fringe, in line with most other states.

That is really not a remarkable decision, but it was widely reported as making a big change in the law, and some of that reporting was done by journalists who had not read the decision, by writers who interviewed lawyers who had not read the decision, and by others who commented on the decision without having read it. The perceptions of the decision were incorrect, and these perceptions caused landowners and developers to become unreasonably hopeful about what they could achieve with a takings claim and, unfortunately, caused unnecessary anxiety among planners and local commissioners.

What most people do not know is that on remand, without a trial ever having been held, the California appellate court found there was not a taking because the church could still conduct camping activities on the site during the two-year moratorium. The church never got a dime. End of case.

The *Nollan* case is important in understanding *Dolan* but, as I noted above, has had no real impact. Planners who really understand *Nollan* have actually used it to their advantage. In that case, Jim and Marilyn Nollan, as a condition of their contract to purchase a small beach house and lot, were required to replace the beach house with a much larger house (to help property values increase for the seller who owned dozens of lots along the shorefront). The Nollans went to the California Coastal Commission for a permit and, as a condition of the permit, the commission required them to set aside a public access easement along the beach.

The case made its way to the U.S. Supreme Court, and the Court held that there was no "essential nexus" between what the enabling legislation expressly permitted and what was being required. The court acknowledged, however, that a visual easement from the street down to the water, or even a viewing platform, could have been required, both of which were expressly or impliedly within the reach of the enabling statute. But, because the statute did not say anything about access *along* the beach, the commission could not require it. Not too remarkable. There was some speculation that the decision turned on the notion of the Nollans being required to give up one of the sticks in their bundle of rights (namely the right to exclude someone from entering their property), but that interpretation would not be consistent with preserving the view from the street and creating access to preserve that view.

This was Justice Scalia's first opinion after he joined the Court. It was a five-to-four decision. Some of us speculated that it may originally have been a five-to-four decision going the other way, and that the majority opinion was, in the draft stages, the dissenting opinion. The opinion certainly reads that way. It also includes a string cite of substantive due process cases that does not seem to make any sense. It turns out that my esteemed colleague, Michael Berger, who so ably represented First English and filed an amicus brief in *Nollan,* had those same citations in his brief, carefully categorized and distinguished. It appears that some clerk lumped them together, causing considerable confusion ever since—not only among law students who have been dragged kicking and screaming through reading those cases and trying to find a common thread (there is not one), but even among land-use lawyers.

Every time the Supreme Court coins a new phrase, like "essential nexus," you can be sure that there will be years of pulling at little strings in the decisions that follow, trying to figure out what lies behind that term. By my reckoning, one new term in a big Supreme Court land-use case will enable each land-use lawyer to buy a new car during the three years following the decision.

The *Lucas* decision was also mishandled by the media and very little follow up was done. David Lucas was the hapless purchaser of two waterfront lots, separated by a developed lot, along the substantially developed shorefront of Isle of Palms, South Carolina, just north of Charleston. Actually, he was one of the developers and may have been cashing out his position with the purchase. He bought in 1986. In 1988, the South Carolina legislature adopted a long-considered law prohibiting development in areas where erosion historically had occurred, and

Lucas was left without the ability to build anything. He sued, and although the South Carolina legislature later adopted an "escape hatch" in the statute, the litigation was too far along.

Although Lucas lost at the state level, he won in the Supreme Court. The Court held that a property owner whose property was rendered "valueless" by regulation (whatever that is) had a right to money damages for a new type of "categorical" taking—a type of regulatory taking that would be treated by the courts as if it were a physical-invasion taking, such as the type Ms. Loretto experienced when a shoebox-sized cable television junction box was placed on top of her apartment building without her permission.[17] (She eventually won one dollar in damages—I have often wondered if her lawyer was on a one-third contingent fee. . . .)

There was quite a bit of hullabaloo with the *Lucas* decision, but my review of the cases over the two years since *Lucas* reveals very few decisions that have been influenced directly by the *Lucas* categorical taking. There may be more as the courts work their way through the "whole parcel" rule—in *Loveladies Harbor, Inc. v. United States,*[18] for example, the developers developed most of the site and made a profit, but a portion of the site standing alone could not be developed and ultimately the U.S. government acquiesced in a large award of damages to the property owner.

But what is really great about the *Lucas* case is not the troubling facts or the Supreme Court's coining of the new type of taking (thanks for the new car), but what happened afterwards. Gideon Kanner can tell the story—in fact he can tell any story a lot better than I can—and so I refer you to Chapter 15, which tells it all.

When we look at the real effect of all these takings decisions, we see land-use commentators who cried wolf once too often. The press reports these decisions in an inflammatory way without good knowledge. The spin doctors on both sides do their thing through the media and through their writings and, after a year or two of seeing no discernible change in state and local court decisions, the planners shrug their shoulders and say there is no wolf at the door.

It is not surprising, therefore, that the reaction to *Dolan* has been muted and intellectually reasonable. Planners immediately recognized problems in the City of Tigard's regulatory efforts, and many have told me at several post-*Dolan* workshops across the country that they generally would not require that an interest in land be dedicated along a floodway if the same planning result could be reached through merely prohibiting development. The plain fact is that planners are not what Professor Daniel Mandelker would call "police-power hawks." They are moderates, and in many of their small town and rural locales they reflect the moderate-to-conservative views of the general populace. The majority of planners I have come to know are probably quite sympathetic to the economic interest of the private property owners affected by regulation.

Most planners will see *Dolan* as merely evolutionary: they will wait to see whether anyone shakes a copy of the decision at them at the next planning board meeting and whether the state and local courts apply it to cases closer to home. In the meantime, the large majority of planners are really not all that concerned about exactions for bikeways and pedestrian paths, because they are not requiring them in their own plans and regulatory systems, at least not the way the City of Tigard did. Instead, planners have used Intermodal Surface Transportation Efficiency Act (ISTEA) funds to acquire such rights of way, or they have provided regulatory incentives for voluntary dedication, or, as most highly effective planners do, they have taken the developers aside and cajoled the "voluntary" dedication out of them. I remember one particularly effective planner who, fifteen years ago, before affordable housing programs became popular, would take condominium developers aside and tell them if they wanted their project approved, they should offer to provide some affordable units in their projects. Am I condoning random extortion? Of course not, but much good can come from a little backroom bartering.

In short, one of the effects of *Dolan* for the planning community is to force consideration of other financing mechanisms. While the commentators are wrestling with whether *Dolan* will promote impact fees, orchestrated financing techniques have been increasingly emphasized in recent years, partly driven by federal, state, and local fiscal austerity. For example, the Hackensack Meadowlands Development Commission (which I, along with Jim Nicholas and Julian Juergensmeyer, represent in the implementation of its Special Area Management Plan) is orchestrating many types of financing techniques—including transfer of development rights, development fees, impact fees, and general revenues—to create a $1 billion fund for the Environmental Improvement Plan (EIP). The EIP will spend most of its money on cleaning up so-called "orphan" landfills, which are Superfund sites that have no owners who can be found, and a good part of the rest of the money on wetland projects. An essential part of this orchestration of financing techniques, which is still in the development stage, is to create value in wetlands that are to be preserved and wetlands that are to be restored. This avoids the takings problem.

Earlier I noted that understanding a little about *Nollan* would help you understand *Dolan*. There is some affinity between the two, beyond the rhyme in their names. In *Nollan*, the concept of "essential nexus" was focused on the quality and character of the connection between the enabling statute and the required exaction. As there was no connection between the two, the relationship never rose to the required "essential nexus" level.

In *Dolan*, the Court found the requisite nexus, at least regarding the quality of the connection. The Court did not question whether regulating for flood damage protection and regulating for transportation management were permissible objectives of the state enabling statute.

What the *Dolan* Court was concerned about, however, was the "rough proportionality" between what the statute allowed the city to do and what was exacted. This is a question of quantity and magnitude. Even during oral argument, the Chief Justice observed that increasing the impervious surface by expanding the size of the building and paving the parking lot would necessarily increase runoff. (I mentally cheered him along, hoping he would draw the distinction between velocity and volume in the runoff calculus, but I was not to be satisfied on that front.) What the Court wanted to know, however, was whether there were any site-specific studies showing that the area set aside for the floodway and the bikepath/pedestrian walkway was necessary to avoid flooding and to overcome traffic impacts, respectively. The case is now on remand to answer these questions, though as this book goes to press, there has not been much activity on the local level and rumor has it that Florence Dolan and her son Dan may not expand their plumbing-supply store anyway because of too much competition in the marketplace.

III. Planners Will Plan a Little More Than They Have in the Past

As the details in the *Dolan* case have sunk in, planners recognize that they must not only document what they do, they must also do something to document. In the *Dolan* case, there was no site-specific analysis of the increased volume or velocity of stormwater that would flow off the site as a result of the larger building and increased paved parking area. There also was no analysis about the number of people who might use the bikepath/walkway, or the proportion of the expanded store's customers who would forego using cars. Planners know how to do these analyses, having done them many times before, and they will do even more when the case demands.

Reportedly, that is exactly what is going on in the City of Tigard as we write. The city has requested more site-specific studies by the applicant. Planners have learned over the years to ensure the existence of the "reasonable relationship" or "essential nexus" or whatever other term is chosen to identify the qualitative aspects of the relationship between the enabling law and local regulation. And now they are simply going to become more focused on the quantitative relationship between the development that is allowed and whether the impacts from that development warrant the exactions imposed.

IV. Regrettably, We Are Unlikely to See Increased Use of Eminent Domain

Regulators are notoriously frugal. If they can get something for free, they want it. But if they have to pay for it, they usually do not want it. Assuming there was insufficient evidence to support an uncompensated dedication, a city could readily take, at low cost, a bikepath and pedestrian walkway by using its power of eminent domain. I cannot imagine that a 15-foot-wide strip on a 70,000-square-foot parcel of land in an area that is legally and physically undevelopable and causes virtually no adverse impact on the property's development potential would be valued at any substantial amount. But local officials are opposed to using their eminent domain power for anything but absolutely necessary public improvements, such as street widenings and utility easements.

It is not economically efficient to try a case like *Dolan*. I would guess the case cost more than $500,000 to litigate. Planners could buy miles of bike and pedestrian paths for the cost of trying a case and going through one or more appeals.

V. Planners Have Not Forgotten One of the "Where's Waldo" Lessons of Nollan

Somewhat hidden in the *Nollan* decision and lurking in the *Dolan* decision is the principle that conditions are appropriate when necessary to grant approval for a project that, lacking such conditions, would not pass muster. Planners can talk softly, asking in whispers for dedications, and carry the big stick of denial. But not many planners do that, though they know such recourse is available to them. Instead, the typical dance that takes place over the negotiation of conditions focuses on what is necessary to get the project approved, not to prevent it from being denied. That positive approach worked well for planners long before *Nollan* and *Dolan* and continues to do so today.

VI. Planners Do Not Supply Free Lunches

Dolan requires site-specific analysis to determine the "quality" of the nexus between the dedication/condition and the development's impact. Planners lack the staff, time, and money for the work that *Dolan* apparently requires. And they are unlikely to add staff or increase budgets.

The developers will buy their own lunch. Planners will require that applicants do impact analyses at their own expense. And, in some jurisdictions, developers may be required to pay the cost of an independent review by the government.

Extreme examples are extreme examples, but here is one from my recent experience. Planners have become deft at making eager developers jump for jellybeans. I have just finished a project for the expansion of a regional shopping mall straddling two towns with two planners and two separate sets of commissions. It is a big project, with over $100 million in improvements to a profitable mall. The principal objective is to bring the first store of a certain national, upscale, department store chain to New England.

I might be violating a confidence of my client to tell you how many millions of dollars were spent in getting the approvals, but I will just estimate it at "several" million dollars. And that is just for approval of the site plans, not the detailed architecture, design, and engineering. At the last count, there had been over three hundred revisions to the site plans, and the developer, in the process of obtaining the discretionary approvals, analyzed a watershed of hundreds of acres and an off-site watercourse thousands of feet long, even though we knew that the volume and velocity of runoff would not increase as a result of the expansion and that the water quality would probably improve. Because one of the towns questioned the impact of runoff, the developer ultimately capitulated not only by doing the study, but by undertaking a $1.8 million off-site improvement program.

The largesse heaped upon the other town[19] included road improvements and the installation, without any charge, of a sewer system to several dozen homes, even though the mall expansion project would not have any impact on the septic systems of the surrounding homes.

The plain fact is that local planners know the economic value of development projects quite well, and they know how much discretion they have in approving and disapproving projects. This calculus of profit and discretion yields leverage. Sometimes there is not any leverage; other times, there is enormous leverage that, in the political process of land-use approvals, has not changed as a result ot *Lucas* or *Nollan* or *Dolan* or any of the other cases of recent years.

The political reality remains that not only will developers buy their own lunch, they are likely to buy the local government's lunch, as well.

VII. Conclusion

Dolan will prove to be only a slight body check to developers and planners skating through the land-development game. The effect will be felt on planners, but they have already learned new moves and will continue to do so. *Dolan* will not help many developers score, but with the strong showing of the Republicans during the midterm elections in 1994, the property rights movement will be better positioned to change the rules of the game in ways that truly disadvantage planners.

Notes

1. 114 S. Ct. 2309 (1994).
2. 235 N.E.2d 897 (N.Y. 1968).
3. 30 N.Y.2d 359, 285 N.E.2d 291, *appeal dismissed,* 409 U.S. 1003 (1972).
4. 15 Cal. App. 4th 1737, 19 Cal. Rptr. 2d 468 (Ct. App. 1993), *judg. vacated,* 114 S. Ct. 2731 (1994), B055523 (Cal. Ct. App. 2d Dist., Div. 5 Dec. 23, 1994) *judg. reaffirmed.*
5. See discussion of *Ehrlich* in Chapter Four, authored by Daniel J. Curtin.
6. 277 U.S. 183 (1928).
7. 438 U.S. 104 (1978).
8. 447 U.S. 255 (1980).
9. 450 U.S. 621 (1981).
10. 473 U.S. 172 (1985).
11. 477 U.S. 340 (1986).
12. 436 U.S. 658 (1978).
13. 445 U.S. 622 (1980).
14. 482 U.S. 304 (1987).
15. 483 U.S. 825 (1987).
16. 112 S. Ct. 2886 (1992).
17. Loretto v. TelePrompTer Manhattan CATV Corp., 458 U.S. 419 (1982).
18. 28 F.3d 1171 (Fed. Cir. 1994).
19. Courts have described the developer's mandated generosity in other terms. *See, e.g.,* JED Associates, Inc. v. Town of Sandown, 430 A.2d 129 (N.H. 1981).

CHAPTER ❖ 11

Assessing the Impact of *Dolan v. City of Tigard* on Local Governments' Land-Use Powers

Otto J. Hetzel and Kimberly A. Gough

I. Introduction

The Supreme Court's decision in *Dolan v. City of Tigard,*[1] issued in June, 1994, was the Court's fifth major pronouncement in the last seven years addressing the government's role in regulating land use and property development. *Dolan* follows the Court's 1992 decision in *Lucas v. South Carolina Coastal Council,*[2] and its 1987 trilogy, *Keystone Bituminous Coal Association v. DeBenedictis,*[3] *First English Evangelical Lutheran Church v. County of Los Angeles,*[4] and *Nollan v. California Coastal Commission.*[5] These cases have clearly signalled the Court's determination to provide greater protection for private property rights and, in the case of *Dolan,* to require that any imposition of costs on private property owners be roughly proportional to the impact caused by the development activity involved. Gone are the days when local governments could freely impose dedications or exactions that transfer public costs to landowners.

Dolan's emphasis on greater precision in preparing findings to justify imposing costs on developers increases applicable procedural requirements, and will frequently require quantification in findings related to particular properties to justify imposing costs on landowners. Failure of local governments to carefully review existing developmental regulations and requirements in light of these cases, and to act more conservatively before proceeding with past practices, could have costly consequences. There is now a real potential of damage claims and an increased likelihood of incurring significant legal costs. Thus, it behooves local governments to assess accurately how these recent decisions (particularly *Dolan* and its potential impact) affect their role in regulating development activities.[6]

This chapter attempts to provide a framework to aid local governments in that assessment, considering the various exactions, dedications, and conditions many of them impose through controls on property use and development. *Dolan*'s tests potentially affect local government requirements, whether the development activity involves new tract development, new commercial construction, or even rehabilitation of existing structures. Requirements imposed to obtain local approval of changes in land use should be reviewed to ensure closer matching of local government demands to the public effects of the proposed development.

The obvious concern for local governments is how to ensure that exactions, dedications, and other government requirements or conditions, triggered by requested changes in property use, are brought within the scope of local government's police powers, as now defined. In other words, how much of what might be considered public costs may still be imposed on private landowners because of proposed land-use plans? The need for landowners to obtain approval for such changes has provided the opportunity for local governments to exact commitments from property owners, often in excess of the actual effects the development will produce. These impositions have generally involved low-visibility decisions, infrequently challenged until recently, because of the long odds and high costs involved in successfully "fighting city hall." With *Dolan*, the potential for successfully resisting local government demands may be perceived by developers as far improved.

Local governments clearly face an era of reduced revenues to support governmental activities. While these circumstances may increase the temptation to pass along costs to private property owners, the consequences of overreaching could be expensive. The necessity of devoting limited resources to compensate for misjudgments in what was presumed to be a valid means of obtaining public cost contributions from private landowners will need to be more carefully considered. The tenor of the Court's new respect for property rights should not be underestimated. Hindsight judicial review, such as that displayed in *Dolan*, can impose compensation costs for what had been previously consid ered a regulatory taking of property. Increased precision in findings will be needed. Decisions that are simply poorly documented, but ultimately justifiable, can be as costly as situations involving excessive demands that are not sufficiently related to the governmental concerns involved.

In *Dolan*, a substantial part of the city's failure was the inadequate documentation and quantification of findings necessary to justify imposing public costs on Mrs. Dolan. Despite plausible determinations that the bicycle pathway would reduce traffic demands from the expected increase in business, and that increased protection from flooding would be needed to offset greater runoffs from the proposed paving of the adjacent parking lot, the Court found these justifications insufficient to require dedication of private property for the public easements. The issue has now become the types of exactions, dedications, and conditions that will be found acceptable and within local governments' regulatory police powers.

Before examining that issue, this chapter provides a brief historical analysis of the Court's handling of takings cases, followed by a review of the doctrinal developments that led to the *Dolan* decision. After an analysis of the rationale used by the Court in this five-to-four decision, an assessment of *Dolan*'s impact on local governments' exactions, dedications, and conditions is provided.

Although one should be cautious about using the rationale provided in a close decision as clear guideposts for the future, there is some basis for believing that this Court's reactions to property rights issues are becoming more predictable, as was demonstrated by Professor Douglas Kmiec, who accurately foresaw the result in *Dolan*.[7] Once the decision was handed down, however, press reports struggled to assess its significance.[8] The evaluations ranged from reports of "gloom and doom" for local governments to assessments of relatively little impact.[9]

What is clear from the trend in these recent cases is that exercise of regulatory police powers on property use will no longer survive without clear justification for the governmental action. The fallout from the Court's efforts to enunciate new tests for justifying costs that local governments can impose on property use is likely to have significant effects on urban and environmental policy and affordable housing considerations. In light of renewed congressional efforts to expand protection of private property rights and to prevent governments from imposing costs on property owners (especially those related to environmental restrictions), local governments face new challenges in financing public improvements and imposing land-use regulations without incurring condemnation costs.[10]

II. Background: Takings Law

A. Eminent Domain and Police Powers

Local governments' police powers have been the justification for imposing public costs on property owners. Courts have for many years permitted a broad scope in the use of these powers, which are based on local governments' authority to regulate to protect the health, safety, morals, and general welfare of the public.[11] A government may regulate the use and enjoyment of private property, or even deprive the owner of its beneficial uses without compensation (other than the sharing of the resulting benefits) as long as health and safety concerns can be demonstrated. Only when there are constitutional "takings" beyond the authority permitted by governmental police powers are property owners entitled to compensation for the loss of beneficial use of their property. These constitutional protections are provided to ensure that "burdens which, in all fairness and justice, should be borne by the public as a whole"[12] are compensated by the government imposing the burden.

The Fifth Amendment provides that "[n]o person shall . . . be deprived of . . . property without due process of law; nor shall private property be taken for public use, without just compensation."[13] The second clause, otherwise known as the "takings clause," does not on its face identify the exact type of governmental action that will constitute a taking. Reconciling the dual objectives of governmental regulation and property-rights protection has not been without considerable difficulty.

In *Pennsylvania Coal Co. v. Mahon,* Justice Oliver Wendell Holmes attempted to bring clarity to the clause when he made his landmark declaration that "while property may be regulated to a certain extent, if regulation goes too far it will be recognized as a taking."[14] Although the 1922 decision in *Pennsylvania Coal* laid the foundation for the regulatory takings doctrine, it failed to articulate a clear standard for its application. The Supreme Court did not decide another major takings clause case for over fifty years, until 1978 in *Penn Central Transportation Co. v. City of New York.*[15] Thereafter, it was not until its 1987 trilogy of decisions that the Court turned its attention again to the law of takings.

As the Supreme Court has swung to the right in recent years, primarily due to appointments from the Reagan and Bush administrations, there has been a resurgence in its protection of property rights.[16] The Court's 1992 decision in *Dolan* and *Lucas v. South Carolina Coastal Council*[17] reflects the Court's changing perspective on property rights, and the *Dolan* dissenting Justices summed up, "property owners have surely found a new friend today."[18]

The eminent domain power permits the government to acquire, confiscate, or otherwise take private property for public use without an owner's consent. Belonging to every government, the power of eminent domain "is an incident of sovereignty and requires no constitutional recognition."[19] The Fifth Amendment simply operates as a check on this power. Unlike the power of eminent domain, exercise of the police power does not require government to compensate for its acquisition of, or imposition on, private property.[20] The police power allows government to regulate to protect the health, safety, morals, and general welfare of the public.[21]

In *Pennsylvania Coal Co. v. Mahon,* the Court recognized the line between police power interference with property and an interference that, "when it reaches a certain magnitude, . . . must be an exercise of eminent domain."[22] Given that somewhat inexact standard, the Supreme Court has occasionally seemed to blur the line between eminent domain and police powers.[23]

B. The Takings Clause

Because just compensation is required only when a government "takes" private property, the critical issue is whether a "taking" has occurred. When government commences formal condemnation procedures, a taking is obviously contemplated and compensation is required. Likewise, "[w]hen it can be determined that government regulation as applied to a specific parcel is so restrictive that it has effectively taken that property, and the government has not exercised any formal eminent domain proceedings, a landowner may [institute inverse condemnation proceedings to recover compensation]."[24]

1. HISTORICAL DEVELOPMENT

The government's ability to regulate property provides the underlying basis for the takings clause of the Fifth Amendment.[25] Neither colonial nor revolutionary America accepted the principle that property owners were entitled to compensation when the government took private property.[26] The author of the takings clause, James Madison, wrote with concern for preservation of property rights, "Government is instituted no less for protection of the property, than of the persons of individuals."[27] However, Madison "intended the clause to apply to only direct, physical taking of property by the federal government."[28] In fact, the original version of the takings clause states, "No person shall be . . . obliged to relinquish his property, where it be necessary for public use, without just compensation."[29]

2. THE ELEMENTS

A dissection of the literal terms of the Fifth Amendment's takings clause yields four elements: private property, public use, just compensation, and, of course, a taking. Private property has been defined as "property as belongs absolutely to an individual, and of which he has the exclusive right of disposition."[30] "[V]irtually every kind of property, whether real or personal, tangible or intangible, and every variety or degree of interest in property"[31] is subject to the takings clause.

The "public use" requirement of the Fifth Amendment arguably has no practical significance in contemporary takings law,[32] as the level of review demanded for this requirement was significantly diminished by the Supreme Court in *Berman v. Parker*.[33] The *Berman* Court proclaimed that "when the legislature has spoken, the public interest has been declared in terms well-nigh conclusive."[34] The Court reaffirmed that position in *Hawaii Housing Authority v. Midkiff*, in which the Court explained that "where the exercise of the eminent domain power is rationally related to a conceivable public purpose, the Court has never held a compensated taking to be proscribed by the [Takings] Clause."[35]

The "just compensation" element of the takings clause, on the other hand, is often the subject of dispute, as the Fifth Amendment "does not outline any definite standards of fairness for determining just compensation."[36] Just compensation is ordinarily equivalent to the fair market value of the property at the time of the taking, calculated as:

> [T]he price that an informed and knowledgeable purchaser would offer a willing seller for the land and any buildings, structures, or other improvements considered to be a part of the property, with neither party being under any duress or compulsion. Market value is generally considered in terms of the property's highest and best use which would be reasonably possible in the near future.[37]

The factors that determine fair market value include market demand, economic development in the area, specific plans to develop the land, particular uses permitted by zoning ordinances, perceived compatibility with neighboring areas, and the actual use of the property at the time of the taking.[38]

The final element, "a taking," is the most conceptually difficult and constitutionally significant. Some argue that the framers of the Constitution intended the just compensation requirement to apply only to actual, physical seizures of private property by the government. However, the takings clause has not been limited to forbidding the government from outright acquisitions of land without compensation.[39] Although there is no doubt that the government has the constitutional authority to regulate property,[40] there is some point at which regulation will be recognized as a compensable taking.

III. Supreme Court Takings Jurisprudence

The law of takings has not been analyzed under a single framework or theory, which the Supreme Court itself has candidly recognized. "The question of what constitutes a 'taking' for purposes of the Fifth Amendment has proved to be a problem of considerable difficulty."[41] This difficulty was acknowledged in 1979, when then Justice Rehnquist stated:

> [T]his court has generally "been unable to develop any 'set formula' for determining when 'justice and fairness' require that economic injuries caused by public action be compensated by the government, rather than remain disproportionately concentrated on a few persons." Rather, it has examined the "taking" question by engaging in essentially ad hoc, factual inquiries that have identified several factors—such as the economic impact of the regulation, its interference with reasonable investment backed expectations, and the character of the governmental action—that have particular significance.[42]

Consistent with this inability to develop a bright line test to define when governmental action requires compensation, the Supreme Court's jurisprudence has produced uncertain and incompatible results.[43]

A. Early Law

Early takings cases held that a property owner was not entitled to compensation unless the government physically seized the property.[44] Courts focused on nuisances created by property owners, and not the diminution in value of the property resulting from the governmental action. A representative case is *Mugler v. Kansas*,[45] in which the Court held that a statute that prohibited the manufacture of liquor did not amount to a taking of a distillery, despite the fact that the manufacturer's property was rendered practically worthless as a result of the regulation. The government could prohibit the property owner from using his property in a manner that damaged others, without having to compensate the owner for the value of the prohibited use.[46] Believing that governmental action in the form of regulation could not rise to the level of a Fifth Amendment taking, the Court stated:

> The power which the States have of prohibiting such use by individuals of their property as will be prejudicial to the health, morals, or the safety of the public, is not—and, consistently with the existence and safety of organized society, cannot be—burdened with the condition that the State must compensate such individual owners for pecuniary losses they may sustain, by reason of their not being permitted, by a noxious use of their property, to inflict injury upon the community.[47]

Mugler and its progeny[48] established the rule that a state's "interest in preventing activities similar to public nuisances is a substantial one, which in many instances [does] not require compensation."[49] The rationale for this nuisance exception to the takings clause is "the simple theory that since no individual has a right to use his property so as to create a nuisance or otherwise harm others, the State has not 'taken' anything when it asserts its power to enjoin nuisance-like activity."[50]

B. The Regulatory Takings Doctrine

The *Mugler* Court did not consider diminution in value in its analysis; but, this consideration was the principal issue in *Pennsylvania Coal Co. v. Mahon*.[51] The Court first conceded that government could not function if it were required to pay for each decline in property value caused by regulation. Recognizing that private property rights must yield to the police power of the state, the Court then analyzed whether the law was a valid exercise of the police power by balancing the public benefit against the private loss caused by the statute.[52] Stating that a reduction in value of property was a relevant factor in its decision, the Court held that the public benefit fell short of justifying the private loss.[53]

Subsequently, the Court developed a multifactor balancing approach for analyzing takings cases, which included diminution of value.[54] The Court in *Penn Central Transportation Co. v. New York City*[55] employed a three-prong balancing test to analyze the takings issue. The Supreme Court identified three factors of "particular significance" to the takings issue: the character of the governmental action; the extent to which the regulation interfered with distinct investment-backed expectations; and the economic impact of the regulation on the property owner. Balancing these factors, the *Penn Central* Court concluded that the law did not effect a compensable taking.

The facts in *Penn Central* showed that although the regulation interfered with the property's economic value, it did not prevent a reasonable return on investment. Additionally, the Court found that the transferable development rights, which allowed development elsewhere, mitigated any economic losses caused by the regulation.[56] As a consequence of *Penn Central*, the Court began consistently to include diminution in value as a factor in determining whether regulations constituted a taking.[57]

Later, in *Agins v. City of Tiburon*,[58] the Supreme Court shifted away from multifactor balancing and toward more definite takings principles.[59] After the plaintiffs in *Agins* acquired a five-acre tract of unimproved land, the city rezoned the property in such a way that the plaintiffs could build no more than five single-family homes on the tract. The plaintiffs claimed the density restriction prevented their plans to develop the property thoroughly, thereby destroying the value of the property. In holding that the zoning ordinance did not constitute a taking, the Court applied the following two-prong test: governmental action effects a taking if it "does not substantially advance legitimate state interests . . . or denies an owner economically viable use of his land." The ordinance complied with the first prong of the test because its purpose was "to protect the residents . . . from the ill effects of urbanization," and because it substantially advanced this purpose. Finding that the land retained economic viability under the second prong, the Court held that the ordinance neither prevented the best use nor prohibited the pursuit of reasonable investment-backed expectations.

The Supreme Court applied the *Agins* two-prong test in the first of its 1987 trilogy, *Keystone Bituminous Coal Ass'n v. DeBenedictis.*[60] In *Keystone,* a coal association alleged that a Pennsylvania law, which prohibited the removal of 50 percent of the coal beneath certain structures, constituted a taking. Because it was designed to minimize harmful subsidence, an important public interest, and because it did not make the association's mining commercially impracticable or unprofitable,[61] the Court held that the regulation did not effect a taking.

C. The Trend toward Categorical Rules

The Supreme Court has identified two discrete categories of regulatory takings that require compensation. An explicit identification of the categories was made in *Lucas v. South Carolina Coastal Council.*[62] If either of these two categories arises from a regulation, a per se taking has occurred and compensation is required, regardless of the regulation's importance.[63] The first category consists of those regulations that "compel the owner to suffer a physical 'invasion' of his property."[64] Those regulations that deny a property owner all economically viable use of the land comprise the second category of regulatory takings.[65] Such regulations are the functional equivalent of a government appropriation of property and are indistinguishable from an actual exercise of eminent domain.[66]

1. PHYSICAL INVASION

In *Loretto v. TelePrompTer Manhattan CATV Corp.,* the Supreme Court announced that physical invasion or occupation of private property is a per se taking.[67] *Loretto* involved a New York law that required landlords to permit installation of cable equipment on their property. Concluding that economic impact, or lack thereof, was irrelevant,[68] the Court stressed that it has long considered physical intrusions to be dispositive in takings cases. The Court refused to extend this physical takings rule, however, in its 1992 decision in *Yee v. City of Escondido*.[69] The Court unanimously held that laws restricting tenant evictions and limiting rent increases in mobile home parks did not result in per se takings because these limitations on an owner's control of his or her property were not the same as physical occupation.

2. DEPRIVATION OF ALL ECONOMICALLY VIABLE USE

The second per se categorical rule announced in *Lucas*, deprivation of all economically viable use, was foreshadowed in earlier cases such as *First English Evangelical Lutheran Church v. County of Los Angeles*.[70] The Court followed its *First English* line of reasoning in deciding *Lucas v. South Carolina Coastal Council*.[71] Justice Scalia, writing for the Court, easily found a compensable taking. Because Lucas had been denied all economically viable use of his property, the Court thereby invoked the second per se categorical rule.[72]

Although *Lucas* created another category of per se takings, as well as diminishing the nuisance exception, the case is likely to affect only a handful of situations. Few, if any, land-use regulations result in rendering an owner's land economically worthless. More important is the *Lucas* Court's acceptance of a balancing test for those cases that do not fall within the purview of the two categorical rules.[73] When the governmental action is not as obvious as a physical invasion or a complete deprivation of economically viable use, the cases will be decided by analyzing the economic impact of the regulation and the extent to which the regulation has interfered with distinct investment-backed expectations.[74]

IV. Land Dedications, Exactions, and Conditions after Dolan

Development exactions are another method by which governments exercise their police powers. Development exactions are levies imposed on persons developing their property as a condition of carrying out a project within a municipality.[75] Dedication of land was the first development exaction used by local governments to shift the increased infrastructure costs to developers; today, it is still the most common type of exaction employed by local governments.[76] It is commonplace for state and local governments to require that developers, in exchange for building permits, dedicate some of their land for parks, open spaces, streets, sidewalks, sewers, schools, and other public uses. Courts generally upheld the constitutionality of such dedications,[77] at least until the recent challenges occurred.

A. *Nollan,* a Precursor to *Dolan*

In *Nollan v. California Coastal Commission,*[78] the Nollans applied to the commission for a permit to allow them to demolish a cottage on their beachfront property and replace it with a larger home. The commission agreed to issue the permit on the condition that the Nollans dedicate a ten-foot wide easement to the state, which would allow the public to access a portion of the Nollans' private beach while walking along the coast. The condition was imposed because the commission feared that the newly constructed house would contribute to "the development of 'a "wall" of residential structures' that would prevent the public 'psychologically . . . from realizing a stretch of the coastline exists nearby that they have every right to visit.' "[79]

Justice Scalia, writing for a five-to-four majority,[80] held that the easement was a "permanent physical occupation" and thus was a taking.[81] The inquiry did not end there, however, as the Court then analyzed whether a compensable taking could be avoided because the easement was only a condition to a development permit.[82] The Court assumed that the commission, under its police powers, could develop regulations that furthered the legitimate public objectives of preventing beach congestion and preserving visual access to the sea. Accordingly, the Court turned to the question of "essential nexus"—whether the government-imposed permit condition substantially advanced a legitimate state objective—and answered it in the negative:

> It is quite impossible to understand how a requirement that people already on the public beaches be able to walk across the Nollans' property reduces any obstacles to viewing the beach created by the new house. It is also quite impossible to understand . . . how it helps to remedy any of the congestion on [the beach] caused by construction of the Nollans' new house.[83]

Therefore, the *Nollan* Court concluded that this land dedication was indeed a compensable taking. Justice Scalia stressed that "one of the most essential sticks in the bundle of rights that are commonly characterized as property" is "the right to exclude others."[84]

B. The Court's Opinion in *Dolan*

With *Nollan* serving as precedent, the Supreme Court decided *Dolan v. City of Tigard* on June 24, 1994. According to the Court, certiorari was granted "to resolve a question left open by [the *Nollan* decision] of what is the required degree of connection between the exactions imposed by the city and the projected impacts of the proposed development."[85] Chief Justice Rehnquist, writing for the five-to-four majority, noted:

> Without question, had the city simply required petitioner to dedicate a strip of land along Fanno Creek for public use, rather than conditioning the grant of her permit to redevelop her property on such a dedication, a taking would have occurred.[86]

He then set forth a two-part test, the first of which reaffirmed the *Nollan* test, "whether the 'essential nexus' exists between the 'legitimate state interest' and the permit condition exacted by the city."[87] If the required nexus did indeed exist, the second part of the test would need to be addressed, "whether the degree of the exactions demanded by the city's permit conditions bore the required relationship to the projected impact of petitioner's proposed development."[88]

Chief Justice Rehnquist easily found the first part of the test to be satisfied, stating, "Undoubtedly, the prevention of flooding along Fanno Creek and the reduction of traffic congestion in the Central Business District qualify as the type of legitimate public purposes we have upheld."[89] He also determined that "[i]t seems equally obvious that the required nexus exists between preventing flooding along Fanno Creek and limiting development within the creek's 100-year floodplain."[90] Dolan's redevelopment would "expand the impervious surface on the property and increas[e] the amount of stormwater run-off into Fanno Creek."[91] The required nexus regarding the pathway and reduction of traffic congestion was also found, "In theory, a pedestrian/bicycle pathway provides a useful alternative means of transportation for workers and shoppers[, which will] 'remove potential vehicles from the streets, resulting in an overall improvement in total transportation system flow.' "[92]

Rehnquist then turned to the second part of the test, examining state court decisions for guidance regarding whether the city's findings were constitutionally sufficient to justify the dedication requirements. Rejecting very generalized findings as "too lax" to protect property owners from unconstitutional takings,[93] he, in turn, also rejected state court decisions requiring precise findings and quickly disposed of the standard that requires the exaction to be "directly proportional to the specifically created need."[94] He stated, "We do not think the Federal Constitution requires such exacting scrutiny, given the nature of the interests involved."[95] Determining that an intermediate position was closest to that required by the Constitution, Rehnquist settled for the "reasonable relationship" test, which had been previously adopted by a majority of state courts.[96] Concluding, however, that the term "reasonable relationship" was confusingly similar to the term "rational basis," used in other contexts, he instead substituted "rough proportionality"[97] as the test, defining it thus, "No precise mathematical certainty is required, but the city must make some sort of individualized determination that the required dedication is related both in nature and extent to the impact of the proposed development."[98]

Rehnquist characterized the findings that the city made regarding the required dedications as "rather tentative," and thus constitutionally insufficient to justify the conditions imposed upon Dolan. Concerning the flood control justification, he observed:

> It is axiomatic that increasing the amount of impervious surface will increase the quantity and rate of storm-water flow from petitioner's property. . . . [However, the city] not only wanted petitioner not to build in the floodplain, but it also wanted petitioner's property along Fanno Creek for its Greenway system. The city has never said why a public greenway, as opposed to a private one, was required in the interest of flood control.[99]

Regarding the bicycle pathway, he stated:

> [W]e have no doubt that the city was correct in finding that the larger retail sales facility proposed by petitioner will increase traffic on the streets. . . . But on the record before us, the city has not met its burden of demonstrating that the additional number of vehicle and bicycle trips generated by the petitioner's development reasonably relate to the city's requirement for a dedication. . . . The city has simply found that the creation of the pathway "could offset some of the traffic demand . . . and lessen the increase in traffic congestion." . . .
>
> [This] "is a far cry from finding that the bicycle pathway system will, or is likely to, offset some of the traffic demand." . . . [T]he city must make some effort to quantify its findings . . . beyond th[is] conclusory statement. . . .[100]

V. Doctrinal Analysis of Dolan

A. Doctrinal Shifts

In formulating its rejection of the city's justifications, the *Dolan* Court made three major doctrinal shifts. It created a new terminology to justify a heightened form of judicial scrutiny. Reversing considerable contrary doctrine, it shifted the presumption of constitutionality from the challenging property owner to the government entity attempting to exercise its police powers. Finally, it mandated a newly created form of proportionality requirements for its balancing test.

1. HEIGHTENED JUDICIAL SCRUTINY

The Court stated that "the Takings Clause of the Fifth Amendment, as much a part of the Bill of Rights as the First or Fourth Amendment, should [not] be relegated to the status of a poor relation in these comparable circumstances."[101] The Court's adoption of *Nollan*'s "substantially advanced legitimate state interests" terminology envisions a higher level of scrutiny than that which is normally employed under the "rational basis" test, but nowhere near "strict scrutiny," in which the governmental action will almost invariably be struck down.[102] Indeed, the *Dolan* standard is supposed to provide even less than intermediate-level scrutiny.[103] The Court has generally been deferential to legislative judgments under the rational basis standard of review, but the heightened level of scrutiny contemplated in *Dolan* seems to signify "rational basis" scrutiny with a "significant bite." This heightened judicial scrutiny required by the conservative majority of the Court, according to the dissenters, could provide a "potentially open-ended source of judicial power to invalidate state economic regulations that Members of this Court view as unwise or unfair."[104]

Nollan introduced heightened scrutiny to the rational basis test by requiring the state to show that the regulation "substantially advanced legitimate state interests."[105] The normal level of scrutiny under the rational basis test is "reasonably related" rather than "substantially advanced." In effect, the *Nollan* majority lifted "substantially advanced" from the intermediate level of scrutiny required for gender and legitimacy classifications and grafted it onto the puportedly less restrictive "rational basis" test. In dissent, Justice Blackmun noted the anomaly compared with the ordinary requirement of "rational basis" used to judge local governments' exercise of their political powers.[106] Regarding the standards to be applied in takings clause cases, Justice Scalia stated:

> Our opinions do not establish that these standards are the same as those applied to due process or equal protection claims. To the contrary, our verbal formulations in the takings field have generally been quite different. We have required that the regulation "substantially advance" the "legitimate state interest," sought to be achieved, not that "the State 'could rationally have decided' that the measure adopted might achieve the State's objective."[107]

2. SHIFTING THE PRESUMPTION OF CONSTITUTIONALITY

The dissent in *Dolan* noted that the Court "decides for the first time that the city has the burden of establishing the constitutionality of the governmental action."[108] The majority held that because the City of Tigard made an "adjudicative decision" to condition Dolan's application for a building permit on the dedication, "the burden properly rests on the city."[109] Justice Souter, in dissent, criticized the majority's action:

> [I]t appears that the Court has placed the burden of producing evidence of relationship on the city, despite the usual rule in cases involving the police power that the government is presumed to have acted constitutionally.[110]

The *Dolan* Court also rejected the theory of "reciprocity of advantage," which weighs in favor of the constitutionality of governmental action.[111] As stated in *Pennsylvania Coal,* "reciprocity of advantage . . . has been recognized as a justification for various laws."[112] In *Penn Central,* the Court also stated that reciprocal advantages "undoubtedly mitigate whatever financial burdens the law has imposed . . . and, for that reason, are to be taken into account in considering the impact of the regulation."[113]

Dolan's acceptance of the permit conditions would have provided her with benefits. The city planned to "widen the channel and reinforce the slopes to increase the carrying capacity during serious floods."[114] Without the land dedication, property owners, including Dolan, would be required to expend funds to build a storage facility for the water runoff.[115] Furthermore, with a dedication, Dolan would be relieved of "the duty to pay taxes and the responsibility for tort liability."[116] In addition,

> [t]he City is allowing her at her request to use the floodplain dedication as a full credit against the landscaping requirement that it would otherwise impose. The landscaping will be installed and maintained at public expense. This credit allows use of approximately an additional 7,000 square feet of the site's buildable area for building and parking purposes that would otherwise be committed to open space.[117]

Similarly, the pathway would improve potential customers' street access to Dolan's store, and it would also provide an alternative means of access.[118] "[T]hese improvements will have minimal adverse economic impact, and, quite possibly, will increase the market value of Petitioner's property."[119]

3. THE "ROUGH PROPORTIONALITY" REQUIREMENT

In *Dolan,* the Court determined that the city's "tentative findings" were not constitutionally sufficient to meet its "rough proportionality" test, stating:

> [n]o precise mathematical certainty is required, but the city must make some sort of individualized determination that the required dedication is related both in nature and extent to the impact of the proposed development.[120]

The Court's objection to the city's findings was that the city made no precise determination of the increase in stormwater runoff expected from the new building. It made only the generalized finding that the redevelopment would expand the impervious surface on the property, thereby increasing the runoff. Regarding the pathway dedication, the city had calculated that "the proposed development would generate roughly 435 additional trips per day"[121] and that "its Comprehensive Plan, applied here, relied on studies showing the link between alternative modes of transportation, including bicycle paths, and reduced street traffic congestion."[122] However, the city failed to quantify the number of Dolan's workers and shoppers who would use the pathway, thereby replacing motorists.

Perhaps the city will be able to demonstrate the required proportionality on remand. *Dolan* indicates that local governments will need, in some cases, to hold an adjudicatory proceeding in which it examines witnesses, introduces studies it has conducted, and makes extensive factual findings.

B. Assessing the Practical Impact of *Dolan*

Although the doctrinal shifts are noteworthy, *Dolan* may not have as broad a practical impact on governmental regulatory power as it seems at first blush. However, it is certainly likely to have an impact when local governments are perceived to be overreaching with their police powers to obtain more contributions from developers than can be reasonably justified.

1. LAND DEDICATIONS

The *Dolan* Court certainly did not hold that compensation is required in all cases involving land dedications, noting that, "Dedications for streets, sidewalks, and other public ways are generally reasonable exactions to avoid excessive congestion from a proposed property use."[123] Justice Scalia noted in another context that " 'the common zoning regulations requiring subdividers to . . . dedicate certain areas to public streets, are in accord with our constitutional traditions because the proposed property use would otherwise be the cause of excessive congestion.' "[124]

Development exactions will survive the test set forth by the Court in *Dolan*, provided that the dedications clearly solve problems generated by the owner upon whom they are levied.[125] In endorsing *Simpson v. North Platte*[126] as the basis for its newly propounded test, the *Dolan* Court appears, in fact, to have adopted the reasonable relationship or rational basis test under the guise of its new terminology. This is the standard used by the majority of state courts. If that is a correct assumption, then although there is new terminology, the standard to be applied (based on state cases) may not be such a serious deviation from the requirements currently used by state courts.

Street, sewer, park, and school dedications related to residential developments are likely to be upheld. As noted by the City of Tigard:

> [s]ubdivision dedications have been required since at least 1895. Indeed, cities have been requiring landowners to build and maintain sidewalks for over a century. Thus, 'exactions are now firmly entrenched as a legitimate means of exercising community growth.'[127]

Similarly, street and sewer dedications related to commercial and industrial developments should easily be upheld.

It has been argued that exactions fairly place the costs of growth on the developer who created the need for infrastructure improvements, and reduce the impact of growth on the existing facilities and services of the municipality.[128] Responding to growth is generally seen as a drain on the local community. Thus, the argument goes, putting the cost on those who created the strain is equitable.[129] That proposition has been challenged:

> As a statement of public policy, this assertion reflects at least three underlying assumptions: first, that it is more equitable to allocate the cost of capital and other improvements to the developer than to spread the cost equally on the entire community through general revenue rising devices; second, that because existing development already paid its own way, new development should follow suit; and third, that the local government can accurately measure the true cost imposed on capital infrastructure by growth.[130]

There is a reasonable fear that if courts do not uphold legitimate exactions, "thereby making local governments less likely to adopt them, th[ose] holding[s] might have the unfortunate effect of leading governments to adopt even more regressive and inefficient solutions,"[131] such as stricter growth controls and local excise taxes on development.[132]

2. LAND-USE REGULATIONS

It is apparent that the *Dolan* majority did not intend for its decision to affect legitimate land-use regulations. According to the Court, "[c]ities have long engaged in the commendable task of land use planning, made necessary by increasing urbanization particularly in metropolitan areas such as Portland."[133] Citing *Euclid, Pennsylvania Coal,* and *Agins* with approval, the *Dolan* Court stated that these cases differed from *Dolan* in two respects:

> First, they involved essentially legislative determinations classifying entire areas of the city, whereas here the city made an adjudicative decision to condition petitioner's application for a building permit on an individual parcel. Second, the conditions imposed were not simply a limitation on the use petitioner might make of her own parcel, but a requirement that she deed portions of the property to the city.[134]

Further, the Court noted that "in evaluating most generally applicable zoning regulations, the burden properly rests on the party challenging the regulation to prove that it constitutes an arbitrary regulation of property rights."[135] The Court did not perceive land-use plans as involving adjudicatory proceedings, as it termed the review required for Dolan's permit application. It has been suggested that "[c]ompliance with a comprehensive plan will save even the most burdensome land regulations:"[136]

> To the extent that the legislative body has tied a regulation to a clearly stated plan, one that spells out the public interest pursued, the regulation will have a better chance of surviving whatever level of scrutiny a court decides to apply. . . . The plan, if drafted with integrity, and properly advanced by the regulation, can greatly influence such matters.[137]

The two-prong test set forth in *Agins,* discussed previously, will be used to determine when a land-use regulation has resulted in a taking. According to the Court, land-use regulation and zoning will effect a taking only if "the ordinance (1) 'does not substantially advance a legitimate state interest' or (2) if it 'denies an owner economically viable use of his land.' "[138] The first prong of *Agins* will be difficult for landowners to meet because "[d]eterminations of the legislature regarding . . . the legitimacy of the public interest will be 'clothed with a strong presumption of constitutionality.' "[139] The second prong, as implied in *Lucas,* will be virtually impossible to meet. A land-use regulation rarely, if ever, will deny an owner all economically viable use.

Courts deciding cases after *Dolan* have consistently upheld land-use regulations. In *Harris v. City of Wichita, Sedwick County, Kan.,*[140] the plaintiffs moved for reconsideration of summary judgment that had been granted in favor of the defendants just one day before the Supreme Court handed down its decision in *Dolan.* The plaintiffs in *Harris,* who owned property located at the end of a runway at an air force base, claimed that certain usage restrictions constituted an uncompensated taking. "These restrictions were enacted at the recommendation of the United States Air Force and were based on a 1987 Air

Force study of airplane crashes near Air Force bases."[141] In upholding the summary judgment, the court distinguished *Dolan* as follows:

> In this case, the City and County regulations are land use regulations and do not impose upon plaintiffs the obligation to deed portions of their land to local governments or any other affirmative obligations. Furthermore, the City's and County's decisions were legislative rather than adjudicative in nature. . . . Therefore, *Dolan*'s rough proportionality test does not apply to this case.[142]

Similarly, in *Third & Catalina Associates v. City of Phoenix*,[143] a property owner challenged, as a violation of the takings clause, a fire sprinkler-system retrofit ordinance that was enacted sixteen years after the construction of the owner's building. To install the sprinklers, the owner would have to abate an asbestos problem that would not be a hazard if left undisturbed. Because abatement would cost more than the building was worth, the owner sought exemption from the ordinance. In holding that a taking had not occurred, the Arizona Court of Appeals effectively distinguished *Dolan*, "Here we do not have a situation of private property being pressed into public service as in *Dolan v. City of Tigard*."[144] The court continued:

> To require the City to compensate appellant in order to enforce its sprinkler retrofit ordinance would nullify the City's legitimate police power to protect its citizens from fire hazards. Such a ruling would have far reaching implications—such as preventing the City from ordering a property owner to vacate a structurally unsound building without paying the owner compensation to do so. . . . Appellant has no property right to be exempt from fire safety laws. Merely requiring appellant to spend money to comply with the sprinkler retrofit ordinance is not an unconstitutional taking.[145]

It seems clear that *Dolan* is not likely to affect legitimate land-use regulations, and that legislative determinations on this subject will still be afforded great deference.

3. MONETARY EXACTIONS

Monetary exactions, which, unlike land dedications, do not directly involve any fundamental attribute of real property, are another form of exaction device used by local governments. Originally, municipalities used only "in-lieu fees," which were pooled into a fund and used to finance off-site facilities, such as schools and parks.[146] However, "in lieu fees were limited, by definition, to use only where a [land] dedication would be appropriate."[147] "In contrast, impact fees, which may be defined as charges levied by local government against new development to generate revenue for capital facilities, the need for which is created by the new development, can be used even where the required dedication of land would not be appropriate."[148] Such fees can be assessed against subdivisions, condominiums, apartments, and commercial developments, and can be used to fund "roads, sewers, water systems, schools, parks, drainage systems, police facilities, fire stations and equipment, solid waste disposal sites and resource recovery facilities, libraries and emergency medical facilities."[149] Professor David Callies has described impact fees as follows:

> [M]any local governments have turned to exactions . . . to help pay for those public facilities that growth and development make necessary. Curiously, the basis for such conditions or exactions is not the power to tax, but the power to regulate. . . . The reasoning goes that since most public facilities are for the health, safety, and welfare of the people, the method of paying for them specifically (as contrasted with a general levy or tax that targets no particular facility or purpose) is as an exercise of the police power.[150]

Most recently, municipalities are assessing linkage fees, which require developers of downtown office space to contribute funds toward, or construct housing for, those who will seek employment in the newly constructed facility.[151] "Some cities have gone as far as requiring developers of downtown office space to contribute to job training programs and child care facilities."[152] Likewise, other municipalities have assessed linkage fees that are used to meet their "fair share" affordable housing requirements.[153] In contrast to the more traditional exactions, which are defended as "a means of mitigating the negative physical effects of development," these progressive exactions lessen "the 'social byproducts of new land uses.' "[154]

The Standard City Planning Enabling Act,[155] and nearly all state statutes, expressly authorize local governments to require developers to improve on-site streets and public facilities; additionally, states that expressly authorize fees for off-site improvements are increasing in number.[156] "The majority of jurisdictions, with seeming approval by the United States Supreme Court, apply a two-fold standard for upholding exactions: The development assessed must create the need for the facilities and the payor of the fees must derive some meaningful benefit from their expenditure."[157] The factors in assessing the constitutionality of an exaction include the following:

(a) Whether the local government has adequately documented the estimated costs of acquiring and constructing the needed capital facilities and the inventory of deficiencies found in existing capital facilities.

(b) The formula or methodology used by the local government for determining the proportion of need caused by the new development.

(c) Whether the funds collected are specifically earmarked and segregated into a separate fund. . . .

(d) Whether the actual expenditures are localized by zone or trust fund in order to ensure that residents of the new area or development will actually and substantially benefit from the facilities. . . .

(e) Whether the funds must be spent . . . within a reasonable period or be returned.

(f) Whether [credit is given for] other methods of payment. . . .

(g) Whether the fees exceed the costs needed [for] the new facilities.[158]

These factors appear to be in accord with both *Nollan*'s essential nexus test and *Dolan*'s rough proportionality test.

Cases decided after *Nollan,* but before *Dolan,* consistently held that impact fees are constitutional. In *Commercial Builders of Northern California v. City of Sacramento,*[159] the Ninth Circuit upheld the constitutionality of a city ordinance that conditioned the issuance of permits for certain nonresidential structures on the payment of a linkage fee. Such structures included new construction, additions, and remodeling of office, hotel, research and development, commercial, manufacturing, and warehouse space. The fees, used to expand available low-income housing, were "intended to offset the burdens on the city caused by low-income workers who move there to fill jobs created by the project in question."[160]

In approving these fees, the Ninth Circuit stated, "A purely financial exaction, then, will not constitute a taking if it is made for the purpose of paying a social cost that is reasonably related to the activity against which the fee is assessed."[161] Moreover, the court stated that "nothing in *Nollan* or any other authorities cited by the [plaintiffs] requires the nexus to be more direct than that achieved through the legislative process that the city employed here."[162] *Nollan*'s heightened scrutiny is not applicable to regulations that "do not constitute physical encroachment of land."[163]

Similarly, in *Blue Jeans Equities West v. City & County of San Francisco,*[164] a California appellate court upheld fees imposed by the city's transit impact development fee ordinance, which were required of developers of downtown office space. The fee was used to offset the expected costs of the anticipated increase in use of the transit system generated by the development. The *Nollan* decision itself mentioned that particular attention should be directed toward the nexus requirements when the actual conveyance of property is a condition to the removal of a land-use restriction.[165]

According to the *Blue Jeans* court, "most legal scholars have concluded [that] the *Nollan* strict scrutiny approach is limited to unconstitutional conditions and possessory takings cases."[166] The court stated, "[I]n light of [*Nollan*] and post-*Nollan* case law, we hold that any heightened scrutiny test contained in *Nollan* is limited to possessory rather than regulatory takings cases."[167] As impact fees are subject only to a rational basis test, which requires judicial deference, the court upheld their imposition in *Blue Jeans.*

A California appellate court upheld the validity of imposing school facility fees on a new residential development in *Garrick Development Co. v. Hayward Unified School District.*[168] After recognizing that precedent existed for applying the *Nollan* nexus requirement only in cases of physical invasions,[169] the court held that even if "such a nexus [is] required here, . . . [it] adequately appears," as "there is a clear and close connection between fees imposed for school facilities and new residential construction, the most predictable single source of increased school enrollment."[170]

Conceptual support is also contained in *Yee v. City of Escondido,*[171] in which the Court unanimously held that laws restricting tenant evictions and limiting rent increases in mobile home parks did not constitute a taking because these limitations on an owner's control of his or her property were not the same as physical occupation. The Court then defined physical taking:

> The government effects a physical taking only where it requires the landowner to submit to the physical occupation of his land. . . . Any transfer of wealth from the park owners to incumbent mobile home owners in the form of sub-market rents does not itself convert regulation into physical invasion.[172]

Just a few days after *Dolan* was decided, the Supreme Court vacated the decision in an exactions case, *Ehrlich v. City of Culver City,*[173] and remanded it for further consideration in light of *Dolan.* In the case below, a California appellate court upheld fees imposed by Culver City as a condition of approval of a thirty-unit townhouse development. The developer, Ehrlich, was operating a private recreational club on the property at the time of his permit application; the land-use restriction on the property permitted only community recreational use. The city agreed to change the land-use restriction to residential use on the condition that Ehrlich pay certain fees, which were designated as follows, "(1) a $280,000 fee to mitigate the impact of a land use change (the mitigation fee); and (2) a $33,200 fee in lieu of a requirement that art be placed on the development project (the in lieu art fee)."[174]

Ehrlich claimed an unconstitutional taking. He first challenged the land-use regulations, contending that requiring him to use the property for community recreational facilities deprived him of all economically beneficial use of the property. Quickly rejecting this theory, despite evidence that the club was operating at a loss, the court held, "Property is generally deprived of all economically beneficial use where construction is entirely banned, such as when the property is required to remain as open space. Evidence in the record indicates a community recreational facility could be operated profitably on the property under certain circumstances."[175] Furthermore, the court noted that because "[t]he developer purchased the property with knowledge of the restrictions and with the intent to develop the property as a private tennis club," the land-use restrictions were consistent with his reasonable investment-backed expectations.[176] The developer could also sell the land or leave it vacant.[177]

Ehrlich also challenged the fees. The mitigation fee, which was imposed to alleviate the effects of the loss of land restricted to community recreational use, was found to be rationally related to a legitimate governmental purpose. "Moreover, the use of the funds by the City was expressly limited to the provision of recreational facilities for the community."[178] In upholding the constitutionality of the fees, the court stated, "Even if we were to find the 'substantially advance/heightened scrutiny' test of *Nollan* to be applicable, we would conclude that the mitigation fee met this test."[179] The Court appeared to have an even easier time upholding the in-lieu art fee, on the basis that it was mandated by an ordinance that provided that certain high-cost development projects must participate in the city's art program. The ordinance allowed the developer to purchase art and display it on the project's grounds, pay a fee in lieu of doing so, or donate art to the city; Ehrlich chose to pay the fee. The purposes of the ordinance were, among others, to enhance the residents' quality of life, develop cultural and artistic resources, relieve the effects of urbanization, and improve the image and character of the community. Finding this to be within the scope of the city's police powers, and no different from requirements for setback, open space, buffer zone, or landscaping, the court upheld the imposition of the in-lieu art fee.[180]

The *Dolan* decision is not likely to change the takings challenge in *Ehrlich*. First, as the California appellate court already found, the *Nollan* essential nexus requirement was satisfied. Whether the fee exactions meet the rough proportionality test is not as clear. The fees for the loss of recreational use appear to bear the required relationship to the projected impact of Ehrlich's proposed development. Culver City had made an individualized determination that the recreation fees were related both in nature and extent to the impact of the proposed development, and support for such a determination existed in the record, "The need for community recreation facilities has been evidenced by previous staff reports, consultant reports, and public testimony indicating the use and feasibility of such facilities at the subject site."[181] The "[s]taff reports indicated the existing permitted recreation facilities, consisting of tennis courts, paddle tennis courts, swimming pool, running track, aerobics area, jacuzzi, sauna, and related sports club amenities, had an estimated value of at least $800,000."[182] Likewise, "[c]orrespondence from the City's human services director had indicated the property had a history of community recreation use and a land use change would negatively impact the availability, whether public or private, of community recreational facilities in the City."[183] "The City determined that replacement costs for the recreational facilities which had been on the property were as follows: pool—$250,000 to $280,000; paddle tennis courts—$135,000 to $150,000; and tennis courts—$275,000 to $300,000."[184] The city did not, however, require Ehrlich to pay replacement costs for all of these amenities. Instead, "[t]he fee was related to the cost of constructing four tennis courts at another location ($275,000 to $300,000)."[185] The in-lieu art fee, however, may be more difficult to sustain, unless it can be defended as a city-wide, rather than individually focused, exaction.

In *Trimen Development Co. v. King County,*[186] the Supreme Court of Washington upheld the city's conditioning of a subdivision plat approval on the dedication of land for open space or on the payment of a fee in lieu of such a dedication. Trimen, which had opted to pay the fee, challenged the condition as an uncompensated taking. Rejecting Trimen's claim, the court specifically cited *Dolan* and its rough proportionality requirement, holding that "the fees imposed in lieu of dedication were reasonably necessary as a direct result of Trimen's proposed development."[187]

The court acknowledged that the county did not conduct a site-specific study. However, it found the county could rely on a comprehensive assessment of park needs conducted in 1985.[188]

The *Dolan* decision should have little effect on cases involving in-lieu monetary exactions, as long as the fees are related in both nature and extent to the proposed development.[189] Examples of such fees legitimately imposed on residential developments include those to fund roads, sewers, water systems, schools, parks, drainage systems, police facilities, fire stations and equipment, libraries, and emergency medical facilities. In-lieu exactions on commercial and industrial developments that would appear to be permissible include fees for environmental waste disposal sites and child care facilities. Courts may have more difficulty with justifications for monetary exactions such as in-lieu fees for job training programs and "fair share" affordable housing requirements. However, when such fees are part of a negotiated arrangement in which the developer has received benefits, it is not clear that such an arm's-length agreement could be successfully attacked on the basis of *Dolan*.

VI. Conclusion

A great deal of constitutional history and Supreme Court jurisprudence has been devoted to the degree of protection that should be afforded to private property. The right of private ownership and use of property are basic American concepts, but the police powers doctrine has long established that such rights are not without limitation. Although the pendulum may have swung rather far to the local government's side for an expansive reading of its police powers, the recent decisions of the Supreme Court have started to interject some limits on the extent to which public costs can be imposed on landowners by local governments.

Local governments are faced with truly overwhelming costs for maintaining their public infrastructure, let alone needing to deal with loss of housing and degradation of the environment at a time when federal funding is in precipitous decline due to more conservative control of Congress. The remedy of increasing property taxes has been described as "either politically unpopular or illegal."[190] In light of the financial constraints and increased needs currently experienced by local governments, those entities will continue to seek methods of financing infrastructure needs. Although they can continue to impose certain land-dedication requirements, regulate land use, and exact impact fees, the *Dolan* decision will certainly be seen as lending an element of uncertainty in doing so. The specter of costly litigation, as well as the additional costs to validate local government dedications and exactions through greater procedural requirements and more extensive and targeted justifications, may discourage some localities from active stimulation of development. Others may be disinclined to proceed when proposed development will generate significant infrastructure costs that may require resort to condemnation and costs of compensation. Conceivably, some development proposals will be denied on the grounds that required infrastructure is not yet in place. If that is *Dolan*'s legacy, that will be unfortunate and certainly not in the interests of the development industry.

Notes

1. 114 S. Ct. 2309 (1994).

2. 112 S. Ct. 2886 (1992).

3. 480 U.S. 470 (1987).

4. 482 U.S. 304 (1987).

5. 483 U.S. 825 (1987).

6. Even before this book, a number of articles and books had been attempting to accurately assess the implications of these decisions. *See, e.g.*, David L. Callies, *Property Rights: Are There Any Left?*, 20 URB. LAW. 597 (1988); Peter W. Salsich, Jr., Keystone Bituminous Coal, First English *and* Nollan: *A Framework for Accommodation?*, 34 WASH. U. J. URB. & CONTEMP. L. 173 (1988).

7. Douglas W. Kmiec, *Clarifying the Supreme Court's Taking Cases—An Irreverent But Otherwise Unassailable Draft Opinion in* Dolan v. City of Tigard, 71 DENV. U. L. REV. 325 (1994). In a satirical fashion, the author summarized prior opinions and predicted the Court's decision in *Dolan* before its issuance.

8. *See, e.g., Court Backs Landowners, Restricts Government*, PLAIN DEALER (Cleveland), June 25, 1994, at A1.

9. "In future cases, this holding may prove to be a significant roadblock for governments with legitimate objectives and limited resources." *Mrs. Dolan and the Bike Path*, WASH. POST, June 26, 1994, at C6. *But see* Joan Biskupic, *Justices Broaden Property Rights, Land-Use Requirements May Be "Takings"*, WASH. POST, June 25, 1994, at A1 (interviewing lawyers who stated that "[t]his is not gloom and doom for local governments" and that "the decision will have relatively little impact").

10. As part of their "Contract With America," House Republicans passed a bill, later sent to the Senate, that would provide greater relief to property owners, particularly in the case of environmental regulations where government action resulted in significant diminution of value. What will ultimately emerge from Congress is hard to predict at this time.

11. *See, e.g.*, Fertilizing Co. v. Hyde Park, 97 U.S. 659, 669 (1878).

12. Armstrong v. United States, 364 U.S. 40, 49 (1960).

13. U.S. CONST. amend. V. The two clauses of this amendment are respectively referred to as the due process clause and the takings clause. Although the Fifth Amendment is directly applicable only to the federal government, its provisions have long been applied to the states by way of the Fourteenth Amendment. Chicago, B. & Q.R. Co. v. Chicago, 166 U.S. 226, 241 (1897); Missouri Pacific Ry. v. Nebraska, 164 U.S. 403, 417 (1896). Additionally, the Fourteenth Amendment, which is applicable to state governments, contains a due process clause that is identical to that provided in the Fifth Amendment. U.S. CONST. amend. XIV, § 1.

14. 260 U.S. 393, 415 (1922).

15. 438 U.S. 104 (1978).

16. Some have observed that property rights gained momentum with Rehnquist's selection as Chief Justice. *See generally* Stephen J. Massey, Note, *Justice Rehnquist's Theory of Property*, 93 YALE L.J. 541 (1984).

17. 112 S. Ct. 2886 (1992).

18. *Dolan,* 114 S. Ct. 2309, 2326 (Stevens, J., dissenting).

19. RICHARD A. EPSTEIN, TAKINGS: PRIVATE PROPERTY AND THE POWER OF EMINENT DOMAIN 18, at 26-27 (1985).

20. "[A] government may regulate use and enjoyment of the owner's property, or, in certain health and safety circumstances, deprive the owner of beneficial uses of it, without compensation other than the sharing of the resulting benefits." THEODORE J. NOVAK, ET AL., CONDEMNATION OF PROPERTY § 1.6, at 6 (citations omitted).

21. *See, e.g., Fertilizing Co.,* 97 U.S. at 669.

22. *Pennsylvania Coal,* 260 U.S. at 413.

23. *See, e.g.,* San Diego Gas & Electric Co. v. City of San Diego, 450 U.S. 621 (1981).

24. *See* NOVAK ET AL., *supra* note 20, § 1.6, at 7. Inverse condemnation is a cause of action in which a property owner institutes an action against the government and attempts to recover just compensation.

25. *See* Herman Schwartz, *Property Rights and the Constitution: Will the Ugly Duckling Become a Swan?,* 47 AM. U. L. REV. 9, 18 (1987); Marla Mansfield, *When "Property Rights" Meet "Public" Rights: The Problems of Labeling and Regulatory Takings,* 65 U. COLO. L. REV. 193, 205 (1994) (footnote omitted).

26. *See* William M. Treanor, Note, *The Origins and Original Significance of the Just Compensation Clause of the Fifth Amendment,* 94 YALE L. J. 694 (1985).

27. *Id.* at 710 (quoting THE FEDERALIST No. 54 (James Madison)).

28. *Id.* at 711 (footnote omitted).

29. *Id.* at 716 n.95. The Bill of Rights, with the Fifth Amendment in its current form, was ratified in 1791.

30. BLACK'S LAW DICTIONARY 1382 (6th ed. 1991).

31. NOVAK ET AL., *supra* note 20, § 2.2, at 10.

32. *See* NOVAK ET AL., *supra* note 20, § 5.5, at 45 (the legislature's discretion "is so wide as to cause many commentators to conclude that the public use requirement has lost all practical meaning as a restriction").

33. 348 U.S. 26 (1954) (holding that the District of Columbia's urban renewal was a public use, although the resulting structures would be operated by private agencies).

34. *Berman,* 348 U.S. at 32.

35. 467 U.S. 229, 241 (1984) (holding that scheme whereby Hawaii transferred lots owned by large landowners to tenants living on them was a public use). The Court further stated that "[t]he 'public use' requirement is . . . coterminous with the scope of a sovereign's police powers." *Id.* at 240. *See also* Poletown Neighborhood Council v. City of Detroit, 304 N.W.2d 455 (Mich. 1981) (holding that condemnation of land to convey it to General Motors as factory site had sufficient public purpose because it would create jobs and tax revenues).

36. NOVAK ET AL., *supra* note 20, § 15.2, at 124 (citing United States v. Cors, 37 U.S. 325, 332 (1949)).

37. *Id.* § 15.2, at 124 (citation omitted).

38. *Id.* § 15.3, at 125 (citation omitted).

39. *See, e.g., Penn Central,* 438 U.S. at 123 n.25 (taking not limited to physical transfers of property).

40. *See* Village of Euclid v. Ambler Realty Co., 272 U.S. 365 (1926).

41. *Penn Central,* 438 U.S. at 123.

42. Kaiser Aetna v. United States, 444 U.S. 164, 175 (1979) (internal citation omitted). *See also Pennsylvania Coal,* 260 U.S. at 415-16 (stressing that takings decisions do not lend themselves to "general propositions").

43. *See Lucas,* 112 S. Ct. at 2894 n.7 (acknowledging that "uncertainty regarding the composition of the denominator in our 'deprivation' fraction has produced inconsistent pronouncements by the Court"). *See also* John A. Humbach, *A Unifying Theory for the Just Compensation Cases: Takings, Regulation and Public Use,* 34 RUTGERS L. REV. 243, 244 (1982) (claiming that takings cases are "a farrago of fumblings which have suffered too long from a surfeit of deficient theories"); Joseph L. Sax, *Takings and the Police Power,* 74 YALE L.J. 36, 37 (1964) (stating cases are "a welter of confusing and apparently incompatible results").

44. *See, e.g.,* Gibson v. United States, 166 U.S. 269 (1897); Transportation Co. v. Chicago, 99 U.S. 635 (1879). *See generally* John N. Groen, *Exploring the Nuisance Exception,* C730 A.L.I.-A.B.A. COURSE OF STUDY, INVERSE CONDEMNATION & RELATED GOV'T LIABILITY 267 (1992) (surveying Nineteenth Century takings law). In the *Legal Tender Cases,* the Court stated as follows: "[T]he Takings Clause has always been understood as referring only to a direct appropriation, and not to consequential injuries resulting from the exercise of lawful power. It has never been supposed to have any bearing upon or to inhibit laws that indirectly work harm and loss to individuals." 79 U.S. (12 Wall.) 457, 551 (1871).

45. 123 U.S. 623 (1887).

46. *Mugler,* 123 U.S. at 668-69.

47. *Id.* at 669.

48. *See, e.g.,* Hadachek v. Sebastian, 239 U.S. 394 (1915) (upholding statute prohibiting brick manufacturer from operating in residential area); Reinman v. City of Little Rock, 237 U.S. 171 (1915) (upholding statute disallowing operation of stable in downtown area); Miller v. Schoene, 276 U.S. 272 (1928) (upholding statute ordering destruction of cedar trees due to trees' adverse effect on apple orchards); Goldblatt v. Hempstead, 369 U.S. 590 (1962) (upholding statute prohibiting excavation of sand below water line).

49. The same perspective was provided in *Keystone,* 480 U.S. at 492.

50. *Id.* at 491 n.20.

51. 260 U.S. 393 (1922).

52. *Pennsylvania Coal,* 260 U.S. at 412-13.

53. *Id.* at 413-14. The public benefit in this case consisted of preventing subsidence of a single home, while the private loss consisted of destroying the company's support estate and making its business commercially impracticable.

54. *United States v. Central Eureka Mining Co.,* 358 U.S. 858, 79 S. Ct. 9 (1958), which exemplifies such an approach, involved a wartime order issued for purposes of conserving labor and equipment. Central Eureka claimed the order effected a taking of its right to mine gold during the life of the order, which thus required compensation. The Court analyzed several factors and

firmly rejected this claim. First, it noted the lack of governmental occupation or possession of the mines. Next, it recognized that the order deprived the owners of the most valuable use of the property. Finally, and most significantly, the Court observed that the order was issued during wartime. This last consideration appeared to be dispositive for the Court's analysis.

55. 438 U.S. 104 (1978). *Penn Central* involved a New York City landmark preservation law, which was designed to preserve the historical and aesthetic integrity of certain buildings that were designated as landmarks. The owner of the so-designated Grand Central Terminal sought a permit to construct an office building above the terminal. When the permit was denied, the owner challenged the law as a compensable taking.

56. *Id.* at 137. For a thorough discussion of transfer of development rights as an alternative, see DAVID L. CALLIES, PRESERVING PARADISE 96-98 (1994).

57. For cases in which the Court has considered economic impact in regulatory takings, see *Nollan,* 483 U.S. at 834; Hodel v. Virginia Surface Mining & Reclamation Ass'n, 452 U.S. 264, 295-96 (1981). *See also* David C. Buck, Note, *"Property" in the Fifth Amendment: A Quest for Common Ground in the Maze of Regulatory Takings,* 46 VAND. L. REV. 1283 (1993) (advocating strict "diminution in value" test for all takings cases).

58. 447 U.S. 225 (1980).

59. *See* Frank Michelman, *Takings, 1987,* 88 COLUM. L. REV. 1600, 1621-22 (1988) (analyzing Court's increasing tendency to set forth more formal, categorical takings rules).

60. 480 U.S. 470 (1987).

61. *Id.* at 495-98.

62. *Lucas,* 112 S. Ct. at 2893.

63. When the Court finds that one of the "two discrete categories of regulatory action" has affected private property, compensation is required "without case-specific inquiry into the public interest advanced in support of the restraint." *Id. But see* Paul F. Haffner, Case Note, *Regulatory Takings—A New Categorical Rule:* Lucas v. South Carolina Coastal Council, 61 U. CIN. L. REV. 1035 (1993) (condemning categorical rules and advocating return to case-by-case approach for takings cases).

64. *Lucas,* 112 S. Ct. at 2893.

65. *Id.* "As we have said on numerous occasions, the Fifth Amendment is violated when land-use regulation 'does not substantially advance legitimate state interests or denies an owner economically viable use of his land.' " *Id.* at 2893-94 (quoting *Agins,* 447 U.S. at 260).

66. *Id.* at 2894-95.

67. 458 U.S. 419, 441 (1992).

68. The dissent stressed the lack of economic impact, noting that "[a]t issue are about 36 feet of cable one-half inch in diameter and two 4" × 4" × 4" metal boxes" amounting to one-eighth of cubic foot of space on a roof. *Id.* at 443 (Blackmun, J., dissenting).

69. 112 S. Ct. 1522 (1992).

70. 428 U.S. 304 (1987). The plaintiff operated a retreat center that was located on the banks of a creek. The effects of a fire had created a serious flood hazard, causing several deaths and destroying many buildings and bridges. As a result, Los Angeles county issued an ordinance temporarily prohibiting construction in the flood area. In analyzing *First English*, the Court abandoned the strict finality requirement, which had previously required the exhaustion of administrative processes or state court remedies. The crux of the holding was that " 'temporary' takings which, as here, deny a landowner all use of his property are not different in kind from permanent takings, for which the Constitution requires compensation." Concluding that "where the government's activities have already worked a taking of all use of property, no subsequent action by the government can relieve it of the duty to provide compensation for the period during which a taking was effective," the Court remanded the case for a determination of whether a taking had in fact occurred. On remand, First English lost, as the court found that the ordinance did not cause a temporary taking of the plaintiff's property. The court stated that the ordinance "substantially advanced the preeminent state interest in public safety" and did not deny all use of the plaintiff's property. 258 Cal. Rptr. 893 (Cal. Ct. App. 1989).

71. 112 S. Ct. 2886 (1992). Lucas had purchased two beachfront lots on a barrier island in 1986 for the purpose of constructing single-family homes. In 1988, South Carolina passed a regulation that sought to protect coastal areas from erosion and ecologically detrimental development. As a result of the regulation, Lucas was prevented from erecting any structures on his property. In arguing against a taking, South Carolina reasoned that because the regulation prevented a harmful use (contribution to erosion) the state was validly exercising its police power. The South Carolina Supreme Court agreed with the state, holding that even though the regulation denied Lucas all use of his property, the *Mugler* nuisance exception precluded finding a compensable taking.

72. Note, however, that this allowed the Court to avoid the extent of devaluation necessary to qualify as a complete destruction of all economically viable use. The Court itself acknowledged its lack of guidance:

> Regrettably, the rhetorical force of our "deprivation of all economically feasible use" rule is greater than its precision, since the rule does not make clear the "property interest" against which the loss of value is to be measured. When, for example, a regulation requires a developer to leave 90% of a rural tract in its natural state, it is unclear whether we would analyze the situation as one in which the owner has been deprived of all economically beneficial use of the burdened portion of the tract, or as one in which the owner has suffered a mere diminution in value of the tract as a whole.

Lucas, 112 S. Ct. at 2894 n.7.

73. *Id.* at 2893 (Court will conduct "case-specific inquiry into the public interest advanced in support of the restraint").

74. *Id.* at 2895 n.8.

75. *See* Donald L. Connors & Michael E. High, *The Expanding Circle of Exactions: From Dedication to Linkage*, 50 LAW & CONTEMP. PROBS. 69, 70 (1987).

76. *Id.*

77. *See, e.g.*, Pengilly v. Multnomah County, 810 F. Supp. 1111 (D. Ore. 1992) (upholding right-of-way dedication requirement); Sudarsky v. City of New York, 779 F. Supp. 287 (S.D.N.Y. 1991) (upholding transit easement dedication); River Birch Ass'n v. City of Raleigh, 388 S.E.2d 538 (N.C. 1990) (upholding required conveyance of recreation area); Boone v. Antrim County Bd. of Road Comm'rs, 442 N.W.2d 688 (Mich. Ct. App. 1989) (upholding required dedication of road in approval of subdivision plat).

78. 483 U.S. 825 (1987).

79. *Id.* at 828-29.

80. It has been argued that Justice Powell's surprise announcement of his retirement on the last day of the Court's 1986 Term changed the fate of takings law. The liberal justices "lost Justice Powell to the conservative wing, suffering defeat five to four." Frank R. Strong, *On Placing Property Due Process Center Stage in Takings Jurisprudence*, 49 OHIO ST. L.J. 591, 615-16 (1988).

81. *Nollan*, 483 U.S. at 832.

82. *Id.* at 834.

83. *Id.* at 838-39.

84. *Id.* at 831 (citations omitted).

85. *Dolan*, 114 S. Ct. at 2312.

86. *Id.* at 2316 (quoting *Nollan*, 483 U.S. at 831).

87. *Id.* at 2317 (citing *Nollan*, 483 U.S. at 837).

88. *Id.* at 2318 (citing *Nollan*, 483 U.S. at 834). The Court indicated it was not required to reach this part of the test in *Nollan* because the first part of the test was not met. *Id.* at 2317.

89. *Id.* (citing *Agins*, 447 U.S. at 260-62).

90. *Id.*

91. *Id.*

92. *Id.* (citations omitted).

93. *Id.* at 2318-19 (citing Jemad, Inc., v. Scarsdale, 218 N.E.2d 678 (N.Y. 1966); Billings Properties, Inc. v. Yellowstone County, 394 P.2d 184 (Mont. 1964)).

94. *Id.* at 2319 (citing Pioneer Trust & Savings Bank v. Mount Prospect, 176 N.E.2d 799, 802 (Ill. 1971) (the first court to develop the "specifi[c] and uniquely attributable" test)).

95. *Id.*

96. *Id.* (citing, for example, Simpson v. North Platte, 292 N.W.2d 297 (Neb. 1980); Jordan v. Menomonee Falls, 137 N.W.2d 442 (Wis. 1965)).

97. *Id.*

98. *Id.* at 2319-20.

99. *Id.* at 2320.

100. *Id.* at 2321-22 (internal citation omitted).

101. *Id.* at 2320.

102. "Strict scrutiny" applies to governmental action based on race and national origin. *See, e.g.*, Rogers v. Lodge, 458 U.S. 613 (1982); Strauder v. West Virginia, 100 U.S. 303 (1880). "Strict scrutiny" also applies to cases involving fundamental rights, such as the right to marriage and the right to personal au-

tonomy. *See, e.g.*, Zablocki v. Redhail, 434 U.S. 374 (1978); Roe v. Wade, 410 U.S. 113 (1973).

103. Intermediate-level scrutiny applies to illegitimacy- and gender-based equal protection claims. *See, e.g.*, Lalli v. Lalli, 439 U.S. 259 (1978); Craig v. Boren, 429 U.S. 190 (1976).

104. *Dolan*, 114 S. Ct. at 2327 (Stevens, J., dissenting).

105. *Nollan*, 483 U.S. at 835 n.3 (citations omitted). In *United States v. Carolene Products Co.*, 304 U.S. 144 (1938), the Court rejected heightened scrutiny in the context of almost all governmental socioeconomic legislation and narrowly limited heightened scrutiny to review of regulations affecting either fundamental constitutional rights or "discrete and insular" minorities. *Id.* at 152 n.4.

106. *Nollan*, 483 U.S. at 865 (Blackmun, J., dissenting).

107. *Id.* at 837 n.3 (internal citation omitted).

108. *Dolan*, 114 S. Ct. at 2323 (Stevens, J., dissenting). It appears, however, that the Court had encroached upon the presumption of constitutionality in earlier opinions.

109. *Id.* at 2320 (citing *Nollan*, 483 U.S. at 836).

110. *Id.* at 2331 (Souter, J., dissenting) (footnote omitted).

111. *Id.* at 2327-28 (Stevens, J., dissenting) (citing Hodel v. Irving, 481 U.S. 704, 715 (1987)).

112. *Pennsylvania Coal*, 260 U.S. at 415.

113. *Penn Central*, 438 U.S. at 137 (citation omitted).

114. *Dolan*, 114 S. Ct. at 2324 (Stevens, J., dissenting) (citing Transcript of Oral Arg. 41-42).

115. *Id.* at 2326 (citing Transcript of Oral Arg. 30-31).

116. *Id.*

117. Brief for the City of Tigard, 1994 WL 123754, at *43, *Dolan* (citations omitted).

118. *Id.* at *42 (citation omitted).

119. *Id.* at *21.

120. *Dolan*, 114 S. Ct. at 2319-20.

121. *Id.* at 2321 (footnote omitted).

122. *Id.* at 2331 (Souter, J., dissenting) (citing Brief for Respondent A-5).

123. *Id.* at 2321.

124. *Id.* at 2331 (Souter, J., dissenting) (quoting Pennell v. San Jose, 485 U.S. 1, 20 (1988) (Scalia, J., concurring in part and dissenting in part)).

125. *See, e.g.*, F&W Assoc. v. County of Somerset, 648 A.2d 482 (N.J. Super App. Div. 1994) (sustaining exaction for land improvements). Other litigation arises out of claims that a regulatory entity lacks proper enabling authority to impose an exaction and that a fee amounts to an invalid tax. While these topics are beyond the scope of this chapter, see the relevant discussions in Cobb v. Snohomish County, 829 P.2d 169 (Wash. Ct. App. 1991), and Bernardsville Quarry, Inc. v. Borough of Bernadsville, 608 A.2d 1377 (N.J. 1992).

126. 292 N.W.2d 297, 301 (Neb. 1980), *cited in Dolan*, 114 S. Ct. at 2319.

127. Brief for City of Tigard, 1994 WL 123754, at *44 n.32 (internal citations omitted).

128. *See* David W. Sweet & Lee P. Symons, *Pennsylvania's New Municipalities Planning Code: Policy, Politics, and Impact Fees,* 94 DICK. L. REV. 61 (1989).

129. Laurie Reynolds, Book Review, *Living With Land-Use Exactions,* 11 YALE J. ON REG. 507, 508-09 (1994).

130. *Id.* at 509.

131. *Id.* at 514.

132. *Id.*

133. *Dolan,* 114 S. Ct. at 2322.

134. *Id.* at 2316.

135. *Id.* at 2320 n.8 (citing *Euclid,* 272 U.S. 365 (1926)).

136. John R. Nolon, *Comprehensive Land Use Planning: Learning How and Where to Grow,* 13 PACE L. REV. 351; (1993) at 393 (and cases cited therein).

137. *Id.*

138. *Agins,* 447 U.S. at 260 (citing *Nectow v. City of Cambridge,* 277 U.S. 183, 188 (1928), and Penn Central, 438 U.S. at 138 n.36).

139. Nolon, *supra* note 136, at 393 (footnote omitted).

140. 862 F. Supp. 287 (D. Kan. 1994).

141. *Id.* at 293.

142. *Id.* at 294.

143. 182 Ariz. 203, 895 P.2d 115 (Ariz. App. 1995).

144. *Id.,* 895 P.2d at 120.

145. *Id.,* 895 P.2d at 120-21.

146. *See, e.g.,* Trent Meredith, Inc. v. City of Oxnard, 170 Cal. Rptr. 685 (1981) (court upheld dedication of land or "fees in lieu" to school district as condition to building permit); Jenad, Inc. v. Village of Scarsdale, 218 N.E.2d 673 (N.Y. 1966) (court upheld same for parks). *See also* Bernard V. Keenan, *The* Nollan *Decision Amidst Land-Use Exactions and Impact Fees,* 25 URB. LAW. 817, 817 (1993) ("fees paid by developers account for approximately 25% of new school construction in fast-growing California suburbs").

147. Theodore C. Taub, *Development Exactions and Impact Fees,* C872 A.L.I.-A.B.A. COURSE OF STUDY, INVERSE CONDEMNATION & RELATED GOV'T LIABILITY 269, 272 (1993).

148. *Id.*

149. *Id.*

150. CALLIES, *supra* note 56, at 37-38.

151. Taub, *supra* note 147, at 290.

152. *Id.*

153. *Id.* With the use of inclusionary zoning, developers are often required to devote a certain percentage of land to low- and moderate-income housing. *See* Reynolds, *supra* note 129, at 515 n.1.

154. Reynolds, *supra* note 129, at 515 n.1.

155. Developed by the Advisory Committee on City Planning, Planning and Zoning U.S. Dept. of Commerce 1928, found in Anderson, American Law of Zoning, §21.11 at 601-02.

156. Taub, *supra* note 147, at 271.

157. *Id.*

158. *Id.* at 283-84.
159. 941 F.2d 872 (9th Cir. 1991), *cert. denied,* 112 S. Ct. 1997 (1992).
160. *Commercial Builders,* 941 F.2d at 873.
161. *Id.* at 876.
162. *Id.*
163. *Id.*
164. 4 Cal. Rptr. 2d 114 (Ct. App.), *cert. denied,* 113 S. Ct. 191 (1992).
165. *Nollan,* 483 U.S. at 841.
166. *Blue Jeans,* 4 Cal. Rptr. 2d at 118.
167. *Id.*
168. 4 Cal. Rptr. 2d 897 (Ct. App. 1992).
169. *Garrick,* 4 Cal. Rptr. at 908 (citations omitted).
170. *Id.*
171. 112 S. Ct. 1522 (1992).
172. *Yee,* 112 S. Ct. at 1524-25.
173. 19 Cal. Rptr. 2d 468 (Ct. App. 1993), *vacated,* 114 S. Ct. 2731 (1994). The dissenters in *Dolan* voted to deny certiorari in *Ehrlich.*
174. *Id.* at 470.
175. *Id.* at 475.
176. *Id.*
177. *Id.* at 476.
178. *Id.* at 475.
179. *Id.* at 476.
180. *Id.* at 480.
181. On remand, in a two-to-one decision, the California Court of Appeals held that Culver City did not violate the developer's constitutional rights in adopting the mitigation and in lieu art fees and that the city's actions were valid in light of *Nollan* and *Dolan. Ehrlich,* No. B055523 (Cal. Ct. App. Dec. 23, 1994), *review granted,* 95 C.D.O.S. 1988 (Cal. Mar. 16, 1995). It seems the California Supreme Court is likely to get the last word, unless the U.S. Supreme Court were to again take up the case.
182. 19 Cal. Rptr. 2d at 473.
183. *Id.*
184. *Id.*
185. *Id.* at 476.
186. 877 P.2d 187 (Wash. 1994).
187. *Id.* at 199. *But see* Henderson Home, Inc. v. City of Bothell, 877 P.2d 176 (Wash. 1994) (finding a park impact "mitigation fee" [exaction] that ignored statutory impact fee requirements to be invalid).
188. *Id.*
189. *See* Home Builders Ass'n of Central Ariz. v. City of Scottsdale, 1995 WL 61490 (Ariz. Ct. App. Feb. 16, 1995) (After remand by the U.S. Supreme Court, taken on the basis of its *Dolan* decision, the Arizona Court of Appeals again upheld a development fee ordinance as consistent with *Dolan*); Waters Landing L.P. v. Montgomery County, 650 A.2d 712 (Md. 1995) (sustaining a development impact tax which it had invalidated when it was originally enacted as an impact fee).
190. *Callies, supra* note 56, at 37.

PART III

Special Issues

CHAPTER ❖ 12

Property Rights Legislation: Some Questions

R. G. Converse

I. Property Rights Legislation: More or Less Unrest?

In the foregoing chapters of this book, the "clash" (as it is often labeled) between the rights of private property owners and the police power has been examined, dissected, categorized, and even proclaimed to have been resolved. This wrestling with the relationship between the liberty Americans enjoy in our private property system and the intrusions by government upon that liberty for the regulation of health, safety, and general welfare of all has reached a point of such frustration (and even anger) that, as a couple of the authors have mentioned, another aspect or relative of takings has appeared on the scene: property rights legislation.

As noted by Douglas Kmiec in chapter five of this book, the "lack of judicial review is partially responsible for the dominating federal presence in much of daily life, from the workplace to schools. And the perception of that federal presence as bloated or unwarranted or worse has now triggered a seismic political change, the likes of which have not been seen in over four decades."[1] For the same reason that Mr. Kmiec advocates the common law of nuisance as the solution to the "takings puzzle," the seismic political change occurring in America is taking the form of property rights legislation: desire for stability and order, and unrest about (and impatience for) social engineering. Thus the question: will property rights legislation achieve that goal or will it merely cause more unrest and impatience with new questions or variations of the old ones? The U.S. House of Representatives has passed, and sent to the Senate for its consideration, The Private Property Protection Act of 1995.[2] A review of that pending legislation should provide some insight about the answer to this question.

II. The Private Property Protection Act of 1995: Definitions

The Private Property Protection Act of 1995, as section 1 of the act proclaims its short title to be, sets out, in section 2, federal policy and direction "that no law or agency action should limit the use of privately owned property so as to diminish its value." Obviously, this is a much broader territory than was staked out for takings jurisprudence in *Pennsylvania Coal v. Mahon*.[3] Section 2 continues, however, to admonish federal agencies, officers, and employees that they *should* exercise their federal authority "to ensure that agency action will not limit the use of privately owned property so as to diminish its value." All of this sounds a little like the planning documents that Dwight Merriam suggests planners recognize as necessary after considering the details of the *Dolan* case. Oh, and yes, Virginia, as Michael Berger notes, there can be partial takings.[4]

To understand this policy and direction (it really seems there is more policy than direction), a few key defined terms must be learned. I previously referred to "property" and "agency action." These terms, along with "agency" and the concept of property use being limited by agency action, are defined in section 10 of the bill.

A. Property

"Property" is defined to mean "land and includes the right to use or receive water." For the moment, accept the definition for what it is and put aside the obvious question: does "land" mean only the dirt, and not include improvements?

B. Agency Action

The terms "agency action" and "agency" are defined by referring to definitions in the U.S. Code,[5] in which "agency" is defined to mean each authority of the U.S. government, regardless of whether it is within, or subject to review by, another agency. However, it does not include Congress, the courts, the governments of U.S. territories or possessions, the government of the District of Columbia, agencies composed of the persons involved in the disputes being determined by them, military courts and commissions, military authority exercised in the field during war or in occupied territory, miscellaneous functions relating to insurance of home mortgages and loans on manufactured housing, certain dispositions of surplus property for public airports, rent controls prompted by World War II or the Korean Conflict, or World War II vintage regulations on the use of foreign currencies and foreign scholarships. "Agency action" includes all or any part of an agency rule, order, license, sanction, relief, or the equivalent or denial thereof, or failure to act.[6]

The concept of property use being limited by agency action is defined in this fashion, "a use of property is limited by an agency action if a particular legal right to use that property no longer exists because of the action."

C. The Twenty and Fifty Percent Rules

Armed with these definitions, the policy and direction of the bill is clear: the federal government should not be exercising its authority in ways that fail to realize the effects its actions have on the values of private property. To implement this policy and direction, however, the bill does not restrict or prevent agency action from reducing or adversely affecting the use of property; rather it sets out in section 3 a right to compensation for the owner whose use of his or her property, or any portion of that property (see, I told you there were partial takings, Virginia!), is limited by an agency action under a specified regulatory law to such extent that the fair market value of that portion is diminished by 20 percent or more. If the limitation on use causes a diminution in value of more than 50 percent, then the property owner can require the federal government to purchase the portion of the property so limited for its fair market value.

D. Specified Regulatory Laws Affected

To appreciate these mandates of compensation in the bill, a few more terms need defining. One such term is "specified regulatory law," which section 10 of the bill defines to include only: section 404 of the Federal Water Pollution Control Act,[7] the Endangered Species Act of 1979,[8] the Food Security Act of 1985,[9] the Reclamation Acts,[10] the Federal Land Policy Management Act,[11] and section 6 of the Forest and Rangeland Renewable Resources Planning Act of 1974.[12]

E. Fair Market Value

Another definition needed to appreciate the extent of the bill's coverage is that of the term "fair market value," which section 10 defines as follows:

> [T]he term 'fair market value' means the most probable price at which property would change hands, in a competitive and open market under all conditions requisite to a fair sale, between a willing buyer and a willing seller, neither being under any compulsion to buy or sell and both having reasonable knowledge of relevant facts, at the time the agency action occurs.

III. Compensation Remedy

A. Effect of the Compensation Remedy on the Substantive Due Process Remedy of Invalidation

A couple of things should be obvious: the power of the federal government to take property is not affected, and the bill takes the Fifth Amendment's compensation approach to federal government takings rather than the substantive due process approach of invalidation. In fact, could it be argued that if the bill were a law, the invalidation remedy in substantive due process takings cases (involving federal takings of "property") would be dead because the bill mandates compensation as the remedy for what the bill defines as government going too far? Also consider that subsection 9(a) states that nothing in the bill is to be construed to limit an owner's right to compensation under the Constitution or other laws of the United States. I cannot believe that such would be the result. It is the Constitution from which substantive due process comes, and its remedy of invalidation must be inherent lest the use of private property becomes more of a lottery than a secure liberty. Another hint that such should not be the result is contained in subsection 3(b) of the bill, which recognizes that agency action could be "otherwise vitiated" (more on that later). Furthermore, the policy and direction statements in section 2 of the bill would become meaningless if the federal government could be as arbitrary as it wished in dishing out agency action as long as it was willing to pay "fair market value," which inevitably will never take into account lost opportunities and associated gains.

Earlier, the suggestion was made to ignore for the time being that the definition of "property" was seemingly limited only to land and water rights. Here is why: If one considers the substance of the agency actions likely under the "specified regulatory laws," it seems that the diminution in value that is likely to occur is only in the value of the land concerned. Usually, the section 404 permits, the habitat of endangered species, and the farm production on wetlands involve only raw land and not improvements, and thus the diminution in value would be only to the land itself. Also, if there are improvements on land that become the subject of agency action that actually reduces the value of the improvements, then the property owner still has the avenue of seeking compensation for that taking (if he or she can prove one has occurred) by making the traditional takings claim.

B. Rescission of the Regulation after Compensation Is Paid

What if the agency wants to rescind its agency action at a later time? Under subsection 3(b) of the bill, once the compensation has been paid to the owner, the property cannot later be used in a way that is contrary to the limitation imposed by the agency action, even if that action is later rescinded or "otherwise vitiated." This provision does not, however, necessarily doom property to a meaningless and useless existence once the limit on its use is gone. The owner of the property (presumably at the time of the request) can elect to refund the amount of compensation, adjusted for inflation, to the U.S. Treasury and thus clear the property from the limit on use.

A couple of questions arise from examining this provision. Suppose the agency action (denial of a section 10(a) permit under the Endangered Species Act, for example) is rescinded, thus allowing development of the property for twenty residential units per acre. Assume also that the owner wants to construct only ten units per acre. Could the property owner refund only half the compensation and limit the development through deed restriction to only ten units per acre, without refunding the balance of the compensation plus the inflation adjustment? I have no answer for this question, but a couple of observations are in order. First, the amount of record keeping associated with this process will be great unless the number of property owners receiving compensation is fairly small. Second, policing the use of all this property (assuming that the number of tracts is large) could spawn a whole new task for some federal agency—perhaps property police, whose task would be to check all this property to ensure the taxpayers are getting their money's worth from these limits on use resulting from agency actions under specified regulatory laws. An alternative would be to use the real property records systems existing in several states to record the limits on use, which would be fine as long as there were mechanisms for dealing with the recordings and for addressing compliance with the limits they contain.

One other question regarding subsection 3(b), which actually now has no federal government implications, is relevant to taxpayers. After the property owner could pay to lift the limitation on use, should the local property tax assessor be able to increase the assessed value of the property for property tax purposes, considering that the only reason the use of the property is then limited is the unilateral decision of the property owner? If that sort of revaluation was allowed, how would the cost to the property owner (which must be incurred to obtain the release of the limit on use) be represented in the valuation? Surely property valuation techniques exist to handle the value part of this analysis, but what about the propriety (even the legality) of such reappraisals? It seems that the same answer should flow as the one that comes from the situation in which property can be rezoned to permit a higher and better use, but the owner chooses not to seek that rezoning. Is his or her property revalued anyway? I think the answer here depends on the provisions of each state's statutes concerning the valuation of real property for property tax purposes.

IV. Exclusions and Exceptions

With the general mandate of the bill behind us, let us now look at the exclusions and exceptions. Aside from those contained in the definitions already covered, there are three sections that provide, in one form or another, exclusions and exceptions to the coverage of the bill.

A. Nuisance

Under section 4 of the bill, if agency action limits a use of property, but that use is already a nuisance as defined by state law or is already prohibited under a local zoning ordinance, then no compensation is due. On its face, that sounds a lot like the *Lucas* pronouncements about background principles of a state's nuisance and property law.[13] However, one should consider the following question. What if the state or local government adopts an invalid statute or ordinance that limits the use of property, and then a federal agency takes action that results in the same limitation on the use of the owner's property? Is this section of the bill going to mean that the owner must sue to invalidate the state or local government law before he or she can seek compensation from the federal agency? The answer to this question must be yes. Surely the Republican House members would not expose the federal treasury (and the American taxpayers) to being the "payor of choice," so to speak. Rather, if the use is already limited at the state or local level, how can the property owner complain about federal agency action until (and unless) the owner obtains local permission to make that use of the property. Federalism should run both ways.[14] Also, if the owner cannot get the local limit on use reversed, but is able to obtain compensation from the state or local government, then he or she should not be able to collect again from the federal government for the same limit on use.

B. Health and Safety

Section 5 of the bill includes a general health and safety exception, and another (for the courts) defined "federal navigational servitude," except to the extent that the navigational servitude is interpreted to apply to wetlands. The health and safety exception provides that agency action is not compensable when it has as its primary purpose the prevention of an identifiable hazard to public health or safety, or damage to specific property (other than the property with the limited use). The bill does not indicate what is necessary to demonstrate "primary purpose." Are the self-serving preliminary statements and preambles, which Justice Scalia scorned in *Lucas,* sufficient, or is there another nexus analysis on the horizon? Section 5 does not say who carries the burden of proof on demonstrating the primary purpose of the agency action. Hopefully, common sense would solve that issue; the agency taking the action is in the best position to articulate at least the prima facie case for its primary purpose in taking the action. What if the owner is able to show that although the agency action may have a legitimate primary purpose, that purpose can be achieved through different agency action that does not impact the owner's property, at least not to the same degree? That issue does not appear to be covered by the bill.

Also worth noting is that section 5 addresses the prevention of *identifiable* hazards and damage. Could this requirement (that the hazard or damage sought to be prevented be identifiable) provide the answer, for example, to those who advocate that the listings under the Endangered Species Act are based on faulty or no biology? Also note that there must be specific property (other than the property being regulated) to which damage is being prevented. Again the burden of proof on these issues will be important and, just as the Court required in *Dolan,*[15] that burden of proof should be on the agency. The agency is supposed to be better informed and equipped about these issues; indeed, a policy of the bill is that the agency take its action in such manner as to not diminish the value of privately owned property.

V. The Procedure to Obtain Compensation

Section 6 of the bill establishes a procedure for the property owner to request compensation. The agency may bargain with the owner about the amount of compensation and, if no or insufficient compensation is paid by the agency, the owner can require binding arbitration or sue in court. There are fairly short time periods (at least compared with the amount of time it takes to process a takings claim through the state or federal courts or both) for the procedure to take place.

The process is started by the agency giving appropriate notice, as mandated by section 8 of the bill, to owners of private property whenever that agency takes action limiting the use of such property. The notice must explain an owner's rights under the bill, and "the procedures directly affected for obtaining any compensation that may be due" the owner under the bill. Under subsection 6(a), the owner has 180 days after receiving actual notice of the agency action to make a compensation request to the "agency whose agency action resulted in the limitation [on the use of the owner's property]." An initial question that will arise is whether failing to meet the 180-day deadline is fatal to the owner's request for compensation, if the owner read about the agency action in the newspaper but never got a notice from the agency because the agency either failed to send one or believed it gave one in an "appropriate" manner, though it failed to actually reach the owner. Sounds like a good jury question.

After the owner has timely requested compensation, a 180-day period for negotiations follows, but only if the agency wants to bargain. Subsection 6(b) clearly states that the agency "may bargain with the owner to establish the amount of compensation." What if the agency refuses to bargain, or waits until 150 days have passed and only then will bargain? Indeed this may be a real possibility, as the agency's means of "leveling the playing field." In other words, the agency could take 150 days or so to investigate and get its best value case prepared (or its best face to tell the owner that it believes it is exempt from the bill's coverage) and then commence talks. The owner may then feel that he or she has had to wait for what seems like forever, and now is squeezed into making a decision on short notice or facing the alternatives. Before we look at the alternatives, however, one thought crosses the mind: could the agency's refusal to negotiate itself be an agency action that diminishes the value of the owner's property (by an amount representing the value of the use of the property for the period of time the agency failed to negotiate)?

If within 180 days after the property owner makes a request the parties fail to reach agreement about the right to, and amount of, compensation, the owner's alternatives are to seek either binding arbitration under subsection 6(d) or compensation in a civil action under subsection 6(e). The procedures governing the binding arbitration are those set forth in Title IX of the U.S. Code, and the award made pursuant to that arbitration must include a reasonable attorney's fee and arbitration costs (including appraisal fees). The agency must then "promptly pay any award to the owner." If the owner does not choose arbitration, or, if having arbitrated, the agency does not promptly pay, then the owner can maintain a civil action against the agency to obtain "appropriate relief," which is the diminution in value in the first instance and enforcement of the arbitration award in the latter. Also recoverable in the civil action is interest on the amount of any compensation, calculated from the time of the limitation on property use. Thus, the bill provides a fairly tidy and simple process.

Now, with an award or judgment in the bag, it is time to collect—and promptly—right? This aspect of the bill may be the most problematic part. First of all, section 7 of the bill states, "Notwithstanding any other provision of law, any obligation of the United States to make any payment under this Act shall be subject to the availability of appropriations." Surprised? You should not be. Being subject to appropriations is the torment of the private sector when dealing with the government. If Congress fails to appropriate the money, a private party cannot collect—generally.

In the bill, however, is some hope (maybe). Subsection 6(f) provides that the owner's arbitration award or civil suit judgment "shall, notwithstanding any other provision of law, be made from the annual appropriation of the agency whose action occasioned the payment or judgment." Beyond the scope of this chapter, but interesting to note, is this question: can the U.S. Congress, by statute, bind the budget decisions and appropriations of future Congresses and the President? Assuming without deciding, as the courts do, that this is a valid provision, subsection 6(f) of the bill contains a few more gems. If one agency takes action because of a requirement imposed by another, then the agency taking such action and making payment may seek partial or complete reimbursement from the appropriated funds of the other agency. This subsection also provides that the head of an agency may transfer or reprogram any appropriated funds available to the agency and, if insufficient funds exist for the payment, that "it shall be the duty of the head of the agency to seek the appropriation of such funds for the next fiscal year." What if he or she does not do so? Would a section 1983 action lie for the failure?

VI. Conclusion

So what about this aspect, or relative, of takings that has appeared? Will it alleviate the frustration and anger that have reached such heights that they prompted the passage of this legislation by the U.S. House of Representatives? The passage may indeed be a source of some relief, as the governed can point to it as at least one example of our system of government working: the governed, through the ballot box, signaled a change was needed and then a change was proffered. It does seem that the bill can provide more immediate and less costly relief when the actions of government go too far and, by doing so, may even cause government to rethink its proposed actions to find less economically devastating means of achieving the ends it finds necessary to pursue.

It also seems that many of the issues this book sets out concerning traditional takings jurisprudence will persist in complying with, and seeking the benefits of, the Private Property Protection Act of 1995. For example, ripeness questions will continue to plague property owners in the form of determining the nature of a "final disposition" in the definition of agency action. Questions about limitations on parts of property, and about agencies taking action in phases to avoid the 20 percent threshold, will be the equivalent to partial takings issues in traditional takings cases. Also, just as in takings cases, the question of what constitutes a nuisance under state law will remain. Even the determination of a proper nexus will be present when examining whether an exception to the bill's coverage exists regarding a particular agency action, such as when the agency claims its action involves preventing either an identifiable hazard to public health or safety, or damages to specific property.

The bill's approach has certain benefits. There is certainty achieved in the partial takings case with the 20 percent threshold and the 50 percent condemnation trigger. The bill identifies the particular federal statutes under which agency action can occur, and thus identifies those concerns that Congress feels are legitimate governmental interests. Finally, the apparent speed and precision the bill provides for obtaining and determining the amount of compensation should not be overlooked.

Only passage and implementation of this bill and corresponding bills in the states (several of which have already done so[16]) will prove their worth. If they achieve stability and order, and lessen the unrest and impatience for social engineering that Americans expressed in 1994, then this is the "conclusion" to takings. Otherwise, there will be more to come.

Notes

1. See chapter 5 of this book, at 108.
2. H.R. 925, 104th Cong., 1st Sess. (1995).

3. 260 U.S. 393 (1922).

4. See chapter 7 of this book.

5. 5 U.S.C.A. § 551 (West 1977 & Supp. 1995).

6. Each of these items is likewise defined, and it is interesting to note that the definition of "order" uses the term "final disposition." Could this be the next round of ripeness arguments? See chapter 3 of this book, by Thomas Roberts.

7. 33 U.S.C.A. § 1344 (West 1986 & Supp. 1995).

8. 16 U.S.C.A. § 1531 (West 1985 & Supp. 1995).

9. 16 U.S.C.A. § 3821 (West 1985 & Supp. 1995).

10. 43 U.S.C.A. § 371 (West 1986 & Supp. 1995).

11. 43 U.S.C.A. § 1701 (West 1986 & Supp. 1995).

12. 16 U.S.C.A. § 1604 (West 1985 & Supp. 1995).

13. Lucas v. South Carolina Coastal Council, 112 S. Ct. 2886, 2900 (1992).

14. See section C of chapter 5 of this book.

15. Dolan v. City of Tigard, 114 S. Ct. 2309, 2319 (1994).

16. In 1995, at least three states passed laws requiring that compensation be paid for regulations, beyond that required by the Fifth Amendment and corresponding provisions of those states' constitutions. *See* H. R. 863, 1995 Fla. Reg. Sess. (Fla. 1995) (enacted May 18, 1995); Texas Private Real Property Rights Preservation Act, 1995 Tex Gen. Laws S. B. 14 (to be codified at TEX. GOV'T CODE ANN. § 2007 (West 1995)); Protection of Private Property Act, WASH. REV. CODE § 36. 70A.370 (Supp. 1992). The Arizona legislature passed a compensation bill, ARIZ. REV. STAT. ANN. (1992) but the state's voters rescinded the law in a statewide referendum.

A number of states have passed bills requiring state agencies or the state attorney general to conduct assessments of the economic impact of regulations; such laws differ from the Florida, Texas, and Washington laws listed above in that they do not mandate compensation beyond that required by the Constitution. Rather, like the National Environmental Policy Act environmental impact statement, they call for a takings impact statement. *See, e.g.*, DEL. CODE ANN. tit. 29, § 605 (1992); IDAHO CODE § 67-8003 (1994); IND. CODE § 4-22-2-32 (1994); MISS. CODE ANN. §§ 17-1-3, 95-3-29 (1994); MO. REV. STAT. §§ 536.017, 536.018 (1994); TENN. CODE ANN. § 12-1-201 (1994); UTAH CODE ANN. §§ 63-90a-1-63-90a-4, §§ 78-34a-1-78-34a-4 (1994); W. VA. CODE §§ 22-1A-1-22-1A-6 (1994).

CHAPTER ❖ 13

Open-Space Preservation after *Dolan*

Christopher J. Duerksen and Richard Paik

I. Introduction

As urbanization continues its inexorable march into the nation's hinterlands, rural areas and open spaces dwindle and become increasingly precious. In seeking to preserve these open spaces, planners command a broad array of tools. These include purchases of strategic parcels, transfer-of-development-rights programs, restrictive zoning regulations, clustered-development regulations, set-aside requirements, and requirements for the dedication of open spaces. This chapter examines the various tools that have been used for preserving recreational, scenic, agricultural, and other types of open spaces, and then analyzes the *Dolan* decision and its likely effects on the practice of planning for open-space protection.

II. Open-Space Preservation Tools

Local governments command a number of techniques to protect open spaces, and these are profiled briefly in the following sections.

A. Acquisition Approaches

1. FEE SIMPLE PURCHASE

Various interests in land include rights of possession and access, and rights to various uses such as mining, hunting, or construction. When one party owns the entire bundle of these rights, such party owns the land "in fee simple." Acquisition of land in fee simple gives the purchaser full title to, and possession of, all rights associated with the purchased property, subject only to the constraints imposed by nuisance laws and valid public regulations. Fee simple ownership provides the simplest and most effective means of effecting control; when government owns the land, government controls its development, redevelopment, and preservation. Government entities may derive funding for acquisition from a number of sources, including general tax revenues, open-space bond issues, lottery funds, or special sales tax levies. Once the government entity assumes fee simple ownership of the land, it possesses a broad range of options: the government may reconvey selected interests in the land, restrict future uses, lease the land, or otherwise control the bundle of property rights in a manner appropriate to its intended objectives.

Federal, state, and local government entities commonly use fee simple purchase for properties to be reserved for parklands. State and national park systems, for example, consist of lands containing natural resources that are best protected through government management; when such resources are valuable, government may determine that those resources should not be subjected to the broad range of unforeseeable threats that may arise under private ownership. In such cases, acquisition in fee simple provides the surest method for land protection.

2. EASEMENT PURCHASES AND PURCHASES OF DEVELOPMENT RIGHTS

Easements are severable rights or interests in land. The severable nature of easements allows a landowner to convey or reserve specific rights associated with a property, apart from other essential rights of possession and use. There are two distinct types of easements. Positive easements grant an affirmative right to use property in a specified manner, or to interfere with the title holder's otherwise enforceable property rights. A right of access across a property is a common example of a positive easement. In contrast, negative easements affix restrictions upon the landowner's property rights. Negative easements do not grant affirmative rights; the "purchaser" of a negative easement simply affixes a restriction. Particular restrictions vary in accordance with the objective: in open-space preservation planning, negative easements may prohibit uses that are incompatible with existing agricultural uses, prevent new construction that obstructs views, prohibit development that encroaches upon wetlands or wildlife habitat, or effect other such protective goals. Private landowners frequently donate such easements to nonprofit land trusts for preservation purposes. Such donations qualify grantors for federal income-tax deductions. Section II.A.4 of this chapter presents a further discussion of this practice of easement donation.

Applying the easement principle that recognizes the separability of distinct rights in land, local governments can initiate purchase-of-development-rights programs, which are essentially government easement purchases whereby local governments pay landowners to forfeit certain land development rights. Local government purchasers can identify the specific type and intensity of development rights to be purchased, as well as the rights to be retained by the landowner. While such programs may raise valuation issues, the concept provides an inexpensive alternative to fee simple acquisition for preserving low-intensity uses of land.

King County, Washington, located in the Seattle metropolitan area, provides a good example of a successful purchase-of-development-rights program. Designed to preserve agricultural land in the face of metropolitan growth pressures, this program drew upon a $50 million bond issue to provide for the county's purchase of development rights for properties facing development pressures, with purchase priorities determined in accordance with the intensity of such pressures. Participation in the program was voluntary for eligible landowners. Purchase prices were calculated as the difference between appraised highest and best uses and appraised values under farmland uses; upon purchasing development rights, the county recorded restrictive covenants on the property deeds, limiting development rights to 5 percent of the property's nontillable area.

Purchase-of-development-rights programs are best administered when development pressures are not so strong that they inflate the values of development rights, and when the agricultural or other residual uses of the land remain profitable: essentially, government should "buy low" to maximize its cost savings. Purchase-of-development-rights programs effect significant cost savings (relative to a fee simple purchase program) by reducing acquisition costs and by enabling property to remain on local tax rolls. In addition, the purchase of development rights does not incur government obligations for management and maintenance, and the property remains in productive use. Such programs, however, raise issues involving the effect of zoning on valuation. For instance, when a property is zoned for agricultural use, why should the value of the property's "development rights" exceed its agricultural use value? On the other hand, when a property is zoned for a higher intensity of use, should a government spend money to purchase development rights when it could simply downzone the property to a less intensive use classification? Issues like these raise legal questions that should be fully explored before establishing a purchase-of-development-rights program.

3. PURCHASE AND SELLBACK OR LEASEBACK ARRANGEMENTS

Government entities may use the purchase and subsequent resale or leasing of property to direct land development patterns and preserve open space. A government may acquire property in fee simple and retain certain development rights—essentially affixing a restrictive easement to the property—and then reconvey the property but not the retained rights. Alternatively, government may purchase property and then lease it, subject to conditions and restrictions as provided in the lease. These arrangements, known as "purchase and sellback" and "purchase and leaseback" arrangements, enable the government to recover at least a portion of its acquisition costs while exercising direct control over the type of development activity that occurs on the purchased property.

The California Coastal Conservancy, charged by the state with the task of assisting in the protection of undeveloped coastal lands, administers a successful program that provides grants to land trust organizations for the purchase and resale—subject to conservation restrictions—of agricultural and other open lands. The experience of the state-funded program is that agricultural lands purchased at full market value can be resold with conservation restrictions that allow for agricultural and other open-space uses at nearly the original purchase price. The program thus minimizes costs while keeping land in productive use.

The California State Parks Department also administers a successful purchase and leaseback program for agricultural lands in various areas of the state. In Santa Cruz County, the state purchased the 2,300-acre Wilder Ranch, of which 635 acres are leased to eleven farmers for agricultural purposes; these areas produce 15 percent of the nation's brussels sprouts. The state maintains the remainder of the ranch for a variety of recreational and open-space uses. The state parks department believes that the success of this and other similar projects has helped dispel a prevailing belief that agricultural and recreational uses are incompatible with one another.

4. USE OF LAND TRUSTS IN OBTAINING OPEN-LAND PARCELS

Private land trusts are private, nonprofit organizations that pursue various land stewardship functions. When public planning objectives coincide with private land-trust objectives—typical objectives include agricultural protection, habitat conservation, and recreational land protection—local planning jurisdictions can coordinate their efforts with these organizations. Although land trusts are private entities and play no regulatory role, they command a broad array of preservation strategies and provide valuable partners to public entities endeavoring to protect valued land resources. For example, when government budgets are insufficient to acquire critical tracts within given time frames, land trusts may be able to purchase and hold such properties for future government acquisition. In addition, land trusts can provide significant cost savings. As tax-exempt charitable organizations, land trusts may acquire lands through charitable donations or bargain sales, which may prove financially beneficial to grantor landowners, who will derive tax benefits from such transactions. When the land trust resells such low-cost acquisitions to the government, the trust may be able to recoup its own costs while still helping the government realize considerable savings.

Another land preservation technique that land trusts can use involves the limited development of land. Limited development is effective when the trust can identify portions of a parcel that are critical to preservation efforts, and isolate other portions of the tract upon which suitable development would not conflict with identified preservation objectives. The trust can then identify the most appropriate forms of development and then sell or lease the developable areas for such uses, subject to various restrictions.

In Colorado, a private trust used this approach to preserve a 3,200-acre property known as the Evans Ranch. This ranch contains forested areas providing habitat for a variety of species, including mountain lion, elk, black bear, and mountain goat. Initially zoned for residential use in 2-acre-minimum lots, Colorado Open Lands divided the property into five topographically separate ranch areas and identified appropriate areas for limited development. The next step was to affix covenants limiting development rights to one dwelling unit within 40-acre envelopes, as well as positive easements providing common recreational use rights to the owners of all five ranches. Colorado Open Lands then sold the five ranch parcels, recapturing most of its initial investment.

In another Colorado example, the Nature Conservancy collaborated with the Phantom Canyon Ranch Company to preserve, just north of Fort Collins, a 16,000-acre scenic area featuring a wild river canyon, a reservoir, and surrounding wilderness areas. The Nature Conservancy established a 2,700-acre preserve by purchasing more than 1,100 acres and acquiring conservation easements restricting the use of an additional area. On the remaining 13,300 acres, the Phantom Canyon Ranch Company made use of restrictive covenants and restrictions to create four working-ranch parcels of 800 to 1,200 acres, and a limited number of smaller home sites carefully situated to preserve physical characteristics such as ridge lines, hills, woodlands, wildlife habitat, and other elements, as well as the privacy and views of the property owners.

B. Police Power Techniques

1. LARGE-LOT ZONING

Zoning ordinances commonly require minimum lot sizes. In suburban single-family residential areas, minimum lot sizes typically range from one-quarter acre to two acres. In preserving agricultural areas, forests, wetlands, floodplains, and other valued open spaces, minimum lot sizes may require forty or more acres per dwelling unit. Some communities in midwestern states such as Illinois, Michigan, and Wisconsin have required minimum lot sizes of 160 acres and more. Large-lot zoning provisions may also feature sliding scales by which the number of units allowed varies with the size of the farm parcel. Such systems generally permit more units at lower densities on larger parcels (for example, more than thirty acres) while permissible densities increase for smaller tracts, with the objective of retaining sufficient open lands to ensure the continued viability of farming.

2. CLUSTERING

Cluster zoning allows developers to construct buildings in high-density clusters on small portions of a site while preserving large open areas on other portions of the site. Under cluster zoning ordinances, maximum densities are calculated not for individual lots, but for overall development sites. Rather than requiring minimum lot sizes to foster uniform spacings between buildings, cluster zoning allows tight clusters of buildings in some areas, with other portions of the parcel set aside for open space or recreational uses. Clustering thus provides larger areas for open space and other amenities while minimizing the land area required for roads and other infrastructure.

3. TRANSFER OF DEVELOPMENT RIGHTS

Transfer-of-development-rights (TDR) programs encourage the maintenance of low-density land uses by establishing an off-site market for the sale of unused development rights. The concept allows for the transfer of development rights from one area to another; a landowner in a "sending area" sells development rights to another landowner in a "receiving area," who thus augments his or her development rights in excess of otherwise permissible limits. In this manner, local governments can maintain low-density land uses without depriving property owners of the value of their development rights. Typically, a successful TDR program involves three essential elements: (1) a "sending area" where low-density land uses are to be preserved; (2) a two-tiered density standard for the sending area, which imposes a base maximum allowable development intensity while allowing landowners to retain transferable rights to a higher development intensity standard; and (3) a "receiving area" in which landowners may augment their development rights with additional rights purchased from owners of land in the sending area.

While the TDR concept has been applied in a number of jurisdictions, the Montgomery County, Maryland, and New Jersey Pinelands Reserve programs provide the essential prototypes for the concept. Located in suburban Washington, D.C., Montgomery County has used a TDR program to protect agricultural lands against strong urban growth pressures. The Montgomery County program incorporates the three basic TDR elements: (1) the identification of a "sending area" comprising the county's best agricultural lands; (2) downzoning in the sending area from 5-acre-minimum lots to 25-acre-minimum lots, with landowners retaining transferable development rights equal to their original 5-acre lot development rights; and (3) the identification of a "receiving area," in which landowners may augment their development rights with additional rights purchased from owners of land in the sending area. As of September, 1994, Montgomery County's TDR program has overseen the exchange of roughly 5,800 TDRs, resulting in the preservation of 29,000 acres of agricultural and open-space land.

The Pinelands National Reserve in New Jersey has administered one of the nation's most successful TDR programs for natural area protection. Established by federal legislation, the Pinelands National Reserve encompasses one million acres of land in sixty local government jurisdictions containing forests, wetlands, and agricultural areas devoted to cranberry and blueberry production. In response to suburban growth pressures, the federal government created the Pinelands Reserve and authorized the creation of the Pinelands Planning Commission, a regional government entity assigned to prepare a comprehensive management plan for the Pinelands, as well as regulations to protect large tracts of open space. The commission's Pinelands Plan embraced the TDR concept with its Pinelands Development Credit (PDC) program.

The PDC program allocates transferable development credits (TDCs) to sending areas in allotments that vary with the nature of the land. For example, because wetlands possess minimal development potential, owners of wetland tracts are awarded the minimum allocation of one-quarter credit (one residential dwelling unit) per forty-nine acres. On the other hand, owners of agricultural lands possessing greater development value are awarded the maximum allocation of one credit (four dwelling units) per forty-nine acres. Receiving areas, designated by each local government, permit developers to increase their development densities by four residential units for each PDC purchased.

Overall, the PDC program created 5,625 TDCs (development rights for 22,500 dwelling units) potentially available for transfer from sending areas, and allowable density bonuses of up to 46,000 units in receiving areas. To date, the program has successfully facilitated transactions involving more than 1,000 development rights, accounting for the preservation of 10,000 acres of wetlands, agricultural lands, and other sensitive areas vital to the character of the Pinelands Reserve.

4. URBAN GROWTH BOUNDARIES

Growth management policies can direct new development and limit municipal annexations to designated growth areas. Such policies typically define limits for extensions of urban services, thereby discouraging uncontrolled sprawl in open, rural areas. In the Portland, Oregon, metropolitan area, for example, a regional government entity has delineated an urban growth boundary, administered by local governments in compliance with state legislative mandates. This program has proven generally successful in confining growth to the areas within the boundary. Within the boundary, development has often bypassed previously "urbanized" areas and moved to outlying "urbanizable" areas (areas within the boundary defined as available and suitable for urban development upon the extension of urban services), but the program has generally succeeded in keeping development within the growth boundary, by containing leapfrog development, preserving outlying areas for agricultural and other less intensive uses, and maintaining order in the pattern of metropolitan growth.

5. EXACTIONS AND LAND DEDICATIONS

When new development creates needs for increased public services or infrastructure (schools, roads, recreational facilities, and so on), many local governments impose dedication requirements, fees in lieu thereof, impact fees, and other exactions as conditions for permit approvals. These types of conditions are used to ensure that new developments pay their own way by bearing the costs of their public service and infrastructure needs. Thus, when new development threatens to strain a community's available recreational facilities, developers might be required to dedicate a specified number of parkland acres for every hundred residents of a residential project. In the alternative, developers might pay a fee into a dedicated open-space fund that would be used to purchase recreational open-space land in the general vicinity of the project.

The law of exactions, though not entirely consistent across jurisdictional lines,[1] essentially requires that when public agencies require property, money, or other concessions as conditions for development approvals, such exactions bear reasonable relationships to the legitimate public purposes that would have justified denials of the proposed developments. The Supreme Court's decision in *Dolan v. City of Tigard*,[2] focuses on the constitutional validity of a development approval conditioned on a dedication of open land for public use. The discussion below examines the case and presents some conclusions regarding the decision's impact on land dedications, exactions, and the practice of open-space planning in general.

III. Dolan: *New Requirements*

A. The Case

In reviewing Ms. Florence Dolan's application for a building permit, the City of Tigard administered the standards set forth in section 18 of its legislative code[3] (CDC) requiring that the city condition its approval on Dolan's agreement to: (1) dedicate open land located in the 100-year floodplain and (2) dedicate land, including lands included in the floodplain dedication requirement, for development and use as a public recreational bicycle trail. Then, in the review of Dolan's application for a variance from these provisions, the CDC requires that the planning commission grant requested variances when the applicant shows that:

> owing to special circumstances related to a specific piece of the land, the literal interpretation of the applicable zoning provisions would cause "an undue or unnecessary hardship" unless the variance is granted.[4]

In finding the city's application of such standards unconstitutional, the Court makes two key points, as contained in the following passage:

> Rough proportionality best encapsulates what we hold to be the requirement of the Fifth Amendment. No precise mathematical calculation is required, but the city must make some sort of

> individualized determination that the required dedication is related both in nature and extent to the impact of the proposed development.[5]

The Court's first point requires a showing that the dedication relates in extent as well as in character to the public purpose served; the extent of the dedication must bear a roughly proportional relationship to the achievement of its objectives. The Court's second point requires an individualized determination of the requisite relationship. These two points chart a new course in planning law, and have important implications for the evolving practice of open-space protection planning, as discussed below.

B. Rough Proportionality

The roughly proportional requirement is actually more of a clarification than a significant change in the law of exactions. At the outset of its opinion, the Court states that its objective in granting certiorari was "to resolve a question left open by our decision in *Nollan* . . . of what is the required degree of connection between the exaction imposed by the city and the projected impacts of the proposed development."[6] Without issuing a definitive ruling on the issue, the *Nollan* decision used terms such as "essential nexus" and "substantial relationship" to describe the applicable standard in considering the validity of exactions and dedications; the Court's interchangeable use of such terms prompted assertions from property owners that *Nollan* established a more rigorous standard regarding the requisite connection between the impacts of proposed developments and dedications required as conditions to development approvals. *Dolan* refutes this assertion. In identifying "rough proportionality" as the proper test, the Court essentially adopts the majority view among the states:

> We think the "reasonable relationship" test adopted by a majority of the state courts is closer to the federal constitutional norm than either of those [tests] previously discussed. But we do not adopt it as such, partly because the term "reasonable relationship"' seems confusingly similar to the term "rational basis" which describes the minimal level of scrutiny under the Equal Protection Clause of the Fourteenth Amendment. We think a term such as "rough proportionality" best encapsulates what we hold to be the requirement of the Fifth Amendment.[7]

Thus, the "rough proportionality" language simply makes a semantic adjustment to a test that had already been applied in the majority of jurisdictions. The significance of this point lies in the Court's affirmance of the majority view of exactions and dedications, thus clarifying the semantic confusion surrounding the applicable standard left in the wake of the *Nollan* decision.

C. Individualized Determinations

The Court's second point signals a more significant departure from the established law of dedications. The individualized determination requirement is new, and essentially reverses the traditional approach in cases in which land-use exactions raise questions of constitutional law.

The traditional approach is as stated in *Nollan v. California Coastal Commission:*

> [a] permit condition that serves the same legitimate police-power purpose as refusal to issue the permit should not be found to be a taking if the refusal to issue the permit would not constitute a taking. . . . [T]he Commission's assumed power to forbid construction of the house in order to protect the public's view of the beach must surely include the power to condition construction upon some concession by the owner, even a concession of property rights, that serves the same end. If a prohibition designed to accomplish that purpose would be a legitimate exercise of the police power rather than a taking, it would be strange to conclude that providing the owner an alternative to that prohibition which accomplishes the same purpose is not.[8]

This approach presumes the constitutional validity of land-use regulations enacted pursuant to the government's police power; the burden falls upon the party challenging an exaction ordinance to show the total absence of the required rational nexus, or rough proportionality. This approach applies to land-dedication requirements as well as other types of police power regulations. For example, in the case of *College Station v. Turtle Rock Corp.*, the Texas Supreme Court, considering the validity of a parkland dedication requirement, stated that "the court must consider whether there is a reasonable connection between the increased population arising from the subdivision development and the increased park and recreation needs in this neighborhood. The burden rests on [the applicant] to demonstrate that there is no such reasonable connection."[9]

Dolan appears to reverse this approach. *Dolan* begins with the premise that a required dedication of property interests constitutes a taking of private property requiring just compensation; in the absence of compensation, such requirements are invalid unless the governmental entity can show an appropriate justification. Rather than scrutinizing Ms. Dolan's attempt to demonstrate that the city's dedication requirements bear insufficient relationships to their stated objectives, the Court instead evaluates the *city's* attempts to show that such relationships do exist.

This approach essentially presumes that dedication requirements invoke the government's power of eminent domain rather than its police power authority to regulate the use of land. While the *Nollan* Court ultimately treated the dedication requirement at issue as an exercise of eminent domain rather than police power authority, the Court chose this analytical framework only after finding that no relationship *whatsoever* existed between the dedication and the government's stated purpose, thus rebutting the presumption of validity that would have been available to a land-use regulation enacted pursuant to police power authority. After so finding, the Court expressly recognized its departure from normal principles of land-use jurisprudence, "We therefore find that the Commission's imposition of the permit condition cannot be treated as an exercise of its land-use power for any of these purposes."[10]

The situation in *Dolan,* however, differs from that of *Nollan.* In *Dolan,* the Court did not find, as a prerequisite to its departure from police-power jurisprudence, that the dedication requirement was entirely unrelated to the city's stated public purpose; the Court essentially eliminated the presumption of constitutionality ordinarily given land-dedication requirements. As a result, under *Dolan,* the burden of proof falls upon the governmental entity to make individualized determinations that every administration of a land-dedication requirement (the Court attempts to limit the scope of this requirement to "adjudicative" rather than "generally applicable" land-dedication requirements, as discussed in section IV of this chapter) effects a roughly proportional advancement of the public purpose that would have justified a permit denial. In this analysis, qualitative findings and quantitative formulae for calculating valid dedication requirements are no longer sufficient to support land-use exactions, for such findings and formulae do not address the specific impacts of individual developments.

In defending its dedication requirement, the City of Tigard relied on specific findings that Dolan's proposed expansion would increase traffic flow by 435 trips per day, and a general finding, set forth in the city's comprehensive plan, that bicycle and pedestrian pathway systems reduce the number of automobile trips.[11] Despite the majority's assurances that "no precise mathematical calculation is required,"[12] the

Court nonetheless found that Tigard had not carried its burden of making an individualized determination of rough proportionality. Although the city had in fact found that bicycle and pedestrian circulation systems would reduce traffic, in its brief the city stated only that its exaction "could" result in decreased traffic.[13] With the burden no longer resting upon the applicant to show that such improvements could *not* reduce traffic, the city's exaction fails to make the requisite individualized determination of rough proportionality.

IV. Scope of Dolan's *Individualized Determination Requirement*

Dolan's effect on open-space planning will depend on the scope of application of its individualized determination requirement. The Court attempts to define its intended scope when it distinguishes *Dolan* from traditional zoning cases such as *Euclid v. Ambler Realty Co.*,[14] *Pennsylvania Coal Co. v. Mahon*,[15] and *Agins v. Tiburon*[16] on the grounds that

> [t]he sort of regulations discussed in the cases just cited, however, differ in two relevant particulars from the present case. First, they involved essentially legislative determinations classifying entire areas of the city, whereas here the city made an adjudicative decision to condition petitioner's application for a building permit on an individual parcel. Second, the conditions imposed were not simply a limitation on the use petitioner might make of her own parcel, but a requirement that she deed portions of the property to the city.[17]

Although the second of these distinctions provides meaningful guidance, the first is based on vague delineations and may foster uncertainty for those attempting to understand the scope of the individualized determination requirement. These distinctions, and the applicable scope of the individualized determination requirement, are discussed below.

A. The Right to Exclude Others

With its second distinction, the Court singles out those actions in which the government entity requires a dedication—an actual right of physical occupation or invasion—of property. Absent a dedication requirement, the Court indicates that a mere restriction on building construction in certain portions of the Dolan parcel would have been upheld:

> The city . . . not only wanted petitioner not to build in the floodplain, but it also wanted petitioner's property along Fanno Creek

> for its greenway system. The city has never said why a public greenway, as opposed to a private one, was required in the interest of flood control. The difference to petitioner, of course, is the loss of her ability to exclude others. As we have noted, this right to exclude others is "one of the most essential sticks in the bundle of rights that are commonly characterized as property."[18]

This language signals that the public access requirement—as opposed to the set-aside required for a private greenway—triggered the Court's analysis. Thus, land-use regulations that restrict development rights but do not interfere with the landowner's right to exclude others remain unaffected by this case. Such regulations will continue to receive the traditional presumption of validity given to police power regulations; *Dolan*'s effect is limited to the law of dedication[19] requirements.

B. Adjudicative Decisions

The other factor the Court uses to define the scope of the individualized determination requirement involves the "adjudicative" nature of the city's action:

> In evaluating most generally applicable zoning regulations, the burden properly rests on the party challenging the regulation to prove that it constitutes an arbitrary regulation of property rights. . . . Here, by contrast, the city made an adjudicative decision to condition petitioner's application for a building permit on an individual parcel. In this situation, the burden properly rests on the city.[20]

Thus, according to the Court, when the zoning body administers a "generally applicable" regulation, the developer must prove the unconstitutionality of the challenged regulation. When, however, the zoning body renders an "adjudicative" decision regarding permissible development approvals, the burden shifts; the public agency must prove, for each contested approval decision, that the imposed exaction bears an essential nexus, and is roughly proportional, to the needs generated by the proposed development.

This attempt to distinguish between "adjudicative" and "generally applicable" regulations creates significant uncertainty. The distinction is entirely undefined. Few land-use regulations—and even fewer land-dedication requirements—are "generally applicable" to *all* lands within a jurisdiction. Land-use regulations vary in accordance with specific zoning classifications; for example, two-acre minimum lot sizes that apply in certain residential districts will probably not apply in high-density commercial districts. Similarly, regulations that apply to all lands adjacent to floodplains, airports, steep slopes, coast lines, or other such features only apply when stated conditions are present. Such regulations are not universally applicable throughout jurisdictions: are they nonetheless "generally applicable?" As a further illustration of the ambiguity of the distinction, street-dedication conditions for subdivision approvals would seem to be generally applicable[21] in an intuitive sense; yet, the Court provides no basis for distinguishing between these exactions and the Tigard exaction.[22]

The Court's distinction might gain clarity had the city devised a unique requirement for application only to Dolan's parcel, but the city simply administered a legislative mandate applying to all development within and adjacent to the 100-year floodplain. As Justice Souter notes in dissent, "this case raises no question about discriminatory, or 'reverse spot' zoning, which 'singles out a particular parcel for different, less favorable treatment than the neighboring ones.' "[23]

The most readily discernible distinction between adjudicative actions and the administration of generally applicable regulations lies in the difference between an application for development approvals—to be reviewed under generally applicable land-use codes—and an application for a variance or other form of special relief. In *Dolan,* the fact that the dispute involved a variance application provides the only factor characterizing the city's action as "adjudicative" rather than merely administrative. Justice Souter makes this point, "The majority characterizes this case as involving an 'adjudicative decision' to impose permit conditions . . . but the permit conditions were imposed pursuant to Tigard's Community Development Code. . . . The adjudication here was of Dolan's requested variance from the permit conditions otherwise required to be imposed by the Code."[24]

Despite the clarity of Justice Souter's distinction, this was not what the majority intended. Two factors support this interpretation. First, if all "adjudicative" actions involving applications for special relief fall within the individualized determination requirement, then *Dolan* would overturn solidly entrenched principles of land-use law. In reviewing applications for variances, special exceptions, conditional use permits, and the like, the courts in virtually all jurisdictions have long presumed the constitutional validity of the applicable land-development regulations. In such proceedings, applicants generally assume the burden of showing that unique hardships or special conditions justify permit approvals, despite a project's nonconformance with enumerated conditions for approvals "as of right." Then, in judicial review of variance decisions, the burden again falls upon the applicants to rebut a presumption of validity given the ordinances.[25] When the burden shifts to the "adjudicating" governing agency to show why a variance should *not* be granted, a highly ironic result ensues. In the forum designed to enable the *applicant* to show that his or her application justifies special treatment, the government agency would bear the burden of showing why the individual parcel *should* be subject to the applicable regulations set forth in the legislative code. It is unlikely that the Court intended this essential shifting of burdens.

The second and more persuasive indication that the Court did not intend the distinction suggested by Justice Souter lies in the Court's statement that "the city made an adjudicative decision to condition petitioner's application for a *building permit* on an individual parcel."[26] This indicates that the Court focused not on the difference between "adjudicative" variance proceedings and the general application of land-use regulations, but rather on the distinction between requirements that are in some sense "jurisdiction-wide" and those that are administered to a more specifically defined range of properties. As discussed above, this distinction creates an area of uncertainty, to be resolved through the gradual evolution of the law of land dedications.

C. Dedications for Open Space: What Remains?

As described above, *Dolan* appears to presume the invalidity of land-dedication requirements when property owners challenge such requirements in an "adjudicative" forum. Despite this apparent alteration of land-use jurisprudence, however, government entities need not abandon land-dedication requirements as a means for open-space preservation. The *Dolan* Court struck down the city's *application* of its dedication conditions; it did not invalidate the ordinance provisions themselves. Thus, local governments assume new risks and burdens only in their manner of applying such requirements. *Dolan*'s individualized determination rule arises when a landowner triggers the requirement by challenging the administration of dedication requirements. Before such challenges, the government agency remains free to impose dedication requirements. It is only when local governments must act upon applications for relief from dedication requirements that they must determine on individualized bases the roughly proportional relationships between such dedications and the alleviation of a need for open space or other public amenities caused by the proposed development. When the government finds such determinations costly, difficult, or even tenuous, it may opt to grant the requested relief, thus avoiding the new requirements set forth in *Dolan*.

V. Implications for Open-Space Planning Practice

Dolan's impacts on the law of dedications may shift local government approaches to open-space protection. While these shifts will vary in accordance with the nature of the political and economic contexts of each particular jurisdiction, the following sections describe the various shifts that may flow from the *Dolan* decision.

A. Legal Effects

As an initial matter, it is clear that *Dolan* will exert few impacts on the law and application of most open-space preservation techniques. *Dolan* will have no effect on acquisition approaches (described in section II.A of this chapter), whether such approaches involve fee simple interests, easements, or development rights; purchase by definition involves compensation, and thus raises none of the Fifth Amendment rights at issue in *Dolan*.

Likewise, Dolan will have a very limited impact on most of the police power techniques described in section II.B. Measures involving large-lot zoning, clustering requirements, TDR programs, and urban growth management boundaries all restrict land development rights without any accompanying physical invasions or encroachments upon the right to exclude others, which the Court clearly identifies as the essential factor in triggering its framework for protecting property rights against uncompensated takings of property. In short, among the police power regulations listed in section II.B, *Dolan* changes the law only as it relates to exactions and land dedications.

B. Practical Effects

Since *Dolan*'s individualized showing requirement will apply only to land-dedication requirements, its effect on acquisition and other police power practices will be limited to an increased use of such, as a result of changes in the law of dedications. The following forecasts the likely practical reactions to *Dolan*.

1. GOVERNMENT'S SIMPLEST RESPONSE TO *DOLAN* IS TO ABANDON LAND-DEDICATION REQUIREMENTS AND REQUIRE DEVELOPERS TO SET ASIDE PRIVATE OPEN SPACES

By simply requiring set-asides—in effect, requiring private rather than public greenways, as implicitly sanctioned by the *Dolan* majority—the government avoids interference with the right to exclude others, steers clear of the individualized showing requirement, and regains the presumption of validity accorded police power regulations, subject only to the traditional rational nexus test. Local governments can invoke a broad range of public uses to justify set-aside regulations. These include environmental protection, tree protection, agricultural industry protection, aesthetic objectives, and, as long as set-aside lands remain in private control, wetland and floodplain protection.

2. WHEN GOVERNMENTS POSSESS ADEQUATE FUNDS, THEY MAY CHOOSE TO AVOID *DOLAN* ISSUES BY SIMPLY RELYING ON ACQUISITION STRATEGIES TO ACHIEVE OPEN-SPACE PRESERVATION

As ex-urban migrants continue to place increasing value on the retention of rural open spaces and character, they may provide unequivocal mandates—and new funding sources—for open-land acquisition. Many communities throughout the United States have approved sales and excise taxes, open-space acquisition bond issues, lottery funding programs, and other such funding sources for open-space acquisition; such measures promise to play an increasing role in public open-space preservation efforts.

3. SOME GOVERNMENT ENTITIES WILL ALLOCATE THE ADDITIONAL RESOURCES NECESSARY TO SATISFY THE INDIVIDUALIZED FINDINGS OF ROUGH PROPORTIONALITY MANDATED BY *DOLAN*

Although *Dolan* does not subject dedication requirements themselves to greater facial scrutiny, when landowners challenge the application of such requirements, governments will have to justify their dedication requirements by showing that such are related in character, and roughly proportional in extent, to a legitimate public purpose.

In most cases this requirement should not be too difficult to satisfy. The *Dolan* decision indicates that the city of Tigard might have satisfied its obligations if it had simply used the word "would" instead of "could" in stating that the relationship between the required bikepath dedication and the reduction of traffic volume, "The finding of fact that the bicycle pathway system 'could offset some of the traffic demand' is a far cry from a finding that the bicycle pathway system will, or is likely to, offset some of the traffic demand."[27] When open-space dedications are at issue, readily available national standards and studies identify typical open-space burdens created by new development; through simple application of these standards, in most cases governments should be able to demonstrate the requisite proportional relationships at minimal cost.

Governments may encounter more difficulty, however, in demonstrating the requisite relationships when developments involve nonresidential or very low-density residential uses. Regarding commercial and industrial property, local governments will have to demonstrate either that additional traffic congestion justifies the dedication of land for trails or pathways, or that employees will generate new demands for recreational or other types of open space. Also, when developers propose to build at extremely low densities (for example, development on forty-acre lots, as are required in agricultural districts), governments may be hard-pressed to show that such development generates the need for significant open-space dedications.

4. WHEN THE GOVERNMENT DOES NOT WISH TO ASSUME NEW COSTS, OR TO RISK LOSING LEGAL CHALLENGES, THE GOVERNMENT MAY SIMPLY EXERCISE ITS POLICE-POWER AUTHORITY TO DENY DEVELOPMENT REQUESTS

When public open spaces or other services fail to satisfy public needs, dedication requirements imposed as conditions to approvals essentially give the developer an option under which an otherwise properly deniable project may receive an approval in exchange for a land dedication. When the government perceives that this option simply invites litigation and further shortfalls in its public open spaces, however, the government may find it easier to simply say no to development without offering the dedication option. In effect, the local government simply relies more heavily on its police-power tools; when proposed developments generate new needs for open space or other public resources, the government administers development regulations requiring permit denials. This approach produces an ironic result for developers: when local governments face shortages of open spaces or other resources, the stricter judicial scrutiny given dedication requirements as a result of *Dolan* may eliminate potential avenues for obtaining development approvals.

5. GOVERNMENTS CAN APPLY ALL THE ABOVE APPROACHES IN COMBINATION WITH INCREASED GOVERNMENT RELIANCE ON PRIVATE LAND TRUSTS

When governments wish to acquire land or positive access easements, or when they wish to restrict development rights, they can enlist private land trusts to serve as third-party recipients of easement donations—providing tax benefits for landowner/donors—or as cost-saving conduits for eventual government purchases in the manner described in section II.A of this chapter.

V. Conclusion

The Court's articulation of its "rough proportionality" test clarifies one point of land-use law. At the same time, however, the Court's "individualized determination" requirement appears to depart from customary principles of land-dedication rules, and the scope of this requirement creates significant new areas of uncertainty. Faced with this uncertainty, local government entities seeking to preserve dwindling open spaces will have to exercise increased prudence in attempting to require land dedications as conditions for development approvals. In many cases, government entities may simply apply alternative means to achieve their objectives. Such alternatives encompass a broad array of tools, involving public acquisition approaches as well as police power regulations restricting or denying development permits. In many cases, however, governments will retain their land-dedication requirements; eventually, land developers will challenge such provisions. When this occurs—at least when "adjudicative" governmental actions are in dispute—the government may have to show that the application of each challenged land-dedication requirement bears a rough proportion to the advancement of a legitimate police power purpose. The scope of these "adjudicative" actions is somewhat ambiguous at this time; the ultimate scope and effect of *Dolan*'s individualized determination requirement will emerge only with the gradual evolution of a new body of case law applying *Dolan*'s principles.

Notes

1. The law of impact fees, in particular, varies from state to state. The use of impact fees to accomplish a broad range of purposes is well established in states such as California, Texas, and Florida; in many states, however, authorization to impose local impact fees remains open to question. Further, the tests for impact fee legality varies: as the *Dolan* Court notes, while the majority of states agree on applicable legal standards, states such as Illinois and California vary slightly.
2. 114 S. Ct. 2309 (1994).
3. The city's Community Development Code provides:

> The development shall facilitate pedestrian/bicycle circulation if the site is located on a street with designated bike paths or adjacent to a designated greenway/open space/park. Specific items to be addressed: (i) Provision of efficient, convenient and continuous pedestrian and bicycle transit, circulation systems, linking development by requiring dedication and construction of pedestrian and bike paths identified in the comprehensive plan.

TIGARD, O., COMMUN. DEV. CODE [hereinafter CDC] § 18.86.040.A.1.b (1990), *quoted in Dolan,* 114 S. Ct. at 2313. The following provision sets forth a more specific directive:

> Where landfill and/or development is allowed within and adjacent to the 100-year floodplain, the city shall require the dedication of sufficient open land area for greenway adjoining and within the floodplain. This area shall include portions at a suitable elevation for the construction of a pedestrian/bicycle pathway within the floodplain in accordance with the adopted pedestrian/bicycle plan.

CDC § 18.120.180.A.8, *quoted in Dolan,* 114 S. Ct. at 2314.

4. *Dolan,* 114 S. Ct. at 2313. (quoting CDC § 18.134).

5. *Id.* at 2319-20.

6. *Id.* at 2312.

7. *Id.* at 2318. The Court cites a number of state court holdings requiring that public entities show "reasonable relationships" between exactions and the impacts of proposed developments, including: Simpson v. North Platte, 292 N.W.2d 297 (Neb. 1980); Jordan v. Menomonee Falls, 137 N.W.2d 442 (Wis. 1965); Collis v. Bloomington, 246 N.W.2d 19 (Minn. 1976); College Station v. Turtle Rock Corp., 680 S.W.2d 802 (Tex. 1984); Call v. West Jordan, 606 P.2d 217 (Utah 1979).

8. 483 U.S. 825, 836 (1987).

9. *College Station,* 680 S.W.2d at 806-07. *See also,* Goldblatt v. Town of Hempstead, 369 U.S. 590, 596 (1962), United States v. Carolene Products Co., 304 U.S. 144, 154 (1938).

10. *Nollan,* 483 U.S. at 839. *Nollan* also recognized that required easement dedications effect unconstitutional takings requiring just compensation when not imposed as conditions for development approvals. 483 U.S. at 836. In *Nollan,* however, the Court based its holding on its finding of no relationship whatsoever between the exaction and the purpose that would have justified a permit denial:

> It is quite impossible to understand how a requirement that people already on the public beaches be able to walk across the Nollans' property reduces any obstacles to viewing the beach created by the new house.

483 U.S. at 838-39.

11. *See Dolan,* 114 S. Ct. at 2331 (Souter, J., dissenting) (citing City of Tigard Comprehensive Plan as cited in Brief for Respondent A-5).

12. *Id.* at 2319-20.

13. *Id.* at 2315. The Court also stated that the city had failed to identify the requisite connection between the required dedication and the city's interest in flood control:

> The city has never said why a public greenway, as opposed to a private one, was required in the interest of flood control. . . . We conclude that the findings upon which the city relies do not show the required reasonable

relationship between the floodplain easement and the petitioner's proposed new building.

Id. at 2320. As Justice Souter notes in his dissent, however, the city's purpose in requiring public access was directed to the bicycle and pedestrian pathway objective, and not to the floodplain protection objective: "[T]he city of Tigard never sought to justify the public access portion of the dedication as related to flood control. . . . [T]he Court unsurprisingly finds a recreation area to be unrelated to flood control." *Id.* at 2330.

14. 272 U.S. 365 (1926).

15. 260 U.S. 393 (1922).

16. 447 U.S. 255 (1980).

17. *Dolan,* 114 S. Ct. at 2316.

18. *Id.* at 2320.

19. Exactions encompass a broader range of conditions than dedications, and include, in addition to dedications, impact fees and fees-in-lieu of dedications. For the purposes of this chapter's discussion, "dedication" and "exaction" are used interchangeably.

20. *Dolan,* 114 S. Ct. at 2319 n.8.

21. *C.f.* Board of Supervisors of West Marlborough Twp. v. Fiechter, 566 A.2d 370 (Pa. Commw. Ct. 1989) (holding that required street dedication would require just compensation, as "the record contains no indication that the two-lot subdivision, or its development, could produce an impact or burden on the public which could possibly provide a police power justification for demanding that the landowner make a special, uncompensated contribution to the adjacent local street").

22. In footnote 8, the Court acknowledges its shifting of burdens and defines the scope of its rule by distinguishing between adjudicative and legislative government actions. 114 S. Ct. at 2320 n.8. As Justice Souter notes, however, the city was in fact administering its legislative mandates. The city's legislative code provides:

> The development shall facilitate pedestrian/bicycle circulation if the site is located on a street with designated bike paths or adjacent to a designated greenway/open space/park. Specific items to be addressed [include]: (i) Provision of efficient, convenient and continuous pedestrian and bicycle transit-circulation systems, linking developments by requiring dedication and construction of pedestrian and bike paths identified in the comprehensive plan. If direct connections cannot be made, require that funds in the amount of the construction costs be deposited into an account for the purpose of constructing paths.

114 S. Ct. at 2313 n.1, (quoting CDC § 18.86.040A.1.b.). In addition,

> [w]here landfill and/or development is allowed within and adjacent to the 100-year floodplain, the city shall require the dedication of sufficient open land area for greenway adjoining and within the floodplain. This area shall include portions at a suitable elevation for the construction of a

pedestrian/bicycle pathway within the floodplain in accordance with the adopted pedestrian/bicycle plan.

114 S. Ct. at 2313 (quoting CDC § 18.120.180A.8).

Thus, two separate code provisions require the dedication of land for pedestrian and bicycle use and floodplain protection. These requirements apply to all sites lying adjacent to planned circulation systems identified in the city's comprehensive plan, and to all sites adjacent to 100-year floodplains. These requirements are hard and fast standards set forth in the city's legislated code. Despite this, the Court did not consider them "generally applicable."

23. *Dolan,* 114 S. Ct. at 2331 n.1 (Souter, J., dissenting).

24. *Id.* (Souter, J., dissenting).

25. *See, e.g.,* Kraemer & Sons, Inc. v. Sauk County Bd. of Adjustment, 515 N.W.2d 256 (Wis. 1994); Kingwood Twp. Volunteer Fire Co. v. Bd. of Adjustment of the Twp. of Kingwood, 640 A.2d 356 (N.J. Super. Ct. Law Div. 1993); Hewette v. Carbondale Zoning Bd. of Appeals, 634 N.E.2d 1223 (Ill. App. Ct. 1994); Trademark Homes v. Avon Lake Bd. of Zoning Appeals, 634 N.E.2d 685 (Ohio Ct. App. 1993).

26. *Dolan,* 114 S. Ct. at 2316 (emphasis added).

27. *Id.* at 2322 (quoting Dolan v. City of Tigard, 854 P.2d. 437, 447 (Or. 1993, Petersen, dissenting).

CHAPTER ❖ 14

Substantive Due Process and Land Use: The Alternative to a Takings Claim

Kenneth B. Bley

I. Introduction

Section 1 of the Fourteenth Amendment to the federal Constitution states that no state "shall deprive any person of life, liberty, or property, without due process of law." Laws regulating the use of land can run afoul of this prohibition. When they do, a remedy can be sought under 42 U.S.C. § 1983, one of the federal civil rights acts.[1]

The simple words of the due process clause do not lead to simple and straightforward results in land-use cases. Instead, they lead to a number of questions, including: What is property? What does "due process" mean? What is the application to land-use cases? What is the relationship between the due process clause and the takings clause? What are the conditions precedent to recovery when a violation of the due process clause is alleged? What are the remedies available? Where can they be sought? This chapter will attempt to answer these and other, similar questions.

II. The Meaning of "Property"

In the land-use context, the prohibition contained in the due process clause comes into play only when a state attempts to deprive a person of "property." If there is no property involved, then the protection provided by the due process clause is not invoked. Land is often thought of as the quintessential example of property—real property—but, as demonstrated below, not all courts have agreed that the landowner is entitled to the protection of the due process clause merely because of the ownership of land.

State law determines what constitutes property in the land-use context.[2] However, property is defined by its attributes and not by what a state chooses to label it.[3] The right to use and enjoy land is a property right.[4] Goodwill may constitute property.[5] A right to renew a land-use permit is a species of property.[6] A legal, nonconforming, vested right is also property.[7] Procedural rights create property rights when they impose significant, substantive restrictions on decision making.[8]

There is no property right in having land rezoned.[9] However, in *Village of Arlington Heights v. Metropolitan Housing Development Corp.*,[10] which involved a village council's refusal to rezone, and in *City of Eastlake v. Forest City Enterprises, Inc.*,[11] which involved a referendum on rezoning, the Supreme Court analyzed the denials of rezonings to see if they violated the landowner's right to due process.[12]

The Supreme Court has addressed the question of whether a claimant has a property right. For example, it stated in *Board of Regents v. Roth*[13] that "[t]o have a property right in a benefit, a person must have more than an abstract need or desire for it. He must have more than a unilateral expectation of it. He must, instead, have a legitimate claim of entitlement to it." In *Perry v. Sinderman*,[14] the Court addressed the same issue.

Roth and *Perry* arose when college professors claimed their civil rights had been violated when they were fired without a hearing. Some courts have interpreted *Roth* and *Perry* to mean that there can be no property right when the approving authority has discretion about whether to grant or deny approval, because the landowner has only a mere expectation.[15]

Generally no one—neither the landowner nor a neighbor—has a vested right to have existing zoning remain unchanged.[16] Thus, no claim for relief is stated against a city that wrongly refuses to enforce zoning regulations applicable to neighboring land,[17] that grants a variance resulting in noisy trucks using the lot next door,[18] or that changes the use of one block in an urban renewal project to the detriment of the owner of land in a neighboring block.[19] Moreover, a neighbor does not have a right to complain of a change in the zoning of a lot, even though the rezoning devalues the neighbor's lot,[20] nor does a state procedure calling for noticed hearings give a competitor a property right regarding someone else's land-use approval.[21]

III. The Relation between the Due Process Clause and the Takings Clause

In *Agins v. City of Tiburon*, the Supreme Court identified the situations in which land-use regulations can take property:

> The application of a general zoning law to a particular piece of property effects a taking if the ordinance does not substantially advance legitimate state interests, see *Nectow v. Cambridge,* 277 U.S. 183, 188 (1928), or denies an owner economically viable use of his land, see *Penn Central Transp. Co. v. New York City,* 104, 138, n. 36 (1978).[22]

The takings clause does not, by itself, apply to the states.[23] Instead, it is made applicable to the states through the Fourteenth Amendment.[24] Thus, there is an immediate relationship between the due process and the takings clauses.

This relationship is made clear upon consideration of *Nectow v. City of Cambridge,*[25] the cite given as authority for the first prong of the *Agins* test. *Nectow* involved a claim that the zoning applied to a specific piece of property was invalid. The Court stated that "[t]he attack upon the ordinance is that, as specifically applied to plaintiff in error, it deprived him of his property without due process of law in contravention of the Fourteenth Amendment. *Euclid v. Ambler Co.* . . ."[26]

Village of Euclid v. Ambler Realty Co.,[27] the case that upheld the validity of comprehensive zoning, was not based on the Fifth Amendment and did not assert that the imposition of zoning, with its severe (from Ambler Realty's point of view) restrictions on allowable uses, constituted a taking of Ambler Realty's property. Instead, the zoning was "assailed on the grounds that it is in derogation of section 1 of the Fourteenth Amendment of the federal Constitution in that it deprives appellee of liberty and property without due process of law. . . ."[28]

Thus, the authority for the first prong of the *Agins* takings test was no authority at all; it was a case based solely on the due process clause. In other words, governmental actions that do not substantially advance a legitimate state interest constitute a violation of the substantive due process clause. In fact, the early land-use cases, often cited to support or oppose the argument that a land-use regulation could result in a taking of property, were all based on the due process clause.[29]

The Supreme Court held in *First English Evangelical Lutheran Church v. County of Los Angeles*[30] that a land-use regulation could effect a taking that mandated the payment of just compensation. The Court cited *Pennsylvania Coal Co. v. Mahon*[31] in support of this proposition.[32] But *Pennsylvania Coal* was not a takings case; it held that Pennsylvania's Kohler Act, which required that coal mine owners leave certain coal in place, was invalid because it went too far and did not provide for compensation. It was, in other words, a substantive due process case, holding that certain governmental actions, designed to achieve a legitimate aim, asked too much of an individual property owner and thus could be upheld only if the power of eminent domain—rather than the police power—were employed.

Some courts have recognized that there is a relationship—indeed, an overlap—between claims brought under the takings clause and those brought under the due process clause, and have carefully differentiated between them, defining the claims as follows:

1. Just compensation takings claim: Plaintiff claims that the zoning applied to his or her land constitutes a taking of property without just compensation in contravention of the Fifth Amendment, the remedy sought being the just compensation.
2. Due process takings claim: Plaintiff claims that the zoning applied to his or her property goes too far and destroys the value of the property to such an extent that it amounts to a taking by eminent domain without due process of law. The remedy sought is invalidation of the zoning regulation.
3. Arbitrary and capricious due process claim: Plaintiff claims that the zoning regulation is arbitrary and capricious because it does not bear a substantial relation to the public health, safety, moral, or general welfare.[33]

The opinion in *Eide v. Sarasota County*[34] contains a more extensive discussion of the three categories and the case law supporting the distinctions, as does an article by Douglas Kmiec.[35]

A failure to recognize the difference between just compensation due process claims and arbitrary and capricious due process claims has led to confusion and an incorrect decision in more than one case.

IV. Denial of Substantive Due Process

Violation of the due process clause may result in liability for undue interference with the use of land, not merely because it deprives the land of all value, but also because the regulation itself is arbitrary, capricious, or unreasonable. As stated by the court in *Blaylock v. Schwinden*,[36] "[s]ubstantive due process refers to certain actions that government may not engage in, no matter how many procedural safeguards it employs."

The Supreme Court outlined the limits of the police power in *PruneYard Shopping Center v. Robins*,[37] when it stated that "[t]he guaranty of due process, as has often been held, demands only that the law shall not be unreasonable, arbitrary or capricious, and that the means selected shall have a real and substantial relation to the objective sought to be obtained."

Some courts go even further and hold that substantive due process is violated only if the action complained of is invidious or irrational.[38]

Other courts have held there can be no violation of substantive due process unless the governmental action shocks the judicial conscience.[39] However, in *Pearson v. City Grand Blanc,*[40] the court limited the test set forth in one of those cases, *G.M. Engineers,*[41] and in *McKinney v. Pate,*[42] the court held that the "shocks-the-conscience" test "has no place in a civil case for money." In addition, the federal courts analyze a claim that governmental action has violated the federal right to be free of arbitrary and capricious behavior more strictly than do state courts.[43]

In short, the courts have been all over the map when it comes to the issue of substantive due process. For example, in those jurisdictions that hold there is no property right if a discretionary approval is involved, there can be no violation of substantive due process.[44] Also, the ability to state a claim for relief under the takings clause does not mean there can be no claim stated for violation of substantive due process.[45] The denial of a permit to which the applicant is entitled constitutes a denial of substantive due process.[46] A mistaken interpretation of state law does not, in itself, constitute a violation of substantive due process.[47] Notwithstanding the numerous courts holding that the presence of discretion is tantamount to the absence of a property right, a number of cases have held that discretionary acts can create liability if they are performed in an arbitrary and capricious manner.[48]

Denying a land-use approval merely because neighbors object to a project is a violation of substantive due process.[49] However, in *Church of Jesus Christ of Latter-Day Saints v. Jefferson County,*[50] the court held there can never be a violation of substantive due process when legislative (that is, political) actions are involved. Other courts have taken a middle ground, holding that city councils may take the public's desires into consideration.[51]

The imposition of unconstitutional conditions when granting a land-use approval is a denial of substantive due process.[52] The Supreme Court's decisions in *Dolan v. City of Tigard*[53] and *Nollan v. California Coastal Commission*[54] are actually substantive due process cases, based on the analysis set forth in Section III of this chapter. Justice Stevens also seems to think so, as indicated in his dissent in *Dolan.*[55] The imposition of a condition that can be satisfied only by actions of other private individuals not under the applicant's control is also a violation of substantive due process.[56]

A number of other cases have dealt with actions that violate a landowner's right to substantive due process. These include: the refusal to issue a water permit based on a false assertion that a water shortage exists;[57] the denial of a land-use approval for reasons unrelated to the use or size of a lot,[58] for reasons not allowed by state law,[59] or for reasons related to personal or political concerns;[60] and the revocation of a permit in retaliation for successfully seeking judicial review.[61] However, *Nestor Colon Medina & Sucesores, Inc. v. Custodio*[62] holds that retaliation for political opposition should be analyzed as a violation of First Amendment rights, rather than a violation of substantive due process.

Zoning cannot be used to depress the value of land to reduce the expense of condemnation.[63] But limiting the use of land that is subject to flooding is a rational response to a potential problem, and does not constitute a denial of substantive due process merely because the factual basis for the limit may be incorrect.[64]

Denial of a permit for failure to comply with a reasonable condition precedent is not a denial of substantive due process,[65] nor is it irrational to require that land be developed pursuant to a specific plan adopted by a municipality.[66] Further, it is not irrational to impose reasonable conditions on a permit.[67]

Similarly, preservation of environmental resources such as lakes,[68] beaches,[69] endangered species,[70] and open spaces[71] is rational, as is protection against erosion.[72]

It is not irrational to maintain moderate residential density and to provide adequate parking,[73] to regulate modular housing,[74] or to differentiate between mobile homes and other forms of manufactured housing.[75] It is not irrational to impose rent control on mobile home parks,[76] to limit condominium conversion to preserve rental housing,[77] or to require that rent-controlled apartments be rented within sixty days.[78]

Maintaining public safety, property values of surrounding land, and aesthetics, and avoiding traffic congestion, adverse impacts to streets, and noise, are all rational bases for denying a given land use.[79] Also, courts have held that it is not unreasonable to set height limits on buildings.[80]

Delay, by itself, does not constitute a denial of due process.[81] The delay associated with normal processing of land-use approvals does not result in liability,[82] nor does delay resulting from litigation initiated by the government.[83] Of course, if a delay prevents the use of the land for too long, it becomes unreasonable.[84] Delay that results from a government's refusal to correct problems has been held unreasonable.[85]

V. Ripeness

Williamson County Regional Planning Commission v. Hamilton Bank[86] requires that land-use cases be ripe before they are ready for adjudication. A land-use case is ripe if both a final governmental decision has been made, and existing state remedies (particularly those for inverse condemnation) have been used.[87]

A. Finality of Decision

In general, there can be neither a taking nor a denial of due process until the allegedly improper governmental action is final, so that its full impact can be determined.[88] Thus, a landowner must seek all available means of relief from the governmental agency responsible for such action before the issue is considered ripe for judicial review under 42 U.S.C. § 1983 (which generally means making more than one application for relief in the form of a variance).[89] However, when an "arbitrary and capricious" due process claim is made, rather than a claim that a taking has occurred, only one development application must be made; there is no requirement that a second application be submitted.[90]

Even if it is unlikely that relief will be granted, a claim is not ripe for adjudication regarding an "as applied" due process takings claim until at least one development application is submitted and denied.[91] There is no need, however, to seek a variance when state law prohibits its issuance.[92]

Some courts have stated that a case is not ripe until the landowner has sought a rezoning.[93] However, a case is ripe for adjudication when the claim for relief is that a denial of a rezoning constitutes a violation of the right to substantive due process,[94] or when there is no issue about the inability to develop property for anything other than single-family homes.[95]

Finally, there is no need to apply for a development approval when a law is attacked as facially invalid.[96]

B. Existing State Remedies

The takings clause does not prohibit the taking of property; it requires only that just compensation be paid when a taking occurs.[97] Therefore, the existence of a state compensation mechanism means there can be no violation of the takings clause.[98]

However, when the allegedly improper action involves an "arbitrary and capricious" due process claim, the unconstitutional violation is complete when the action takes place, and the availability of an adequate state remedy is irrelevant.[99] As expressed in *Restigouche, Inc. v. Town of Jupiter*,[100] "[a] property owner has been denied substantive due process, however, the moment a governmental decision affecting his property has been made in an arbitrary and capricious manner, regardless of whether he is later compensated for that violation."

VI. Remedies for Denials of Substantive Due Process

In *First English Evangelical Lutheran Church of Glendale v. County of Los Angeles*,[101] the Supreme Court held that when government takes land through regulation, it is required to pay just compensation.[102] The landowner has no right to have an otherwise valid governmental action set aside.[103]

Justice Brennan, in his famous dissent in *San Diego Gas & Electric Co. v. City of San Diego*,[104] noted that under the takings clause, compensation would be required for a temporary taking caused by a regulation that went too far.[105] He also noted that a regulation that violated the due process clause—an arbitrary and capricious due process claim—did not invoke the takings clause. Instead,

> [a] different case may arise where a police power regulation is not enacted in furtherance of the public health, safety, morals, or general welfare so that there may be no "public use." Although the government may not be forced to pay just compensation under the Fifth Amendment, the landowner may nevertheless have a damage cause of action under 42 U.S.C. § 1983 for a Fourteenth Amendment due process violation.[106]

A plaintiff who succeeds in an action under 42 U.S.C. § 1983 will be entitled to compensatory damages.[107] This can include recovery for "mental and emotional distress."[108] Recovery can also include attorneys' fees incurred in the state court proceedings that were required to issue a wrongfully withheld permit.[109] The plaintiff must mitigate his or her damages,[110] and failure to prove actual damages will result in the award of nominal damages.[111] Damages under 42 U.S.C. § 1983 are a question of federal law; therefore, limitations on the amount imposed by state law do not apply.[112]

Punitive damages are also available against individuals "where the defendant's conduct is shown to be motivated by evil motive or interest, or when it involves reckless or callous indifference to the federally protected rights of others."[113] Federal standards control the award of punitive damages.[114]

Punitive damages are not generally available against municipalities.[115] However, they may be available when "the taxpayers are directly responsible for perpetrating an outrageous abuse of constitutional rights."[116]

Finally, attorneys' fees and experts' costs are available to a prevailing plaintiff in actions under 42 U.S.C. § 1983.[117]

VII. Conclusion

Most land-use lawyers think in terms of recovering for land-use regulations that go too far under the takings clause. The Supreme Court has erected a number of hurdles to bringing such actions. Seeking relief for a violation of the due process clause removes some—but not all—of those hurdles. A failure to understand the similarities and differences between the takings and the due process clauses guarantees problems; understanding them does not guarantee success, but it goes a long way toward presenting a claim that can succeed.

Notes

1. Extensive literature concerning the use of 42 U.S.C. § 1983 in land-use cases exists. A complete discussion of all aspects of land-use litigation under that statute, including a substantial bibliography, can be found in KENNETH B. BLEY, USE OF THE CIVIL RIGHTS ACTS TO RECOVER DAMAGES FOR UNDUE INTERFERENCE WITH THE USE OF LAND (1994), and in the Resource Manual produced by the Lincoln Institute of Land Policy for its course entitled "Land Use and the Constitution: The New Realities" given in San Francisco in August, 1994.

2. First Assembly of God of Naples, Florida, Inc. v. Collier County, 20 F.3d 419 (11th Cir. 1994); Key West Harbour Dev't Corp. v. City of Key West, 987 F.2d 723 (11th Cir. 1993); Mackensie v. City of Rockledge, 920 F.2d 1554 (11th Cir. 1991); Landmark Land Co. of Oklahoma, Inc. v. Buchannan, 874 F.2d 717 (10th Cir. 1989); Downtown Auto Parks, Inc. v. City of Milwaukee, 938 F.2d 705 (7th Cir. 1991); Gunkel v. City of Emporia, 835 F.2d 1302 (10th Cir. 1987); Littlefield v. City of Afton, 785 F.2d 596 (8th Cir. 1986); Shelton v. City of College Station, 754 F.2d 1251 (5th Cir. 1985), *rev'd on other grounds,* 780 F.2d 475 (5th Cir.), *cert. denied,* 477 U.S. 905 (1986); Decarion v. Monroe County, 853 F. Supp. 1415 (S.D. Fla. 1994); Everett v. City of Tallahassee, 840 F. Supp. 1528 (N.D. Fla. 1992); La Societe General Immobiliere v. Minneapolis Community Dev't Agency, 827 F. Supp. 1431 (D. Minn. 1993); Bender v. City of St. Ann, 816 F. Supp. 1372 (E.D. Mo. 1993); Mays-Ott Co., Inc. v. Town of Nags Head, 751 F. Supp. 82 (E.D.N.C. 1990); Milens v. Richmond Redevelopment Agency, 665 F.2d 906 (9th Cir. 1982); Wattentar v. Lepper, 636 F. Supp. 331 (S.D.N.Y. 1986); Sucr. Suarez v. Gelabert, 541 F. Supp. 1253 (D.P.R. 1982), *aff'd,* 701 F.2d 231 (1st Cir. 1983).

3. Brookpark Entertainment, Inc. v. Taft, 951 F.2d 710 (6th Cir. 1991).

4. Nollan v. California Coastal Comm'n, 483 U.S. 875 (1987); River Park, Inc. v. City of Highland Park, 23 F.3d 164 (7th Cir. 1994); Harris v. County of Riverside, 904 F.2d 497 (9th Cir. 1990); Polenze v. Parrott, 883 F.2d 551 (7th Cir. 1989).

5. WAM Properties, Inc. v. DeSoto County, 758 F. Supp. 1468 (M.D. Fla. 1991).

6. Reed v. Village of Shorewood, 704 F.2d 943 (7th Cir. 1983).

7. Greene v. Town of Blooming Grove, 879 F.2d 1061 (2d Cir. 1989). *See also* Resolution Trust Corp. v. Town of Highland Beach, 18 F.3d 1536 (11th Cir.

1994) (vested right is a property right even though it arose because of mistaken interpretation of state law).

8. Wedges/Ledges of California, Inc. v. City of Phoenix, 24 F.3d 56 (9th Cir. 1994); Parks v. Watson, 716 F.2d 646 (9th Cir. 1983).

9. Jacobs, Visconsi & Jacobs v. City of Lawrence, 715 F. Supp. 1000 (D. Kan. 1989), *aff'd*, 927 F.2d 1111 (10th Cir. 1991).

10. 429 U.S. 252 (1977).

11. 426 U.S. 668 (1976).

12. DANIEL MANDELKER ET AL., FEDERAL LAND USE LAW, REFUSALS TO REZONE § 2.02[2] [d] (1994).

13. 408 U.S. 564, 577 (1972).

14. 408 U.S. 593 (1972).

15. Orange Lake Associates, Inc. v. Kirkpatrick, 21 F.3d 1214 (2d Cir. 1994); L.M. Everhart Construction, Inc. v. Jefferson County Planning Comm'n, 2 F.3d 48 (4th Cir. 1993); Biser v. Town of Bel Air, 991 F.2d 100 (4th Cir.), *cert. denied*, 114 S. Ct. 182 (1993); Gardner v. City of Baltimore, 969 F.2d 63 (4th Cir. 1992); Silver v. Franklin Twp. Bd. of Zoning Appeals, 966 F.2d 1031 (6th Cir. 1992); Spence v. Zimmerman, 873 F.2d 256 (11th Cir. 1989); RRI Realty Corp. v. Incorporated Village of Southampton, 870 F.2d 911 (2d Cir.), *cert. denied*, 493 U.S. 893 (1989); Bateson v. Geisse, 857 F.2d 1300 (9th Cir. 1988); Dean Tarry Corp. v. Friedlander, 826 F.2d 210 (2d Cir. 1987); Sullivan v. Town of Salem, 805 F.2d 81 (2d Cir. 1986); Scott v. Village of Kewaskum, 786 F.2d 338 (7th Cir. 1986); Riverview Investments, Inc. v. Ottawa Community Improvement Corp., 769 F.2d 324 (6th Cir. 1985); Sylvia Dev't Corp. v. Calvert County, 842 F. Supp. 183 (D. Md. 1994); Triomphe Investors v. City of Northwood, 835 F. Supp. 1036 (N.D. Ohio 1993); Nello L. Teer Co. v. Orange Country, 810 F. Supp. 679 (M.D.N.C. 1992); Moore v. City of Edgewood, 790 F. Supp. 1561 (M.D. Fla. 1992); Koncelik v. Town of East Hampton, 781 F. Supp. 152 (E.D.N.Y. 1991); Crooked Lake Dev't, Inc. v. Emmet County, 763 F. Supp. 1398 (W.D. Mich. 1991); Jacobs, Visconsi & Jacobs Co. v. Lawrence, 715 F. Supp. 1000 (D. Kan. 1989), *aff'd*, 927 F.2d 1111 (10th Cir. 1991); Long Grove Country Club Estates, Inc. v. Village of Long Grove, 693 F. Supp. 640 (N.D. Ill. 1988); Yale Auto Parts, Inc. v. Johnson, 593 F. Supp. 329 (D. Conn. 1984), *aff'd*, 758 F.2d 54 (2d Cir. 1985).

16. 1 Robert M. ANDERSON, AMERICAN LAW OF ZONING § 4.28 (3d ed. 1986); Orange Lake Associates, Inc. v. Kirkpatrick, 21 F.3d 1214 (2d Cir. 1994) (owner); Ellentuck v. Klein, 570 F.2d 414 (2d Cir. 1978) (neighbor); Aquino v. Tobriner, 298 F.2d 674 (D.C. Cir. 1962) (owner); Stratford v. State-House, Inc., 542 F. Supp. 1008 (E.D. Ky. 1982), *aff'd mem.*, 722 F.2d 742 (6th Cir. 1983) (neighbor); Sachetti v. Blair, 536 F. Supp. 836 (S.D.N.Y. 1982) (neighbor). *But see* Nemmers v. City of Dubuque, 716 F.2d 1194 (8th Cir. 1984) (landowner had vested right to zoning under Iowa law).

17. Gagliardi v. Village of Pawling, 18 F.3d 188 (2d Cir. 1994).

18. Barbian v. Panagis, 694 F.2d 476 (7th Cir. 1982).

19. Beacon Syracuse Associates v. City of Syracuse, 560 F. Supp. 188 (N.D.N.Y. 1983).

20. Mehta v. Surles, 905 F.2d 595 (2d Cir. 1990). *See also* MacNamara v. County Council, 738 F. Supp. 134 (D. Del.), *aff'd mem.*, 922 F.2d 832 (3d Cir. 1990).

21. West Farms Associates v. State Traffic Comm'n, 951 F.2d 469 (2d Cir. 1991), *cert. denied*, 112 S. Ct. 1671 (1992). *But see* Everett v. City of Tallahassee, 840 F. Supp. 1528 (N.D. Fla. 1992); Selinger v. City Council, 216 Cal. App. 3d 259, 264 Cal. Rptr. 499 (Ct. App. 1989) (statute providing for automatic approval of land-use application after specified period unconstitutionally deprives neighbors of procedural due process right).

22. 447 U.S. 255, 260 (1980).

23. Pumpelly v. Green Bay & Mississippi Canal Co., 80 U.S. (13 Wall.) 166 (1871); and Barron v. Mayor and City Council of Baltimore, 32 U.S. (7 Pet.) 243 (1837).

24. Dolan v. City of Tigard, 114 S. Ct. 2306 (1994).

25. 277 U.S. 183, 185 (1928).

26. *Nectow*, 277 U.S. at 185 (citation omitted).

27. 272 U.S. 365 (1926).

28. *Village of Euclid*, 272 U.S. at 395.

29. Mugler v. State of Kansas, 123 U.S. 623, 661 (1887) (a court will declare a statute unconstitutional if "a statute purporting to have been enacted to protect the public health, the public morals, or the public safety, has no real or substantial relation to those objects"); Welch v. Swasey, 214 U.S. 91, 105 (1909) ("If the means employed, pursuant to the statute, have no real, substantial relation to a public object which government can accomplish, if the statutes are arbitrary and unreasonable, and beyond the necessities of the case, the courts will declare their invalidity."); Reinman v. City of Little Rock, 237 U.S. 171, 177 (1915) (ordinance will be upheld unless "clearly unreasonable and arbitrary"); Hadacheck v. Sebastian, 239 U.S. 394, 411 (1915) (ordinance upheld based on the reasoning in *Reinman*).

30. 482 U.S. 304 (1987).

31. 260 U.S. 393 (1922).

32. *First English*, 482 U.S. at 316.

33. Pearson v. City of Grand Blanc, 961 F.2d 1211, 1215-16 (6th Cir. 1992).

34. 908 F.2d 716, 720-22 (11th Cir. 1990), *cert. denied*, 498 U.S. 1120 (1991).

35. Douglas W. Kmiec, *Disentangling Substantive Due Process and Takings Claims*, *in* 1991 ZONING AND PLANNING LAW HANDBOOK ch. 7 (Kenneth H. Young, ed. 1991).

36. 862 F.2d 1352, 1354 (9th Cir. 1988). *See also* Nectow v. City of Cambridge, 277 U.S. 183 (1928); Village of Euclid v. Ambler Realty Co., 272 U.S. 365 (1926).

37. 447 U.S. 74, 84-85 (1980). *See also Village of Arlington Heights*, 429 U.S. at 263 (landowner has "right to be free from arbitrary or irrational zoning actions," such as a refusal to rezone in this case).

38. Anderson v. Douglas County, 4 F.3d 574 (8th Cir. 1993); Nestor Colon Medina & Sucesores, Inc. v. Custodio, 964 F.2d 32 (1st Cir. 1992); Condor Corp.

v. City of St. Paul, 912 F.2d 215 (8th Cir. 1990); Harding v. County of Door, 870 F.2d 430 (7th Cir. 1989); Lemke v. Cass County, 846 F.2d 469 (8th Cir. 1987); Coniston Corp. v. Village of Hoffman Estates, 844 F.2d 461 (7th Cir. 1988).

39. Licari v. Ferruzzi, 22 F.3d 344, 347 (1st Cir. 1994) ("egregiously unacceptable, outrageous, or conscience shocking"); G.M. Engineers & Associates, Inc. v. West Bloomfield Twp., 922 F.2d 328 (6th Cir. 1990).

40. 961 F.2d 1211 (6th Cir. 1992).

41. G.M. Engineers & Assocs., Inc. v. West Bloomfield Twp., 922 F.2d 328 (6th Cir. 1990).

42. 20 F.3d 1550, 1556 (11th Cir. 1994).

43. Resolution Trust Corp. v. Town of Highland Beach, 18 F.3d 1536 (11th Cir. 1994); Gardner v. City of Baltimore, 969 F.2d 63 (4th Cir. 1993); Pearson v. City of Grand Blanc, 961 F.2d 1211 (6th Cir. 1992) (more deference to be given local legislative actions than local administrative actions); Coniston Corp. v. Hoffman, 844 F.2d 461 (7th Cir. 1988); Pace Resources, Inc. v. Shrewsbury Twp., 808 F.2d 1023 (3d Cir.), *cert. denied*, 482 U.S. 906 (1987); Sylvia Dev't Corp. v. Calvert County, 842 F. Supp. 183 (D. Md. 1994); Everett v. City of Tallahassee, 840 F. Supp. 1528 (N.D. Fla. 1992); Triomphe Investors v. City of Northwood, 835 F. Supp. 1036 (N.D. Ohio 1993).

44. Sylvia Dev't Corp. v. Calvert County, 842 F. Supp. 183 (D. Md. 1994); Orange Lake Associates, Inc. v. Kirkpatrick, 825 F. Supp. 1169 (S.D.N.Y. 1993), *aff'd*, 21 F.3d 1214 (2d Cir. 1994).

45. United States v. James Daniel Good Real Property, 114 S. Ct. 492 (1993); Soldal v. Cook County, 113 S. Ct. 538 (1992); Pearson v. City of Grand Blanc, 961 F.2d 1211 (6th Cir. 1992). *But see* Rocky Mountain Materials & Asphalt, Inc. v. El Paso County, 972 F.2d 309 (10th Cir. 1992); Miller v. Campbell County, 945 F.2d 348 (10th Cir.), *cert. denied*, 112 S. Ct. 1174 (1991); First Bet Joint Venture v. City of Central City, 818 F. Supp. 1409 (D. Colo. 1993). *See also* Roberts & Shearer, *Land-Use Litigation: Takings and Due Process Claims*, 24 URB. LAW. 833 (1992).

46. Bateson v. Geisse, 857 F.2d 1300 (9th Cir. 1988) (building permit); Bello v. Walker, 840 F.2d 1124 (3d Cir.) (building permit), *cert. denied*, 488 U.S. 868 (1988); Sullivan v. Town of Salem, 805 F.2d 81 (2d Cir. 1986) (certificate of occupancy); Cunningham v. City of Overland, 804 F.2d 1066 (8th Cir. 1986); Littlefield v. City of Afton, 785 F.2d 596 (8th Cir. 1986) (building permit); L & H Sanitation, Inc. v. Lake City Sanitation, Inc., 769 F.2d 517 (8th Cir. 1985) (solid waste disposal permit); Sanderson v. Village of Greenville, 726 F.2d 284 (6th Cir. 1984) (use permit); Scott v. Greenville County, 716 F.2d 1409 (4th Cir. 1983) (building permit); Parks v. Watson, 716 F.2d 646 (9th Cir. 1983) (street vacation); Reed v. Village of Shorewood, 704 F.2d 943 (7th Cir. 1983) (failure to renew liquor license); Wilkerson v. Johnson, 699 F.2d 325 (6th Cir. 1983); TLC Dev't, Inc. v. Town of Branford, 855 F. Supp. 555 (D. Conn. 1994) (site plan); Koncelik v. Town of East Hampton, 781 F. Supp. 152 (E.D.N.Y. 1991) (subdivision map); Decarion v. Monroe County, 853 F. Supp. 1415 (S.D. Fla. 1994); Mays-Ott Co., Inc. v. Town of Nags Head, 751 F. Supp 82 (E.D.N.C. 1990) (extension of building permit); Mount Sinai Medical Center of Greater Miami, Inc. v. City of Miami Beach, 706 F. Supp. 1525 (S.D. Fla. 1989) (revocation of building permit);

Bannum, Inc. v. City of Memphis, 666 F. Supp. 1091 (W.D. Tenn. 1987) (certificate of occupancy); Anderson-Myers, Inc. v. Roach, 660 F. Supp. 106 (D. Kan. 1987); Acorn Ponds of North Hills v. Incorporated Village of North Hills, 623 F. Supp. 688 (E.D.N.Y. 1985) (certificate of occupancy); Mindich Developers, Inc. v. Hunziker, 622 F. Supp. 1513 (S.D.N.Y. 1985) (building permit); Southern Cooperative Dev't Fund v. Driggers, 527 F. Supp. 927 (M.D. Fla. 1981) (subdivision map), *aff'd*, 696 F.2d 1347 (11th Cir.), *reh'g denied*, 703 F.2d 582 (11th Cir.), *cert. denied*, 463 U.S. 1208 (1983); Mother Goose Nursery Schools, Inc. v. Sendak, 502 F. Supp. 1319 (N.D. Ind. 1980), *reaff'd*, 591 F. Supp. 897 (N.D. Ind. 1984), *rev'd on other grounds*, 770 F.2d 668 (7th Cir. 1985); Katris v. City of Waukegan, 498 F. Supp. 48 (N.D. Ill. 1980). *See also* Brady v. Town of Colchester, 863 F.2d 205 (2d Cir. 1988) (denial of permit that was not even required).

47. Chesterfield Dev't Corp. v. City of Chesterfield, 963 F.2d 1102 (8th Cir. 1992); Creative Environments, Inc. v. Estabrook, 680 F.2d 822 (1st Cir.), *cert. denied*, 459 U.S. 989 (1982); Decarion v. Monroe County, 853 F. Supp. 1415 (S.D. Fla. 1994); Biser v. Town of Bel Air, 778 F. Supp. 249 (D. Md. 1991), *aff'd*, 991 F.2d 100 (4th Cir.), *cert. denied*, 114 S. Ct. 182 (1993).

48. Village of Arlington Heights v. Metropolitan Housing Dev't Corp., 429 U.S. 252 (1977); Nectow v. City of Cambridge, 277 U.S. 183 (1928); Jacobs, Visconsi & Jacobs v. City of Lawrence, 927 F.2d 1111 (10th Cir. 1991); Executive 100, Inc. v. Martin County, 922 F.2d 1536 (11th Cir.), *cert. denied*, 112 S. Ct. 55 (1991); Herrington v. County of Sonoma, 834 F.2d 1488 (9th Cir. 1987) (denial of subdivision application), *reh'g denied*, 857 F.2d 567 (9th Cir. 1988), *cert. denied*, 489 U.S. 1090 (1989); Everett v. City of Tallahassee, 850 F. Supp. 1528 (N.D. Fla. 1992) (refusal to rezone); Creekside Associates, Inc. v. City of Wood Dale, 684 F. Supp. 201 (N.D. Ill. 1988) (refusal to annex and rezone); Lutheran Day Care Center v. Snohomish County, 119 Wash. 2d 91, 829 P.2d 746 (1992) (conditional use permit).

49. Washington *ex rel.* Seattle Title Trust Co. v. Roberge, 278 U.S. 116 (1928); Eubank v. City of Richmond, 226 U.S. 137 (1912); Del Monte Dunes at Monterey, Ltd. v. City of Monterey, 920 F.2d 1496 (9th Cir. 1990); Geo-Tech Reclamation Industries, Inc. v. Hamrick, 886 F.2d 662 (4th Cir. 1989); Marks v. City of Chesapeake, 883 F.2d 308 (4th Cir. 1989); Wheeler v. City of Pleasant Grove, 664 F.2d 99 (5th Cir. 1981), *cert. denied*, 456 U.S. 973 (1982); Schulz v. Milne, 849 F. Supp. 708 (N.D. Cal. 1994); Browning-Ferris Industries of St. Louis, Inc. v. City of Maryland Heights, 747 F. Supp. 1340 (E.D. Mo. 1990); McCollum v. City of Powder Springs, 720 F. Supp. 985 (N.D. Ala. 1989); Mindich Developers, Inc. v. Hunziker, 622 F. Supp. 1513 (S.D.N.Y. 1985).

50. 721 F. Supp. 1212 (N.D. Ala. 1989).

51. Corn v. City of Lauderdale Lakes, 997 F.2d 1369 (11th Cir. 1993), *cert. denied*, 114 S. Ct. 1400 (1994); Midnight Sessions, Ltd. v. City of Philadelphia, 945 F.2d 667 (3d Cir. 1991), *cert. denied*, 112 S. Ct. 1668 (1992); Nelson v. City of Selma, 881 F.2d 836 (9th Cir. 1990); Greenbriar, Ltd. v. City of Alabaster, 881 F.2d 1570 (11th Cir.), *reh'g en banc denied*, 893 F.2d 346 (11th Cir. 1989); Moore v. City of Edgewood, 790 F. Supp. 1561 (M.D. Fla. 1992); Koncelik v. Town of East Hampton, 781 F. Supp. 152 (E.D.N.Y. 1991); Pearson v. City of Grand Blanc, 756

F. Supp. 314 (E.D. Mich. 1991), *aff'd on other grounds*, 961 F.2d 1211 (6th Cir. 1992).

52. Littlefield v. City of Afton, 785 F.2d 596 (8th Cir. 1986); Parks v. Watson, 716 F.2d 646 (9th Cir. 1983); Jade Aircraft Sales, Inc. v. City of Bridgeport, 849 F. Supp. 510 (D. Conn. 1994); Epstein v. Township of Whitehall, 693 F. Supp. 309 (E.D. Pa. 1988).

53. 114 S. Ct. 2306 (1994).

54. 483 U.S. 825 (1987).

55. *Dolan*, 114 S. Ct. at 2326-29.

56. Sederquist v. City of Tiburon, 765 F.2d 756 (9th Cir. 1985).

57. Lockary v. Kayfetz, 917 F.2d 1150 (9th Cir. 1990).

58. Curto v. City of Harper Woods, 954 F.2d 1237 (6th Cir. 1992).

59. TLC Dev't, Inc. v. Town of Branford, 855 F. Supp. 55 (D. Conn. 1994).

60. Brady v. Town of Colchester, 863 F.2d 205 (2d Cir. 1988); Bello v. Walker, 840 F.2d 1124 (3d Cir.), *cert. denied*, 488 U.S. 868 (1988).

61. Carr v. Town of Dewey, 730 F. Supp. 591 (D. Del. 1990).

62. 964 F.2d 32 (1st Cir. 1992).

63. Urbanizadora Versalles, Inc. v. Rivera Rios, 701 F.2d 993 (1st Cir. 1983); Oberndorf v. City and County of Denver, 653 F. Supp. 304 (D. Colo. 1987), *aff'd*, 900 F.2d 1434 (10th Cir.), *cert. denied*, 498 U.S. 845 (1990); Kaiser Dev't Co. v. City and County of Honolulu, 649 F. Supp. 926 (D. Haw. 1986).

64. Terrace Knolls v. Dalton, Dalron, Little & Newport, 571 F. Supp. 1086 (N.D. Ohio 1983).

65. D.C.A. Dev't Corp. v. Ogden City Municipal Corp., 965 F.2d 827 (10th Cir. 1992); Carolan v. City of Kansas City, 813 F.2d 178 (8th Cir. 1998); Decarion v. Monroe County, 853 F. Supp. 1415 (S.D. Fla. 1994); Leonard Partnership v. Town of Chenango, 779 F. Supp. 223 (N.D.N.Y. 1991).

66. Kawaoka v. City of Arroyo Grande, 796 F. Supp. 1320 (C.D. Cal. 1992), *aff'd*, 17 F.3d 1227 (9th Cir.), *cert. denied*, 115 S. Ct. 193 (1994).

67. Hartland Sportsman's Club, Inc. v. Town of Delafield, 827 F. Supp. 562 (E.D. Wis. 1993).

68. Bourne v. Tahoe Regional Planning Agency, 829 F. Supp. 1203 (D. Nev. 1993); Stephans v. Tahoe Regional Planning Agency, 697 F. Supp. 1149 (D. Nev. 1988).

69. Esposito v. South Carolina Coastal Comm'n, 939 F.2d 165 (4th Cir. 1991), *cert. denied*, 112 S. Ct. 1671 (1992); McNulty v. City of Indialantic, 727 F. Supp. 604 (M.D. Fla. 1989).

70. Del Monte Dunes at Monterey, Ltd. v. City of Monterey, 920 F.2d 1496 (9th Cir. 1991).

71. Kaiser Dev't Co. v. City and County of Honolulu, 649 F. Supp. 926 (D. Haw. 1986).

72. Zilber v. Town of Moraga, 692 F. Supp. 1195 (N.D. Cal. 1988).

73. Curto v. City of Harper Woods, 954 F.2d 1237 (6th Cir. 1992); Burrell v. City of Kankakee, 815 F.2d 1127 (7th Cir. 1987).

74. Horizon Concepts, Inc. v. City of Balch Springs, 789 F.2d 1165 (5th Cir. 1986).

75. Grant v. Seminole County, 817 F.2d 731 (11th Cir. 1987); Clark v. Winnebago County, 817 F.2d 407 (7th Cir. 1987).

76. Levald, Inc. v. City of Palm Desert, 998 F.2d 680 (9th Cir. 1993), *cert. denied,* 114 S. Ct. 924 (1994); Adamson Cos. v. City of Malibu, 854 F. Supp. 1476 (C.D. Cal. 1994).

77. Traweek v. City and County of San Francisco, 659 F. Supp. 1012 (N.D. Cal. 1984), *aff'd on other grounds,* 920 F.2d 589 (9th Cir. 1990).

78. Help Hoboken Housing v. City of Hoboken, 650 F. Supp. 793 (D.N.J. 1986).

79. Kawaoka v. City of Arroyo Grande, 17 F.3d 1227 (9th Cir. 1994), *cert. denied,* 115 S. Ct. 193 (1994); Corn v. City of Lauderdale Lakes, 997 F.2d 1369 (11th Cir. 1993), *cert. denied,* 114 S. Ct. 1400 (1994); Nelson v. City of Selma, 881 F.2d 836 (9th Cir. 1989).

80. Welch v. Swasey, 214 U.S. 91 (1909); Albery v. Reddig, 718 F.2d 245 (7th Cir. 1983).

81. Bello v. Walker, 840 F.2d 1124 (3d Cir.), *cert. denied,* 488 U.S. 868 (1988); Schafer v. City of New Orleans, 743 F.2d 1086 (5th Cir. 1984); Quinn v. Bryson, 739 F.2d 8 (1st Cir. 1984); Chiplin Enterprises v. City of Lebanon, 712 F.2d 1524 (1st Cir. 1983).

82. Kawaoka v. City of Arroyo Grande, 796 F. Supp. 1320 (C.D. Cal. 1992), *aff'd,* 17 F.3d 1227 (9th Cir.), *cert. denied,* 115 S. Ct. 193 (1994); Herrington v. County of Sonoma, 790 F. Supp. 909 (N.D. Cal. 1991), *aff'd,* 12 F.3d 901 (9th Cir. 1993); Zilber v. Town of Moraga, 692 F. Supp. 1195 (N.D. Cal. 1988) (eighteen months not unreasonable as matter of law); Walker v. City of Kansas City, 691 F. Supp. 1243 (W.D. Mo. 1988) (two years not unreasonable as matter of law); Anastasio v. Planning Board, 209 N.J. Super. 499, 507 A.2d 1194 (Sup. Ct. App. Div. 1986).

83. Estate of Himelstein v. City of Fort Wayne, 898 F.2d 573 (7th Cir. 1990).

84. Urbanizadora Versalles, Inc. v. Rivera Rios, 701 F.2d 993 (1st Cir. 1983) (no use of land allowed for fourteen years); Eaton v. City of Solon, 598 F. Supp. 1505 (N.D. Ohio 1984); Anastasio v. Planning Board, 197 N.J. Super. 457, 484 A.2d 1358 (Sup. Ct. Law Div. 1984).

85. Q.C. Construction Co., Inc. v. Gallo, 649 F. Supp. 1331 (D.R.I. 1986).

86. 473 U.S. 172 (1985).

87. *See generally* R. Jeffrey Lyman, *Finality Ripeness in Federal Land-Use Cases from* Hamilton Bank *to* Lucas, 9 J. LAND USE & ENVT'L L. 101 (1993); Bruce I. Wiener, *Obstacles and Pitfalls for Landowners: Applying the Ripeness Doctrine to Section 1983 Land Use Litigation,* 7 J. LAND USE & ENVT'L L. 387 (1992); Michael M. Berger, *The "Ripeness" Mess in Federal Land Use Cases or How the Supreme Court Converted Federal Judges into Fruit Peddlers,* 1991 INST. ON PLAN. ZONING & EMINENT DOMAIN, ch. 7 (1991); Stuart Minor Benjamin, *The Applicability of Just Compensation to Substantive Due Process Claims,* 100 YALE L. J. 2667 (1991); Brian W. Blaeser, *Closing the Federal Courthouse Door on Property Owners: The Ripeness and Abstention Doctrines in Section 1983 Land Use Cases,* 2 HOFSTRA PROP. L. J. 73 (1988); Michael M. Berger, *"Ripeness" Test for Land Use Cases Needs Reform: Reconciling Leading Ninth Circuit Decisions Is an Exercise in Futility,* 11 ZONING & PLAN. L. REP., No. 8, 57 (Sept. 1988); Frederic S. Schwartz, *The Post-Deprivation*

Remedy Doctrine of Parratt v. Taylor *and its Application to Cases of Land Use Regulation*, 21 GEORGIA L. REV. 601 (1987).

88. This is certainly true when the plaintiff is asserting a "just compensation" due process claim, but has a much more limited application when the plaintiff is asserting an "arbitrary and capricious" due process claim.

89. MacDonald, Sommer & Frates v. Yolo County, 477 U.S. 340 (1986) (denial of single subdivision map application does not constitute final determination of allowable use); Williamson County Regional Planning Comm'n v. Hamilton Bank, 473 U.S. 172 (1985) (failure to seek variances from restrictions that prohibited approval of subdivision map precluded recovery for either a taking or denial of due process). *See also* Kawaoka v. City of Arroyo Grande, 17 F.3d 1227 (9th Cir.), *cert. denied*, 115 S. Ct. 193 (1994); Triple G Landfills, Inc. v. Bd. of Commissioners, 977 F.2d 287 (7th Cir. 1992); Smithfield Concerned Citizens for Fair Zoning v. Town of Smithfield, 907 F.2d 239 (1st Cir. 1990); Eide v. Sarasota County, 895 F.2d 1326 (11th Cir. 1990), *cert. denied*, 498 U.S. 1120 (1991); Beacon Hill Associates II Limited Partnership v. Loudoun County Bd. of Supervisors, 875 F.2d 1081 (4th Cir. 1989); Unity Ventures v. Lake County, 841 F.2d 770 (7th Cir.), *cert. denied sub nom Alter v. Schroeder*, 488 U.S. 891 (1988); Shelter Creek Dev't Corp. v. City of Oxnard, 838 F.2d 375 (9th Cir.), *cert. denied*, 488 U.S. 851 (1988); Diamond Waste, Inc. v. Monroe County, 796 F. Supp. 1511 (M.D. Ga. 1992) (at least one application for land-use approval and at least one for variance, unless shown to be futile, are required before substantive due process or equal protection violation is ripe for adjudication); Martino v. Santa Clara Valley Water Dist., 703 F.2d 1141 (9th Cir.), *cert. denied*, 464 U.S. 847 (1983); Fry v. City of Hayward, 701 F. Supp. 179 (N.D. Cal. 1988).

90. Herrington v. County of Sonoma, 834 F.2d 1488 (9th Cir. 1987), *reh'g denied*, 857 F.2d 567 (9th Cir. 1988), *cert. denied*, 489 U.S. 1090 (1989).

91. Kawaoka v. City of Arroyo Grande, 17 F.3d 1227 (9th Cir.), *cert. denied*, 115 S. Ct. 193 (1994); Southern Pacific Transp. Co. v. City of Los Angeles, 922 F.2d 498 (9th Cir. 1990), *cert. denied*, 112 S. Ct. 382 (1991); Greenbriar, Ltd. v. City of Alabaster, 881 F.2d 1570 (11th Cir.), *reh'g en banc denied*, 893 F.2d 346 (11th Cir. 1989); Unity Ventures v. County of Lake, 841 F.2d 770 (7th Cir.), *cert. denied sub nom Alter v. Schroeder*, 488 U.S. 891 (1988); Herrington v. County of Sonoma, 834 F.2d 1488 (9th Cir. 1987), *reh'g denied*, 857 F.2d 567 (9th Cir. 1988), *cert. denied*, 489 U.S. 1090 (1989); W. Birkenfeld Trust v. Bailey, 827 F. Supp. 651 (E.D. Wash. 1993).

92. Kawaoka v. City of Arroyo Grande, 17 F.3d 1227 (9th Cir.), *cert. denied*, 115 S. Ct. 193 (1994); Seguin v. City of Sterling Heights, 968 F.2d 584 (6th Cir. 1992); Greenbriar, Ltd. v. City of Alabaster, 881 F.2d 1570 (11th Cir.), *reh'g en banc denied*, 893 F.2d 346 (11th Cir. 1989); Herrington v. County of Sonoma, 834 F.2d 1488 (9th Cir. 1987), *reh'g denied*, 857 F.2d 567 (9th Cir. 1988), *cert. denied*, 489 U.S. 1090 (1989). *But see*, Shelter Creek, 838 F.2d 375 (9th Cir.) (planning commission frequently disregarded the law) *cert. denied*, 488 U.S. 851 (1988).

93. Tahoe-Sierra Preservation Council, Inc. v. Tahoe Regional Planning Agency, 911 F.2d 1331 (9th Cir. 1990), *cert. denied*, 499 U.S. 943 (1991); Celentano v. City of West Haven, 815 F. Supp. 561 (D. Conn. 1993); Stephans v. Tahoe Regional Planning Agency, 697 F. Supp. 1149 (D. Nev. 1988). *See also* Southern Pa-

cific Transp. Co. v. City of Los Angeles, 922 F.2d 498 (9th Cir. 1990) ("variance" is undefined and may include general plan amendment or zone change) *cert. denied,* 112 S. Ct. 382 (1992). *Contra,* Tahoe-Sierra Preservation Council v. Tahoe Regional Planning Agency, 938 F.2d 153 (9th Cir. 1991).

94. Resolution Trust Corp. v. Town of Highland Beach, 18 F.3d 1536 (11th Cir. 1994); Pearson v. City of Grand Blanc, 961 F.2d 1211 (6th Cir. 1992); Executive 100, Inc. v. Martin County, 922 F.2d 1536 (11th Cir.), *cert. denied,* 112 S. Ct. 55 (1991); Nelson v. City of Selma, 881 F.2d 836 (9th Cir. 1989); Dubac v. Green Oak Twp., 810 F. Supp. 867 (D. Mich. 1992); Diamond Waste, Inc. v. Monroe County, 792 F. Supp. 812 (M.D. Ga. 1992). *See also* P.L.S. Partners v. City of Cranston, 696 F. Supp. 788 (D.R.I. 1988) (no need to seek conditional-use permit when claim is denial of substantive due process).

95. Greenbriar, Ltd. v. City of Alabaster, 881 F.2d 1570 (11th Cir.), *reh'g en banc denied,* 893 F.2d 346 (1989). *But see* Acierno v. Mitchell, 6 F.3d 970 (3d Cir. 1993); Taylor Investment, Ltd. v. Upper Darby Twp., 983 F.2d 1285 (3d Cir.), *cert. denied,* 114 S. Ct. 304 (1993); Southview Associates, Inc. v. Bongartz, 980 F.2d 84 (2d Cir. 1992), *cert. denied,* 113 S. Ct. 1586 (1993); Rocky Mountain Materials & Asphalt, Inc. v. El Paso County, 972 F.2d 309 (10th Cir. 1992); Glendon Energy Co. v. Borough of Glendon, 836 F. Supp. 1109 (E.D. Pa. 1993).

96. Yee v. City of Escondido, 112 S. Ct. 1522 (1992); Agins v. City of Tiburon, 447 U.S. 255 (1980); Levald, Inc. v. City of Palm Desert, 998 F.2d 680 (9th Cir. 1993), *cert. denied,* 114 S. Ct. 924 (1994); Southern Pacific Transp. Co. v. City of Los Angeles, 922 F.2d 498 (9th Cir. 1990), *cert. denied,* 112 S. Ct. 382 (1991); Adamson Cos. v. City of Malibu, 854 F. Supp. 1476 (C.D. Cal. 1994).

97. Williamson County Regional Planning Comm'n v. Hamilton Bank, 473 U.S. 172, 194 (1985).

98. *Hamilton Bank,* 473 U.S. at 194.

99. Zinermon v. Burch, 494 U.S. 113 (1990); Sierra Lake Reserve v. City of Rockland, 987 F.2d 662 (9th Cir. 1993); Southview Associates, Ltd. v. Bongartz, 980 F.2d 84 (2d Cir. 1992), *cert. denied,* 113 S. Ct. 1586 (1993); Southern Pacific Transp. Co. v. City of Los Angeles, 922 F.2d 498 (9th Cir. 1990), *cert. denied,* 112 S. Ct. 382 (1991); Sinaloa Lake Owners Assoc. v. City of Simi Valley, 882 F.2d 1398 (9th Cir. 1989), *cert. denied,* 494 U.S. 1016 (1990); Watts v. Burkhart, 854 F.2d 839 (6th Cir. 1988); Smith v. City of Fontana, 818 F.2d 1411 (9th Cir.), *cert. denied,* 484 U.S. 935 (1987); Brown v. Texas A & M University, 804 F.2d 327 (5th Cir. 1986); Littlefield v. City of Afton, 785 F.2d 596 (8th Cir. 1986); Epstein v. Twp. of Whitehall, 693 F. Supp. 309 (E.D. Pa. 1988); Williams v. City of St. Louis, 783 F.2d 114 (8th Cir. 1986); Rivervale Realty Co., Inc. v. Town of Orangetown, 816 F. Supp. 937 (S.D.N.Y. 1993). *But see* Rocky Mountain Materials & Assoc., Inc. v. Board of County Commissioners, 972 F.2d 309 (10th Cir. 1992); Lemke v. Cass County, 846 F.2d 469 (8th Cir. 1988); Ochoa Realty Corp. v. Faria, 815 F.2d 812 (1st Cir. 1987); PFZ Properties, Inc. v. Rodriguez, 739 F. Supp. 67 (D.P.R. 1990), *aff'd on other grounds,* 928 F.2d 28 (1st Cir. 1991), *cert. improvidently granted,* 112 S. Ct. 1151 (1992); Park View & Gravel, Inc. v. Town Bd., 625 F. Supp. 456 (E.D. Wis. 1985).

100. 845 F. Supp. 1540, 1547 n.8 (S.D. Fla. 1993).

101. 483 U.S. 304 (1987).

102. Before First English, several state supreme courts had held that land-use regulations could never take land so as to require the payment of just compensation; instead, those courts held that a regulation that went too far constituted a violation of the due process clause and could be remedied only through invalidation. *See, e.g.*, Agins v. City of Tiburon, 24 Cal. 3d 266, 598 P.2d 25, 157 Cal. Rptr. 372 (1979), *aff'd on other grounds*, 447 U.S. 255 (1980); Fred F. French Investing Co. v. City of New York, 39 N.Y.2d 587, 350 N.E.2d 381, 385 N.Y.S.2d 5, *app. dismissed and cert. denied*, 429 U.S. 990 (1976).

This view has begun to return. *See, e.g.*, Hensler v. City of Glendale, 8 Cal. 4th 1, 876 P.2d 1043, 32 Cal. Rptr. 244 (1994); Tampa-Hillsborough County Expressway Authority v. A.G.W.S. Corp., 640 So. 2d 54 (Fla. 1994); Orion Corp. v. State, 109 Wash. 2d 621, 747 P.2d 1062 (1987), *cert. denied*, 486 U.S. 1086 (1988).

103. Presault v. Interstate Commerce Comm'n, 494 U.S. 1 (1990).

104. 450 U.S. 621, 636-61 (1981).

105. *San Diego Gas & Electric*, 450 U.S. at 653.

106. *Id.* at 656 n.23.

107. First English Evangelical Lutheran Church v. County of Los Angeles, 482 U.S. 304 (1987); Memphis Community School Dist. v. Stachura, 477 U.S. 299 (1986) (no abstract value to be assigned to constitutional rights); Carey v. Piphus, 435 U.S. 247 (1978); Hammond v. County of Madera, 859 F.2d 797 (9th Cir. 1988) (rental value of land taken together with proximately caused damages resulting from denial of substantive due process); Herrington v. County of Sonoma, 790 F. Supp. 909 (N.D. Cal. 1991) (return on difference in value, measured by one-year treasury bills for appropriate time using complicated formula based on probability of approval) *aff'd*, 12 F.3d 901 (9th Cir. 1993); Westborough Mall, Inc. v. City of Cape Girardeau, 757 F. Supp. 1022 (E.D. Mo. 1991) (decreased value of leasehold); Smith v. Village of Maywood, 699 F. Supp. 157 (N.D. Ill. 1988) (lost rentals); P.L.S. Partners v. City of Cranston, 696 F. Supp. 788 (D.R.I. 1988) (increased and extra costs); Heritage Homes of Attleboro, Inc. v. Seekonk Water District, 498 F. Supp. 463 (D. Mass. 1980), *aff'd*, 648 F.2d 761 (1st Cir.), *judgment vacated and remanded on another point*, 454 U.S. 81 (1981), *modified and aff'd*, 670 F.2d 1 (1st Cir.), *cert. denied*, 457 U.S. 1120 (1982). *But see* Burlington Assembly of God Church v. Zoning Bd., 247 N.J. Super. 285, 588 A.2d 1297 (Sup. Ct. Law Div. 1990) (no consequential damages allowed under 42 U.S.C. § 1983; only just compensation measure used for a taking).

108. *Carey*, 435 U.S. at 262.

109. Mindich Developers, Inc. v. Hunziker, 622 F. Supp. 1513 (S.D.N.Y. 1985).

110. Meyers v. City of Cincinnati, 14 F.3d 1115 (6th Cir. 1994).

111. Zinermon v. Burch, 494 U.S. 113 (1990); Carey v. Piphus, 435 U.S. 247 (1978); County of Munroe v. United States Dep't of Labor, 690 F.2d 1359 (11th Cir. 1982); Burt v. Abel, 585 F.2d 613 (4th Cir. 1978); Cordeco Dev't Corp. v. Santiago Vasquez, 539 F.2d 256 (1st Cir.), *cert. denied*, 429 U.S. 978 (1976).

112. Patrick v. City of Florala, 793 F. Supp. 301 (M.D. Fla. 1992).

113. Smith v. Wade, 461 U.S. 30, 56 (1983). *See also* Cunningham v. City of Overland, 804 F.2d 1066 (8th Cir. 1986); Fox Valley Reproductive Health Care Center, Inc. v. Arft, 454 F. Supp. 784 (E.D. Wis. 1978) (allegation that town board had adopted restrictive ordinance with full knowledge of its unconstitutionality); Cordeco Dev't Corp. v. Santiago Vasquez, 539 F.2d 256 (1st Cir.), *cert. denied*, 429 U.S. 978 (1976); Silver v. Cormier, 529 F.2d 161 (10th Cir. 1976); Winograd v. Clear Lake City Water Authority, 811 S.W.2d 147 (Tex. Ct. App. 1991).

114. Hill v. Marshall, 962 F.2d 1209 (6th Cir. 1992). *See generally, Punitive Damages in Actions for Violations of Federal Civil Rights Acts*, 24 A.L.R. FED. 608 (1975).

115. City of Newport v. Fact Concerts, Inc., 453 U.S. 247 (1981).

116. *Fact Concerts*, 453 U.S. at 267 n.29.

117. 42 U.S.C. § 1988 (1994).

CHAPTER ❖ 15

Not with a Bang, but a Giggle: The Settlement of the *Lucas* Case

Gideon Kanner

The *Lucas* case,[1] a veritable storm center during the 1991 U.S. Supreme Court Term, settled quickly and anticlimactically following the Court's holding that—absent a common law nuisance—a land-use regulation that precludes any reasonable use of privately owned property amounts to a taking. While the case was pending before the Supreme Court, the press falsely depicted *Lucas* as an apocalyptic confrontation pitting the forces of conservatism against the environment.[2] It was, of course, nothing of the sort.

Conceptually, *Lucas* was a rather pedestrian confrontation between a landowner and overreaching government regulators who, in the name of protecting the environment, forbade all reasonable use of the affected land, thus rendering it useless and worthless. David Lucas had paid $1 million for the last two vacant beachfront lots on the Isle of Palms in South Carolina, intending to build one home for himself and one for sale. But the South Carolina Coastal Council (Coastal Council) adopted regulations forbidding all construction on the two lots, even though all others in the area had been improved with expensive private homes. Lucas thus became the "odd man out"—forbidden to do what all his neighbors had done earlier without hindrance.

David Lucas's claim of regulatory taking of his land was upheld by the trial court, reversed by the South Carolina Supreme Court,[3] and reversed again by the U.S. Supreme Court, in an opinion holding that—absent a common law nuisance—a regulation forbidding all reasonable use of private land amounts to a taking. Following the U.S. Supreme Court's reversal, the case was remanded for a hearing to allow the regulators to prove, if they could, that any use of the land by Lucas would constitute a common law nuisance.

At first, the South Carolina regulators insisted they could meet the common law nuisance standard. Cotton C. Harness, general counsel for the Coastal Council, was quoted as saying he was confident that "we can go to court and demonstrate that there is a threat to the environment."[4] But Mr. Harness proved to be overly optimistic. The South Carolina Supreme Court promptly found that Lucas's proposed construction of the two homes did not amount to a nuisance, and remanded the case to the trial court to reassess damages.[5]

Originally, the trial court had awarded Lucas about $1 million in damages on the theory that the draconian coastal regulations constituted a full taking of his fee simple title. But in 1990, while the *Lucas* case was pending on appeal, the regulations were amended to allow landowners subject to them to apply for "special permits" for construction of habitable structures seaward of the established no-building line.[6]

The state supreme court thought this option reopened the question of the extent of the taking; Lucas would now be able to apply for a special permit, so the taking would be a temporary one.[7] The opinion tacitly assumes that once confronted with Lucas's application, the Coastal Council would issue the permit, and does not consider the possibility that it might deny the permit and pay the full amount of compensation for a total, permanent taking.

Thus, a remand was necessary to reassess damages for the period between the enactment of the Coastal Act (1988) and the date of the opinion (1992). But the valuation trial never took place; the case settled. The total settlement came to $1.5 million, and consisted of payment of $425,000 for each lot, plus interest and legal fees.[8] After payment of his mortgage and costs, David Lucas cleared less than $100,000.[9]

The State of South Carolina thus became the owner of Lucas's lots.

If the *Lucas* litigation had the elements of high drama, particularly while it was pending before the U.S. Supreme Court, its aftermath following the settlement quickly degenerated into a bureaucratic farce. Having acquired Lucas's lots, South Carolina promptly executed a neck-snapping, intellectual about-face. The lots, which only a year earlier were depicted as a "threat to life and property" if built upon, underwent a sudden metamorphosis. By July 17, 1993, Bachman C. Smith, III, another lawyer for the Coastal Council, was quoted as saying that—given the built-up character of the area surrounding Lucas's lots—"it is reasonable and prudent to allow houses to be built."[10]

So much for the "threat to life and property."

Of course, that left the state with the question of what to do with the lots. In what turned out to be probably the Coastal Council's only display of prudence in this entire wretched mess, the Coastal Council decided it would not attempt to develop the lots itself, but would market them to developers.

To say that the state was optimistic would be a gross understatement. Though it paid Lucas $425,000 for each lot, it announced that it intended to turn a profit and that public bids for the lots would begin at $450,000.[11]

"I hear people are standing in line waiting to buy those lots," said Coastal Council spokeswoman Donna Gress.[12] But reality was not kind to Ms. Gress's rosy projections.

It turned out that the highest comparable sales in the local market indicated a value of only $425,000 per lot—exactly the settlement amount. Moreover, because the amended 1990 regulations provided that in the event of beach erosion any improvements might have to be moved, no one in the market was willing to pay even $425,000 per lot. Speaking with unassailable logic, local realtor David Crosby was quoted as saying, "I think $450,000 is probably a little high for a lot in which you're going to have a variance to build on it."[13] Randy Walker, another local realtor, was more acerbic, "It's asking a lot for a guy to spend $450,000 under the premise that he may have to move his house some day if the agency decides to tell him to."[14]

The state decided to market the lots itself to save itself a broker's commission. But in a lesson on the pitfalls awaiting amateurs, its functionary who had driven from Columbia to the Isle of Palms to put up "For Sale" signs had to turn back when he learned that local regulations forbade them.

The only timely bid the state received on its first effort to sell was from Andy Guagenti, one of Lucas's neighbors, who offered $315,000 for one of the lots to keep it vacant and protect his view.[15] Though this would have achieved precisely the result for which the state fought during this litigation, it declined Guagenti's bid. Instead, after extending time and soliciting additional bids, the state accepted $392,500 per lot from Congaree Construction Company, owned by John C. Gwinn, who bought the land with the intention of developing it.[16]

Thus, once it found itself picking up the tab, the state abandoned its claims of threats to life and property. It was unwilling to forego even $77,000 to assure that one of Lucas's lots would remain vacant—precisely what the state told three levels of courts it wanted to accomplish as vitally necessary.

The moral of it all is, primarily, the familiar truism that there is no such thing as a free lunch. It is amazing how our environmental government servants recognize the merit of that eternal verity when they have to pay the price of the vaunted public benefits out of their own agency budget, rather than being able to stiff an innocent bystander.

But given the tone of the reporting of the *Lucas* case while it was pending before the U.S. Supreme Court, another villain emerges: the press. Aside from Jane Lehman's *Washington Post* story, which a few newspapers reprinted, no major newspapers or magazines—certainly none of those that had carried on hysterically in 1992 about how a Supreme Court decision in favor of David Lucas might doom property regulation root and branch—reported South Carolina's ignominious intellectual and moral retreat. The only coverage of these events was by the local newspaper, the *Charleston Post and Courier.*

Thus, we learn that when it comes to judging the importance of a story, it evidently all depends on whose ideological ox is being gored, and whose "spin" the press wants to present to the public—which leaves one loose end: whatever happened to the media's vaunted principle that "the public has a right to know"?

Notes

1. Lucas v. South Carolina Coastal Council, 112 S. Ct. 2886 (1992).

2. *See* Gideon Kanner, Lucas *and the Press: How to Be Politically Correct on the Taking Issue, in* AFTER *Lucas:* LAND USE REGULATIONS AND THE TAKING OF PROPERTY WITHOUT COMPENSATION, (David L. Callies ed. 1993).

3. Lucas v. South Carolina Coastal Council, 404 S.E.2d 895 (S.C. 1991).

4. CORNELIA DEAN, *When a Shoreline Home May Be a Public Nuisance,* N.Y. TIMES, July 4, 1992, sec.1, at 6.

5. Lucas v. South Carolina Coastal Council, 424 S.E.2d 484 (S.C. 1992).

6. S.C. CODE ANN. § 48-39-290 (D) (1) (Supp. 1991).

7. *Lucas,* 424 S.E.2d at 486.

8. Jane Lehman, *Accord Ends Fight Over Use of Land,* WASH. POST, July 17, 1993, at E1.

9. *Id.* at E7.

10. *Id.*

11. Bill Steiger, *State Selling 2 Isle Lots,* CHARLESTON POST AND COURIER, Aug. 27, 1993, at 1-B.

12. *Id.*

13. *Id.*

14. Bill Steiger, *State Extends Bidding for 2 Isle of Palms Lots,* CHARLESTON POST AND COURIER, Oct. 5, 1993, at 1-B.

15. *Id.*

16. CHARLESTON POST AND COURIER, Nov. 1, 1993.

PART IV

Comparative Takings Law

CHAPTER ❖ 16

Compensation Aspects of the "Takings Issue" in German and American Law: A Comparative View

Carl-Heinz David

I. Introduction

Compensation for a taking of private property rights in land is considered to be a core issue for protecting individual human rights within modern democratic and law-ruled constitutional systems. The scope of this principle is not obvious, but results from various political and legal considerations that differ from country to country and change with time. A comparison between the American "takings issue" and the broader German compensation system for expropriation, which covers issues similar to an American "taking," reveals the underlying general ideas and principles that form the structure and framework for adapting existing constitutional and legal systems to pressing political, social, and environmental changes that require a political, legal, and administrative response.

Considering the professional and public reaction to the sequence of U.S. Supreme Court takings decisions (starting in the early 1920s and continuing until the major changes of the recent past), a foreign observer might get the impression that after the recent *Lucas* and *Dolan* decisions, the takings issue is not so much a purely dogmatic legal or judicial point of argument, but has instead gained the character of an actual legal rule entitling private landowners to claim compensation from public authorities, with possibly major impacts on already hard-pressed public budgets. In addition, the effects of changes in environmental or social public policies may make it more difficult (or impossible) to implement a taking in the future. Restricting public compensation payments and managing social changes without exorbitant public outlays is a political and legal problem in Germany, too. For example, adapting farming activities to environmental requirements, or changing the present distribution of tasks between public authorities and private enterprises involved in the waste disposal sector to comply with new environmental requirements (for example, replacing disposal by combustion) might affect ownership and entrepreneurship, and thus result in compensation claims.

II. Different Legal Approaches

The compensation systems of both the American and German legal systems have a constitutional background. Since the French Revolution of 1789, the constitutional evolution of each system has taken a different direction.[1]

Historical background provides a basis for understanding the common general principles and roots that form the foundation for the constitutional guarantee of property rights. In Germany, which during the past two hundred years[2] has had various constitutions representing different forms of government (ranging from monarchy to dictatorship to democracy), property rights have been constitutionally guaranteed with similar wordings, but different meanings. Even the two democratic constitutions of 1919 and 1949 varied considerably.

The present constitutional concept, which is based on the German Basic Law (Grundgesetz) of 1949, considers the constitutional guarantee of property rights a cornerstone within a democratic and social governmental structure ruled by law (demokratischer und sozialer Rechtsstaat). The guarantee of property rights is part of a human rights system (Grundrechte). It therefore has a major role in protecting individual liberty and freedom, which implicates more than safeguarding the substance and value of real property against unconstitutional devaluation.

In Germany, the takings issue is not restricted to impacts on land-related property rights. The constitutional doctrine of expropriation extends the concept of compensable property rights to other legal positions, including rights related to holding and operating an enterprise, copyrights, and trademark rights. Certain legal rights, though related to the land, are legally severed from landownership rights. Examples of such rights include mining and water-use rights.[3] Changes in these areas of legislation do not legally touch landownership rights.

Unlike the takings issue in the United States, the compensation issue in Germany is part of the wider issue of state liability for covering damages deriving from state activities,[4] caused either intentionally or unintentionally by public action. Any claim for compensation needs an explicit legal or constitutional basis. Thus, compensation can come from a public budget only if a specific law or legal principle allows for it.

In Germany and in the United States, such legal rules and principles are the rare exception and, if they do exist, are narrowly interpreted by the courts. A basic constitutional principle is that in cases of condemnation (in German terminology, "classic" expropriation—klassische Enteignung) compensation must be paid. But to understand the dogmatic system of state-granted compensation in Germany, one must keep another constitutional principle in mind: the state's liability for damage from deliberate or unlawful action of its officials. (Amtspflichtverletzung, Art. 34 of the Constitution (GG), and Section 839 of the Civil Code (BGB).) The two principles are related. For instance, an expropriation might turn out to be illegal, or an action by a civil servant might be considered unlawful but beyond his personal responsibility (for example, if the damage was caused accidentally).

Moreover, under both principles, the legal basis for granting compensation goes back to a more general legal principle defined in the first concise absolutist European codification, the Prussian General Land Law of 1794. The principle of sacrifice (Aufopferungsprinzip) states that if individual rights and benefits clash with public welfare rights and duties, the latter must take priority over the former; however, the state must compensate those who sacrifice their specific right or advantages for the common good.[5]

The above-mentioned regulation is no longer valid, as the Federal Constitutional (Supreme) Court recently affirmed in a major decision in which it held that this principle of sacrifice has the legal rank of only an ordinary law, and is not an independent constitutional principle. Initially this ruling appeared to apply only to some marginal cases.[6] But with time, it has achieved rising importance because it allows the judiciary to decide cases requiring compensation under conditions of hardship without defining the exact borderline of expropriation. (This is discussed further in section VII.B.2 of this chapter.)

Moreover, this decision forms the legal and argumentative background for granting compensation in those cases in which administrative or legislative impacts on property rights (other than physical or "classic" takings) attain the status of an expropriation requiring compensation. The German category of cases falling within "sacrifice-related expropriation" (versus the "classic expropriation" category) are comparable to the American category of "regulatory takings." The implications of the legal doctrines outlined are disputed, giving rise to a legal system with some contradictions.

III. Different Categories of Relevant Cases

Though the basic issues are similar, the subjects covered by the German and U.S. judiciaries differ widely. Therefore, a direct comparison of key decisions would not serve a useful purpose.

The futility of such a comparison is partly due to procedural differences. There are three High Courts on the federal level in Germany, with well-defined competencies restricting their power of review. The Federal Constitutional Court is only one actor, though in a key position, in this judicial field.[7]

To a certain degree, the various judicial systems reflect the differences in the respective legislative, administrative, and judicial branches related to public liability for takings compensation. Despite the more detailed legal system, Federal Courts' decisions are needed to secure the uniformity of the federal legal order. But due to the more detailed constitutional and ordinary (federal and state) German law system, the major Federal Courts' decisions appear to cover more specific subjects. For instance, they may interpret actual regulations of the ordinary law (for example, how the expropriation regulations of the Federal Building Code must be applied), or they may define legal criteria for restricting or extending the state's liability in accordance with the constitution. Though the scope appears to be broader, the strategy used to handle the compensation issue in Germany is similar to that in the United States: to be open-minded in formulating general principles, but restrictive in applying them to grant actual compensation.

IV. Different Constitutional Concepts for Defining "Takings" Criteria

The U.S. Constitution's Fifth Amendment states that private property must not be taken for public use without just compensation. The wording of the analogous Article 14 of the Basic Law (Grundgesetz)[8] is more detailed. It differentiates between (1) expropriation (paragraph 3 of the article), which requires a specific compensation procedure, reflecting a fair balance between public and private interests in the public weal, and (2) determination by law of the content and limits of property rights (paragraph 1 of the article), which does not require compensation. Further, the German Constitution explicitly states that private property rights carry an obligation for the owner and that use of those rights must also serve the public weal, thus implicating the so-called social obligation of property rights (Sozialpflichtigkeit des Eigentums, paragraph 2 of the article).

The German constitutional concept of property rights protection posits that a physical taking or an administrative, legislative, or public action may adversely affect property rights. For both public authorities and private landowners, the key legal issue regarding compensation is whether an impact must qualify legally as an expropriation, or fall under the determination of the content or social obligation of property rights.

Many categories of legislative regulations, or planning/administrative decisions based on such regulations, only define the legal content of property rights and do not provide any compensation consequence. This is also true of most regulations concerning town planning and building, and related planning/administrative decisions, such as binding zoning plans or planning permissions.[9] Constitutional law might form the legal framework for interpreting the applicable planning or building law (particularly to avoid unconstitutionality), but it does not provide an independent basis for deciding the case and for granting compensation, thus amending or supplementing the detailed urban planning and building legislation.[10]

Whether a piece of land lacks a potentially lucrative use is not considered as an absolute legal criterion for expropriation. In Germany, land might not be usable because of a so-called social obligation: for example, the land might be located in an area of outstanding natural beauty or contain a historical monument or specific landmark (see discussion in section VII.B.2 of this chapter).

While a property owner in the United States is considered to have a bundle of property rights, in Germany ownership is considered as a virtually comprehensive legal position, though it might be subject to rather far-reaching private or public restrictions.[11] Thus, to own property and to be limited by private or public restrictions or exactions (servitudes, for example) that bar some property uses is no contradiction to the German concept of ownership.

Two doctrines help distinguish between expropriation and the determination of the content of property right. The first theory, applied by the Federal Civil Court, determines whether the impact in question qualifies as an expropriation by considering whether it specially relates to the specific situation of the property. The second theory, applied by the Federal Administrative Court, considers whether the impact is both "hard and unbearable" (schwer und unerträglich) for the affected landowner. The common background for both doctrines is the abovementioned[12] principle related to sacrifice. Both doctrines reach the same result in most cases, as relevant criteria to be considered are cross-related. Both require comparison of the impacted landowner with other landowners in similar positions.[13]

In assessing the impact of regulations protecting areas of scenic beauty, monuments, or landmarks, the doctrine focusing on the relevance of the given situation allows for a clearer determination. In other cases not characterized by a specific physical or environmental situation, the requirement that the impact be both hard and unbearable for the landowner makes for an easier decision about whether a compensable expropriation has occurred.

Only the Federal Constitutional Court has the jurisdiction to find a legal regulation unconstitutional and therefore invalid. The other two federal civil/administrative courts have the jurisdiction to find only that a regulation is constitutional. They first try to interpret the relevant regulation in accordance with the constitution. Only if this fails is the case to be submitted to the Federal Constitutional Court for ruling on unconstitutionality and invalidity. Decisions stating that a specific law or regulation does not comply with the constitutional requirements of Art. 14 GG are rather rare but, if released, always have a major impact on judicial and administrative practice.

At first glance, the American "takings" concept appears to have something in common with the German doctrine stressing the "hard and unbearable" criteria, as it considers the total loss of any vital land use. But when examined more closely, it might have an even closer relationship to the other German doctrine that focuses on the specific situation of the property. The situation is defined not only by the physical circumstances, such as natural beauty, but also by the legal valuation, given by general police power, public welfare benefits, or specific legislation pursuing or explaining more general political goals.

V. American "Takings" Categories and Their German Parallels—Freilich and Garvin Distinguish among Three Types of Regulatory Takings

Freilich and Garvin[14] make distinctions among three types of regulatory takings: physical takings, title takings, and economic takings. According to German understanding, the distinction between the first and second categories is not quite obvious, as some of the impact from a title taking appears to be a preliminary stage of a yet to be implemented physical taking.

For example, there may be land in agricultural use that is suitable for private housing and is designated for road construction. The designation already devalues the land significantly. Physically, nothing may change for years, until the land is formally transferred to the road authority, the road work begins, the road is completed, and the traffic starts. Germans would understand some of the cases of physical and title taking (as used in American terminology) as a preliminary stage of classic expropriation, raising questions about whether the compensation for devaluation caused by the mere designation can be separately claimed, or whether the owner can claim that the authority takes over the land in this early stage and must compensate the landowner for the land value (plus compensable side damages, if any).

Under the American takings doctrine, one of the major differences between a physical taking and the other two types of takings is that in the latter, the nexus between (1) restrictions and infringements upon ownership, and (2) the public purpose advanced, must be proved. Though the legal argument is based on constitutional principles, the takings issue, for a German observer, loses much of its purely constitutional character and becomes (due to the nexus requirement) related to the various, widely differing, specific fields of legislation involved, so that the two different legal systems appear to converge.

Without doubt, the "economic taking" is the most difficult category of the three to understand, as it suggests that there exists an absolute, economically measurable criterion to prove a taking. The "loss of all economic viable use" issue always appears to relate to cases in which, before the "takings" event, the land had an obvious and considerable economic use—as reflected, for example, by the price paid for the acquisition. So far, there is a clear parallel to the German doctrine, which considers private usefulness of property (Privatnützigkeit des Eigentums) as a core issue of constitutional property rights protection. However, German doctrine defines this in legal, not economic, terms. The criterion is strongly related to what a common sense landowner must accept regarding the property. For instance, if someone owning a piece of land on a recently discovered prehistoric site wants to develop the property as a large recreation area, he probably could be stopped, even if a specific protective designation is not yet in place.

VI. Public Purposes Justifying "Taking" and "Expropriation"

In German law, the term "Enteignung" (expropriation) has been expanded during a long period of constitutional history based on judicial and jurisprudential considerations, so that it now unquestionably comprises both classic and regulatory takings aspects.

A substantial justification for allowing expropriation is that it is done for the public weal (or for the public welfare, using a more common terminology). Because everything done by public administrative and planning authorities can be considered to be in the public good,

German legal doctrine requires that the public benefit justifying expropriation must be more specific: that is, there must be an actual and definite public benefit, represented in an approved specific project or plan. For example, simply adding land, presently earmarked for no particular public purpose, to a municipality's land reserve to meet future land demand would not justify an expropriation. However, the outcome would be totally different if the land were needed for a specific school development designated by a binding zoning plan.

Expropriation does not allow a transfer from one private person to another. This can pose difficulties if land is needed for both private and public purposes. In the *Boxberg* decision[15] it was held that land could not be compulsorily taken from a farmer to construct a large racing test field for Mercedes cars, even though there was a major public interest in the project to advance regional development and employment. The court suggested that an expropriation based on an explicit state law might have solved the problem, because then the public weal would have been definitely and specifically determined by the legislature (federal state) itself.

Expropriation for the implementation of urban plans and schemes is generally held to be in accordance with expropriation requirements. The private landowner involved is protected, particularly by the procedural rule that expropriation is permitted only if the owner is neither able nor willing to implement the plan himself (to comply with housing redevelopment requirements, for instance). In such a case, the expropriation burdens the municipality with the financial risk of implementing the plan; if it fails to do so, it must return the property to the owner.

A case comparable to *Hawaii Housing Authority v. Midkiff*[16] would raise difficult constitutional questions in Germany, because implementing land-reform goals is likely *not* to be a subject of Article 14 GG of the Constitution, but of Article 15 GG, which deals with "socialization."

The police power in Germany has lost much of its legal and political importance in the legislative and administrative arena. Beginning with a key decision of the Prussian Administrative Law Court more than a hundred years ago,[17] the general police power has been replaced by increasingly detailed legislation forming specific legal bases for the various fields of administration. The Constitution reflects this in a detailed distribution of legislative power to the federal and the federal/state legislatures, which continuously have had to adapt the scope of private property rights to new political demands (such as environmental requirements), under scrutiny of the constitutional judiciary.

The various legal restrictions a landowner faces when he wants to construct a house have given rise to major discussions about whether the legal principle of liberty to build (Baufreiheit) still exists, or whether it has been replaced by a rule that permission to build must be granted by the authorities within the framework of the law. The Federal Courts maintain the principle despite the many existing restrictions. This has some major consequences on the extent to which legislatures can change land-related legislation without amending Art. 14 of the Constitution.

VII. Compensation Regulations Covering "Regulatory Taking" Matters in German Law

A. General Function

The existence of compensation regulations related to "regulatory takings" cases strongly influences the administrative practices of the authorities, who, of course, try to avoid administrative decisions or actions with clear compensation consequences. The existence of such regulations does not seem to frequently result in high payments to landowners, thus burdening the public (federal, state, local) budgets considerably, although no precise statistics are available. Moreover, the courts tend to be restrictive in interpreting such regulations in favor of private claimants.

Because regulations implying the existence of expropriation without compensation would be unconstitutional, there is strong pressure on legislators to cope with that matter. Such compensation regulations do not explicitly state whether compensation is granted for constitutional or other reasons, such as state courtesy to mitigate a specific hardship.

B. Various Compensation Regulations

1. URBAN PLANNING LEGISLATION

The most detailed takings-related compensation regulations are provided by the Federal Building Code (FBC),[18] which regulates urban planning and its implementation. The code covers both classic expropriation (FBC §§ 85–122) and regulatory takings, for which compensation is due. In particular, sections 39–44 of the FBC provide compensation for the following:

- Damages suffered by landowners who rely on the continuity of legally-binding land-use plans
- Damages resulting from land-use plans that designate areas for public purposes (recreation areas, for example) or areas for which the owner must tolerate public walking or riding rights, or public utilities

- Damages resulting from "downzoning" of a legally permitted land use[19]
- Damages resulting from development freezes or postponements of building applications lasting longer than four years (FBC § 14)

Specific regulations exist for the reallocation of land (Umlegung, FBC § 45), special urban (block) redevelopment (Sanierung), and large-area urban developments (Entwicklungsgebiete, FBC § 136). A landowner whose property falls under such categories might face serious restrictions in using, transferring, or disposing of his property. Permission for a transfer or improvement of land might be required. Rent controls might apply. The land might be exchanged for a site at a comparable location in the designated area.

The land value is frozen when the proceedings start. In newly developed areas, up to 30 percent of the original land can be taken away to satisfy public infrastructure requirements. All computations regarding exchange of land equal in value are based on the land value at the beginning of the proceedings, when the increase in value caused by the expectation of public investment or made by public investment has not yet taken place. Most of these impacts are considered as resulting from the social obligation related to private property, and are deemed to be in the interest of the landowner, who reasonably understands that without public infrastructure he could not make economically viable use of the land. The deduction of a certain portion of the owner's land is considered to be in the interest of both the public and the owner, so no compensation is due. Compensation payments are used only marginally to reach solutions, when an exchange of land does not work for legal or factual reasons. (For example, it may be that the site was so small that the owner cannot receive in return a site equal in value and large enough to fit into the new land-use structure envisioned by the renewal plan.)

2. LEGISLATION TO PROTECT AREAS OF SCENIC BEAUTY

Before the recently heightened level of environmental awareness, this field of law was widely considered as requiring no regulations for compensation, because it was thought that authorities never need cross the legal borderline of defining the content and social obligation of property rights. Areas earmarked for full environmental protection were either acquired by the authority in advance, or the designation was made with the full consent of the owners involved. With growing environmental awareness, it became obvious that regulations and measures needed to protect areas of outstanding natural beauty might rise to the level of an expropriation.

The federal states tried to solve the problem by introducing regulations that simply stated that if a public action had the effect of being an expropriation, compensation must be paid. The scope and the constitutionality of such regulations was controversially upheld by various federal state and state law courts. This issue will probably require future consideration by the Federal Constitutional Court. Until now, the courts have avoided submitting the issue to Federal Constitutional Court by trying to interpret the regulations as being in accordance with the Constitution.[20] These regulations likely do not comply with the constitutional requirement for expropriation, as they do not define the scope and extent of compensation as required by the Constitution in Article 14, Abs. 3, Section 2. Therefore, the regulations are interpreted as being applicable only in nonexpropriation cases, by arguing that they regulate a type of balance payment in cases where the content of property rights is determined, but where a particular hardship exists under the principle of sacrifice.

The law courts avoid defining the constitutionally determined borderline of expropriation, but continue to apply criteria very similar to that formerly used to define expropriation. The scope of social obligation requires an evaluation and weighing of the conflicting public and private interests: would a wise landowner who reasonably takes aspects of public welfare into consideration refrain from the intended land use? Criteria considered include legally admitted uses already implemented in the past, and uses that appear suitable on the site. The weighing might have the result that major public concerns (nature conservancy, for example) require the landowner to accept the loss of all vital economic land use without compensation. But the preceding question, which the courts explicitly must consider, is whether the land use the owner claims to be impacted was legally admitted when the taking became effective.

3. LEGISLATION ON HIGHWAY AND ROAD PLANNING

Legislation on highway and road construction is a paradigm for compensation regulation in similar areas, such as railway tracks, air fields, airports, and waste disposal projects.[21] The authority in charge oversees a specific planning procedure (Planfeststellungsverfahren), allowing it to concentrate all needed planning and administrative decisions in one final administrative decision. This procedure allows the authority to overrule conflicting municipal plans or decisions, and considerably restricts a private owner's legal position to stop any impacts from the projected construction and its later use.[22] The final decision does not transfer existing private property rights to the authority, but is a prerequisite for expropriation (if required) because a voluntarily negotiated land transfer fails.

The only issue still to be settled in the expropriation proceedings is the amount of compensation. Thorny compensation problems such as the following may arise. What is the relevant property to be compensated—just the piece of land required for road construction, or adjacent land as well, which can no longer be economically used for the purpose for which the whole property had been suited? Which side effects must be compensated (for example, when a farm building is separated from parts of the farmland)? What impacts have resulted from changes of the road or long-lasting construction? In Germany, a favorable location (for example, a business at a crossroads) is not part of the ownership right of the adjacent land, but only a favorable opportunity that can be discontinued without touching private property rights. On the other hand, access to light and air is considered to be part of the property right and therefore, if impacted by the construction, loss of that right must be compensated.

Any category that might require compensation is related to the legal requirement of the German planning law (with a constitutional background) that public and private interests have to be fairly valued and balanced (Abwägungsgebot) to justify impacts on private property rights. This means a compromise between the public interests pursued and the private interests involved must be reached. This requirement is particularly necessary for urban planning,[23] but also applies to road and highway construction, which sometimes has major, unavoidable impacts on private property even though the impacts might not rise to the level of an expropriation. To meet the requirement to fairly weigh and balance private and public interests, the law on administrative proceedings provides compensation for major, unavoidable impacts of the scheme.[24] The law does not provide an exact definition of "major impacts," but given the dogmatic background, it is beyond doubt that the borderline of expropriation must not yet be crossed.

VIII. Can Any Conclusions Be Drawn from the American-German Comparison?

The constitutional and legal frameworks of the American and German governments, especially as they relate to legislative, administrative, and judicial systems, differ considerably. But in both countries, the constitutional protection of property rights and the political need for managing economic, social, and environmental change result in the necessity of distinguishing between those restrictions or infringements imposed by government regulations or actions on private property rights that require compensation, and those that do not.

The constitutional principles protecting private property rights against expropriation without compensation appear to provide a basis in both countries for expanding claims for compensation beyond the historically, politically, and legally uncontroversial concept of total physical taking of property to satisfy the public need for land, especially for infrastructure that is obviously for the public's benefit.

The German constitutional doctrine appears to be in a comparatively more advantageous position, because the compensation consequences of regulatory restrictions, infringements, and genuine takings of private property rights are explicitly considered by the Constitution itself. Unlike the American stance of applying and expanding the constitutional guarantee of property rights to instances beyond a physical taking, German constitutional doctrine accepts the exclusion of compensation for those cases that are not clearly expropriations. This doctrine is supported by a legislative strategy that provides compensation for both expropriation cases and cases of particular hardship. In Germany, the compensation determination turns on the interpretation of the specific laws and legal principles on the ordinary law level, thus reducing the need to refer directly to the Constitution. In particular, legislation has focused on areas such as urban planning, nature conservation, and landmark preservation, and has also provided regulations on the administrative procedure for major public land-consuming projects, such as road and highway construction.

Although in both countries the constitutions are the last resort for deciding whether to grant or deny compensation, determining the cases that merit compensation is primarily done at the legislative level in Germany. The German system allows different levels of protection for property rights according to the specific scope of the various areas of legislation involved. Typically, courts restrictively interpret these regulations. An advantage of the German strategy of shifting from a constitutional level to the sub-constitutional (that is, federal or federal state) level of legislation is that it allows for flexibility in determining the legal prerequisites for compensation claims, but leaves open final recourse to constitutional principles.

Though the American takings doctrine appears to have more uniformity in the legal principles applied, greater predictability in public decisionmaking, and better judicial control in refining constitutional doctrine, the recent reference in the *Lucas* case to the existing "background principles in the state's law of property" and the present legislative discussion about the "Private Property Rights Protection Act" reveal a rising relevance of the sub-constitutional level of legislation. The American and German political and legal strategies appear to converge considerably in their efforts to cope with the takings issue. To allow decisions on a case-by-case basis, both the American and German judiciaries resort to weighing the clashing public and private interests involved. However, major differences appear in the final valuation of public interests as they relate to the impacted private interests.

Avoiding the overburdening of public budgets and restricting private claims of compensation can be accomplished by explicitly addressing the compensation issue through legislation. German experience demonstrates that prudent administrative practice, along with proper judicial control, can restrict public compensation to the core areas targeted by the legislation.

Notes

The research for this chapter has been generously supported by the Deutsche Forschungsgemeinschaft, Bonn.

1. Art. 17 Déclaration des droits de l'homme et du citoyen de 28.8.1789; *Cf.* Justus Wilhelm Hedemann, *Die Fortschritte des Zivilrechts im XIX.* Jahrhundert, 2.Teil, Entwicklung des Bodenrechts von der französischen Revolution bis zur Gegenwart, S. 117 ff, (1930, reprint 1968); W. Böhmer, *Die rechtsgeschichtlichen Grundlagen der Abgrenzungsproblematik von Sozialbindung und Enteignung,* DER STAAT, 182 (1985).

2. Compare the following constitutional provisions: Art. 9 of the preußischen rev. Verfassung (1850), Art. 153 of the Weimarer Reichsverfassung (1919), and Art. 14 of the GRUNDGESETZ [Constitution] [GG] (1949).

3. *Cf.* Judgment of July 15, 1981, Bundesverfassungsgericht [BVerfG] (Naßauskiesung), NEUE JURISTISCHE WOCHENSCHRIFT 745 (1982): A landowner obtained permission to exploit gravel, which because of the potential impact on the groundwater, was based on the regulations protecting water resources. As the respective legislation changed, the authority stopped the exploitation. The landowner argued this would be a case of expropriation and therefore implicate compensation. The Federal Constitutional Court held that the water resources are not part of the private (land) property rights, but are subject to a public order for the use of water resources. This can be changed by legislation without affecting the constitutional guarantee of private property rights. But courts must consider whether compensation for reasons other than expropriation (such as the principle of sacrifice) is due.

4. *See* F. Ossenbühl, *Staatshaftungsrecht* (1991).

5. *See* §§ 74, 75 Einleitung prALR (1794); *cf.* ALLGEMEINES LANDRECHT FÜR DIE PREUßISCHEN STAATEN VON 1794 (H. Hattenhauer ed. 1994).

6. A major case in this category was the following: Judgment of July 14, 1981, BVerfG BVerfGE 58, 137 (Pflichtexemplar). By law every publisher has to give a copy of his publications, free of charge, to a specific library that collects all publications produced in Germany. This is not considered to be an expropriation and therefore is not to be compensated. Even a publisher who produces a few copies of a fancy edition of an art book at the cost of several thousand Deutsche Mark is obliged to deliver one copy to this library. The publisher might be compensated; not based on expropriation, but on the abovementioned principle of sacrifice.

7. In the area of expropriation law, three Federal Courts exercise jurisdiction. They are the Federal Constitutional Court (Bundesverfassungsgericht [BVerfG]), the Federal Administrative Court (Bundesverwaltungsgericht [BVerwG]), and the Federal Civil Court (Bundesgerichtshof in Zivilsachen) [BGH Z.]). (There is only one federal level of jurisdiction; thus all federal courts are to be considered as "high" or "supreme" courts regarding their task to enable a uniform interpretation of federal law all over the country.) The involvement of three federal courts in the compensation issue might be confusing, but it derives from a constitutional requirement: Art. 14, Abs. 3 GG requires civil law courts to decide on compensation for expropriation, though the underlying administrative decisions might be reviewed by the administrative courts. To align the judicial review, common civil/administrative judicial bodies are formed on federal state and federal levels (Kammern/Senate für Baulandsachen, §§ 217 ff. Federal Building Code). Only the Federal Constitutional Court has the jurisdiction to declare a (federal or state) law as unconstitutional and therefore null and void (Verwerfungskompetenz). If a court doubts the constitutionality of a law, the case must be submitted to the Federal Constitutional Court.

8. Article 14 of the Grundgesetz (Property, Inheritance, and Expropriation) states:

> (1) Property and the right of inheritance shall be guaranteed. Their substance (content) and limits shall be determined by law.
> (2) Property entails obligation. It should also serve the public weal.
> (3) Expropriation shall only be permissible in the public weal. It may be ordered by or pursuant to a law that determines the kind and extent of compensation. Compensation shall reflect a fair balance between the public interest and the interests of those affected. In case of dispute regarding the amount of compensation, recourse may be had to the ordinary courts.

9. An exception exists for those cases explicitly regulated, as explained in section VII. B.1. of this chapter.

10. Generally, planning cases do not fall within the jurisdiction of the (Federal) Constitutional Court, but instead are within the jurisdiction of the

other federal Courts, which are in charge of the review of the (sub-constitutional) ordinary federal legislation (such as the Federal Building Code).

11. The Civil Code (Bürgerliches Gesetzbuch) restricts the landowner to certain legal forms, and beyond those the landowner cannot restrict his ownership position at will.

12. See section II of this chapter regarding different legal approaches.

13. For more detail, see section VII.B.2. of this chapter.

14. *See* R.H. Freilich & E.A. Garvin, *Taking after* Lucas: *Growth Management, Planning and Regulatory Implementation Will Work Better Than Before, in* AFTER *LUCAS:* LAND USE REGULATION AND THE TAKING OF PROPERTY (D.L. Callies ed. 1993).

15. Judgment of Mar. 24, 1987, BVerfG, NEUE JURISTISCHE WOCHENSCHRIFT 1251 (1987).

16. 467 U.S. 229 (1984) (state law requiring sale of privately owned residential land from lessors to lessees to reduce the concentration of fee simple land ownership held to be a public use within meaning of Fifth Amendment).

17. In the *Kreuzberg* decision, it was held that based on the police clause, permission to build could not be denied for aesthetic reasons (obstruction of the view of the "Kreuzberg" monument), but instead specific legal enabling legislation was required. This signalled the beginning of a specialized town planning and building law in Germany.

18. German designation of the code is "Baugesetzbuch" (abbr. BauGB). *Cf.* GERMAN PLANNING AND BUILDING LAWS, (C. H. David, ed. 1995). For an English outline of the German planning system, see LAW AND PRACTICE OF URBAN DEVELOPMENT IN THE FEDERAL REPUBLIC OF GERMANY, (C. H. David, ed. 1993).

19. Compensation claims are granted only within seven years after the potential land use first was permitted. After that time, the owner can claim only the difference between the existing land-use value and the value after downgrading (FBC § 42, Abs. 2). This allows the authority to downgrade binding land-use plans if the landowner did not take advantage of the plan in the past without compensation of the loss of potential land value created by the plan.

20. A recent decision of the Federal Civil Court (Judgment of July 7, 1994, Deutsches Verwaltungsblatt 104 (1995)) outlines the present state of discussion. The case concerns a quarry that was exploited for sixty years and that after that time attracted rare fauna and flora. A public statute protected the area, allowing only hunting and some other similar use. The owner's application for a commercial use was rejected based on the statute. The owner saw his property devalued by half a million dollars and argued that his quarry was the only one out of ten similar quarries in the region to be covered by the statute restricting private land use. The lower court held that the owner had the advantage of exploiting the quarry for many years, and actually created the basis for the rare environment that restricts his land-use potential today. The court accepted the reasons given by the authority for selecting his quarry for the designating statute and not the other ten. The Federal Civil Court held the compensation regulation (§ 7 of the Landscape Law of the State North-Rhine Westfalia) to be in

accordance with the federal Constitution, but held that the lower court failed to adequately weigh public and private interests according to legal requirements, and to consider that the owner was unfairly burdened by a sacrifice in comparison with the other ten quarry owners. The lower court will have to consider these matters.

21. To implement environmental plans or protective designations (see section VII. B.2. of this chapter) requiring "classic expropriation" different, less-effective procedures are applied. General (federal states) legislation exists regulating the scope and procedure of expropriation, as well as the compensation to paid.

22. *Cf.* § 75 Abs. 1, 2 S.1 of the Law on Administrative Proceedings (Verwaltungsverfahrensgesetz); for English translation of the law, see THE RULE OF LAW IN PUBLIC ADMINISTRATION AND ADMINISTRATIVE JURISDICTION (H. Siedentopf et al. eds., 1994).

23. *See* subsection 6, Federal Building Code: "In preparing land-use plans, public and private interests are to be duly weighed and fairly balanced."

24. *See* § 75 Abs. 2, S.1 of the Law on Administrative Proceedings.

CHAPTER ❖ 17

If Tigard Were an English City: Exactions Law in England Following the *Tesco* Case

Malcolm Grant

I. Introduction

The close parallels between the approaches of municipalities in the United States and Great Britain in securing contributions from developers for off-site public goods were identified in an article by Callies and Grant, published in 1991.[1] It noted the extent to which similar fiscal pressures were driving municipalities on both sides of the Atlantic to adopt remarkably similar practices in their negotiations with developers, despite the significant differences in the legal frameworks limiting their powers. The highest courts in both countries have recently had an opportunity to review those frameworks, and they have adopted approaches that are diametrically opposed. Whereas the Supreme Court of the United States in the *Dolan*[2] case sought to establish the requisite relationship between the conditions imposed on a land-use permit and the projected impact of the proposed development, the English House of Lords, in *Tesco Stores Ltd. v. Secretary of State for the Environment*,[3] abdicated all responsibility for that task. Indeed, one of the two leading (and concurring) judgments directly quotes the observation made by Callies and Grant that

> "[t]he necessity to avoid falling foul of the 'taking' doctrine has meant that United States local governments have always had to be in a position to justify their rules in case of constitutional challenge, and hence to pursue openness and economic transparency. . . ."
>
> [N]o English court would countenance having the merits of a planning decision judicially examined in this way. The result may

> be some lack of transparency, but that is a price which the English planning system, based upon central and local political responsibility, has been willing to pay for its relative freedom from judicial interference.[4]

This is a significant departure from British jurisprudence of recent years; indeed, it is nothing less than a wholesale retreat from a series of recent attempts to establish judicial oversight of the process that has come to be known in Britain as "planning gain." In this chapter, I explore the course followed in these recent decisions and the confusions inherent in them. I also explore the extent to which the House of Lords is justified in its assumption that the systems of central and local political responsibility that lie at the heart of the English planning system can act as an effective surrogate protector of private property.

II. If Tigard Were an English City

The best starting point for both of these lines of inquiry, particularly for the benefit of American readers unfamiliar with the English system, is to consider how Ms. Dolan's application for a permit would have been determined under English law.

Florence Dolan owned a plumbing and electrical supply store in Tigard, Oregon. She wanted to redevelop the site, and planned initially to double the size of the store and pave the thirty-nine-space parking lot, and later to construct an additional building for complementary businesses. The city's planning commission granted her application for a permit, subject to conditions requiring the dedication of the portion of her property lying within the 100-year floodplain (for improvement of a storm drainage system along Fanno Creek), and the dedication of an additional fifteen-foot strip of land adjacent to the floodplain (for a pedestrian/bicycle pathway). She requested a variance, on the ground that her proposed development would not conflict with the policies of the comprehensive plan. When that failed, she appealed unsuccessfully to the land-use board of appeals. From there, her challenge was routed through the courts.

The city's attempt to rely on land-use planning powers to secure these requirements would not be thought unusual in England, where the process of "planning gain," an expression commonly used to encompass all forms of exactions, has proved every bit as controversial as in the United States.

Table 1 summarizes the different approaches taken in Tigard and in England (where there is a national system of planning control, but

Table 1. SUMMARY OF APPROACHES TAKEN BY CITY OF TIGARD IN *DOLAN* CASE, AND THOSE THAT WOULD BE TAKEN IN UNITED KINGDOM IN SAME CASE

Action	*Tigard*	*United Kingdom*
Proposals to expand hardware store	Proposals consistent with the city's Community Development Code (CDC) enacted under state legislation, but permit required from City Planning Commission that imposed conditions required by the CDC. Variance possible only when shown that undue or unnecessary hardship would otherwise result.	Requires permit ("planning permission") regardless of policies and allocations in the development plan. Uniform control system imposed by national legislation, the Town and Country Planning Act, 1990.
Process	Planning commission's order approved by city. Right to appeal to Land-Use Board of Appeals, pursued on question of law about whether city's dedication requirements were related to the impact of the proposed development.	Application to local planning authority, which would consult with other interested parties (for example, the National Rivers Authority (NRA) on floodplain protection). Authority not bound by NRA's technical advice, but in practice it is highly persuasive. If authority attempted to impose a higher standard than sought by NRA, would need to be able to defend it on appeal; if sought a lower standard without good reasons, NRA could request central government intervention. Authority entitled to refuse permission altogether (for example, due to appropriateness of development to this location, or dissatisfaction with design), or to impose conditions. If permission refused or conditions imposed, applicant has right of appeal to Secretary of State for the Environment, which amounts to a full review of the merits. Subsequent appeal, on point of law only, can be made to the High Court.

Action	*Tigard*	*United Kingdom*
Criteria for granting permit	The CDC, coupled with the capacity to grant a variance (the validity of which the Supreme Court chose specifically not to address).	Starting point is the development plan for the area: it has no direct legal force, but is a primary factor taken into account in decisionmaking. It will normally contain policies on floodplain protection, and may have policies on pathways. If so, plan will provide policy backing for proposed conditions, but not itself render them valid. Other material considerations include statements of national policy (for example, on floodplain protection and cycling (see PLANNING POLICY GUIDANCE 13, *Transport* (1994)).
Validity of conditions on permit	Must find (1) an essential nexus between legitimate state interests and the condition, and (2) some rough proportionality between the required dedication and the impact of the proposed development: there must be an individualized determination that the required dedication is related both in nature and extent to the impact of the proposed development.	No clear guidance in the national legislation, and no constitutional protection for private property. But a series of leading cases seek a similar balance: a planning condition will be valid only if it (1) relates fairly and reasonably to the permitted development, (2) is not manifestly unreasonable in content (for example, confiscatory), and (3) is imposed for a planning purpose. Also, policy advice issued by central government to local planning authorities about different types of conditions (Dept. of Environment Circular 1/85, *The Use of Conditions in Planning Permissions*) would form the basis for an appeal against the local planning authority's determinations.
Other approaches		The local planning authority may simply refuse permission altogether. However, if the redevelopment was in general accordance with the development plan, this is an unlikely result because the applicant could appeal to the Secretary of State. Instead, the authority might seek to negotiate an agreement and to secure the dedications by that method.

local discretion in its application).[5] The proposal to expand the store and pave the parking area could be carried out lawfully[6] under English planning law only if planning permission had been granted for it. England formally abandoned zoning in 1948, and substituted for it a system of development plans containing provisions that are indicative, rather than legally binding, coupled with a comprehensive system of discretionary control over all development.[7] For planning permission, Ms. Dolan would have to apply to the local government, to which was assigned the relevant functions as "local planning authority" under the Town and Country Planning Act, 1990.[8] In deciding whether to grant or refuse that application, and whether conditions will attach to the grant of permission, the authority would not be bound by the development plan. At the heart of England's discretionary system of control is a requirement that the local planning authority "have regard to the provisions of the development plan, so far as material [to the application] and to any other material considerations."[9] This is extremely broad discretion. It is not qualified like the Tigard variance provisions, which require the applicant to show that undue or unnecessary hardship would result if the code were applied. As a matter of law, English local planning authorities enjoy wide discretionary power. The development plan is a statement of agreed-upon policies for the exercise of control over land-use change, not a code of legal rules.

However, there is a powerful system of checks over the exercise of that power, deriving from the administrative framework. Local planning authorities are locked within a network of administrative relationships that strongly affect the outcome of their deliberations. These relationships are both horizontal (for example, a requirement to take into account representations made by another public or private body when determining a planning application), and vertical (for example, the oversight powers of the Secretary of State for the Environment that allow him to take over entire responsibility for an application that the authority proposes to grant—the so-called "call-in" power—and to entertain appeals of authorities' refusals of permission). These relationships are underpinned by law, and it is not surprising that the role of the courts in English planning law has developed into one primarily of ensuring compliance with these rules while setting fairly broad limits to jurisdiction. At the heart of the English land-use planning system lies broad statutory discretionary power, which must be exercised in light of policies adopted by central and local government, the observance of which is, in turn, overseen not by the courts but through the administrative processes of appeal and call-in.

A. Floodplain Protection

The protection of floodplains provides an example of this administrative network in operation. Responsibility for the protection of water resources is vested in a special agency of national government, the National Rivers Authority (NRA).[10] The NRA must be consulted when local planning authorities formulate their development plans, and these plans are expected to contain policies concerning the control of development in flood-risk areas. The policies must establish the standards of protection required in relation to the degree of risk of flooding.[11] The Secretary of State for the Environment has issued guidance to all local planning authorities, in the form of a circular[12] in which he requests they consult the NRA on any applications for planning permission for development affecting floodplains. The circular advises local authorities about the problems arising from impermeable surfaces, and indicates that when alleviation works are required to prevent any unacceptable flood risk from new development, then the cost of undertaking such works must rest with the developer. The NRA has also issued guidance to local planning authorities, stressing that it looks to those authorities:

> to resist development in such locations [that is, floodplains], while redevelopment of existing sites will only be considered where the LPA, in consultation with the NRA, is satisfied that the developer will provide appropriate mitigation and/or protection measures. There may also be opportunities to enhance or restore the natural floodplain when redevelopment takes place.[13]

The importance of this advice lies in the administrative arrangements for its enforcement. A local planning authority is entitled to refuse—without any compensation liability—an application for planning permission if a threat to floodplain protection exists that the applicant is unwilling or unable to alleviate. The circular says nothing about the transfer of land by a developer, but if that is needed to implement the necessary works (such as the construction of mitigation measures), then doing so is implicit in the advice. If permission is refused, or if the developer believes the authority's requirements are excessive, the developer is entitled to appeal to the Secretary of State, where the whole application is reexamined on its merits by an independent planning inspector (effectively a technically qualified planning judge). The Secretary of State's policy guidance, and the local development plan, provide the policy framework for the decision on appeal. If the local planning authority is found to have acted unreasonably, it may be ordered to pay the developer's appeal costs.

B. Cycleways

On cycling, the policy framework is less developed. Nonetheless, there is national policy guidance that encourages local planning authorities to devise policies and proposals for cycleways, and to aim to provide an effective network of cycle routes. The guidance provides that plans should "indicate routes along which measures will be encouraged to make cycling safer and more attractive," and that "provision of cycle routes and cycle priority measures should be encouraged in new development."[14] The policy is easily applied when the development comprises a large housing estate: cycleways, like highways and sewers, become part of the on-site physical infrastructure that a developer is required to provide. But the policy becomes more problematic with small-scale projects like the one Ms. Dolan proposed. The linear character of a cycleway makes it impossible for planners to rely solely on the opportunities arising from new development, especially when the objective is to run a cycleway through an already built-up area. Nonetheless, redevelopment provides an opportunity to induce developers to adapt to the new requirements. But how?

III. The Tools of Exactions: Planning Conditions and Planning Agreements

English planning legislation offers two routes to exactions: a "planning condition" imposed on planning permission, or a "planning obligation," which is an agreement between the landowner and the local planning authority,[15] and which then runs with the land. The legislation that confers the power to impose planning conditions is silent about their lawful extent: it simply provides that the local planning authority is entitled to impose such conditions as it sees fit.[16] There is no constitutional limit, but the courts have devised their own tests for validity. The first steps were taken in 1958, with Lord Denning's famous dictum:

> [A]lthough the planning authorities are given very wide powers to impose "such conditions as they think fit" . . . the law says that those conditions, to be valid, must fairly and reasonably relate to the permitted development. The planning authority are not at liberty to use their powers for an ulterior object, however desirable that object may seem to them to be in the public interest.[17]

This test is a restatement of a basic principle of English judicial review, which seeks to ensure that statutory powers are exercised only for the purposes of the legislation conferring them. It also introduces an element of proportionality. Subsequent case law has developed these principles and linked them to another basic rule of judicial review, to produce the so-called "*Newbury*[18] principles." Under those principles, a planning condition, to be valid, must (1) be imposed for a planning purpose, (2) fairly and reasonably relate to the development for which permission is being given, and (3) be reasonable, in the sense of being a condition that a reasonable local authority, properly advised, might impose. This last test is more one of doctrine than economic reasonableness, and more a safeguard against arbitrariness than overprescription[19].

This doctrine confines planning conditions to a narrow role, and this effect is reinforced by the policies adopted by the Secretary of State for the Environment in relation to their use. Local planning authorities are advised, for example, that they should not impose conditions requiring the payment of money or the transfer of land, based on the apparent assumption that such a condition would be manifestly unreasonable and beyond their powers.[20] This approach may have worked well with a regime in which developers could rely upon central and local government to provide all off-site public goods necessary for the development, but it has become increasingly at odds with the development requirements of the last quarter of the twentieth century, when these burdens have in fact fallen upon the private sector. Despite a somewhat belated acceptance by the courts that similar ends might be pursued by means of a passive condition,[21] the rule against direct imposition of exaction requirements by condition remains intact today.

The practical consequence of this rule has been that local planning authorities and developers have resorted to other means: exactions have been negotiated in connection with the formal processes of obtaining planning permission, but have been kept off the formal record and have remained outside the provisions relating to appeals to the Secretary of State. Hence, ironically, a rule that was established to protect developers from manifestly unreasonable demands has (1) had the actual effect of removing from them the capacity to challenge unreasonable demands through planning appeal,[22] and (2) removed this important part of the planning process from the public record.

A. Planning Agreements and Obligations: The Background

During the 1970s, the principal tool for exactions in England became that of planning agreements, a device provided in what was then section 52 of the Town and Country Planning Act, 1971. As originally conceived, a planning agreement was a statutory version of the restrictive covenant between freehold owners of adjoining land, which under English property law is capable of giving rise to a proprietary right enforceable by and against successors-in-title to the original covenantors. Section 52 adapted that model to the requirements of public bodies, by allowing an agreement to be made for the purpose of restricting the use or development of land, and to be enforced by the local planning authority as if it owned land that benefitted from the agreement. It was, on the face of it, an unlikely vehicle for securing exactions, yet it was pressed into widespread service for this purpose, especially when the former requirement that every agreement must have the Secretary of State's approval was dropped in 1968.

The pragmatic and incremental character of its use for what was coming to be known as "planning gain" meant that little thought was given (in the 1970s) to how the powers should be controlled by the courts. Any relevant litigation that existed tended to regard it as an uncontroversial phenomenon. But public concern was growing nonetheless, and was clearly reflected in a special report of the Government's Property Advisory Group in 1980.[23] That report came to the clear conclusion that planning gain should have no part in the planning process, except in certain special cases. In contrast with today's concerns, the report saw planning gain almost exclusively as an unwarranted infringement of developers' and landowners' rights. The report, criticized at the time for that somewhat simplistic characterization,[24] simply assumed, without critical examination, that local authority regulation of land use should be slotted within a quasi-judicial model. The report overlooked the greater subtlety of the bargaining model that was emerging in local government, and which has now led to significant long-term changes in the way in which both local and central government understand the allocation of financial responsibility for off-site infrastructure. Hence the report failed to address two issues properly.

First, it did not consider the need to establish guidelines for the wholly legitimate use of the process to secure contributions toward provision of necessary off-site infrastructure or other related benefits. The advisory group was heavily influenced by the anecdotal instances of abuse that were starting to emerge, where it was charged that some local planning authorities were seeking extortionate and unrelated contributions. This led the advisory group to take a narrow and negative view of the bargaining process.

Second, the advisory group largely overlooked the phenomenon of the willing contributor, and the possibility that this might require a different approach, in terms of both policy and law, from that of the unwilling contributor seeking the protection of the courts from extortionate demands. A notable distinction between the patterns of litigation in the United States and the United Kingdom is that whereas challenges to exactions in the United States have, in the main, been mounted by property owners and developers, in the United Kingdom the initiative has come primarily from rival developers. This reflects several important points of difference. The first is the consensual nature of the process in the United Kingdom. Developers' contributions are not exacted unilaterally; they are negotiated, and agreed upon by the contributor in return for the promise of planning permission. Another difference is the highly competitive character of a particular area of recent British development activity—the construction of large retail malls, often on out-of-town or edge-of-town sites. The tight policies in force against a proliferation of these developments have meant that permissions are effectively rationed, and the first developer to secure a permission in a particular area has a good chance of securing a trading monopoly. Hence the importance of litigation to try to maintain the status quo ante.

This background also helps explain why the focus of much of the recent litigation has been on the potential for misuse of power by local governments, in response to inducements by developers: the courts have been prey to an underlying fear that, without proper judicial oversight of the process, planning might become simply a process of buying and selling planning permissions. Lord Justice Lloyd, in *Bradford City Council v. Secretary of State for the Environment*,[25] first gave voice to this concern when he stated that he regarded it as "axiomatic" that planning permissions could not be bought or sold. Subsequently, in the Court of Appeal in *Tesco Stores Ltd. v. Secretary of State for the Environment*, Lord Justice Steyn elevated the concern to

> a principle which is part of the very alphabet of our planning law. The philosophy of the bazaar has been rejected. The governing principle is that planning permission may not be bought and sold. . . . It is, in the language of Dworkin, a principle and not a rule. It is fuzzy round the edges. The application of the principle gives rise to difficult problems.[26]

This provides a useful starting point for our understanding of contemporary judicial confusion, because it forces us to confront the relationship between rules of law and rules of policy, and the balance between administrative and judicial oversight of the planning process. The principle enunciated by Lord Justice Steyn was, in the British constitutional structure, best captured as a rule of policy rather than law, and the expression "fuzzy round the edges" might be better applied to the attempt of the courts to convert this perfectly sensible policy into a legal rule. Their search for a special formula has led to some of the very worst jurisprudence we have seen from the courts in planning law.

1. THE THEORETICAL BASES: CONTRACT

Planning agreements and obligations are novel instruments that straddle both public and private law, and the courts have consistently failed to develop an appropriate framework for assessing their validity. Contract as a basis for planning is as old as statutory planning itself. Planning agreements first appeared in the Housing, Town Planning etcetera Act 1909, reflecting the limited interventionist powers conferred by that act, and the extent to which its implementation was thought to rest upon consensus and the voluntary agreement of landowners. But in 1909, the landowners held all the power, and the thought that special protection might have been necessary to save them from the blackmailing tendencies of rapacious town clerks was untenable. The power to enter into agreements was intended to allow legal expression to be given to the natural philanthropy of the landed classes.

Therefore, the presence of contracts in planning legislation today owes more to history than to conscious design. When a private treaty is used as an instrument of public planning, the consequence is inevitably confusion between the regimes (and their underlying philosophies) that should govern the arrangements. To private lawyers, a planning agreement is a contract, to which the appropriate judicial approach is the laissez-faire function of enforcing promises. In general, it is no part of contract law to review the adequacy of consideration, or to overturn promises on the grounds that one of the parties did not have a good bargain. Under a contract law approach, the only significance of the statutory power is to ensure that a planning agreement runs with the land, notwithstanding the absence of any dominant tenement, and notwithstanding that the agreement may be positive in its nature. Hence the role of the statutory provisions is to enhance the contracting power of the local authority: a landowner may agree to provide infrastructure or to cede land to the authority in return for a grant of planning permission, in the same way that a plumber may agree to repair the local authority's central heating system in return for money.

The 1991 amendments to the relevant legislation, which allowed developers to offer planning benefits unilaterally, effected a further shift in balance between private and public law. The scope of the statutory power was broadened: the agreement no longer need be for the purpose of restricting or regulating the use or development of land; it may contain positive covenants and it may provide for the payment of money. Yet to balance this increased freedom, the Secretary of State was given power to override covenants when they no longer serve any purpose—even to the extent of relieving the original covenantor of an obligation otherwise still binding in contract. Hence the planning obligation is even more a hybrid instrument than its wholly bilateral predecessor. In the case of a unilateral obligation, there is no exercise of any statutory power, unless and until the local planning authority or the Secretary of State grants planning permission on the basis of it, or attempts to enforce it. Up to that point, there can be no issue about the validity of the obligation in public law, simply because there has been no exercise of a statutory power. As we shall see, this new statutory framework was eventually to provide the courts with an opportunity to set aside their earlier approach.

2. THEORETICAL BASES IN PUBLIC LAW

In public law, the considerations are different. Planning agreements/obligations are, in practice, almost invariably linked to the grant of planning permission. The argument is that planning permission is not a market commodity to be bought and sold, but the outcome of a process of decisionmaking by a publicly elected and accountable body. The function of a planning agreement is to enhance the public powers, not to supersede them. Local planning authorities (and the Secretary of State when exercising his oversight functions of call-in and appeal) must be held squarely to the powers conferred on them by statute and, in construing those powers, the courts consider two primary objectives.

The first we may call the "private protective function" of ensuring that applicants for planning permission are protected from the arbitrary exercise of power. This is the function performed by the Court in *Dolan v. City of Tigard*. The second arises from the broader public interest in ensuring that planning authorities remain within their statutory powers, even when there is no cry for protection from the landowner most intimately affected by the exercise of power, or indeed from the public at large.

The "sale" of a planning permission may be thoroughly popular for the benefits it brings to a hard-pressed community; it may even have (though this is unlikely) the unbridled support of rival developers, and the unanimous cross-party backing of councillors. And it may provide an ideal planning solution to a series of complex but unconnected problems. Yet it would still be wrong in terms of legal principle, because the payment of an unrelated inducement to a local planning authority cannot constitute a material consideration in their decision about whether to grant planning permission. Unless the deal is limited to providing public goods that are material to the development under consideration, it is beyond the powers of the local planning authority to use it as a basis for granting planning permission. The issues are wider than the obvious risk of collusive dealing between landowner and local planning authority, which may have adverse third-party impacts and against which the courts must act. It is also clear law—though the practical limits of the doctrine are far from clear[27]—that a local authority cannot by agreement fetter the future exercise of its powers.

These tests are all examples of a public protection function of the courts. To some extent, it overlaps with the function of private protection. But its range is far broader. Perhaps it was a sense of unease about this function, and a reluctance to allow public planning to be undertaken too widely through private treaty, that prompted the decision by Parliament in 1947 to insist that ministerial consent to all planning agreements be obtained.[28] That requirement led to few agreements being made, and thus to its repeal in 1968; but that repeal removed any government oversight. In attempting to plug that gap, the courts appear to have confused the functions of private protection and public protection. In particular, their wish to protect developers from excessive demands led them to apply the tests for validity of planning conditions to planning agreements, instead of simply examining the validity of a planning permission granted on the back of such an agreement. This result meant that the protection was misplaced. It ignored the voluntariness of the bargaining process, and led to the irony of the courts being invited, in a suit brought by a developer, to protect the rival developer from obligations he freely offered to undertake.

B. The Roots of Contemporary Confusion

A major cause of this confusion has been the somewhat sporadic nature of the courts' consideration of the issues. Two different lines of thought have emerged, but more as a result of a relatively undeveloped series of judicial observations than of conflicts of principle. The first challenge to the use of a planning agreement came in 1977, with an unreported dictum of Justice Walton in *Western Fish Products v. Penwith District Council*,[29] "[T]he purpose of an agreement under section 52 is that it will enable the local planning authority to control matters which it might otherwise have no power to control by the imposition of conditions on any planning permission." The same line was taken by the Court of Appeal in *Windsor and Maidenhead Royal Borough Council v. Brandrose Investments, Ltd.*, in which Lord Justice Lawton pronounced that

> Section 52(1) empowers a local planning authority to make agreements to achieve ends which they could not achieve without the consent of an applicant for planning permission.[30]

Similarly, for Justice Popplewell in *R. v. Wealden District Council, ex parte Charles Church South East, Ltd.*, the applicable rules were obvious:

> It is clear, as a matter of law, that a council cannot impose a condition requiring the gratuitous provision of land for public use as a condition of planning permission. However, it is also perfectly clear that while it cannot be done as a matter of condition it may well be done as matter of negotiation. Equally, I take the view that the matters to be considered under section 52 are different from the rules governing planning conditions. Otherwise it is difficult to see what the purpose of section 52 is.[31]

However, in 1985, the Court of Appeal took a quite different line. In *Bradford City Council v. Secretary of State for the Environment*,[32] counsel for the Secretary of State had conceded that the objective sought by an invalid condition (road widening at the developer's expense) could have been achieved equally well by a planning agreement. The Court of Appeal was unhappy with that notion. Lord Justice Lloyd (in whose judgment the other two members of the Court concurred) said

> [i]f the condition was manifestly unreasonable, and so beyond the powers of the planning authority to impose it, whether or not the developers consented, it must follow that it was also beyond the powers of the planning authority to include the condition as "an incidental or consequential provision" of an agreement restricting or regulating the development or use of land under section 52.[33]

There is clearly a logical difficulty with that phrase "it must follow": such an assertion assumes that the statutory powers that it elides are identical, and they are not. There is no difficulty with the proposition that the presence or absence of a developer's consent to a planning *condition* is immaterial. It is not part of the statutory planning system, and any attempt to override the statutory criteria by reference to some form of estoppel against the owner is a confusion of doctrine. But with a planning *agreement* or *obligation*, the developer's consent is fundamental: without it, there can be no obligation.

The confusion is compounded by the fact that there is no necessary correlation between judicial formulations of manifest unreasonableness, and economic perceptions of reasonableness. A common case is that of the developer whose site cannot be unlocked for development until road improvements are carried out, not only to meet the increased traffic generated by the development, but also to remedy existing deficiencies. The local authority with responsibility for highways may have no relevant provision in its capital program; if the developer is willing to contribute toward the cost, the authority would be willing to put the works in the program, although it may still be some time before the additional public sector finances would be available to allow the works to proceed. There are many other calls for capital spending, and the authority has the duty of fixing its own priorities. If, however, the developer will meet the full costs, the works can be brought forward, perhaps even to the current financial year. Hence, the process is not merely consensual: it is also voluntary in the sense that the developer's economic interests are best served by bringing the site forward for early development, if the developer makes a sufficient contribution to off-site infrastructure costs. In development transactions, land-appropriate discounts are made in anticipation of the off-site costs that development will require. Any suggestion that such a developer, exercising free economic choice, should require the avuncular protection of the courts is simply untenable.

Bradford hints that the courts would be willing to draw a distinction—as a matter of law—between planning benefits that are reasonable in scale, and those that go beyond any reasonable relationship. According to Lord Justice Lloyd:

> That is not to say that this might not have been a case for a more limited agreement under section 52. A contribution towards the cost of widening Meadway [a local highway providing access to the development site] might well have been reasonable, due to the increased use of the road resulting from the development, and the benefit to the occupiers of the residential development: see Circular 22/83, *Planning Gain,* where the considerations are well set out in paras. 6–8. See also paras. 3 and 6 of Appendix A. But I need not pursue that consideration further. For there is all the difference in the world between a provision of a section 52 agreement requiring a contribution from a developer towards the cost of widening a highway and a provision which requires the entire works to be carried out at his risk and expense.[34]

This passage is a clear statement of *policy,* drawing as it does directly from the circular; but it would be wrong to regard it as a valid or workable principle of law, by which the validity of a planning obligation might be assessed. Establishing a satisfactory relationship between any particular planning benefit and the planning permission proposed to be granted goes way beyond the traditional function of the courts in English planning law, and it is an odd approach to an agreement to which a developer is *ex hypothesi* a voluntary signatory. The legal or economic arguments upon which that proposition is predicated remain unclear. Yet it caused severe difficulties for several subsequent decisions, as courts struggled to apply it to the terms of planning agreements that had been entered into consensually, but that were now being attacked by rival developers or residents' groups.[35]

C. The New Approach

Four major decisions between 1993 and 1995, culminating in the *Tesco* case, have now cut through these earlier confusions. First, the distinction between unilateral exaction and voluntary contribution was acknowledged by the Court of Appeal in *R. v Plymouth City Council, ex parte Plymouth and South Devon Cooperative Society.*[36] The local planning authority had agreed to grant planning permission to a major retailer (J Sainsbury plc) for construction of a 76,000-square-foot store, in return for a package of benefits worth nearly £5 million. A rival developer challenged the decision, arguing that the benefits offered by Sainsbury went beyond what was necessary to overcome any planning objections to the proposal. The court unanimously rejected that challenge, holding that there was no such test of "necessity."[37]

It is curious that the court did not simply discard the *Newbury* test. Instead, individual members of the court applied it in two quite different ways. Lord Justice Russell referred to the *Newbury* test as relating to a planning condition, and then observed, literally in parentheses, that "the same must be true of a section 106 obligation." He went on to question whether each of the planning obligations proposed satisfied the *Newbury* test. For Lord Justices Evans and Hoffmann, the relevance of the *Newbury* test was not to the validity of a planning obligation at all, but to the definition of what was a "material consideration" under section 70. This is a neat adaptation, but the two approaches are fundamentally at odds. This now appears to have been recognized, first by a differently constituted Court of Appeal in *Good v. Epping Forest District Council,*[38] which rejected without qualification the application of the *Newbury* tests to planning agreements, insisting that the only applicable tests for validity were those found in the statutory power itself; and second, in the *Tesco* decision, where the break was signalled by (1) Lord Keith's observation that "I do not think that reference to the *Newbury* case is particularly helpful for the purpose of deciding whether a planning obligation is a consideration material to the determination of a planning application with which the obligation was associated,"[39] and (2) by Lord Hoffmann, who although party to the decision in the *Plymouth* case, now found himself "bound to agree" with Lord Keith that "the parallel is by no means exact"[40] and therefore sought to explain its use in *Plymouth* as a "convenient judicial paraphrase of the effect of section 70(2)."

A significant feature of these cases has been the courts' desire to adapt the previous judicial doctrine to the realities of current planning and development practice, and to use the legislative amendments of 1991 as a justification for a fresh approach. For example, in the *Plymouth* case, Lord Justice Evans[41] drew upon arguments in the *Encyclopedia of Planning Law and Practice*[42] to conclude that market conditions had changed from the times when the public sector provided all public goods, and that development control had, under some circumstances, become a process of exchange. Likewise, Lord Hoffmann in *Tesco* characterized the planning bargaining process as a means of capturing the external costs of development.

Implicit in these approaches is a healthy retreat from the private protection function, which was taken furthest by a ruling of the Court of Appeal in 1994 in *R. v. South Northamptonshire District Council ex parte Crest Homes, Ltd.*[43] In that case, the court rejected an application by a developer to set aside the policy of the local planning authority requiring developers to contribute to the costs of off-site infrastructure related to their developments. The court was willing to uphold the requirements, notwithstanding (1) that the basis of contribution was not an assessment of the actual off-site requirements generated by the development, but a 20 percent tax on enhanced development values in the land, and (2) that any surplus generated by this means was to be held "for the common good of that part of the district of South Northamptonshire adjacent to the development."

These dramatic changes in judicial approach have all been based on a realization that the traditional doctrines were not only muddled but also at odds with the contemporary requirements of all parties to the land development process. These changes have strengthened the hand of local governments that wish to secure developers' contributions to off-site costs, and lifted the threat of legal challenge to deals going beyond that which is necessary simply to meet legitimate planning objections to a particular development. When a developer is a willing contributor, there is a new regime of contractual laissez-faire. When a developer is an unwilling contributor, the alternative of refusing to pay and appealing over the head of the local authority to the Secretary of State remains.

Nevertheless, there is still a perception that the courts have gone too far, and have lost sight of the public protection function. In the *Plymouth* case, the Court of Appeal was unanimous in deciding that there was no risk of planning permissions being bought and sold, "the test of materiality, strictly applied, is a sufficient safeguard against its abuse."[44] Yet in the *Tesco* case in the Court of Appeal, one of the Lords Justice, agreeing with academic criticism of the *Plymouth* case, asserted that it "comes perilously close to emasculating the principle that planning permission may not be bought and sold."[45] The only safeguard that is now retained is the requirement that any benefits offered by a developer be "material" to the development, a test that leaves to the local planning authorities a broad range of discretion. Benefits that are "excessive," in the sense of not being necessary simply to overcome planning objections, are not thereby rendered immaterial. Hence, some benefit completely unrelated to the development will probably be necessary to actuate the courts to intervene in any public protective role in the future. The courts have now squarely acknowledged that there can be no effective judicial review of planning agreements, and that earlier efforts to do so under a private protection theory were doctrinally inadequate.

D. An Administrative Alternative to Judicial Protection

In the British planning system, an administrative alternative to judicial protection is an entirely appropriate stance. The courts are ill-equipped to second-guess local planning authorities about matters involving judgment and degrees of distinction. But such an alternative is not necessarily the final word. The integrity of the planning system is a matter of concern for central government, and it is noteworthy that government policy on the use of planning obligations takes a more restricted view of those obligations than the courts.[46] In particular, government insists that any benefits incorporated into such obligations be proportionate, as well as material, to the development, and also be appropriate for the developer to bear. A balanced policy can secure the public protection purpose, provided it is observed in practice. Therein lies the rub, because national planning policies work best in defining a relationship between local planning authorities and developers. They have little impact when those parties are *ad idem*.

Should this prove too problematic, the only obvious course presently open to policymakers is to extend the terms of an existing administrative device, the Town and Country Planning (Consultation and

Development Plans) Direction, 1992,[47] to require notification to the Secretary of State of all planning applications in which permission is proposed to be granted on the basis of a planning obligation, whether proffered by the developer or required by the local planning authority. The notification should explain how the terms of the proposed obligation relate to the circular. The notification would also, as with other notifications under the Direction, be accompanied by public advertisement.

Also, the Secretary of State would be enabled to call-in cases that appear, to him, to go beyond the terms of the circular. If, within twenty-one days, he neither does so nor issues a further holding direction, then the local planning authority would be free to grant permission as proposed. Call-in need not be an automatic response: indeed, in most cases the evaluation would be a paper exercise and call-in would be rare. Exposing planning negotiations to a review procedure in this way could be expected to moderate the more excessive tendencies, and to encourage a more even application of government policy in a highly complex area.

IV. If Tigard Were in England

Finally, back to Ms. Dolan. Under existing law, the local planning authority could not have imposed on her permit the conditions that Tigard imposed. However, they could have refused her permission altogether, though she would have a right to appeal to the Secretary of State. The Secretary would normally be expected to uphold any reasonable requirements of the NRA relating to floodplain protection, though it would be willing to review the technical case for its imposition and design. Alternatively, whether in return for a speedy permission or additional rights elsewhere on the site, Ms. Dolan might have entered into negotiations to provide the sought-after facilities by means of a planning obligation. The courts would not protect her from any demands of the local planning authority that she believed to be excessive, nor would another developer be able to challenge her grant of permission should she agree to meet the authority's requirements (or even exceed them). Her remedy against excessive demands would lie within the administrative system, by appeal to the Secretary of State, where the merits—not just the legalities—of the demands could be examined, if necessary at a public hearing with expert witnesses and with legal representation.

Notes

1. D. Callies & M. Grant, *Paying for Growth and Planning Gain: An Anglo-American Comparison of Development Conditions, Impact Fees and Development Agreements*, 23 URB. LAW. 221 (1991).

2. Dolan v. City of Tigard, 114 S. Ct. 2309 (1994).

3. [1995] 2 All E. R. 636 (H.L.).

4. *Id.* at 658-59 (Hoffman, L., concurring).

5. There is a single national system for England and Wales, administered respectively by (for England) the Secretary of State for the Environment, through the Department of the Environment (DOE), and (for Wales) the Secretary of State for Wales, through the Welsh Office (WO). For Scotland, there is separate legislation (the Town and Country Planning (Scotland) Act, 1972), but it is based on the same general principles and is administered by the Secretary of State for Scotland.

6. If development is commenced without permission, or there is a failure to comply with a condition attached to a planning permission, the local planning authority is entitled to take enforcement action requiring the breach to be remedied, and it also has special power to apply to the court for an injunction to stop any ongoing breach. Town and Country Planning Act, 1990, §§ 172, 187B (Eng.).

7. The Town and Country Planning Act, 1947, has subsequently been reenacted in consolidation form (taking in all later amendments) on three occasions: in 1962, in 1971 and, in the current primary legislation, the Town and Country Planning Act, 1990, which applies throughout England and Wales.

8. In comparison with the United States, local government structures and functions in England and Wales are relatively uniform, but there are differences between areas with a single, so-called "unitary" council, and those with a two-tier structure. Hence, planning legislation allocates functions to the "local planning authority," and then identifies which council in a two-tier structure is to have which function. There is unitary local government in Greater London and six other metropolitan areas, and all planning functions are allocated to the single council (unless there is a special urban development corporation for part of the area whose function is to secure regeneration, and to which all functions relating to the control of development are normally allocated). Elsewhere, in so-called "shire England," there are normally two tiers: a county council, which has those functions that can only be regulated across a wider territory, such as long term ("strategic") planning, highways and transportation functions, minerals extraction, and waste disposal; and a district council, which has all the other functions. Ms. Dolan's application would go to a district council. These structures are presently under review: An all-unitary structure will be introduced to Wales in 1996 and, over the next two years, in parts of shire England, pursuant to recommendations by the Local Government Commission for England.

9. Town and Country Planning Act, 1990, § 70 (2) (Eng.). In 1991, Parliament attempted to elevate the status of the development plan in decisionmaking, and hence to diminish this broad discretion, by inserting a new section 54A in the Town and Country Planning Act, 1990, to require that determinations must be made "in accordance with the development plan, unless material considerations indicate otherwise." This is a fine distinction that has generated much debate and litigation. It has affected the practice of decisionmakers, but its legal effectiveness is limited.

10. The NRA was established by the Water Act, 1989, upon the privatization of the water industry in England and Wales, and its functions are now to be found in the Water Resources Act, 1991, and the Water Industry Act, 1991. The Environment Bill, 1995, presently before Parliament, proposes that a new, integrated, national environment agency be established in 1996, and that all the functions of the NRA be transferred to it.

11. If a local planning authority fails to reflect NRA policies properly in its development plan, the NRA is entitled to lodge a formal objection and, if necessary, to pursue it at a public hearing (known as a "public local inquiry") that must be held to inquire about objections to the draft plan.

12. Department of Environment (DOE) Circular 30/92, *Development and Flood Risk* (1992).

13. NRA, *Guidance Notes for Local Planning Authorities on the Methods of Protecting the Water Environment through Development Plans* (NRA, 1994).

14. PLANNING POLICY GUIDANCE 13, *Transport*, 4.15, 4.16 (1994).

15. These were traditionally known as "planning agreements," until the Planning and Compensation Act, 1991, changed the legislation to allow them to be furnished unilaterally by landowners, and renamed them "planning obligations" (Planning and Compensation Act, 1991, §12, substituting new § 106 in the Town and Country Planning Act, 1990).

16. Town and Country Planning Act, 1990, § 70(2) (Eng.).

17. *Pyx Granite Co., Ltd. v. Minister of Housing and Local Government*, [1958] 1 Q.B. 554.

18. Following the decision by the House of Lords in *Newbury District Council v. Secretary of State for the Environment*, [1981] App. Cas. 578 (H.L.).

19. The safeguard against excessive requirements is the developer's right of appeal to the Secretary of State, who may review the requirements of a planning condition on the merits.

20. DOE Circular 1/85, *The Use of Conditions in Planning Permissions*, 58 (1985).

21. The so-called "Grampian condition" (from *Grampian Regional Council v. City of Aberdeen District Council* [1984] J.P.L. 590 (House of Lords)) is a passive condition, under which some stage of a development (such as its commencement, or its occupation) is prohibited until a precondition is met. The precondition may be the provision of some item of off-site infrastructure, but the condition does not impose the burden of providing it directly on the developer. The House of Lords has recently given strong support to Grampian conditions. *British Railways Board v. Secretary of State for the Environment* [1993] 3 P.L.R. 125 (H.L.).

22. The developer may agree to contribute at the level sought by the local planning authority and enter into an agreement/obligation accordingly; or appeal to the Secretary of State for planning permission. Hence the appeal is not confined to the issue of quantum.

23. *Planning Gain* (Her Majesty's Stationery Office, 1980).

24. *See, e.g.*, M. Grant, *False Diagnosis, Wrong Prescription*, 51 TOWN & COUNTRY PLANNING 59 (1982); *Urban Planning Law*, 374-75 (Sweet and Maxwell, 1982).

25. 53 P.P. & C.R. 55 (Court of Appeal 1986).

26. [1994] 1 P.L.R. 97, 118 (C.A. 1994).

27. *See, e.g.*, R.v. London Borough of Hammersmith and Fulham, ex parte Beddowes [1987] 1 All E.R. 369 (High Court).

28. The background of this decision is discussed in M. GRANT, URBAN PLANNING LAW 363 (Sweet and Maxwell 1981).

29. Although this case was unreported, it was noted in Grant, *id.* at 367-68.

30. [1983] 1 W.L.R. 509 (C.A.).

31. 59 P.P. & C.R. 150, 158-59 (High Court 1989).

32. 53 P.P. & C.R. 55 (C.A. 1986).

33. *Id.* at 66.

34. *Id.* at 66.

35. For example, see *R. v. Gillingham Borough Council, ex parte F. Parham, Ltd.*, [1988] J.P.L. 336 (High Court), in which the court proved willing to apply the third of the *Newbury* tests, but not the first two; and *R. v. Wealden District Council, ex parte Charles Church South East, Ltd.*, 59 P.P. & C.R. 150 (High Court 1989).

36. [1993] 2 P.L.R. 75 (C.A.).

37. Also worth noting is the observation by Lord Justice Hoffmann that it would be bizarre to allow the doctrine of proportionality "to be invoked by a trade competitor to destroy a planning permission granted to a rival who does not complain that his liberty to deal with his land has been disproportionately restricted." *Id.* at 88.

38. [1993] 3 P.L.R. 135 (C.A.).

39. [1995] 2 All E.R. 636, 646 (H.L.).

40. *Id.* at 656.

41. [1993] 2 P.L.R. 75, 84 (C.A.).

42. 2 ENCYCLOPEDIA OF PLANNING LAW AND PRACTICE § P106.08 (M. Grant ed. 1995).

43. [1994] 3 P.L.R. 47 (C.A.).

44. [1993] 2 P.L.R. 75, 84 (C.A.) (Evans, L.J.).

45. [1994] 1 P.L.R. 97, 118 (C.A. 1994) (Steyn, L.J.).

46. *See* DOE Circular 16/91, *Planning and Compensation Act, 1991: Planning Obligations*.

47. *See* DOE Circular 19/92, *Town and Country Planning General Regulations, 1992: The Town and Country Planning (Consultation and Development Plans) Directions, 1992*.